Learning
Japanese
Kanji

THE 520 MOST ESSENTIAL CHARACTERS

Glen Nolan Grant

T0161183

TUTTLE Publishing

Tokyo | Rutland, Vermont | Singapore

"Books to Span the East and West"

Tuttle Publishing was founded in 1832 in the small New England town of Rutland, Vermont [USA]. Our core values remain as strong today as they were then—to publish best-in-class books which bring people together one page at a time. In 1948, we established a publishing office in Japan—and Tuttle is now a leader in publishing English-language books about the arts, languages and cultures of Asia. The world has become a much smaller place today and Asia's economic and cultural influence has grown. Yet the need for meaningful dialogue and information about this diverse region has never been greater. Over the past seven decades, Tuttle has published thousands of books on subjects ranging from martial arts and paper crafts to language learning and literature—and our talented authors, illustrators, designers and photographers have won many prestigious awards. We welcome you to explore the wealth of information available on Asia at www.tuttlepublishing.com.

Published by Tuttle Publishing, an imprint of Periplus Editions (HK) Ltd.

www.tuttlepublishing.com

Copyright © 2013 by Periplus Editions (HK) Ltd.

All rights reserved. No part of this publication may be reproduced or utilized in any form or by any means, electronic or mechanical, including photo-copying, recording, or by any information storage and retrieval system, without prior written permission from the publisher.

Library of Congress Cataloging-in-Publication Data

Grant, Glen Nolan.
Tuttle Learning Japanese Kanji : the innovative method to learn the 520 most essential Japanese kanji characters / by Glen Nolan Grant ; illustrations by Ya-Wei Lin.
    p. cm.
 ISBN 978-4-8053-1168-4 (pbk.)
1. Japanese language--Writing. 2. Chinese charac-ters--Japan. 3. Japanese language--Textbooks for foreign speakers--English. I. Lin, Ya-Wei. II. Title.
 PL528.G723 2012
 495.6'82421--dc23
                                        2012018073

ISBN: 978-4-8053-1666-5
(Previously published as ISBN: 978-4-8053-1168-4)

Distributed by

North America, Latin America & Europe
Tuttle Publishing
364 Innovation Drive
North Clarendon, VT 05759-9436 U.S.A.
Tel: 1 (802) 773-8930; Fax: 1 (802) 773-6993
info@tuttlepublishing.com; www.tuttlepublishing.com

Japan
Tuttle Publishing
Yaekari Building, 3rd Floor
5-4-12 Osaki
Shinagawa-ku
Tokyo 141 0032
Tel: (81) 3 5437-0171 Fax: (81) 3 5437-0755
sales@tuttle.co.jp; www.tuttle.co.jp

Asia Pacific
Berkeley Books Pte. Ltd.
3 Kallang Sector #04-01
Singapore 349278
Tel: (65) 6741-2178; Fax: (65) 6741-2179
inquiries@periplus.com.sg
ww.tuttlepublishing.com

First edition
24 23 22 21   5 4 3 2 1   2106TP
Printed in Singapore

TUTTLE PUBLISHING® is a registered trademark of Tuttle Publishing, a division of Periplus Editions (HK) Ltd.

ACKNOWLEDGMENTS

This book is the result of a collaborative effort. Sincere thanks to Eric Oey of Periplus Editions for steering everything in the right direction, as well as to Bob Graham, Calvert Barksdale, Sandra Korinchak, William Notte, Nancy Goh, Angie Ang and the entire editorial and design departments of Tuttle Publishing for their stellar work with the manuscript. Watai Yuko, Niimi Emiko, Nakano Mariko, Watai Fumiko, Murray Grant, Cathy Grant, Damon Vignale, as well as Numamura Shimpei, Rick Havlak and Shaun Culham all offered welcome assistance. Special thanks are also owed to Junko Lucas and Fujitake Rika, for lending their voices to the sound recordings, Matt Pinneo, for his excellent job designing the online interactive software, and to the very talented Ya-Wei Lin, whose wonderful illustrations helped bring each of the stories to life.

This book is dedicated to Mr. H.B. (Henry Barrie) and Mrs. Wilma Grant, for their incredible support and encouragement.

To Download or Stream Bonus Material.

1. You must have an internet connection.
2. Type the URL below into your web browser.

https://www.tuttlepublishing.com/tuttle-learning-japanese-kanji

For support email us at info@tuttlepublishing.com.

Contents

Chapter 4

Chapter 5

Chapter 6

Chapter 7

Chapter 11

Chapter 12

Chapter 13

Chapter 17

Chapter 18

Chapter 19

Chapter 20

Chapter 21

Chapter 22

The **online interactive software** offers you animated stroke-order information and pronunciations for all 520 kanji. See the Download Notice.

Visit the Learning Japanese Kanji page at **www.tuttlepublishing.com** to download Index 4 and other updates and bonus items.

To Download or Stream Bonus Material.

1. You must have an internet connection.
2. Type the URL below into your web browser.

https://www.tuttlepublishing.com/tuttle-learning-japanese-kanji

For support email us at info@tuttlepublishing.com.

INTRODUCTION

This book can help you greatly reduce the time and effort involved in learning to read Japanese. It does so by introducing a method that is both effective and easy to use in memorizing the meanings and pronunciations of *kanji*, the array of characters that are used in the language to symbolize everything from abstract ideas to concrete nouns.

Learning any of the kanji, you will find, is a two-step process, requiring that you remember both the *visual* aspect of a character (so you can recognize it when you see it) and the *aural* aspect (so you will know how to say and, thus, read it). The method presented here will show you how to tackle both of these aspects from the outset, and by so doing enable you to immediately get down to the practical (and fun!) business of recognizing and reading kanji on everything from street signs to newspapers. By the time you finish this book, in fact, you will be able to boast of a Japanese vocabulary numbering in the thousands of words.

Kanji and the Japanese Writing System

Kanji (literally, "Chinese characters") arrived in Japan along with Buddhism and other aspects of Chinese culture approximately 1,500 years ago. As with many concepts introduced into the country from abroad, this writing system was gradually shaped and modified over the centuries to better suit the Japanese themselves. Kanji today comprise one part of written Japanese, being used alongside a pair of much simpler phonetic syllabaries, *katakana* and *hiragana*. Katakana are generally employed to denote foreign words, as well as various technical and scientific terms. Hiragana, on the other hand, have a largely grammatical function, and are used for everything from verb endings to particles. As you can see from the examples below, katakana and hiragana are visually similar; they never contain more than four strokes. Kanji, however, are more varied; they can have anywhere from one to more than 20 strokes.

Hiragana:	か	き	く	け	こ
Katakana:	カ	キ	ク	ケ	コ
Kanji:	東	曜	秋	語	意

Written Japanese is thus a mixture of three elements, and a single sentence can have all three present, as in the following example.

アフリカで水牛とキリンを見ました。

I saw a water buffalo and a giraffe in Africa.

Number and Frequency of Kanji

As katakana and hiragana can be learned quickly (there are only around fifty of each), this book will focus exclusively on learning kanji. It's worth keeping in mind that the Japanese Ministry of Education has stipulated that high school students in Japan are expected to learn 2,136 characters (the so-called "general-use" kanji) by the time they graduate. Magazines and newspapers can employ upwards of 3,000 kanji, although these "extra" characters are often accompanied by hiragana showing how they are to be pronounced; without this, most Japanese would often be unsure of both the meaning of the character in question and its pronunciation.

Despite there being so many kanji, it is important to understand that some are used far more frequently than others. The 500 most common, for example, make up approximately 80% of the kanji you will see. The 1,000 most common bring this figure to over 90%. Learning the 520 kanji presented in this volume, therefore, will offer great immediate benefit.

The Composition of Kanji

In general, kanji dictionaries divide characters into groups that share a common part (called a "radical"). As you can see below, the kanji in the first row all share the same left-hand radical 亻. The kanji in the second row share the same top 宀, while the radical in the third row (夂) appears in various positions.

At times this book will break kanji apart into fragments smaller than radicals. To keep things simple, all radicals and parts that make up a kanji – *but are not themselves kanji* – are called components, and will always be presented in a separate text box immediately before the first character in which they appear.

Stroke Order

Stroke order refers to the sequence of lines that are used to correctly write out a kanji. Knowing this order is important for several reasons. First, it will help train you to quickly count the number of strokes in a character, and thus make it easier to locate unfamiliar kanji (or those for which pronunciations may have been forgotten) in a kanji dictionary. It will also aid you in breaking down characters visually, making it easier to see the components that will help you recall a kanji's meaning. Stroke order diagrams accompany each entry in this book. The accompanying online interactive software, in addition, provides an animated graphic showing each character being written in its proper order.

An Overview of *On-yomi* and *Kun-yomi*

On-yomi and **kun-yomi** are the two main branches of pronunciation (or "readings", as they are called) that are present in modern day Japanese. **On-yomi** are sometimes called the "Chinese readings" of the kanji, as these were the initial pronunciations attached to the characters when they first arrived from China. The **kun-yomi**, on the other hand, developed from within Japan, and are thus referred to as "Japanese readings". This, along with the fact that different **on-yomi** for the same character sometimes arrived from China centuries later, helps explain how a single kanji in Japanese can sometimes have more than one of each type of reading.

Clearly, memorizing these various pronunciations and knowing when to use them are two of the most difficult tasks in learning Japanese.

There are, however, reasons to be optimistic. Over 60% of the kanji have only a single **on-yomi**, or one **on-yomi** and one **kun-yomi**. In addition, when multiple **on-** or **kun-yomi** are present, there is usually only one dominant reading for each. This book will help you determine the most important pronunciations to be learned by classifying every reading as either "common" or "less common". Those that are less common do not merit being learned at this stage of your language study; they are presented only for future reference.

An interesting aspect of Japanese (and an unlucky one for us in this volume!) is that the most complex kanji in terms of pronunciation are often amongst the most simple to write. Do not get discouraged, therefore, when thorny characters such as "person" (Entry 2), "one" (Entry 3), "sun" (Entry 6), and "large" (Entry 17) all show up in the first chapter, as these can be classified with the most difficult in the language. Be patient with such characters, and take comfort in knowing that by the time you finish this book you will have dealt with the trickiest entries in the entire range of the general-use kanji.

Rules for Using *On-yomi* and *Kun-yomi*

There are some useful ground rules that you should keep in mind when learning to read single kanji and compounds (words formed from several kanji put together):

1. Kanji in most compounds are usually read with their **on-yomi**. Note, that when the pronunciations for **on-yomi** are given, these are conventionally written in katakana, and indicated by uppercase letters in English.

KANJI	PRONUNCIATION	MEANING
火山	**KA·ZAN** カ・ザン	*volcano*
家具	**KA·GU** カ・グ	*furniture*
弓道	**KYŪ·DŌ** キュウ・ドウ	*(Japanese) archery*
同時	**DŌ·JI** ドウ・ジ	*simultaneous*

2. Compounds only rarely mix **on-yomi** and **kun-yomi**. Note here that **kun-yomi** are conventionally written in hiragana, and indicated by lowercase letters in English.

KANJI	PRONUNCIATION	MEANING
中古車	CHŪ·KO·SHA チュウ·コ·シャ	*used car*
十二月	JŪ·NI·GATSU ジュウ·ニ·ガツ	*December*
小春	ko·haru こ·はる	*Indian summer*
花見	hana·mi は な·み	*cherry blossom viewing*

3. Kanji in compounds that are accompanied by hiragana are almost always read with their **kun-yomi**.

KANJI (+ HIRAGANA)	PRONUNCIA-TION	MEANING
切り下げる	ki·ri sa·geru き·り さ·げる	*to devalue*
売り家	u·ri ie う·り いえ	*"House for sale"*
名高い	na daka·i な だか·い	*renowned*
立ち止まる	ta·chi do·maru た·ち ど·まる	*to stand still*

4. Kanji that appear alone (that is, they are not part of a compound in a sentence) are usually read with their **kun-yomi**.

KANJI (+ HIRAGANA)	PRONUNCIATION	MEANING
小さい	chii·sai ちい·さい	*small*
犬	inu いぬ	*dog*
東	higashi ひがし	*east*
来る	ku·ru く·る	*to come*

You may have noticed words such as "usually" and "almost always" in the above rules. One thing you will soon learn about kanji is that they seem to take delight in turning up exceptions to every rule. The best thing to do is make use of these exceptions as a means to memorize the words in which they appear. Put another way, you will be much further ahead if you learn to love headstrong words that live by their own rules!

Voiced and Unvoiced Sounds

An important consideration in learning to read Japanese is understanding the difference between voiced and unvoiced consonant sounds. Think of this difference by saying aloud the English words "brink" and "bring"; the "k" of "brink" is unvoiced, while the "g" of "bring" is voiced (you need to vibrate your vocal cords to say it). This is the same distinction, for example, between the Japanese sounds "**ka**" and "**ga**" (か and が). What you need to know is that certain kanji can turn from being unvoiced to voiced, depending on where they appear in a compound. The first entry of the previous section above provides an example: the unvoiced **on-yomi SAN** (サン) changes to the voiced **ZAN** (ザン) in the first sample word shown. Although there are an assortment of rules that explain when such changes take place, it is best to develop a "feel" for when these phonetic transformations might occur. Once this happens, your ear will develop to the point where certain compounds begin sounding more natural with one of their kanji voiced.

Irregular Readings

It sometimes occurs in Japanese that a kanji compound has an irregular reading. Known as *jukujikun*, such readings have no relation to the normal on- or **kun-yomi** of their component kanji. Rather, these irregular readings are assigned to entire compounds rather than to their component kanji.

You will encounter the first of these in Entry 2. In all three such irregular readings shown there, the reading of the kanji "人" is completely different from what we would expect it to be normally. In a sense, this is much like the problem foreigners face when learning English; the pronunciation of the word "cough", for example, has little connection with the normal sound of the letters from which it is made. Fortunately there are not many irregular readings to be learned (less than fifty appear in this book), but as they are all in common use it is best to come to grips with them the moment they are encountered, by memorizing them as individual words. All irregular readings in this book will be presented separately from the "Common words and compounds" section, to make it clear that these are some truly oddball pronunciations.

A Method for Memorizing the Visual and Aural Aspects of Kanji

As we have seen, kanji are typically more visually complex than hiragana and katakana. Because of this, a good way to simplify the task of committing kanji to memory is to look at their constituent parts. We will do just that, breaking the characters down piece-by-piece and assigning meanings to these components based exclusively on *how they look*. When these various components then join together to build kanji, we will make use of short stories featuring the pieces as "actors", accompanied by drawings to help solidify the appearance of the characters in a unique way. This part of our memorization approach, therefore, will focus exclusively on the visual aspect of each kanji.

For the aural side of the equation, we need to take one other difference between the **on-** and **kun-yomi** into account when devising our memorization strategy: there are far fewer **on-yomi** to learn than **kun-yomi**. This is because **on-yomi** are not often complete words on their own – it helps to think of them as short "blocks" of sound that in most cases form words only when they are strung together. (It is worth keeping in mind, though, that the kanji for numbers are a notable exception to this.) Given that roughly 300 **on-yomi** suffice to cover the entire range of Japan's 2,136 general-use characters, a single reading can be attached to many different kanji. **SHŌ** (ショウ), for example, is an **on-yomi** for more than 60 characters. We will be taking advantage of this aspect of Japanese to cut down on the work involved in memorizing these readings.

Our basic plan for committing both the **on-yomi** and **kun-yomi** to memory will be to come up with English keywords that approximate their sounds as closely as possible, and to use these in sentences that also contain a word encompassing the general meaning of the character.

As an example, the kanji for "two" has an **on-yomi** of **NI** (ニ), and a **kun-yomi** of **futa** (ふた). If we choose the word "knee" to suggest **NI**, and the phrase "**who ta**ns" for **futa**, a possible sentence might be the following: "**TWO knee**s? **Who ta**ns only those?". This second side to our approach, therefore, will focus exclusively on the aural aspect of a kanji.

A useful shortcut will involve using the same **on-yomi** keyword every time a kanji having that reading appears (recall that many kanji can share the same **on-yomi**). In the preceding example, therefore, the word "knee" will be used each time a kanji with the **on-yomi** "NI" crops up, and will simply be combined with the different **kun-yomi** and meaning of the new kanji. A major advantage of this approach is that it will make easily confused **on-yomi** such as **HŌ** (ホウ) and **HO** (ホ) absolutely distinctive in your mind, as you will have assigned different keywords to each of these. Given their importance (they will need to be used over and over again with different kanji), the creation of **on-yomi** keywords will be left up to you once a few examples have been provided at the beginning of Chapter 1 – your sentences will be more memorable if these words have a distinct personal meaning for you. The **On-Yomi** *Keyword Table* at the end of the book will help you manage your list of these keywords as it grows, and is designed to be filled in as you encounter each **on-yomi** in the pages ahead. By keeping all these readings in one place, you can refer to them quickly when needed.

The **kun-yomi**, on the other hand, are far greater in number, and therefore best learned individually. Fortunately, they tend to be more distinctive than the **on-yomi**, and are, as a result, often easier to remember once a unique keyword phrase has been created. In order to help with the workload in this respect, suggestions for

kun-yomi keywords are provided through the first ten chapters of this book, but you should not hesitate to use an idea of your own should one spring immediately to mind.

Presentation of the Entries in This Book

Each entry will offer one kanji along with a word embracing its broadest possible meaning, followed by a grid showing its stroke order. Next, you'll see a list of the components making up the character, together with reference numbers indicating the points at which these have been introduced earlier in the book. After a short background section describes the various shades of meaning the character conveys, a story (when required) and illustration are presented to help you memorize the kanji visually. A pronunciation section then lists the most common **on-** and **kun-yomi** for the character followed by readings that you will encounter less frequently. Entries conclude with a section showing the character's use in a number of common Japanese words, and a sample sentence in which the kanji is featured.

There is an important point to keep in mind with respect to the "Common words and compounds" table in each entry: any word or compound consisting of kanji you have already learned will be shown in **bold face**. This will allow you to focus on reviewing those words you have previously encountered. One useful way to review would involve covering up the right-hand columns in the table with your hand or a piece of paper, then drawing it back to reveal the individual kanji meanings, pronunciation, and the overall meaning of the word in question.

In order to make your task a bit more manageable – you'll be mastering 520 of the most important kanji in Japanese, after all! – the book is divided into chapters of 20 to 30 entries

each. This will allow you to periodically review a reasonable number of characters before proceeding onward. Short review sections at the end of each chapter will help you check your learning, along with cumulative exercises following Chapters 5, 10, 16 and 22. Use these reviews to see exactly how far you've come in your mastery of the kanji, and to find out which entries to return to for more practice, if you need it. You'll find answer keys, along with indices listing kanji by stroke count, English meaning and pronunciation at the end of the book. Remember that all of the **on-yomi** are presented in katakana and employ upper-case Roman letters for romaji. The **kun-yomi** are written with hiragana, and have lower-case Roman letters for romaji.

To add an audio aspect to your kanji learning, the accompanying online interactive software contains pronunciations for all the **on-** and **kun-yomi** found in this book, as well as for the sample sentences and common words in each entry; it will be particularly useful in helping you to select your **on-yomi** keywords. An animated graphic is also provided to show you how each kanji is written using the proper stroke order.

Learning to read kanji is fascinating; the characters, so different from those used in our own writing system, have a mysterious quality that attracts everyone who studies Japanese. As you progress through this book and see how kanji are easily able to present even the most complex ideas, it is worth keeping in mind that you are not only setting out to learn a new means of written communication, but another way of conceptualizing the world around you. It's an exciting task, and by using the present book as your guide you will find this process to be not only interesting, but fun. So let's jump right in – and start learning Japanese kanji!

Kanji #1 — 20

KANJI #1

MOUNTAIN

Meaning

Mountain. Our first kanji is one of those wonderful characters whose meaning is obvious at a glance. As kanji such as these are best learned from a simple picture, there is no need for an accompanying story. A number of characters in the book will fall into this category.

Common Pronunciations

Common **ON** reading: **SAN** (サン)
Common **kun** reading: **yama** (やま)

This kanji has only one **on-yomi** and one **kun-yomi** (the pronunciation of which – together with all others in this book – can be heard on the accompanying online interactive software). To suggest these sounds, let's use the word "SANDWICH" for **SAN**, and "yam appetizer" for **yama**. As "sandwich" will now be a permanent keyword for all kanji sharing the reading **SAN**, turn to the

on-yomi table in the back of the book and write "Sandwich" in the space next to **SAN**. Remember that only **on-yomi** (not **kun-yomi**) should be entered in the table.

We now need to link the *meaning* of the kanji to its *sounds* by using the words "mountain", "sandwich", and "yam appetizer" in a sentence. Let's try this: I had a **yam a**ppetizer and a **SAND**WICH on the Mountain. For future review, write this sentence in the box below.

Now for some common words that make use of this kanji. There's no need to worry for the moment about being unable to recognize the other characters, as they will all be learned over the course of the book; at this stage, try to see how the meanings of individual kanji combine to form more complex words (look especially at the fourth example below). This is a useful skill, as it will help foster an intuitive feel for the meanings of unfamiliar compounds that you encounter in the future. It is also one of the most rewarding aspects of learning to read the language. Understanding the logic that went into the formation of a compound not only makes it easier to remember, but offers fascinating insight into the minds of the people who devised it hundreds – if not thousands – of years earlier.

Remember that the uppercase letters and *katakana* here indicate **on-yomi**, with lowercase letters and *hiragana* indicating **kun-yomi**. Recall as well from the introduction that this is our first instance of a character whose unvoiced reading can sometimes become voiced (in examples 3 - 4, where the **on-yomi** changes from **SAN** to **ZAN**). Note how the first kanji of the entry below is presented in **bold face** – indicating that this is a word you now know.

Common Words and Compounds		
山	*mountain*	**yama** や ま
一山	one + mountain = *a pile of something*	hito·**yama** ひ と・や ま
高山	tall + mountain = *alpine*	KŌ·**ZAN** コ ウ・ザ ン
火山	fire + mountain = *volcano*	KA·**ZAN** カ・ザ ン
山村	mountain + village = *mountain village*	**SAN**·SON サ ン・ソ ン

Each entry concludes with a sample sentence featuring the character under discussion; any unfamiliar kanji in these sentences are introduced later in the book.

SAMPLE SENTENCE:

山　に　木　が　あ り ま せ ん 。

yama　**ni**　**ki**　**ga**　　**arimasen.**

mountain　tree　　　are not

= *There are no trees on the mountain.*

KANJI #2

 人　**PERSON**

ノ	人							

Meaning

Person/Human being. Another visually simple kanji for which no story is required. When appearing at the end of country names, this kanji denotes an individual's nationality.

Common Pronunciations

Common **ON** reading: **JIN** (ジ ン); **NIN** (ニ ン)
Common **kun** reading: **hito** (ひ と)

As mentioned in the introduction, 人 is a character that challenges every student of Japanese. As there are few patterns to its distribution of readings, words containing it often need to be memorized individually. **JIN**, however, tends to signify that a person belongs to a certain subgroup of humanity, while **NIN** indicates a person engaged in an activity specified by the kanji preceding it. Look for **JIN** in the first position and at the end of words signifying countries, and be aware that the **kun-yomi** is always voiced (changes from **hito** to **bito**) when it appears outside of the first position, as it does in the sixth compound below.

We now need our keywords and sentence for the three readings. For **JIN** and **NIN** let's choose "JEANS" and "NINCOMPOOP". As you did in the previous entry for 山, turn to the **on-yomi** table at the end of the book, but this time write "Jeans" in the space next to **JIN** and "Nincompoop" in the space next to **NIN**. For the **kun-yomi** "**hito**" we'll use "**heat o**pen". We can now throw everything together into the sentence "That Person is a **NIN**compoop because they **heat o**pen their **JEANS**". For future review, write this sentence in the box below.

Here are our initial encounters with irregular readings. Note that the irregular reading in the first two examples belongs to 人; as you will learn in the next two entries, "一" and "二" are read with their normal **kun-yomi**. In the final compound, both readings are irregular. All three of these words are best thought of as special cases, and memorized individually.

IRREGULAR READINGS

一人	one + person = *one person*	**hito·ri** ひ と・り
二人	two + person = *two people*	**futa·ri** ふ た・り
大人	large + person = *adult*	**otona** お と な

COMMON WORDS AND COMPOUNDS

人	*person*	**hito** ひ と
白人	white + person = *caucasian*	**HAKU·JIN** ハ ク・ジ ン
人口	person + mouth = *population*	**JIN·KŌ** ジ ン・コ ウ
三人	three + person = *three people*	**SAN·NIN** サ ン・ニ ン
四人	four + person = *four people*	**yo·NIN** よ・ニ ン
村人	village + person = *villager*	**mura·bito** む ら・び と
外国人	outside + country + person = *foreigner*	**GAI·KOKU·JIN** ガ イ・コ ク・ジ ン

SAMPLE SENTENCE:

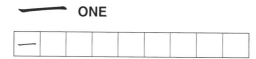

あの	人	の	手	は	小さい	です。
ano	**hito**	**no**	**te**	**wa**	**chii·sai**	**desu.**
that	person		hand		small	

= *That person's hands are small.*

KANJI #3

ONE

一						

Meaning
One. It's hard to find an easier kanji to remember than this!

Remembering this kanji
Despite its simplicity, we need to complicate things a little in order to make use of this character in other kanji. As a result, this character will mean the "top of a hamburger bun" when appearing over all other parts of another character, and the "bottom of a hamburger bun" when it

shows up beneath them. But what of a horizontal line found in the middle of a character? Well, that would be the patty (which vegetarians may wish to picture being made of tofu).
"*In the beginning, there was ONE shapeless... bun.*"

Common Pronunciations
Common **ON** readings: **ICHI** (イ チ); **ITSU** (イ ツ)
Common **kun** reading: **hito** (ひ と)

Though this is the simplest kanji in a visual sense, knowing when to use which of its readings can be tricky. Now that we have some understanding of the difference between voiced and unvoiced consonant sounds, however, it's much easier for us to make sense of it all. Basically, whenever this kanji appears as the first character in a compound it is almost always read with its **on-yomi**, and its pronunciation of **ICHI** or **ITSU** will depend on whether the initial sound of the following kanji is voiced or voiceless (look closely at the sixth compound of the common words section below to see how the sound of **ITSU** "doubles up" with the sound of the next kanji in this situation). Don't worry if this sounds complicated for now; rest assured it will soon become intuitive as compounds begin sounding more natural with one reading or the other.

We now need a sentence with all three common readings together with the word "one". To suggest the sounds **ICHI** and **ITSU**, let's use "**EACH EEL**" and "**EAT SOUP**". Write these in their respective places in the **on-yomi** table at the back of the book. For the **kun-yomi** "hito", we'll use "**he tol**d". Let's choose the following sentence: "One," **he** told us, "**EACH EEL** must **EAT SOUP**." As before, write this sentence in the box below for future reference.

Less Common Pronunciations
Less common **ON** reading: none
Less common **kun** reading: none

Here is another irregular reading; the word "day" appears in brackets to make the logic behind the compound clearer by indicating a secondary meaning of 日 (Entry 6).

IRREGULAR READING		
一日	one + sun (day) = *first day of the month*	**tsuitachi** ついたち

Note that the same compound is shown below with a different pronunciation and meaning. Context will determine which is the appropriate

reading to apply; when 一日 is seen at the top of a newspaper page, for example, it clearly refers to the first day of the month and would thus be read "**tsuitachi**" (ついたち).

COMMON WORDS AND COMPOUNDS		
一	*one*	**ICHI** イチ
一つ	*one (general counter)*	**hito·tsu** ひと・つ
一日	one + sun (day) = *one day*	**ICHI·NICHI** イチ・ニチ
一月	one + moon (month) = *January*	**ICHI·GATSU** イチ・ガツ
同一	same + one = *identical*	**DŌ·ITSU** ドウ・イツ
一回	one + rotate = *once*	**IK·KAI** イッ・カイ
一時	one + time = *one o'clock*	**ICHI·JI** イチ・ジ

SAMPLE SENTENCE:

一時　　　に　会いましょう。
ICHI·JI   **ni**   **a·imashō.**
One o'clock   let's meet
= *Let's meet at one o'clock.*

KANJI #4

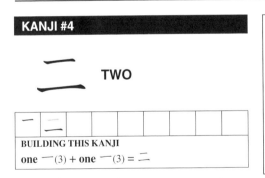

TWO

一	二					

BUILDING THIS KANJI
one 一(3) + one 一(3) = 二

Meaning
All things to do with two, including the ideas of "double" and "**bi-**", etc. Note that the top line is drawn slightly shorter.

Remembering this kanji
On day **TWO**, things began to emerge in the form of a hamburger-like object.

Common Pronunciations
Common **ON** reading: **NI** (二)
Common **kun** reading: **futa** (ふた)

After that bruising encounter with the pronunciation of 一, things become much simpler with 二, although as you can see below there are also three irregular readings that need to be learned with this character. To suggest our **on-yomi**, let's use "**KNEE**", and for our **kun-yomi**, "**who tans**".

After entering KNEE in your **on-yomi** table, write the following sentence in the box below: "Two **KNEES**? **Who ta**ns only those?"

Less Common Pronunciations
Less common **ON** reading: none
Less common **kun** reading: none

Here are three irregular readings that will be frequently encountered.

IRREGULAR READINGS		
二日	two + sun (day) = *second day of the month*	**futsuka** ふつか
二十日	two + ten + sun (day) = *twentieth day of the month*	**hatsuka** はつか
二十歳	two + ten + annual = *twenty years old*	**hatachi** はたち

COMMON WORDS AND COMPOUNDS		
二	*two*	**NI** 二
二つ	*two (general counter)*	**futa**·tsu ふた・つ
二月	two + moon (month) = *February*	**NI**·GATSU 二・ガツ
二十	two + ten = *twenty*	**NI**·JŪ 二・ジュウ
二百	two + hundred = *two hundred*	**NI**·HYAKU 二・ヒャク
二時	two + time = *two o'clock*	**NI**·JI 二・ジ
二週間	two + week + interval = *two weeks*	**NI**·SHŪ·KAN 二・シュウ・カン

SAMPLE SENTENCE:

二月　の　オーストラリア　は
NI·GATSU　no　ōsutoraria　wa
February　　　　Australia
美しい。
utsuku·shii.
beautiful
= *Australia is beautiful in February.*

KANJI #5

三　　THREE

一	二	三					

BUILDING THIS KANJI
one 一(3) + one 一(3) + one 一(3) = 三

Meaning
Three/Triple/Tri-, etc.

Remembering this kanji
On day THREE, the full hamburger - in all its glory - came into being.

Common Pronunciations
Common **ON** reading: **SAN** (サン)
Common **kun** reading: none

It's now time to begin making use of our key short-cut for learning the **on-yomi**. As we have already created a keyword for **SAN** (recall the **on-yomi** for "山" in Entry 1), we will now use that same word here. Let's keep things simple and have "Three **SANDWICHES**" as our phrase. As always, write this in the box below.

Less Common Pronunciations
Less common **ON** reading: none
Less common **kun** readings: **mi**- (み つ); **mi** (み)

Here we have our first examples of some less common readings, in this case the two **kun-yomi** "mi-" and "mi". Keep in mind that "less common" does not equate with "unimportant," as to read Japanese fluently these pronunciations will all have to be learned in time. At this stage, however, it is far more useful to solidify the common readings in your memory and take up the others when they are encountered in the future. When you reach that stage, the appropriate phrase for the respective kanji (e.g. "Three SANDWICHES") can simply be extended to accommodate additional mnemonic words.

In the present example, the first **kun-yomi** appears in only two words, and always "doubles up" in the same way "**ITSU**" (the **on-yomi** for "一") does when preceding voiceless consonant sounds (this is indicated by the short dash after mi). In a sense, this reading is unusual enough to merit the words being learned as if they were irregular readings: 三日 [**mik·ka** (みっ·か)] "the third day of the month", and 三つ [**mit·tsu** (みっ·つ)] the general counter for "three". The second less common reading is more typical of the pronunciations you will find in this section. The words in which it occurs are

obscure; it is enough to be aware that such less common readings exist for some of the kanji in this book, but that you don't need to worry about them for now.

COMMON WORDS AND COMPOUNDS		
三	*three*	**SAN** サン
三人	three + person = *three people*	**SAN·NIN** サン·ニン
三月	three + moon (month) = *March*	**SAN·GATSU** サン·ガツ
三時	three + time = *three o'clock*	**SAN·JI** サン·ジ
三十	three + ten = *thirty*	**SAN·JŪ** サン·ジュウ
三千	three + thousand = *three thousand*	**SAN·ZEN** サン·ゼン

SAMPLE SENTENCE:

三人　　が　早く　来ました。
SAN·NIN **ga** **haya·ku** **ki·mashita.**
Three people　　early　came.
= *Three people came early.*

KANJI #6

SUN

Meaning
This is a kanji with two primary meanings that are clearly related: "sun" and "day". The character will become most familiar to you through its use in the days of the week, and as the initial kanji in the compound for Japan.

This is another character, incidentally, for which we do not need to make use of a story.

Common Pronunciations
Common **ON** reading: **NICHI** (ニチ); **JITSU** (ジツ)
Common **kun** reading: **hi** (ひ)

日 is another example of a simple-looking kanji that can cause a bit of trouble when it comes to pronunciation. As all three of these readings occur frequently, the best approach is to look for patterns: **NICHI** will be encountered overwhelmingly in the first position (**hi** makes only a few appearances), **JITSU** in the second, and **hi** in the third – where it becomes voiced and pronounced **bi** (び). A perfect example of this odd behavior can be seen in the word Sunday, the final example below. Note also that **NICHI** acts like **ITSU** (from 一) by doubling up any unvoiced consonant sounds that follow it, as can be seen in the more formal rendering of the pronunciation for "Japan", **NIP·PON** (ニッ·ポン), from which the more common **NI·HON** (ニ·ホン) has been derived.

At this point we will now start building our own sentences to memorize pronunciations. First, think of a word to approximate the **on-yomi NICHI** (a

German philosoper, perhaps?) and the **on-yomi** JITSU (a martial art, maybe?). Whichever words you decide to use, don't forget to write them in the **on-yomi** table at the back of the book. When it comes to the **kun-yomi**, suggestions will be provided for each one ahead (they can be tough to dream up at times). Don't hesitate, however, to use your own ideas if another word springs immediately to mind. For the present character, try "**he**lium"; use this together with "sun" and your **on-yomi** keywords to create the sentence you will write in the box below.

Less Common Pronunciations

Less common **ON** reading: none
Less common **kun** reading: **ka** (か)

ka is used only to identify the days of the month from 2-10, 14, 17, 20, 24 and 27.

Here are four irregular readings (the most that will appear for any character in this book). You've already seen the first.

IRREGULAR READINGS

一日	one + day = *first day of the month*	tsuitachi ついたち
昨日	past + day = *yesterday*	kinō きのう
今日	now + day = *today*	kyō きょう
明日	bright + day = *tomorrow*	asu あす ashita あした

COMMON WORDS AND COMPOUNDS

日	*sun; day*	hi ひ
一日	one + day = *one day*	ICHI·NICHI イチ·ニチ
日本	sun + main = *Japan*	NI·HON ニ·ホン NIP·PON ニッ·ポン
休日	rest + day = *holiday*	KYŪ·JITSU キュウ·ジツ
毎日	every + day = *daily*	MAI·NICHI マイ·ニチ
朝日	morning + sun = *morning sun*	asa·hi あさ·ひ
日曜日	sun + day of the week + day = *Sunday*	NICHI·YŌ·bi ニチ·ヨウ·び

SAMPLE SENTENCE:

毎日　　日本語　の　本　を
MAI·NICHI　NI·HON·GO　no　HON　o
　daily　　　Japanese　　　book

読みます。
yo·mimasu.
　read

= *(I) read Japanese books every day.*

COMPONENT #7

JELLY BEAN

Here we have our initial "component". These will always be introduced directly before the first character in which they appear, and will be set apart in a separate text box to indicate that they are **not** themselves kanji on their own.

This little guy, incidentally, can appear at various places and on various angles in a kanji. It can also show up with not only one friend, as in Entry 60, but with two, as in Entry 25.

KANJI #7

白 **WHITE**

BUILDING THIS KANJI
Jelly Bean ╲ + Sun 日 (6) = 白

Meaning

White. To the Japanese, this color symbolizes cleanliness and purity (which helps explain the presence of so many white cars in the country!). As a result, the kanji can appear in words with this shade of meaning. The fourth compound is an example.

Remembering this kanji

As this kanji is composed of a separate character and a component, our first story will help you to memorize it:

I think it's safe to say that any **jelly bean**, no matter what color it is, will turn WHITE if thrown into the **sun**.

Common Pronunciations

Common **ON** reading: **HAKU** (ハク)
Common **kun** reading: **shiro** (しろ)

kun-yomi suggestion: "**she wro**te"

Create your **on-yomi** keyword and enter it in the table at the back of the book. After that, write your sentence to remember the **on-yomi** and **kun-yomi** readings in the box below.

Less Common Pronunciations

Less common **ON** reading: **BYAKU** (ビャク)
Less common **kun** readings: **shira** (しら)

COMMON WORDS AND COMPOUNDS		
白	white (noun)	shiro しろ
白い	white (adjective)	shiro·i しろ·い
白人	white + person = caucasian	HAKU·JIN ハク·ジン
明白	bright + white = obvious	MEI·HAKU メイ·ハク
白鳥	white + bird = swan	HAKU·CHŌ ハク·チョウ
白米	white + rice = polished rice	HAKU·MAI ハク·マイ

SAMPLE SENTENCE:

この 白い 馬 の 名前 は "雪"
kono shiro·i uma no na·mae wa "yuki"
this white horse name "snow"
です。
　desu.
= *This white horse's name is "Snow".*

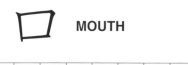

MOUTH

∖	冂	口						

Meaning
Along with the literal meaning of "mouth" and things oral, the kanji also relates to openings in general, from caves and harbors to taps and bottles, for instance.

Remembering this kanji
Has there ever been a more famous MOUTH than that of Dracula? We will use this image of a vampire to suggest the word "mouth" in our stories from now on; a few other simple characters will be treated like this as well.

Common Pronunciations
Common **ON** reading: **KŌ** (コ ウ)
Common **kun** reading: **kuchi** (く ち)

Note how the **kun-yomi** for this kanji can become voiced when it appears in the second position, as it does in the fifth example below.

kun-yomi suggestion: "**coochie** coochie coo"

Create your **on-yomi** keyword and enter it in the table at the back of the book. After that, write your sentence to remember the **on-yomi** and **kun-yomi** readings in the box below.

Less Common Pronunciations
Less common **ON** reading: **KU** (ク)
Less common **kun** readings: none

COMMON WORDS AND COMPOUNDS		
口	*mouth*	**kuchi** く ち
人口	person + mouth = *population*	JIN·KŌ ジ ン・コ ウ
早口	early (fast) + mouth = *rapid speaking*	haya·**kuchi** は や・く ち
口語	mouth + words = *colloquial language*	KŌ·GO コ ウ・ゴ
出口	exit + mouth = *exit*	de·**guchi** で・ぐ ち
口先	mouth + precede = *lip service*	**kuchi**·saki く ち・さ き

SAMPLE SENTENCE:

この 国 の 人口 は 少ない。
kono kuni no JIN·KŌ wa suku·nai.
 this country   population   few
= *This country has a small population.*

COMPONENT #9

PRISON

Though it looks similar to the kanji for "mouth", this component is larger and always completely surrounds whatever happens to be inside it (like a prison should!); this difference can be seen clearly in Entry 9.

KANJI #9

 ROTATE

BUILDING THIS KANJI

Prison □ + Mouth (vampire) 口 (8) = 回

Meaning

Here we see the difference between the "prison" component and the kanji for "mouth". Note that the interior part of this kanji is written following the first two strokes of the prison walls, and becomes enclosed by the final stroke at the bottom. All characters of this type have the same pattern.

The general sense of this kanji relates to the ideas of rotation and going around in both space and time. It can also refer to the vicinity of things (neighborhoods and surroundings, etc), and is well-known to Japanese baseball fans as the character used to denote innings.

Remembering this kanji

It was a great relief for everyone when the **vampire** was finally put in **prison**. It soon became obvious, though, that he could not be kept with the rest of the cons; his offer to "ROTATE the blood" of everyone made them suspicious. The end result, as might be expected, was solitary confinement, a bad enough development for the **vampire** that became even worse when he turned into a bat; flying in endless ROTATIONS apparently brought on some nasty dizzy spells.

Common Pronunciations

Common **ON** reading: **KAI** (カイ)
Common **kun** reading: **mawa** (まわ)

kun-yomi suggestion: "llama wagon"

Create your **on-yomi** keyword and enter it in the table at the back of the book. After that, write your sentence to remember the **on-yomi** and **kun-yomi** readings in the box below.

Less Common Pronunciations

Less common **ON** reading: none
Less common **kun** reading: none

This is a good place to highlight another important aspect of Japanese: the difference between intransitive (intr) and transitive (tr) verbs. Basically, an intransitive verb does not require an object, whereas a transitive verb does. This can be more easily understood by comparing the first two examples given below; a person or thing "goes around" on their own (intransitive), but must have an object to "send around" (transitive). As many Japanese verbs come in such intransitive/transitive pairs (the same kanji accompanied by different *hiragana* attached to the end), it is worth noticing how certain endings often indicate the type of verb; for "**-ru/-su**" pairs such as in the example here, the **-su** verb will always be the transitive.

COMMON WORDS AND COMPOUNDS		
回る (intr)	*to go around*	**mawa·ru** まわ・る
回す (tr)	*to send around*	**mawa·su** まわ・す
一回	one + rotate = *one time*	**IK·KAI** イッ・カイ
二回	two + rotate = *twice*	**NI·KAI** ニ・カイ
引き 回す	pull + rotate = *to pull around*	hi·ki **mawa·su** ひ・き まわ・す
言い 回し	say + rotate = *(turn of) expression*	i·i **mawa·shi** い・い まわ・し

SAMPLE SENTENCE:

私	は	二回	カナダ	へ
watashi	wa	NI·KAI	Canada	e
I		twice	Canada	

行きました。
i·kimashita.
went.
= *I went to Canada twice.*

COMPONENT #10

BALLET

We'll be using this component to mean anything to do with the world of ballet.

KANJI #10

四 **FOUR**

BUILDING THIS KANJI
Prison □ + Ballet ㇯ = 四

Meaning
Four/Quad-, etc. Recall what was noted in Entry 9 regarding the proper stroke order for such characters: the inner part is written after the first two strokes of the prison walls, and enclosed by the final line at the bottom.

Remembering this kanji
Look, I'm not able to say for certain why they threw the **ballet** dancer into **prison**, but I do know one thing: they didn't break him. How could I tell? Well, every afternoon during our exercise period, while the rest of us inmates were either pumping iron or sharpening our shivs, there he'd be, dancing to the FOUR corners of the **prison** walls. We all respected him for it, I suppose; not a single con in those FOUR corners ever laughed at his tights.

Common Pronunciations
Common **ON** reading: **SHI** (シ)
Common **kun** reading: **yon** (よん); **yo** (よ)

Do not choose the word "SHE" for your **on-yomi**, as we will be needing it far more for **kun-yomi**, and a word less abstract (try to think of things, places or people) will always be more memorable and make your sentences easier to create. As you can see from the examples below, this character has a tendency to appear in compounds having a mix of **kun-yomi** and **on-yomi**; this makes it a little trickier than the other kanji for numbers.

kun-yomi suggestions: "try only"; "yodel"

Create your **on-yomi** keyword and enter it in the table at the back of the book. After that, write your sentence to remember the **on-yomi** and **kun-yumi** readings in the box below.

Less Common Pronunciations
Less common **ON** reading: none
Less common **kun** reading: **yo-** (よっ)

This reading is like the less common **kun-yomi** for "three" in that it appears in only two words: 四日 [**yok·ka** (よっ・か)] "the fourth day of the month", and 四つ [**yot·tsu** (よっ・つ)] the general counter for "four". These words are best memorized as is.

COMMON WORDS AND COMPOUNDS		
四	*four*	**SHI** シ
四人	four + person = *four people*	**yo·NIN** よ・ニン
四月	four + moon (month) = *April*	**SHI·GATSU** シ・ガツ
四時	four + time = *four o'clock*	**yo·JI** よ・ジ
四十	four + ten = *forty*	**yon·JŪ** よん・ジュウ
四百	four + hundred = *four hundred*	**yon·HYAKU** よん・ヒャク

SAMPLE SENTENCE:

四月　　に　は　雨　が　多い。
SHI·GATSU ni wa ame ga ō·i.
　April　　　　　rain　　many.

= *There's a lot of rain in April.*

KANJI #11

 MOON

Meaning

As with the kanji for "sun", this character carries two meanings that are clearly related, in this case "moon" and "month." You will become very familiar with this kanji through its use in the names of the months. This is another visually simple character for which no story is required.

Common Pronunciations

Common **ON** reading: **GETSU** (ゲツ); **GATSU** (ガツ)
Common **kun** reading: **tsuki** (つき)

Like **ITSU** (with the kanji " 一 ") and other readings ending in "-TSU", the two **on-yomi** double up any unvoiced consonant sounds that follow. You will encounter **GATSU** primarily in the names of the months.

kun-yomi suggestion: "bought **Sioux kee**psakes"

Create your **on-yomi** keyword and enter it in the table at the back of the book. After that, write your sentence to remember the **on-yomi** and **kun-yomi** readings in the box below.

Less Common Pronunciations

Less common **ON** reading: none
Less common **kun** readings: none

COMMON WORDS AND COMPOUNDS		
月	*moon; month*	**tsuki** つき
一月	one + month = *January*	**ICHI·GATSU** イチ・ガツ
二月	two + month = *February*	**NI·GATSU** ニ・ガツ
三月	three + month = *March*	**SAN·GATSU** サン・ガツ
四月	four + month = *April*	**SHI·GATSU** シ・ガツ
先月	precede + month = *last month*	**SEN·GETSU** セン・ゲツ
月見	moon + see = *moon viewing*	**tsuki·mi** つき・み

SAMPLE SENTENCE:

九月　　に　　月見　　に　行きました。
KU·GATSU ni　tsuki·mi　ni　i·kimashita.
September　　moon viewing　　went

= *I went moon viewing in September.*

明 **BRIGHT**

1	冂	日	日	明	明	明	明

BUILDING THIS KANJI
Sun 日 (6) + Moon 月 (11) = 明

Meaning
Bright/Clear/Light.

Remembering this kanji
"I'm far more **BRIGHT** than you are," said the **moon**.
"Really?" answered the **sun**, smiling. "I find that hard to believe. I'm so **BRIGHT** people have to wear shades; how many people do you notice wearing **moon**glasses."

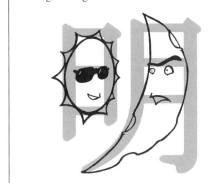

Common Pronunciations
Common **ON** reading: **MEI** (メイ)
Common **kun** reading: **a** (あ); **aka** (あか)

kun-yomi suggestions: "apt"; "stack a…".

Create your **on-yomi** keyword and enter it in the table at the back of the book. After that, write your sentence to remember the **on-yomi** and **kun-yomi** readings in the box below.

Less Common Pronunciations
Less common **ON** reading: **MYŌ** (ミョウ); **MIN** (ミン)
Less common **kun** reading: **aki** (あき)

COMMON WORDS AND COMPOUNDS		
明るい	*bright*	**aka**·rui あか·るい
明かり	*clearness*	a·kari あ·かり
明白	bright + white = *obvious*	**MEI**·**HAKU** メイ·ハク
不明	not + bright = *unclear*	FU·**MEI** フ·メイ

SAMPLE SENTENCE:

月　は　明るい　です。

tsuki wa aka·rui   desu.
moon   bright

= *The moon is bright.*

木 **TREE**

一	十	才	木				

Meaning
Tree/Wood. No story required.

Common Pronunciations
Common **ON** reading: **MOKU** (モク); **BOKU** (ボク)
Common **kun** reading: **ki** (き)

This is another kanji that will require patience to learn. Look for **MOKU** to show up in the first position, however, and **BOKU** in the second. **ki** occurs less often, but appears with equal frequency in the first or second position.

kun-yomi suggestion: "keel" (do not use "key", as this will have far more value as an **on-yomi** keyword).

Create your **on-yomi** keywords and enter them in the table at the back of the book. After that, write your sentence to remember the **on-yomi** and **kun-yomi** readings in the box below.

Less Common Pronunciations
Less common **ON** reading: none
Less common **kun** readings: ko (こ)

Here is a common irregular reading you will often see on clothing tags, etc. The second kanji, incidentally, is not covered in this book.

Such characters will be included only when they form common words in which the pronunciation of the character we are considering has an irregular reading. Irregular readings containing these kanji will be identified with an asterisk (*).

IRREGULAR READINGS		
木綿*	tree + cotton = *cotton (cloth)*	**mo·MEN** も・メン

COMMON WORDS AND COMPOUNDS		
木	*tree*	**ki** き
木曜日	tree + day of the week + sun (day) = *Thursday*	**MOKU·YŌ·bi** モク・ヨウ・び
木星	tree + star = *Jupiter (planet)*	**MOKU·SEI** モク・セイ
大木	large + tree = *large tree*	**TAI·BOKU** タイ・ボク
土木	earth + tree = *civil engineering*	**DO·BOKU** ド・ボク

SAMPLE SENTENCE:

あの 高い 木 の 名前 が 分かります か 。

ano taka·i ki no na·mae ga wa·karimasu
that tall tree name understand
ka.

= *Do you know the name of that tall tree?*

五 **FIVE**

一 丆 五 五

Meaning
Five.

Remembering this kanji
This is how most people feel when their work day ends at **FIVE** o'clock.

Common Pronunciations
Common **ON** reading: **GO** (ゴ)
Common **kun** reading: none

Create your **on-yomi** keyword and enter it in the table at the back of the book. After that, write your sentence to remember the **on-yomi** reading in the box below.

COMMON WORDS AND COMPOUNDS		
五	*five*	**GO** ゴ
五人	five + person = *five people*	**GO·NIN** ゴ・ニン
五月	five + moon (month) = *May*	**GO·GATSU** ゴ・ガツ
五十	five + ten = *fifty*	**GO·JŪ** ゴ・ジュウ
五時	five + time = *five o'clock*	**GO·JI** ゴ・ジ

Less Common Pronunciations
Less common **ON** reading: none
Less common **kun** reading: **itsu** (いつ)

As you might expect, this reading is of most use because of its appearance in two words: 五日 [**itsu·ka** (いつ・か)] "the fifth day of the month," and 五つ [**itsu·tsu** (いつ・つ)] the general counter for "five."

SAMPLE SENTENCE:

五十人 で 山 へ 行きました。
GO·JŪ·NIN de yama e i·kimashita.
fifty people   mountain   went

= *Fifty (of us) went to the mountain.*

KANJI #15

EYE

Meaning
The general meaning is eye. An important secondary usage of the character, however, can be seen when it comes at the end of a number compound such as in the third example below. In these instances it is read with its **kun-yomi** and indicates the "-th" suffix in words such as "fourth" and "seventh" (it also expresses the related endings of "first", "second" and "third" in such compounds).

Remembering this kanji
In the interests of full disclosure, it should be said that the Cyclops lobbied long and hard to be this book's representative for "EYE". Well, it looks like his efforts—which included a few thoughtfully chosen gifts—have paid off. Cyclops, you have been placed on an equal footing with Dracula!

Common Pronunciations
Common **ON** reading: **MOKU** (モク)
Common **kun** reading: **me** (め)

me is the more common of the two readings. Remember to use the keyword for **MOKU** that you entered into the **on-yomi** table earlier (from the kanji "木", Entry 13).

kun-yomi suggestion: "**metric**"

Write your sentence to remember the **on-yomi** and **kun-yomi** readings in the box below.

COMMON WORDS AND COMPOUNDS		
目	*eye*	**me** め
目玉	eye + jewel = *eyeball*	**me**·dama め·だま
八回目	eight + rotate + eye = *the eighth time*	HACHI·KAI·**me** ハ チ·カ イ·め
目立つ	eye + stand = *to stand out*	**me** da·tsu め だ·つ
注目	pour + eye = *notice*	CHŪ·**MOKU** チュ ウ·モ ク

SAMPLE SENTENCE:

王子 の 目 は 青い です。
Ō·JI no me wa ao·i desu.
prince   eye   blue

= *The prince's eyes are blue.*

Less Common Pronunciations
Less common **ON** reading: **BOKU** (ボ ク)
Less common **kun** reading: **ma** (ま)

KANJI #16

女 **WOMAN**

Meaning
Woman/Female. No story required.

Common Pronunciations
Common **ON** reading: **JO** (ジ ョ)
Common **kun** reading: **onna** (お ん な)

kun-yomi suggestion: "**own NASA**"

Create your **on-yomi** keyword and enter it in the table at the back of the book. After that, write your

sentence to remember the **on-yomi** and **kun-yomi** readings in the box below.

Less Common Pronunciations
Less common **ON** reading: **NYO** (ニ ョ);
NYŌ (ニ ョ ウ)
Less common **kun** reading: **me** (め)

COMMON WORDS AND COMPOUNDS		
女	woman	**onna** お ん な
女王	woman + king = *queen*	**JO·Ō** ジ ョ·オ ウ
少女	few + woman = *girl*	**SHŌ·JO** ショ ウ·ジ ョ
女心	woman + heart = *a woman's heart*	**onna**·gokoro お ん な·ご こ ろ
雪女	snow + woman = *snow fairy*	yuki·**onna** ゆ き·お ん な
男女	man + woman = *men and women*	DAN·**JO** ダ ン·ジ ョ

SAMPLE SENTENCE:

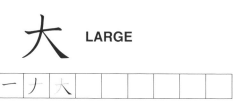

女　の　人　は　木　の　下　で

onna　no　hito　wa　ki　no　shita　de

woman　person　tree　under

止まりました。

to·marimashita.

  stopped

= *The woman stopped under a tree.*

KANJI #17

大　LARGE

一	ナ	大					

Meaning
Large/Big. The meanings of "important" and "great (not always in a positive sense)" can also be implied in words containing this kanji.

Remembering this kanji
Not many things are LARGER than a sumo wrestler, so we'll use this image as our connection to the character from now on.

Common Pronunciations
Common **ON** reading: **DAI** (ダイ); **TAI** (タイ)
Common **kun** reading: ō (おお)

As **DAI** and **TAI** occur with equal frequency (ō much less often) when this kanji appears in the first position, this character presents a special challenge for students of Japanese. When it occupies other positions in a compound, however, **DAI** is far and away the more common reading.

kun-yomi suggestion: "oboe"

Create your **on-yomi** keywords and enter them in the table at the back of the book. After that, write your sentence to remember the **on-yomi** and **kun-yomi** readings in the box below.

Less Common Pronunciations
Less common **ON** reading: none
Less common **kun** reading: none

Here is the irregular reading we met earlier in Entry 2.

IRREGULAR READINGS		
大人	large + person = *adult*	**otona** おとな

COMMON WORDS AND COMPOUNDS		
大きい	*large*	ō·kii おお・きい
大木	large + tree = *large tree*	**TAI**·BOKU タイ・ボク
大好き	large + like = *to really like*	**DAI** su·ki ダイ す・き
大体	large + body = *in general*	**DAI·TAI** ダイ・タイ
大雨	large + rain = *heavy rain*	ō·ame おお・あめ
大切	large + cut = *important*	**TAI·SETSU** タイ・セツ
大学	large + study = *university*	**DAI·GAKU** ダイ・ガク

SAMPLE SENTENCE:

あの　森　には　　大木　　が　多い。

ano　mori　ni wa　TAI·BOKU　ga　ō·i.

that　forest　　　large trees　　many

= *There are many large trees in that forest.*

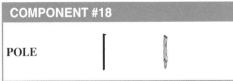

COMPONENT #18

POLE | |

KANJI #18

中 **MIDDLE**

| ＼ | ⼞ | ⼞ | 中 | | | | |

BUILDING THIS KANJI
Mouth (vampire) ⼞ (8) + Pole | = 中

Meaning
A versatile character that expresses the ideas of "middle", "medium", and "average", etc. This kanji can also serve as an abbreviation for China; "日" is used as the equivalent with respect to Japan.

Remembering this kanji
I approached the sleeping **vampire** with the **pole** shaking in my hands: it was now or never. Raising the weapon over his feet I prepared to bring it down, but at the last moment the master's words came back: "How many times must we go over this? Drive it through the MIDDLE of the **vampire**! The MIDDLE!" Yes, I thought, placing the **pole** over the **vampire's** stomach, it would all go perfectly now.

Common Pronunciations
Common **ON** reading: CHŪ (チュウ)
Common **kun** reading: naka (なか)

kun-yomi suggestion: "**knack 'a**"

Create your **on-yomi** keyword and enter it in the table at the back of the book. After that, write your sentence to remember the **on-yomi** and **kun-yomi** readings in the box below.

Less Common Pronunciations
Less common **ON** reading: JŪ (ジュウ)
Less common **kun** reading: none

COMMON WORDS AND COMPOUNDS		
中	*middle*	**naka** なか
中心	middle + heart = *center*	**CHŪ·SHIN** チュウ・シン
中米	middle + rice (America) = *Central America*	**CHŪ·BEI** チュウ・ベイ
中国	middle + country = *China*	**CHŪ·GOKU** チュウ・ゴク
中立	middle + stand = *neutrality*	**CHŪ·RITSU** チュウ・リツ
中古	middle + old = *secondhand*	**CHŪ·KO** チュウ・コ
水中	water + middle = *underwater/in the water*	**SUI·CHŪ** スイ・チュウ

SAMPLE SENTENCE:

車　の　中　に　なに　が　あります　か。
kuruma no naka ni nani ga arimasu ka.
　car　　middle　what　　is
= *What is in your car?*

八 EIGHT

Meaning
Eight.

Remembering this kanji
This is another kanji in the manner of "one" and "mouth" for which it is useful to assign an external meaning, in this case, a volcano: *"I can't be sure, but I think the Krakatoa volcano (which erupted in the 1880's) was one of the EIGHT wonders of the ancient world."*

Common Pronunciations
Common **ON** reading: **HACHI** (ハチ)
Common **kun** reading: none

Create your **on-yomi** keyword and enter it in the table at the back of the book. After that, write your sentence to remember the **on-yomi** reading in the box below.

Less Common Pronunciations
Less common **ON** reading: none
Less common **kun** reading: **yō** (よう); **ya-** (やつ); **ya** (や)

Interestingly, the first two **kun-yomi** readings are like the less common **kun-yomi** for "three" and "four" (Entries 5 and 10, respectively), and are found in only one word each: 八日 [**yō·ka** (よう·か)] "the eighth day of the month," and 八つ [**yat·tsu** (やっ·つ)] the general counter for "eight."

COMMON WORDS AND COMPOUNDS		
八	*eight*	**HACHI** ハチ
八月	eight + moon (month) = *August*	**HACHI·GATSU** ハチ·ガツ
八人	eight + person = *eight people*	**HACHI·NIN** ハチ·ニン
八円	eight + circle (yen) = *eight yen*	**HACHI·EN** ハチ·エン
八時	eight + time = *eight o'clock*	**HACHI·JI** ハチ·ジ

SAMPLE SENTENCE:

八月　　に 秋田 へ 行きましょう。
HACHI·GATSU ni Aki·ta e i·kimashō.
　August　　　Akita　　　let's go
= *Let's go to Akita in August.*

COMPONENT #20

HARPOON

Note how the barbed hook on the bottom of this component distinguishes it from the pole (Component 18).

KANJI #20

 SMALL

亅	丿	小						

BUILDING THIS KANJI

Harpoon 亅 + Eight (volcano) 八 (19) = 小

Meaning

Small/Little.

Remembering this kanji

The dwarf spoke, his words SMALL comfort: "If you be going after the miniature lava whale," he said, "you'd best toss your **harpoon** in that **volcano** over yonder. Your chances of landing him are SMALL, though, given that he's so… SMALL."

Common Pronunciations

Common **ON** reading: **SHŌ** (ショウ)
Common **kun** reading: **chii** (ちい); **ko** (こ)

SHŌ and **ko** are the readings most often found in compounds, **chii** only being used in the first example below.

kun-yomi suggestions: "cheeeese!"; "coat"

Create your **on-yomi** keyword and enter it in the table at the back of the book. After that, write your sentence to remember the **on-yomi** and **kun-yomi** readings in the box below.

Less Common Pronunciations

Less common **ON** reading: none
Less common **kun** reading: **o** (お)

COMMON WORDS AND COMPOUNDS		
小さい	*small*	**chii**·sai ちい·さい
小春	small + spring = *Indian summer*	**ko**·haru こ·はる
小国	small + country = *small country*	**SHŌ**·KOKU ショウ·コク
小高い	small + tall = *slightly elevated*	**ko** daka·i こ だか·い
最小	most + small = *smallest*	SAI·**SHŌ** サイ·ショウ

SAMPLE SENTENCE:

あの 車 はとても 小さい です ね。

ano kuruma wa totemo chii·sai desu ne.

that   car   really   small   isn't it

= *That car is really small, isn't it?*

CHAPTER 1 REVIEW EXERCISES

A. Please match the following kanji to their meanings.

1. 人   a. Rotate
2. 女   b. Large
3. 月   c. Woman
4. 木   d. Mouth
5. 大   e. Person
6. 二   f. Two
7. 回   g. Moon
8. 小   h. Three
9. 三   i. Tree
10. 口   j. Small

B. Please match the following meanings to their
kanji, and these to their **on** or **kun-yomi**.

1. Bright   a. 白   1. **yama**（やま）
2. Five   b. 目   2. **ICHI**（イチ）
3. White   c. 山   3. **me**（め）
4. Four   d. 八   4. **hi**（ひ）
5. Eye   e. 日   5. **GO**（ゴ）
6. Middle   f. 一   6. **HACHI**（ハチ）
7. Mountain   g. 明   7. **SHI**（シ）
8. One   h. 中   8. **aka**（あか）
9. Eight   i. 四   9. **naka**（なか）
10. Sun   j. 五   10. **HAKU**（ハク）

C. Please choose the best answer(s) to the following questions.

1. Which of the following readings apply to
   the kanji 人?
   a. **Ō**（オウ）
   b. **hito**（ひと）
   c. **NIN**（ニン）
   d. **JIN**（ジン）
   e. **hi**（ひ）

2. Where is the most appropriate place to go in
   a spaceship?
   a. 人
   b. 目
   c. 月
   d. 口
   e. 木

3. Which of the following readings apply to
   the kanji 女?
   a. **ZEN**（ゼン）
   b. **SHUN**（シュン）
   c. **uchi**（うち）
   d. **JO**（ジョ）
   e. **onna**（おんな）

4. Which of the following readings apply to
   the kanji 口?
   a. **KŌ**（コウ）
   b. **haru**（はる）
   c. **SHI**（シ）
   d. **kuchi**（くち）
   e. **Ō**（オウ）

5. Which of the following readings apply to
   the kanji 日?
   a. **hi**（ひ）
   b. **to**（と）
   c. **KOKU**（コク）
   d. **JITSU**（ジツ）
   e. **NICHI**（ニチ）

D. Please answer the following questions.
1. Which is the correct reading of 回る?
   a. **mi·ru**（み・る）
   b. **sube·ru**（すべ・る）
   c. **haka·ru**（はか・る）
   d. **mawa·ru**（まわ・る）

2. What is the reading for 一日 when it indicates the first day of a month?
   a. **tama**（たま）
   b. **kuni**（くに）
   c. **uchi**（うち）
   d. **kuchi**（くち）
   e. **tsuitachi**（ついたち）

3. Given that **hitori**（ひとり）is the reading
   for 一人, what is the reading for 二人?
   a. **hatsuka**（はつか）
   b. **futari**（ふたり）
   c. **hatachi**（はたち）
   d. **futsuka**（ふつか）

4. Which of the following does not belong with the others?
   a. 一
   b. 八
   c. 四
   d. 小
   e. 三

5. Which is the correct reading of 白い?
   a. **furu·i** (ふる·い)
   b. **shiro·i** (しろ·い)
   c. **maru·i** (まる·い)
   d. **hiro·i** (ひろ·い)

E. Please match the following compounds and words to their meanings and pronunciations.

1.	三月	a. Twice	1.	**hito·tsu** (ひと·つ)
2.	白人	b. Obvious	2.	**JIN·KŌ** (ジン·コウ)
3.	二回	c. White	3.	**shiro·i** (しろ·い)
4.	小さい	d. Five people	4.	**SAN·GATSU** (サン·ガツ)
5.	明白	e. Small	5.	**chii·sai** (ちい·さい)
6.	人口	f. March	6.	**NI·KAI** (ニ·カイ)
7.	一つ	g. Large tree	7.	**GO·NIN** (ゴ·ニン)
8.	五人	h. One	8.	**TAI·BOKU** (タイ·ボク)
9.	白い	i. Population	9.	**HAKU·JIN** (ハク·ジン)
10.	大木	j. Caucasian	10.	**MEI·HAKU** (メイ·ハク)

CHAPTER TWO

Kanji #21—40

KANJI #21

SHELLFISH

BUILDING THIS KANJI
Eye (Cyclops) 目 (15) + Eight (volcano) 八 (19) = 貝

Meaning

Shellfish/Seashell. As the lack of common words and compounds in the table indicates, this is not the most useful character to learn for its own sake. It often appears as a component in other kanji, however, and for this reason needs to be learned here.

Remembering this kanji

Celebrating his inclusion in this book, the **Cyclops** decided to throw an enormous **SHELL-FISH** barbecue for all his friends. Minotaurs, griffins, nymphs and satyrs…even the sirens showed up (after agreeing to refrain from singing, of course). It was quite a crowd, but the grill the **Cyclops** stretched over a nearby **volcano** was more than enough to accommodate the food. And what a variety of **SHELLFISH** there was! Oysters, mussels, abalone, scallops…everyone agreed it was the best spread since Zeus' clam-bake on Mt. Etna.

Common Pronunciations

Common **ON** reading: none
Common **kun** reading: **kai** (かい)

This character is always unvoiced (**kai**) in the first position, and becomes voiced (**gai**) elsewhere.

    kun-yomi suggestion: "**Kai**ser roll". If you are choosing your own keywords for the **kun-yomi**, do not use the same word you selected for **KAI** (カイ), the **on-yomi** for " 回 " in Entry 9; it is best to keep the two types of readings separate. Create your sentence to remember the **kun-yomi** reading in the box below.

Less Common Pronunciations

Less common **ON** reading: **BAI** (バイ)
Less common **kun** reading: none

COMMON WORDS AND COMPOUNDS		
貝	*shellfish*	**kai** かい
生貝	life + shellfish = *raw shellfish*	nama·**gai** なま・がい
赤貝	red + shellfish = *ark shell*	aka·**gai** あか・がい

SAMPLE SENTENCE:

この レストラン の 赤貝 は 有名

kono   resutoran   no aka·gai wa YŪ·MEI
this   restaurant   ark shell famous

です。

desu.
  is

= *The ark shell in this restaurant is famous.*

COMPONENT #22

POLICE

Our hat will symbolize the police, or any other authority from sheriffs to park rangers.

KANJI #22

六 **SIX**

'	一	六	六				

BUILDING THIS KANJI
Police 一 + Eight (volcano) 八 (19) = 六

Meaning
Six.

Remembering this kanji
Something tells me that if you throw a police hat into a volcano, it will burn. Don't ask me how I know this; it's my SIXTH sense.

Common Pronunciations
Common **ON** reading: **ROKU** (ロ ク)
Common **kun** reading: none

Create your **on-yomi** keyword and enter it in the table at the back of the book. After that, write your sentence to remember the **on-yomi** reading in the box below.

Less Common Pronunciations
Less common **ON** reading: **RIKU** (リ ク)
Less common **kun** reading: **mui** (むい); **mu-** (むっ); **mu** (む)

You may have guessed that these first two **kun-yomi** are found in only one word each: 六日 [**mui·ka** (むい・か)] "the sixth day of the month," and 六つ [**mut·tsu** (むっ・つ)] the general counter for "six."

COMMON WORDS AND COMPOUNDS		
六	*six*	**ROKU** ロク
六人	six + person = *six people*	**ROKU·NIN** ロク・ニン
六月	six + moon (month) = *June*	**ROKU·GATSU** ロク・ガツ
六円	six + circle (yen) = *six yen*	**ROKU·EN** ロク・エン
六時	six + time = *six o'clock*	**ROKU·JI** ロク・ジ

SAMPLE SENTENCE:

六人　は　日本　へ　行きました。
ROKU·NIN wa NI·HON e i·kimashita.
　six people　　Japan　　　went
= *The six people went to Japan.*

KANJI #23

王 KING

| 一 | 丨 | 干 | 王 | | | | |

Meaning

Crowns, scepters, long purple robes…think of kings and royalty when you see this kanji. No story required.

Common Pronunciations

Common **ON** reading: Ō (オウ)
Common **kun** reading: none

Only one reading to deal with here — wouldn't it be nice if all the kanji were this well-behaved? Create your **on-yomi** keyword and enter it in the table at the back of the book. After that, write your sentence to remember the **on-yomi** reading in the box below.

Less Common Pronunciations

Less common **ON** reading: none
Less common **kun** reading: none

COMMON WORDS AND COMPOUNDS		
女王	woman + king = *queen*	JO·Ō ジョ・オウ
王国	king + country = *kingdom*	Ō·KOKU オウ・コク
王朝	king + morning = *dynasty*	Ō·CHŌ オウ・チョウ
王子	king + child = *prince*	Ō·JI オウ・ジ
海王星	sea + king + star = *Neptune (planet)*	KAI·Ō·SEI カイ・オウ・セイ

SAMPLE SENTENCE:
女王 が 日本 へ 行きました。
JO·Ō ga NIHON e   i·kimashita.
Queen   Japan   went.
= *The queen went to Japan.*

KANJI #24

玉 JEWEL

| 一 | 丁 | 干 | 王 | 玉 | | | |

BUILDING THIS KANJI
King 王(23) + Jelly Bean ⟍ = 玉

Meaning

This character appears in the names of a variety of precious stones, including the compounds for rubies, sapphires, and emeralds. It also incorporates the sense of a "ball-like" object, a meaning evident in the final examples below.

Take note of the correct stroke order for this kanji ("King" + "Jelly bean"); the three horizontal lines are **not** written first.

Remembering this kanji

"I wish to reward you for your faithful service," the **king** said to his minister. "There is a **jelly bean** for you at my feet; you may take it if you wish." The man was a little confused by this, of course, until he bent down and saw a JEWEL shaped like a **jelly bean** next to the **king's** shoes. "You might not want to eat that," smiled the **king**. "After all, JEWELS aren't particularly tasty."

Common Pronunciations

Common **ON** reading: none
Common **kun** reading: **tama** (た ま)

Note how often this character changes from the voiceless "**tama**" (た ま) to its corresponding voiced form "**dama**" (だ ま) when in the second position.

kun-yomi suggestion: "hot **tama**le"

Create your sentence to remember the **kun-yomi** reading in the box below.

Less Common Pronunciations

Less common **ON** reading: **GYOKU** (ギョク)
Less common **kun** reading: none

COMMON WORDS AND COMPOUNDS		
玉	*jewel*	**tama** た ま
玉ねぎ	*onion*	tama·negi た ま・ね ぎ
目玉	eye + jewel = *eyeball*	me·dama め・だ ま
水玉	water + jewel = *drop of water*	mizu·tama み ず・た ま
火玉	fire + jewel = *fireball*	hi·dama ひ・だ ま
雪玉	snow + jewel = *snowball*	yuki·dama ゆ き・だ ま

SAMPLE SENTENCE:

玉ねぎ を 切って 下さい。

tama·negi o ki·tte kuda·sai.
onion(s) cut please
= *Please cut the onions.*

HOOK

 HEART

'	㇆	㇂	㇁					

BUILDING THIS KANJI
Jelly Bean ヽ + Hook ㇚ + Jelly Bean ヽ +
Jelly Bean ヽ = 心

Remembering this kanji

There are a couple of ways to capture a HEART. The first is by using kindness; giving gifts such as a trio of **jelly beans** is an example of this method. The second is to simply use a **hook**.

Meaning

This unique-looking character conveys the idea of heart in all its shades of meaning, be it the actual physical organ, the sense of "feelings," or the concept of something's "core."

Common Pronunciations

Common **ON** reading: **SHIN** (シ ン)
Common **kun** reading: **kokoro** (こ こ ろ)

The **kun-yomi** for this kanji always becomes voiced (**gokoro**) when not in the first position (as in the second and fourth examples).

kun-yomi suggestion: "cocoa roast"

Create your **on-yomi** keyword and enter it in the table at the back of the book. After that, write your sentence to remember the **on-yomi** and **kun-yomi** readings in the box below.

COMMON WORDS AND COMPOUNDS		
心	*heart*	**kokoro** こころ
女心	woman + heart = *a woman's heart*	onna·**gokoro** おんな・ごころ
中心	middle + heart = *center*	CHŪ·**SHIN** チュウ・シン
下心	lower + heart = *ulterior motive*	shita·**gokoro** した・ごころ
安心	ease + heart = *peace of mind*	AN·**SHIN** アン・シン
愛国心	love + country + heart = *patriotism*	AI·**KOKU**·SHIN アイ・コク・シン

Less Common Pronunciations
Less common **ON** reading: none
Less common **kun** reading: none

Here is a common irregular reading containing this character, composed of both **kun** and **on-yomi**.

IRREGULAR READINGS		
心地	heart + ground = *feeling*	koko·**CHI** ここ・チ

SAMPLE SENTENCE:

女王　　　によると　　　愛国心　　　は
JO·Ō　　**ni yoru to**　**AI·KOKU·SHIN**　**wa**
queen　　 according to　　 patriotism

大切　　だ　そう　です。
TAI·SETSU da　sō　desu.
 important

= *According to the queen, patriotism is important.*

KANJI #26

 COUNTRY

BUILDING THIS KANJI
Prison 囗 + Jewel 玉(24) = 国

Meaning
Think of "country" here in the sense of a nation state.

Remembering this kanji
Most folks will state that their COUNTRY is like a **jewel**, one that must be protected from external dangers. And so they build walls. But is there a difference between being protected and being in **prison**? It's a thorny question, but perhaps the philosopher Epicurus answered it best: "There may be a **jewel** of a COUNTRY within **prison** walls somewhere, but I'd be willing to bet they'd have lousy food."

Common Pronunciations
Common **ON** reading: **KOKU** (コ ク)
Common **kun** reading: **kuni** (く に)

kun-yomi suggestion: "ty**coon e**ra"

Create your **on-yomi** keyword and enter it in the table at the back of the book. After that, write your sentence to remember the **on-yomi** and **kun-yomi** readings in the box below.

Less Common Pronunciations
Less common **ON** reading: none
Less common **kun** reading: none

COMMON WORDS AND COMPOUNDS		
国	*country*	kuni く に
王国	king + country = *kingdom*	Ō·KOKU オウ・コク
全国	complete + country = *the whole country/ nationwide*	ZEN·KOKU ゼン・コク
入国	enter + country = *to enter a country*	NYŪ·KOKU ニュウ・コク
国内	country + inside = *domestic*	KOKU·NAI コク・ナイ
外国人	outside + country + person = *foreigner*	GAI·KOKU·JIN ガイ・コク・ジン
愛国心	love + country + heart = *patriotism*	AI·KOKU· SHIN アイ・コク・シン

SAMPLE SENTENCE:

あの 国 には 外国人 が 多い。
ano kuni ni wa GAI·KOKU·JIN ga ō·i.
that country   foreigners   many
= *There are many foreigners in that country.*

COMPONENT #27

UMBRELLA

KANJI #27

全 **COMPLETE**

ノ	人	仝	仐	全	全			

BUILDING THIS KANJI
Umbrella 人 + King 王(23) = 全

Meaning
This kanji expresses the idea of wholeness and completion. Note in the sample compounds how both the first and third entries can have different connotations. Although the context will usually make the meaning clear, such ambiguity is a common feature of Japanese.

Remembering this kanji
"You might imagine that the **king's umbrella** bearer has a job that even a COMPLETE idiot could do. Well, you're wrong, because you'd better not let the **king** get wet. Sadly, I learned this the hard way, for one afternoon the **umbrella** I chose had a hole, and a drop of moisture sprinkled the **king's** robe. That was enough to leave me dangling in the dungeon for a week. A tyrant **king**, you say? Perhaps, but the lesson I learned that day has remained with me forever: the **umbrella** must COMPLETELY cover the **king**."

Common Pronunciations
Common **ON** reading: **ZEN** (ゼン)
Common **kun** reading: none

Given that "Zen" (as in Buddhism) is one of the few Japanese words to have entered the English language, feel free to take advantage of this by using it to remember this reading. For the sentence, then, you might employ some Zen-like simplicity: "Complete ZEN".

Create your **on-yomi** keyword and enter it in the table at the back of the book. After that, write your sentence to remember the **on-yomi** reading in the box below.

		COMMON WORDS AND COMPOUNDS
全国	complete + country = *the whole country/ nationwide*	ZEN·KOKU ゼン・コク
安全	ease + complete = *safety*	AN·ZEN アン・ゼン
全校	complete + school = *the whole school/ all schools*	ZEN·KŌ ゼン・コウ
全力	complete + strength = *all one's power*	ZEN·RYOKU ゼン・リョク
全体	complete + body = *the whole*	ZEN·TAI ゼン・タイ
全部	complete + part = *all*	ZEN·BU ゼン・ブ

Less Common Pronunciations

Less common **ON** reading: none
Less common **kun** reading: **matta** (ま っ た); **matto** (ま っ と)

SAMPLE SENTENCE:

田中さん は 全国 を 回る。
Ta·naka-san wa ZEN·KOKU o mawa·ru.
Tanaka-san　　whole country　　go around
= *Tanaka-san is going around the whole country.*

KANJI #28

十

TEN

一	十							

Meaning

Ten. The first two examples of Entry 176 show another use for this character, an interesting application based entirely on its shape.

Remembering this kanji

This is another simple character for which we will assign an external meaning: scarecrow.
In case you're wondering why this particular scarecrow was chosen, the answer is simple: he was rated a perfect TEN in terms of style and poise.

Common Pronunciations

Common **ON** reading: JŪ (ジ ュ ウ)
Common **kun** reading: none

Say hello to the first character for which you should know all the compounds in the main table below. You've already come a long way!

Create your **on-yomi** keyword and enter it in the table at the back of the book. After that, write your sentence to remember the **on-yomi** reading in the box below.

Less Common Pronunciations

Less common **ON** reading: JITSU (ジ ツ)
Less common **kun** reading: **tō** (と お); **to** (と)

tō appears with only one word, 十日 [**tō·ka** (と お・か)] "the tenth day of the month".
　　Two common irregular readings, found earlier with the kanji 二.

IRREGULAR READINGS		
二十日	two + ten + sun (day) = *twentieth day of the month*	**hatsuka** はつか
二十歳	two + ten + annual = *twenty years old*	**hatachi** はたち

COMMON WORDS AND COMPOUNDS		
十	*ten*	**JŪ** ジュウ
十月	ten + moon (month) = *October*	**JŪ·GATSU** ジュウ・ガツ
十一月	ten + one + moon (month) = *November*	**JŪ·ICHI·GATSU** ジュウ・イチ・ガツ
十二月	ten + two + moon (month) = *December*	**JŪ·NI·GATSU** ジュウ・ニ・ガツ
十六	ten + six = *sixteen*	**JŪ·ROKU** ジュウ・ロク
十八	ten + eight = *eighteen*	**JŪ·HACHI** ジュウ・ハチ

SAMPLE SENTENCE:

十月　に は あ の 木 は　美しく
JŪ·GATSU ni wa ano ki wa utsuku·shiku
October   that tree   beautiful
なります。
narimasu.
becomes
= *That tree becomes beautiful in October.*

KANJI #29

早 **EARLY**

BUILDING THIS KANJI
Sun 日 (6) + Ten (scarecrow) 十 (28) = 早

Meaning
Early/Fast. It is important to remember that this kanji expresses both of these ideas.

Remembering this kanji
There isn't much a **scarecrow** can do for exercise, but ours is determined to stay in shape. How so? Well, EARLY each day, once the **sun** is up, he'll launch into a vigorous routine of finger stretches, toe curls, and head rolls. As it's too hot to do this later on, it's fortunate he's an EARLY riser.

Common Pronunciations
Common **ON** reading: **SŌ** (ソウ)
Common **kun** reading: **haya** (はや)

Note the intransitive/transitive verb pair in the table.

kun-yomi suggestion: "**hi ya!**"

Create your **on-yomi** keyword and enter it in the table at the back of the book. After that, write your sentence to remember the **on-yomi** and **kun-yomi** readings in the box below.

Less Common Pronunciations
Less common **ON** reading: **SATSU** (サツ)
Less common **kun** reading: none

COMMON WORDS AND COMPOUNDS		
早い	*early; fast*	**haya·i** は や・い
早まる (intr)	*to be in a hurry*	**haya·maru** は や・ま る
早める (tr)	*to hurry (something)*	**haya·meru** は や・め る
早口	early (fast) + mouth = *rapid speaking*	**haya·kuchi** は や・く ち
早春	early + spring = *early spring*	**SŌ·SHUN** ソ ウ・シ ュ ン
早朝	early + morning = *early morning*	**SŌ·CHŌ** ソ ウ・チ ョ ウ

SAMPLE SENTENCE:

どうして そんな に 早く 来た の
dōshite   sonna   ni haya·ku ki·ta no
　why　　　so　　　　　early　come
です か。
desu   ka.
= *Why did you come so early?*

COMPONENT #30

GOOD FIGURE SKATER

A good figure skater always keeps her leg straight in this position.

KANJI #30

  UPPER

BUILDING THIS KANJI
Good Figure Skater ├ + One (bottom of a bun)
一 (3) = 上

Meaning

This simple-looking character expresses a broad range of ideas relating to the words "upper", "on", and "over", among others; it can refer to anything from goods of high quality to superiors at work. It's a fascinating kanji that is widely used, and one that rewards patient study.

Remembering this kanji
Look at the beautiful posture, with the outstretched leg held perfectly straight; this is a **good figure skater** with complete confidence in her abilities, skating as if the ice were the **bottom of a bun** that would not hurt her if she fell. This is clearly an UPPER-class athlete.

Common Pronunciations

Common **ON** reading: **JŌ** (ジ ョ ウ)
Common **kun** reading: **kami** (か み); **ue** (う え);
nobo (の ぼ); **a** (あ); **uwa** (う わ)

Take a deep breath, as this kanji contains the second largest number of common readings for any character you will encounter in Japanese (you won't have long to wait for the one with the most!). The **on-yomi JŌ**, however, is by far the most frequently used, and the **kun-yomi** readings will often appear with **hiragana** accompaniment (which will offer a clue as to which pronunciation should be used for the kanji).

The verb **a·geru** (あ・げ る) in example 5 below, incidentally, is almost always used in a transitive sense (that is, it "lifts" some object in either a physical or symbolic way), and is best thought of as being paired with the intransitive **a·garu** (あ·がる).

Before proceeding with your sentence, it is useful now to consider one of the most important benefits of the **on-yomi** table: because you will have chosen different keywords for each of the readings, there will be no danger of confusing pronunciations differing only in their use of a "long" versus "short" vowel sound. We encounter the first example of this here, with **JŌ** sounding much like **JO** (the **on-yomi** for "女" in Entry 16), but needing to be memorized as a separate reading.

kun-yomi suggestions: "**ma**ke a **mea**l;" "**tru**e **a**ge;" "**no bo**nes;" "**a**nacon**da**;" "**new wo**k"

Create your **on-yomi** keyword and enter it in the table at the back of the book. After that, write your sentence to remember the **on-yomi** and **kun-yomi** readings in the box below.

Less Common Pronunciations
Less common **ON** reading: **SHŌ** (ショウ)
Less common **kun** reading: none

COMMON WORDS AND COMPOUNDS		
上	*upper*	**kami** かみ
上	*over; on*	**ue** うえ
上る (intr)	*to climb*	**nobo·ru** のぼ·る
上がる (intr)	*to rise*	**a·garu** あ·がる
上げる (tr/intr)	*to lift*	**a·geru** あ·げる
上手	upper + hand = *skillful*	**JŌ·**ZU ジョウ·ズ

SAMPLE SENTENCE:

肉 は テーブル の 上 に あります。
NIKU wa TĒBURU no ue ni arimasu.
meat table on is
= *The meat is on the table.*

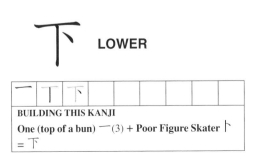

COMPONENT #31

POOR FIGURE SKATER

ト

A poor figure skater lets her leg droop in this position.

KANJI #31

下 **LOWER**

一	丁	下						

BUILDING THIS KANJI
One (top of a bun) 一 (3) + Poor Figure Skater 卜
= 下

Meaning
This obvious partner to the preceding kanji expresses a similarly wide range of ideas, with words in this case relating to the notions of "lower", "under", and "below".

Remembering this kanji
No doubt about it: figure skating crowds are tough, and will not tolerate LOWER-class skaters. In one competition, all it took was a **poor figure skater**'s drooping leg to make the audience hurl the **tops of their buns** at her in disgust.

Common Pronunciations

Common **ON** reading: **KA** (カ); **GE** (ゲ)
Common **kun** reading: **shita** (した); **shimo** (し も); **o** (お); **sa** (さ); **kuda** (く だ)

Here it is: the kanji with the most common readings of all. Although it can be a bit of work trying to come to grips with this character's many angles, keep in mind that the final three **kun-yomi** above are all verb stems, and will thus be accompanied by **hiragana** hinting at the correct pronunciation. When it comes to the readings used for compounds, **KA** or **GE** will be encountered far more than the others, although there are no easily discernible patterns as to when each of these is used.

This kanji illustrates well the difference between intransitive/transitive verb pairs. Refer back to "早" and "上" (Entries 29 and 30). Notice a similarity between the verbs presented there and examples four and five shown here.

suggestions for **kun-yomi**: "**she ta**ckled"; "**she mo**ped"; "**o**rangutan"; "**sa**t"; "barra**cuda**"

Create your **on-yomi** keywords and enter them in the table at the back of the book. After that, write your sentence to remember the **on-yomi** and **kun-yomi** readings in the box below.

Less Common Pronunciations

Less common **ON** reading: none
Less common **kun** reading: **moto** (も と)

IRREGULAR READINGS		
下手	lower + hand = *to be poor at (something)*	**he·ta** へ·た

COMMON WORDS AND COMPOUNDS		
下	*low; below; under*	**shita** した
下りる (intr)	*to come down*	**o·riru** お·りる
下ろす (tr)	*to take down*	**o·rosu** お·ろす
下がる (intr)	*to hang down (on one's own)*	**sa·garu** さ·がる
下げる (tr)	*to lower (something)*	**sa·geru** さ·げる
下さる	*to oblige*	**kuda·saru** く だ·さる
上下	upper + lower = *high and low*	**JŌ·GE** ジョウ·ゲ
天下	heaven + lower = *the whole land*	**TEN·KA** テン·カ

SAMPLE SENTENCE:

木 から 下りて 下さい。
ki   kara   o·rite   kuda·sai.
tree from come down   please
= *Please come down from the tree.*

COMPONENT #32

RABBIT   ＼   ／

ヽ	ヾ	一	十	米	米		

BUILDING THIS KANJI
Rabbit ヾ + Tree 木 (13) = 米

KANJI #32

米   **RICE**

Meaning

(Uncooked) rice. As can be seen in the last five compounds below, this character is used, curiously, to symbolize the Americas (recall how 中 is used in a similar way for China, and 日 for Japan). Note how the fourth example combines two such characters; this occurs frequently in written Japanese.

Remembering this kanji

Interesting fact: Japan has the equivalent of an Easter Bunny! The difference is that this **rabbit** will sneak around behind **trees** until he can dart out and hide RICE for children to find. Unfortunately, as the grains are really small and a lot less interesting than colored eggs, many kids have grown bored with the custom. As a result of this, the tradition of the Japanese RICE **rabbit** is not well-known today.

Common Pronunciations

Common **ON** reading: **MAI** (マイ); **BEI** (ベイ)
Common **kun** reading: **kome** (こめ)

BEI is used as the reading in compounds when this kanji relates to the Americas, with **MAI** the primary choice when it refers to rice.

kun-yomi suggestion: "**comb** acres"

Create your **on-yomi** keywords and enter them in the table at the back of the book. After that, write your sentence to remember the **on-yomi** and **kun-yomi** readings in the box below.

Less Common Pronunciations

Less common **ON** reading: none
Less common **kun** reading: none

COMMON WORDS AND COMPOUNDS		
米	*rice (uncooked)*	**kome** こめ
白米	white + rice = *polished rice*	HAKU·**MAI** ハク・マイ
米国	rice (America) + country = *the United States*	**BEI**·KOKU ベイ・コク
日米	sun + rice (America) = *Japan – U.S.*	NICHI·**BEI** ニチ・ベイ
中米	middle + rice (America) = *Central America*	CHŪ·**BEI** チュウ・ベイ
北米	north + rice (America) = *North America*	HOKU·**BEI** ホク・ベイ
南米	south + rice (America) = *South America*	NAN·**BEI** ナン・ベイ

SAMPLE SENTENCE:

米国　の　牛肉　は　高い。
BEI·KOKU no GYŪ·NIKU wa taka·i.
United States beef expensive
= *U.S. beef is expensive.*

SELF

自

| ′ | 亻 | 冂 | 自 | 自 | 自 | | |

BUILDING THIS KANJI
Jelly Bean ╲ + Eye (Cyclops) 目 (15) = 自

Meaning
This character conveys the important idea of self. Its function becomes clearer if you think of such English words as "self-confidence" and "self-government". When these and other words beginning with "self-" are translated into Japanese, the resulting compound will usually begin with this kanji.

Remembering this kanji
Everyone is aware of a **Cyclops'** weakness for **jelly beans**. It was this, in fact, that saved Hercules; dangling a **jelly bean** over the **Cyclops'** head was enough to make the monster drop his club and lose all sense of SELF. "It was sad, actually," Hercules said at a later press conference. "No SELF-respecting **Cyclops** should act that way. He needs more SELF-control."

Common Pronunciations
Common **ON** reading: **JI** (ジ)
Common **kun** reading: none

Create your **on-yomi** keyword and enter it in the table at the back of the book. After that, write your sentence to remember the **on-yomi** reading in the box below.

Less Common Pronunciations
Less common **ON** reading: **SHI** (シ)
Less common **kun** reading: **mizuka** (みずか)

SHI appears only in the compound 自然 (Self/Nature), the Japanese word for "nature": **SHI·ZEN** (シ・ゼン).

COMMON WORDS AND COMPOUNDS		
自国	self + country = *one's homeland*	**JI·KOKU** ジ・コク
自立	self + stand = *independence*	**JI·RITSU** ジ・リツ
自分	self + part = *oneself*	**JI·BUN** ジ・ブン
自体	self + body = *in itself*	**JI·TAI** ジ・タイ

SAMPLE SENTENCE:

自分 の 車 が 買いたい。
JI·BUN no kuruma ga ka·itai.
oneself   car   want to buy
= *I want to buy my own car.*

COMPONENT #34

GORILLA

KANJI #34

内 **INSIDE**

一	冂	内	内				

BUILDING THIS KANJI
Gorilla 冂 + Person 人 (2) = 内

Meaning
Inside/Interior/Within. This character can also convey the idea of "home."

Remembering this kanji
"You can know nothing of the **gorilla's** ways unless you are INSIDE its world. To truly understand, each **person** must get INSIDE an Acme™ **gorilla** suit—available for a limited time at this low introductory price—and head immediately into the jungle. It is then a simple matter of being accepted by a **gorilla** pod; once this has been done, a **person** can delve easily INSIDE the consciousness of our greatest primate."

Common Pronunciations
Common **ON** reading: **NAI** (ナイ)
Common **kun** reading: **uchi** (うち)

kun-yomi suggestion: "**ooh, cheet**ahs"

Create your **on-yomi** keyword and enter it in the table at the back of the book. After that, write your sentence to remember the **on-yomi** and **kun-yomi** readings in the box below.

Less Common Pronunciations
Less common **ON** reading: **DAI** (ダイ)
Less common **kun** reading: none

COMMON WORDS AND COMPOUNDS		
内	*inside*	**uchi** うち
国内	country + inside = *domestic*	KOKU·NAI コク・ナイ
市内	city + inside = *within the city*	SHI·NAI シ・ナイ
内海	inside + sea = *inland sea*	NAI·KAI ナイ・カイ
車内	car + inside = *inside the car*	SHA·NAI シャ・ナイ
町内	town + inside = *in the town*	CHŌ·NAI チョウ・ナイ

SAMPLE SENTENCE:

その 人 は 国内 で 有名 です。
sono hito wa KOKU·NAI de YŪ·MEI desu.
that person   domestic   famous
= *That person is famous domestically.*

COMPONENT #35

SUPERHERO

KANJI #35

右 **RIGHT**

ノ	ナ	右	右	右			

BUILDING THIS KANJI

Superhero ナ + Mouth (vampire) 口 (8) = 右

Meaning

Right/right-hand side.

Remembering this kanji

Vampires are extremely **RIGHT** wing, demanding unconditional obedience to their authority and strict adherence to traditional ways. Even **superheroes** can turn to the **RIGHT** under their hypnotic influence; they invariably develop a tougher stance on crime and become less likely to wear skin-tight costumes.

Common Pronunciations

Common **ON** reading: none
Common **kun** reading: **migi** (み ぎ)

kun-yomi suggestion: "foa**my gee**se"

Create your sentence to remember the **kun-yomi** reading in the box below.

Less Common Pronunciations

Less common **ON** reading: **YŪ** (ユ ウ); **U** (ウ)
Less common **kun** reading: none

COMMON WORDS AND COMPOUNDS		
右	*right*	**migi** み ぎ
右回り	right + rotate = *clockwise*	**migi** mawa·ri み ぎ まわ·り
右上	right + upper = *upper right*	**migi**·ue み ぎ·う え
右下	right + lower = *lower right*	**migi**·shita み ぎ·し た
右手	right + hand = *right hand*	**migi**·te み ぎ·て
右足	right + leg = *right leg*	**migi**·ashi み ぎ·あ し

SAMPLE SENTENCE:

山口さん は 右 の 目 がかゆい。

Yama·guchi-san wa migi no me ga kayui.

Yamaguchi-san   right   eye   itchy

= *Yamaguchi-san's right eye is itchy.*

KANJI #36

HAVE

| ノ | ナ | ナ | 有 | 有 | 有 | | | |

BUILDING THIS KANJI
Superhero ナ + Moon 月 (11) = 有

kun-yomi suggestion: "Atilla"

Create your **on-yomi** keyword and enter it in the table at the back of the book. After that, write your sentence to remember the **on-yomi** and **kun-yomi** readings in the box below.

Meaning
Have/Possess.

Less Common Pronunciations
Less common **ON** reading: U (ウ)
Less common **kun** reading: none

Remembering this kanji
"Help me!" yelled the **moon**. "I'm going down!" And indeed he was. But just then a **superhero** arrived on the scene.
"I HAVE you, **moon**," he said, flying him higher into the sky before returning to Earth with a smile. "Citizens," he declared before us, "you HAVE your **moon** back."
"Geez," I heard someone whisper, "how many times should we tell this guy that the **moon's** *supposed* to go down?"

COMMON WORDS AND COMPOUNDS		
有る	*to have*	a·ru あ·る
有力	have + strength = *powerful*	YŪ·RYOKU ユウ·リョク
有名	have + name = *famous*	YŪ·MEI ユウ·メイ
私有	private + have = *privately owned*	SHI·YŪ シ·ユウ
公有	public + have = *publicly owned*	KŌ·YŪ コウ·ユウ
国有化	country + have + change = *nationalization*	KOKU·YŪ·KA コク·ユウ·カ

SAMPLE SENTENCE:

エジプト の ピラミッド は 有名

Ejiputo	**no**	**piramiddo**	**wa**	**YŪ·MEI**
Egypt		pyramids		famous

です。
desu.
= *The Egyptian pyramids are famous.*

Common Pronunciations
Common **ON** reading: **YŪ** (ユウ)
Common **kun** reading: **a** (あ)

KANJI #37

肉 **MEAT**

| 一 | 冂 | 内 | 内 | 内 | 肉 | | | |

BUILDING THIS KANJI
Inside 内 (34) + Person 人 (2) = 肉

Meaning
Meat/Flesh. In addition to its literal meaning, this kanji also has a sexual connotation through its appearance in words such as "lust" and "sensuality."

Remembering this kanji
"What is really **inside** a **person**?" Troubled by this question, I embarked on an extended spiritual quest that eventually led me to a remote Himalayan summit. There I fasted, growing weak and delirious until a talking leopard appeared one day and laid a paw on my shoulder. "What are you, nuts?" it said. "Take it from me: there's nothing but MEAT in there."

Common Pronunciations
Common **ON** reading: NIKU (ニク)
Common **kun** reading: none

Create your **on-yomi** keyword and enter it in the table at the back of the book. After that, write your sentence to remember the **on-yomi** reading in the box below.

Less Common Pronunciations
Less common **ON** reading: none
Less common **kun** reading: none

COMMON WORDS AND COMPOUNDS		
肉	*meat*	**NIKU** ニク
人肉	person + meat = *human flesh*	**JIN·NIKU** ジン・ニク
牛肉	cow + meat = *beef*	**GYŪ·NIKU** ギュウ・ニク
肉親	meat + parent = *blood relative*	**NIKU·SHIN** ニク・シン
肉体	meat + body = *the body*	**NIKU·TAI** ニク・タイ

SAMPLE SENTENCE:

あの　　四人　は　　牛肉　　　が
ano　　yo·NIN　wa　GYŪ·NIKU　ga
those four people　　　　　 beef
大好き　です。
DAI su·ki　desu.
really like.
= *Those four people really like beef.*

HALF

`	ˇ	⺍	⺌	半				

BUILDING THIS KANJI
Rabbit ` ˇ + Two 二 (4) + Pole ｜ = 半

Meaning
Half. This character also incorporates a sense of "partial," forming many words that English conveys with the prefix "semi-."

Remembering this kanji
I remember a chef answering a question I once posed. "Yes," she said, "a **pole** *could* split a **rabbit** into **two** HALF sections." I also recall her noting that there would only be HALF the **rabbit** left if it were prepared in such a ridiculous way.

Common Pronunciations
Common **ON** reading: **HAN** (ハ ン)
Common **kun** reading: none

Create your **on-yomi** keyword and enter it in the table at the back of the book. After that, write your sentence to remember the **on-yomi** reading in the box below.

Less Common Pronunciations
Less common **ON** reading: none
Less common **kun** reading: **naka** (な か)

COMMON WORDS AND COMPOUNDS		
上半	upper + half = *upper half*	**JŌ·HAN** ジョウ・ハン
下半	lower + half = *lower half*	**KA·HAN** カ・ハン
半日	half + sun (day) = *half a day*	**HAN·NICHI** ハン・ニチ
半分	half + part = *half*	**HAN·BUN** ハン・ブン
九時半	nine + time + half = *nine-thirty*	**KU·JI·HAN** ク・ジ・ハン
半円	half + circle = *semicircle*	**HAN·EN** ハン・エン

SAMPLE SENTENCE:

木口さん は 半日 ぐらい
Ki·guchi-san wa HAN·NICHI gurai
Kiguchi-san half a day about
新聞 を 読みました。
SHIN·BUN o yo·mimashita.
newspaper read
= *Kiguchi-san read the newspaper for about half a day.*

九 **NINE**

| ノ | 九 | | | | | | |

Meaning
Nine.

Remembering this kanji
This is clearly someone dressed to the **NINES**.

Common Pronunciations
Common **ON** reading: **KYŪ** (キュウ); **KU** (ク)
Common **kun** reading: none

KYŪ is the general reading for this kanji. You are only likely to encounter **KU** in the third and fourth examples below.

Create your **on-yomi** keywords and enter them in the table at the back of the book. After that, write your sentence to remember the **on-yomi** readings in the box below.

Less Common Pronunciations
Less common **ON** reading: none
Less common **kun** reading: **kokono** (ここの)

This is another reading of most use because of its appearance in two words: 九日 [**kokono·ka** (ここの·か)] "the ninth day of the month," and 九つ [**kokono·tsu** (ここの·つ)] the general counter for "nine."

COMMON WORDS AND COMPOUNDS		
九	*nine*	**KYŪ** キュウ
九十	nine + ten = *ninety*	**KYŪ·JŪ** キュウ·ジュウ
九月	nine + moon (month) = *September*	**KU·GATSU** ク·ガツ
九時	nine + time = *nine o'clock*	**KU·JI** ク·ジ

SAMPLE SENTENCE:

中山さん　は　　九月　　に　　日本
Naka·yama-san wa KU·GATSU ni NI·HON
Nakayama-san   September   Japan
へ　行きました
e   i·kimashita.
　　　　went
= *Nakayama-san went to Japan in September.*

KANJI #40

春 SPRING

一	二	三	丰	夫	表	春	春	春

BUILDING THIS KANJI
Three (full hamburger) 三(5) + Person 人(2) +
Sun 日(6) = 春

Meaning
This elegant-looking character refers to the
season of spring. Interestingly, it also carries a
hint of sexuality and amorousness, a meaning
apparent by its presence in the Japanese word for
"puberty," as well as in one of the compounds
below. Make sure in writing this kanji to follow
the order of the components as they are listed
above (three + person + sun).

Remembering this kanji
It's doubtful any **person** looks forward to
SPRING more than I do. As a matter of fact,
on the first day of the season you'll surely see
me in the backyard before dawn, firing up
my barbecue to make the most enormous **full
hamburger** possible. And why do I do that?
Well, it's simple: I'm a **person** who wants to
welcome the SPRING sun properly when it
rises!

Common Pronunciations
Common **ON** reading: **SHUN** (シ ュ ン)
Common **kun** reading: **haru** (は る)

kun-yomi suggestion: "**haru**mph"

Create your **on-yomi** keyword and enter it in the
table at the back of the book. After that, write your
sentence to remember the **on-yomi** and **kun-yomi**
readings in the box below.

Less Common Pronunciations
Less common **ON** reading: none
Less common **kun** reading: none

COMMON WORDS AND COMPOUNDS		
春	*spring*	**haru** は る
小春	small + spring = *Indian summer*	ko·**haru** こ·は る
青春	blue + spring = *youth*	**SEI·SHUN** セ イ·シ ュ ン
売春	sell + spring = *prostitution*	**BAI·SHUN** バ イ·シ ュ ン
春分	spring + part = *vernal equinox*	**SHUN·BUN** シ ュ ン·ブ ン
来春	come + spring = *next spring*	**RAI·SHUN** ラ イ·シ ュ ン

SAMPLE SENTENCE:

日本 の 春 は 美しい。
NI·HON no haru wa utsuku·shii.
 Japan   spring   beautiful.
= *Japan's spring is beautiful.*

CHAPTER 2 REVIEW EXERCISES

A. Please match the following kanji to their meanings.

1.	玉	a.	Ten
2.	全	b.	Country
3.	米	c.	Jewel
4.	貝	d.	Right
5.	肉	e.	Meat
6.	十	f.	Rice
7.	心	g.	Upper
8.	上	h.	Shellfish
9.	右	i.	Heart
10.	国	j.	Complete

B. Please match the following meanings to their
kanji, and these to their **on** or **kun-yomi**.

1.	Nine	a. 内	1.	**HAN** (ハン)
2.	Have	b. 春	2.	**uchi** (うち)
3.	Inside	c. 早	3.	**haru** (はる)
4.	King	d. 九	4.	**YŪ** (ユウ)
5.	Half	e. 下	5.	**ROKU** (ロク)
6.	Spring	f. 有	6.	**haya** (はや)
7.	Self	g. 自	7.	**shita** (した)
8.	Lower	h. 半	8.	**JI** (ジ)
9.	Early	i. 六	9.	**Ō** (オウ)
10.	Six	j. 王	10.	**KYŪ** (キュウ)

C. Please choose the best answer(s) to the following questions.
1. Which of the following readings apply to
the kanji 米?
a. **MAI** (マイ)
b. **kome** (こめ)
c. **SHŪ** (シュウ)
d. **BEI** (ベイ)
e. **to** (と)

2. Which of the following readings apply to
the kanji 上?
a. **nobo** (のぼ)
b. **ue** (うえ)
c. **naka** (なか)
d. **JŌ** (ジョウ)
e. **kami** (かみ)

3. Which of the following readings apply to
the kanji 心?
a. **migi** (みぎ)
b. **SHIN** (シン)
c. **tsuki** (つき)
d. **kokoro** (こころ)
e. **HAN** (ハン)

4. Which of the following is a sushi chef most
likely to put on rice?
a. 王
b. 自
c. 早
d. 貝
e. 国

5. Which of the following readings apply to
the kanji 下?
a. **kuda** (くだ)
b. **KA** (カ)
c. **shita** (した)
d. **o** (お)
e. **GE** (ゲ)

D. Please choose the best answer to the following
questions.
1. Which is the correct reading of 上がる?
a. **to·garu** (と・がる)
b. **a·garu** (あ・がる)
c. **ma·garu** (ま・がる)
d. **sa·garu** (さ・がる)

2. Which answer best captures the meaning
of the compound 米国?
a. Wednesday   d. Oatmeal
b. Vampire   e. Heart failure
c. The United States

3. Which is the correct reading for 九月?
   a. **KU·GATSU** (ク・ガツ)
   b. **kokono·GATSU** (ここの・ガツ)
   c. **KYŪ·GATSU** (キュウ・ガツ)
   d. **kokono·tsuki** (ここの・つき)

4. Which of the following does not belong with the others?
   a. 十
   b. 九
   c. 六
   d. 右

5. Which is the correct reading of 早い?
   a. **aru·i** (ある・い)
   b. **maru·i** (まる・い)
   c. **haya·i** (はや・い)
   d. **ara·i** (あら・い)

E. Please match the following compounds and words to their meanings and pronunciations.

1. 六月	a. Rapid speaking	1. **ROKU·GATSU** (ロク・ガツ)
2. 中国	b. Ulterior motive	2. **JO·Ō** (ジョ・オウ)
3. 早口	c. Queen	3. **GO·JŪ** (ゴ・ジュウ)
4. 五十	d. Early spring	4. **migi·ue** (みぎ・うえ)
5. 中米	e. Upper right	5. **SŌ·SHUN** (ソウ・シュン)
6. 女王	f. Fifty	6. **CHŪ·GOKU** (チュウ・ゴク)
7. 上下	g. June	7. **CHŪ·BEI** (チュウ・ベイ)
8. 早春	h. High and low	8. **shita·gokoro** (した・ごころ)
9. 下心	i. Central America	9. **JŌ·GE** (ジョウ・ゲ)
10. 右上	j. China	10. **haya·kuchi** (はや・くち)

Kanji #41—60

KANJI #41

CAPITAL

BUILDING THIS KANJI

Police 一 + Mouth (vampire) 口 (8) + Small 小 (20) = 京

Meaning

Think of "capital" in the sense of a large metropolis. Though it's not the most common of characters, it is useful to learn this kanji because of its appearance in the compound for Tokyo and other cities.

Remembering this kanji

The CAPITAL can be a pretty intimidating place if you don't know it, and as a **police** officer here I'm always having to help folks with directions. Even **vampires**, who normally wouldn't go near anyone in a **police** uniform, come up to me now and then. It's not surprising, I suppose, that they're overwhelmed by all the buildings and traffic after having come from such **small** Transylvanian villages. But then, it's only natural that everyone – **vampires** included – feels a bit **small** in the CAPITAL.

Common Pronunciations

Common **ON** reading: **KYŌ** (キョウ)
Common **kun** reading: none

Create your **on-yomi** keyword and enter it in the table at the back of the book. After that, write your sentence to remember the **on-yomi** reading in the box below.

Less Common Pronunciations

Less common **ON** reading: **KEI** (ケイ)
Less common **kun** reading: none

COMMON WORDS AND COMPOUNDS		
上京	upper + capital = *come/go to Tokyo*	JŌ·KYŌ ジョウ·キョウ
東京	east + capital = *Tokyo*	TŌ·KYŌ トウ·キョウ

SAMPLE SENTENCE:

中山さん は 上京 しました。

Naka·yama-san wa JŌ·KYŌ shimashita.

Nakayama-san went to Tokyo

= *Nakayama-san went to Tokyo.*

KANJI #42

SEE

BUILDING THIS KANJI
Eye (Cyclops) 目 (15) + Ballet 儿 = 見

Meaning
See/Watch. The idea of "show" can also be expressed. Make sure you notice the difference between this kanji and "貝" (Entry 21).

Remembering this kanji
"I'm tired of living a lie," said the **Cyclops**, throwing down his club before emerging in a tutu. "People need to SEE me for who I really am. They need to SEE I'm not some slob who lounges around belching in a cave littered with sailor bones. They need to SEE the truth: that I…am a **ballerina**!"

Common Pronunciations
Common **ON** reading: **KEN** (ケン)
Common **kun** reading: **mi** (み)

Expect to use the **kun-yomi** when this kanji appears in the first position. The **on-yomi** occurs more often in the second.

kun-yomi suggestion: "**me**an"

Write your sentence to remember the readings below.

Less Common Pronunciations
Less common **ON** reading: none
Less common **kun** reading: none

COMMON WORDS AND COMPOUNDS		
見える (intr)	*to be visible*	**mi**·eru み・える
見る (tr)	*to see; to watch*	**mi**·ru み・る
見せる (tr)	*to show (something)*	**mi**·seru み・せる
見上げる	see + upper = *to look up (to/at)*	**mi** a·geru み あ・げる
月見	moon + see = *moon viewing*	tsuki·**mi** つき・み
見失う	see + lose = *to lose sight of*	**mi** ushina·u み・うしな・う
外見	outside + see = *external appearance*	**GAI·KEN** ガイ・ケン

SAMPLE SENTENCE:

山　の　上　に　小さい　木　が
yama　no　ue　ni　chii·sai　ki　ga
mountain　　upper　　　small　　tree
見えます。
mi·emasu.
is visible
= *A small tree is visible on top of the mountain.*

KANJI #43

止 **STOP**

丨	⼘	⺊	止				

BUILDING THIS KANJI

Good Figure Skater ⺊ + Pole 丨 + One (bottom of a bun) 一 (3) = 止

Meaning

All senses of the meaning "stop". Take care with the stroke sequence of this kanji; the components should be written in the order shown above.

Remembering this kanji

"STOP! STOP!" the audience screamed. It was horrible. The **good figure skater's** posture was perfect, she was skating as if on the **bottom of a bun**, yet was oblivious to the **pole** sticking out of the ice in front of her. To be sure, no one could figure out what a **pole** was doing there in the first place, but no matter; the story must STOP here, as what happened next is too painful to relate.

Common Pronunciations

Common **ON** reading: **SHI** (シ)
Common **kun** reading: **to** (と)

Remember to use the **on-yomi** keyword for **SHI** that you applied to the kanji "四" (Entry 10). Note also how the **kun-yomi** can become voiced when it is used (as in the fourth and fifth examples) in second position, something that occurs frequently with this kanji.

kun-yomi suggestion: "**to**tal"

Write your sentence to remember the **on-yomi** and **kun-yomi** readings in the box below.

Less Common Pronunciations

Less common **ON** reading: none
Less common **kun** reading: none

COMMON WORDS AND COMPOUNDS		
止まる (intr)	*to stop*	**to**·maru と・まる
止める (tr)	*to stop (an object)*	**to**·meru と・める
中止	middle + stop = *discontinue*	CHŪ·**SHI** チュウ・シ
立ち止 まる	stand + stop = *to stand still*	ta·chi **do**·maru た・ち ど・まる
車止め	car + stop = *closed to vehicles*	kuruma **do**·me くるま ど・め

SAMPLE SENTENCE:

こちら に 止まって 下さい。

kochira ni   to·matte   kuda·sai.
  here   stop   please
= *Please stop here.*

COMPONENT #44

COMET

Much like a wandering comet, our friend can appear in a variety of locations: as a slanted or curved line (as opposed to the horizontal "one") on top of a character, at the bottom, or right through the middle. One thing worth keeping in mind is that you should always draw this component from its head to its tail (i.e., in this case, from left to right).

KANJI #44

七 Seven

一	七							

BUILDING THIS KANJI
Comet ⌒ + Hook ∟ = 七

Meaning
Seven. Only two strokes here, but they should be written as the components are listed.

Remembering this kanji
Using a **comet** as his guide, Captain **Hook** sailed the **SEVEN** seas.

Common Pronunciations
Common **ON** reading: **SHICHI** (シ チ)
Common **kun** reading: **nana** (な な)

Note the mix of **on** and **kun** readings in the fourth and fifth examples.

kun-yomi suggestion: "Nana"

Create your **on-yomi** keyword and enter it in the table at the back of the book. After that, write your sentence to remember the **on-yomi** and **kun-yomi** readings in the box below.

Less Common Pronunciations
Less common **ON** reading: none
Less common **kun** reading: **nano** (な の)

This reading appears with only one word (any guesses?): 七 日 [**nano·ka** (な の・か)] "the seventh day of the month".

COMMON WORDS AND COMPOUNDS		
七	*seven*	SHICHI シ チ
七つ	*seven (general counter)*	**nana**·tsu な な·つ
七月	seven + moon (month) = *July*	SHICHI· GATSU シ チ·ガ ツ
十七	ten + seven = *seventeen*	JŪ·**nana** ジュウ·な な
七十	seven + ten = *seventy*	**nana**·JŪ な な·ジュウ
七時	seven + time = *seven o'clock*	SHICHI·JI シ チ·ジ

SAMPLE SENTENCE:
高木さん が 七月 に
Taka·gi-san ga SHICHI·GATSU ni
Takagi-san July
中米 から 来ます。
CHŪ·BEI kara ki·masu.
Central America will come
= *Takagi-san will come from Central America in July.*

KANJI #45

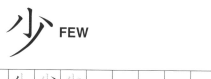

少 FEW

丿	刂	小	少			

BUILDING THIS KANJI
Small 小(20) + Comet 一 = 少

Meaning
Few/Little (in terms of quantity).

Remembering this kanji
"That's not true," said the **comet**. "I mean, let's face it: I'm **small**, and have only a FEW opportunities to meet others. Everyone knows a planet because of its size and where it lives, but I move all over the place; that's why I have so FEW friends. It's got nothing to do with my tail leaving a mess on people's carpets."

Common Pronunciations
Common ON reading: **SHŌ** (ショウ)
Common kun reading: **suku** (すく); **suko** (すこ)

SHŌ will appear in compounds. **Suku** and **suko** are only found in the first and second exam-

ples below. Note the special symbol in example three; Japanese uses this to indicate that a kanji is repeated.

kun-yomi suggestion: "**scoo**ter"; "**sco**ld"

Using your **on-yomi** keyword for 小 (Kanji 20), write your sentence to remember the **on-yomi** and **kun-yomi** readings in the box below.

Less Common Pronunciations
Less common ON reading: none
Less common kun reading: none

COMMON WORDS AND COMPOUNDS		
少ない	*few*	**suku**·nai すく·ない
少し	*a little; a few*	**suko**·shi すこ·し
少々	few + few = *a little*	**SHŌ·SHŌ** ショウ·ショウ
少女	few + woman = *girl*	**SHŌ·JO** ショウ·ジョ
少年	few + year = *boy*	**SHŌ·NEN** ショウ·ネン
最少	most + few = *fewest*	**SAI·SHŌ** サイ·ショウ

SAMPLE SENTENCE:

この 家 に は 物 が 少ない。
kono ie ni wa mono ga suku·nai.
this house　　thing　few
= *There are few things in this house.*

COMPONENT #46

SNOWBOARD

KANJI 46

南 SOUTH

BUILDING THIS KANJI
Ten (scarecrow) 十 (28) + Gorilla 冂 +
Snowboard 丷 + Ten (scarecrow) 十 (28) = 南

Meaning
South.

Remembering this kanji
Stepchildren can often be a problem. The **gorilla** knew this, of course, when she married the **scarecrow**, for all the **scarecrow's** son wanted to do was **snowboard**. Because of this, there was a predictable response when the **gorilla** suggested they travel SOUTH for their vacation.

"I don't want to go SOUTH," said Junior, pouting. "How can I **snowboard** there?"
"Now don't be like that, son," said his father. "You know **gorillas** like warm weather. We're going SOUTH, and that's all there is to it."

Junior said nothing to this, but the **gorilla** knew very well what he was thinking: "I wish Dad had married the polar bear."

Common Pronunciations
Common **ON** reading: **NAN** (ナン)
Common **kun** reading: **minami** (みなみ)

kun-yomi suggestion: "**mean a me**al"

Create your **on-yomi** keyword and enter it in the table at the back of the book. After that, write your sentence to remember the **on-yomi** and **kun-yomi** readings in the box below.

Less Common Pronunciations
Less common **ON** reading: none
Less common **kun** reading: none

COMMON WORDS AND COMPOUNDS		
南	south	minami みなみ
南口	south + mouth = south exit/entrance	minami·guchi みなみ·ぐち
南米	south + rice (America) = South America	NAN·BEI ナン·ベイ
最南	most + south = southernmost	SAI·NAN サイ·ナン
南西	south + west = southwest	NAN·SEI ナン·セイ
南東	south + east = southeast	NAN·TŌ ナン·トウ

SAMPLE SENTENCE

バスターミナル の 南口 で
basutāminaru **no** **minami·guchi** **de**
bus terminal south entrance
会いましょう。
a·imashō.
let's meet
= *Let's meet at the south entrance of the bus terminal.*

KANJI 47

工 **CRAFT**

一	丨	工					

Meaning

Have in mind the ideas of construction and manufacturing when you see this kanji; it's a versatile character that encompasses everything from handicrafts to industrial products. When found at the end of a compound (as in the final example below), this kanji can take on the meaning of "worker", and usually implies a person engaged in some type of manual labor.

Remembering this kanji

There's no better symbol for **CRAFT** than an anvil.

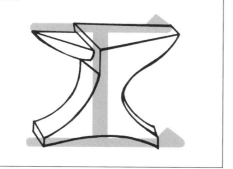

A final reminder about our major timesaving shortcut: your keyword for **KŌ** in this sentence will be the one you have entered in the **on-yomi** table, and that you have already applied to the kanji "口" (Entry 8). Write your sentence to remember the **on-yomi** reading in the box below.

Less Common Pronunciations

Less common **ON** reading: **KU** (ク)
Less common **kun** reading: none

COMMON WORDS AND COMPOUNDS		
人工	person + craft = *artificial*	JIN·KŌ ジン・コウ
人工林	person + craft + grove = *planted forest*	JIN·KŌ·RIN ジン・コウ・リン
工学	craft + study = *engineering*	KŌ·GAKU コウ・ガク
工学士	craft + study + gentleman = *Bachelor of* *Engineering*	KŌ·GAKU·SHI コウ・ガク・シ
刀工	sword + craft = *swordmaker*	TŌ·KŌ トウ・コウ

SAMPLE SENTENCE

これ は 人工 の 島 です ね

kore wa JIN·KŌ no shima desu ne.

this   artificial   island isn't it

= *This is an artificial island, isn't it?*

Common Pronunciations

Common **ON** reading: **KŌ** (コウ)
Common **kun** reading: none

KANJI 48

左 **LEFT**

一	ナ	左	左	左			

BUILDING THIS KANJI
Superhero ナ + Craft 工 (47) = 左

Meaning
Left/Left-hand side. Take note: the writing order of the first two lines differs from that of Entries 35 and 36 ("右" and "有"). It may help to note that in all three cases, the direction of the first stroke matches that of the third.

Remembering this kanji
Craft workers are traditionally **LEFT** wing, and when united can neutralize even a **superhero**, as the illustration makes clear.

Common Pronunciations
Common **ON** reading: none
Common **kun** reading: **hidari** (ひだり)
kun-yomi suggestion: "**heed a ree**f"

Create a sentence to remember the **kun-yomi** reading below.

Less Common Pronunciations
Less common **ON** reading: **SA** (サ)
Less common **kun** reading: none

COMMON WORDS AND COMPOUNDS		
左	*left*	**hidari** ひだり
左回り	left + rotate = *counter-clockwise*	**hidari** mawa·ri ひだり まわ·り
左上	left + upper = *upper left*	**hidari**·ue ひだり·うえ
左下	left + lower = *lower left*	**hidari**·shita ひだり·した
左手	left + hand = *left hand*	**hidari**·te ひだり·て
左足	left + leg = *left leg*	**hidari**·ashi ひだり·あし

SAMPLE SENTENCE

あ の 人 の 左手 を 見 て 下さい。
ano hito no hidari·te o mi·te kuda·sai.
that person   left hand   see   please
= *Please watch that person's left hand.*

高 TALL

'	一	亠	古	古	古	高	高	高
高								

BUILDING THIS KANJI

Police 亠 + Mouth (vampire) 口 (8) + Gorilla
冂 + Mouth (vampire) 口 (8) = 高

Meaning

Tall/High/Best. This kanji is also used to express the idea of "expensive."

Remembering this kanji

The story of King Kong the **gorilla** is well known. What most people don't realize, however, is that it is based on an obscure Transylvanian legend. In it, the angry **gorilla** kidnaps a baby **vampire** and climbs the TALLEST hut in the land. Unfortunately for him, the baby's father is none other than Dracula; the famous **vampire** dons his **police** hat (he is, for reasons yet to be understood, a part-time deputy in this legend) and flies to the rescue. Even today there are inhabitants in the region who hold this story to be true, although most people, to be sure, consider it a TALL tale.

Common Pronunciations

Common **ON** reading: **KŌ** (コ ウ)
Common **kun** reading: **taka** (た か)

Note the intransitive/transitive verb pair below, and how the **kun-yomi** becomes voiced in the sixth example. This often occurs with 高 when it appears in the second or third position.

kun-yomi suggestion: "**tack a**pples"

Write your sentence to remember the **on-yomi** and **kun-yomi** readings in the box below.

Less Common Pronunciations

Less common **ON** reading: none
Less common **kun** reading: none

COMMON WORDS AND COMPOUNDS		
高い	*tall; expensive*	**taka·i** た か・い
高まる (intr)	*to rise*	**taka·maru** た か・ま る
高める (tr)	*to raise*	**taka·meru** た か・め る
高山	tall + mountain = *alpine*	**KŌ·ZAN** コ ウ・ザ ン
高校	tall + school = *high school*	**KŌ·KŌ** コ ウ・コ ウ
円高	circle (yen) + tall = *strong yen*	**EN·daka** エ ン・だ か
最高	most + tall = *highest; the best*	**SAI·KŌ** サ イ・コ ウ

SAMPLE SENTENCE

あ の 高 い 山 は 美 し い で す ね。
ano　taka·i yama wa　utsuku·shii desu　ne.
that　tall　mountain　beautiful　isn't it
= *That tall mountain is beautiful, isn't it?*

COMPONENT #50

BANDAGE

KANJI 50

買

BUY

丨	一	丆	罒	四	丨	冂	冃	買
買	買	買						

BUILDING THIS KANJI

Bandage 罒 + Shellfish 貝 (21) = 買

Meaning

Buy.

Remembering this kanji

As an animal rights activist, I regularly **BUY** **shellfish** in order to set them free. It's heartbreaking for me to go into a store and find them suffering in the tanks, their shells chipped and scarred. I **BUY** as many as possible, naturally, and do my best to help heal them by placing **bandages** on their wounds. But there are so many needing rescue… My only wish is for others to join the cause; after all, I can't **BUY** all the **shellfish** in the world.

Common Pronunciations

Common **ON** reading: none

Common **kun** reading: ka (か)

As nice as it is to have only one main reading to remember for this kanji, mention must be made of a particular quirk in written Japanese that occurs when certain verb stems are used to form nouns. The easiest way to understand this is by comparing the second and third examples below. As you can see, the noun in example 3 has "lost" the **i** (い) that would be present if the kanji were in its **-masu** verb form, **kaimasu**. (買います). It is,

in a sense, implied, based on the **hiragana** ending after 上. Unfortunately, there are no hard and fast rules for this aspect of the language, and it can be frustrating when such words are encountered. Our example, for instance, can be seen variously as "買い上げ," "買上げ," or even "買上" in different dictionaries!

It is worth keeping in mind, however, that not many kanji present such difficulties, and that once a "primary" word (usually the **-masu** form of a verb) has been learned, its related nouns will be easily recognized. Another consolation should be the following: by having reached the stage where you are dealing with such intricacies of the language, you are navigating among the deepest levels of written Japanese.

kun-yomi suggestion: "**cap**"

Create your sentence to remember the **kun-yomi** reading in the box below.

Less Common Pronunciations

Less common **ON** reading: **BAI** (バイ)

Less common **kun** reading: none

COMMON WORDS AND COMPOUNDS		
買う	*to buy*	**ka·u** か・う
買い上 げる	buy + upper = *to buy (up/out)*	**ka·i a·geru** か・い あ・げる
買上げ	buy + upper = *a purchase*	**kai a·ge** かい あ・げ
買い物	buy + thing = *shopping*	**ka·i mono** か・い もの
買い入 れる	buy + enter = *to stock up on*	**ka·i i·reru** か・い い・れる
買い手	buy + hand = *buyer*	**ka·i te** か・い て

SAMPLE SENTENCE

山中さん　　は　　高い　　物　　を　　買う

Yama·naka-san　wa　taka·i　mono　o　ka·u

Yamanaka-san　　　　　　expensive thing　　buy

つもり　です。

tsumori　desu.

plans

= *Yamanaka-san plans to buy something expensive.*

KANJI 51

百

HUNDRED

| 一 | 丶 | 丆 | 丆 | 百 | 百 | | |

BUILDING THIS KANJI
One (top of a bun) 一(3) + White 白(7) = 百

Meaning
Hundred. In a few instances, the idea of "many" is conveyed.

Remembering this kanji
A recent survey found that ONE HUNDRED percent of **white bun tops** are **white**. ONE HUNDRED percent! Rarely is scientific research so conclusive.

Common Pronunciations
Common **ON** reading: **HYAKU** (ヒャク)
Common **kun** reading: none

The thing to watch for here is how **HYAKU** changes phonetically with different numbers.

Note also the **kun-yomi** in examples four and seven. Create your **on-yomi** keyword and enter it in the table at the back of the book. After that, write your sentence to remember the **on-yomi** reading in the box below.

Less Common Pronunciations
Less common **ON** reading: none
Less common **kun** reading: none

COMMON WORDS AND COMPOUNDS		
百	*one hundred*	**HYAKU** ヒャク
二百	two + hundred = *two hundred*	**NI·HYAKU** ニ・ヒャク
三百	three + hundred = *three hundred*	**SAN·BYAKU** サン・ビャク
四百	four + hundred = *four hundred*	yon·**HYAKU** よん・ヒャク
五百	five + hundred = *five hundred*	**GO·HYAKU** ゴ・ヒャク
六百	six + hundred = *six hundred*	**ROP·PYAKU** ロッ・ピャク
七百	seven + hundred = *seven hundred*	nana·**HYAKU** なな・ヒャク
八百	eight + hundred = *eight hundred*	**HAP·PYAKU** ハッ・ピャク
九百	nine + hundred = *nine hundred*	**KYŪ·HYAKU** キュウ・ヒャク

SAMPLE SENTENCE
肉 を 五百 グラム買いました。
NIKU o GO·HYAKU guramu ka·imashita.
meat   five hundred   grams   bought
= *(I) bought five hundred grams of meat.*

KANJI 52

CIRCLE

	ㄇ	ㄇ	円				

BUILDING THIS KANJI
Gorilla ㄇ + Police ⼀ = 円

Meaning
Circle/Round. This kanji is also used to denote the yen, Japan's currency. The connection originated from round one-yen coins.

Remembering this kanji
Every **gorilla** in the park hated the **ranger**, for his snide comments about their grooming habits were known to animals far and wide. It was not surprising, therefore, to hear that he had found himself surrounded by a CIRCLE of angry silverbacks on emerging from his tent one day. No one will know for certain what actually happened to the **ranger**, of course, because the **gorillas** CIRCLED their wagons and refused to cooperate with any investigation.

Common Pronunciations
Common **ON** reading: **EN** (エン)
Common **kun** reading: **maru** (まる)

kun-yomi suggestion: "llama ruins"

Create your **on-yomi** keyword and enter it in the table at the back of the book. After that, write your sentence to remember the **on-yomi** and **kun-yomi** readings in the box below.

Less Common Pronunciations
Less common **ON** reading: none
Less common **kun** reading: none

COMMON WORDS AND COMPOUNDS		
円い	*circular*	**maru**·i まる・い
円高	yen + tall = *strong yen*	**EN**·daka エン・だか
二円	two + yen = *two yen*	**NI·EN** ニ・エン
半円	half + circle = *semicircle*	**HAN·EN** ハン・エン
円安	yen + ease = *weak yen*	**EN**·yasu エン・やす
円周	circle + around = *circumference*	**EN·SHŪ** エン・シュウ

SAMPLE SENTENCE

あの 子 は 　百円 　を なくした。
ano　ko　wa　HYAKU·EN　o　nakushita.
that child　 one hundred yen　 lost
= *That child lost a hundred yen.*

KANJI 53

元 **BASIS**

一	二	ア	元				

BUILDING THIS KANJI
Two 二(4) + Ballet ル = 元

Meaning
This character expresses the idea of a basis or original state of something. When used with its **kun-yomi** before words such as "president," it can be translated as "ex-," or "former."

Remembering this kanji
Two ballet legs are the BASIS of any good performance of Swan Lake. I mean, no one likes to be rude, but every time I watch a one-legged swan take on the role of Princess Odette…well, the very BASIS of the play is called into question for me.

Common Pronunciations
Common **ON** readings: **GEN** (ゲ ン); **GAN** (ガ ン)
Common **kun** reading: **moto** (も と)

GAN occurs only in the first position with a few common words.

kun-yomi suggestion: "**moto**cross"

Create your **on-yomi** keywords and enter them in the table at the back of the book. After that, write your sentence to remember the **on-yomi** and **kun-yomi** readings in the box below.

Less Common Pronunciations
Less common **ON** reading: none
Less common **kun** reading: none

COMMON WORDS AND COMPOUNDS		
元々	basis + basis = *from the first*	moto·moto も と・も と
元日	basis + sun (day) = *New Year's Day*	GAN·JITSU ガ ン・ジ ツ
手元	hand + basis = *at hand*	te·moto て・も と
元気	basis + spirit = *high spirits*	GEN·KI ゲ ン・キ
火元	fire + basis = *origin of a fire*	hi·moto ひ・も と
元来	basis + come = *by nature*	GAN·RAI ガ ン・ラ イ

SAMPLE SENTENCE

元日　な　の　で 人 が 少ない。
GAN·JITSU na　no　de hito ga suku·nai.
New Year's Day because　person　few
= *It's New Year's Day, so there aren't many people.*

KANJI 54

首 NECK

| 丶 | ⸏ | 一 | ⸜ | 宀 | 首 | 首 | 首 | 首 |

BUILDING THIS KANJI
Snowboard ⸜ + Self 自 (33) = 首

Meaning
Neck in its physical sense, as well as the ideas of leader or chief.

Remembering this kanji
His sense of **self** became so wrapped up in his **snowboard** that things started getting weird. After all, carrying a **snowboard** on your NECK at the ski slope is one thing, but wearing it around your NECK at work is another. When this started happening, even his colleagues in the office were concerned enough to seek advice.

"It all has to do with his sense of **self**-worth," said the company psychologist. "What with the recent demotion, his **self** confidence is shaken. He'll get over it eventually."

Common Pronunciations
Common **ON** reading: SHU (シュ)
Common **kun** reading: kubi (く び)

kun-yomi suggestion: "**Scooby** doo"

Create your **on-yomi** keyword and enter it in the table at the back of the book. After that, write your sentence to remember the **on-yomi** and **kun-yomi** readings in the box below.

Less Common Pronunciations
Less common **ON** reading: none
Less common **kun** reading: none

COMMON WORDS AND COMPOUNDS		
首	*neck*	kubi く び
自首	self + neck = *surrender*	JI·SHU ジ・シュ
手首	hand + neck = *wrist*	te·kubi て・く び
足首	leg + neck = *ankle*	ashi·kubi あ し・く び

SAMPLE SENTENCE

高木さん	は	首	に	水
Takagi-san	**wa**	**kubi**	**ni**	**mizu**
Takagi-san		neck		water

を	かけました。
o	**kakemashita.**
	put

= *Takagi-san put some water on his neck.*

KANJI 55

歩 **WALK**

| 1 | ヒ | ιト | 止 | 牛 | 歩 | 芝 | 歩 |

BUILDING THIS KANJI

Stop 止 (43) + Few 少 (45) = 歩

Meaning
Walking/Step/Pace. A secondary meaning of "rate" (as used in a financial sense) is found only with **BU** (ブ), a less-common **on-yomi**.

Remembering this kanji
My WALKING style is a little unorthodox in that I'll **stop**, take a **few** steps, then **stop** once more. It can be frustrating for those WALK-ING with me, I suppose, for what with **stopping** every **few** steps, I rarely make it far beyond my front door.

Common Pronunciations
Common **ON** reading: **HO** (ホ)
Common **kun** reading: **aru** (ある)

kun-yomi suggestion: "**a rou**te"

Create your **on-yomi** keyword and enter it in the table at the back of the book. After that, write your sentence to remember the **on-yomi** and **kun-yomi** readings in the box below.

Less Common Pronunciations
Less common **ON** readings: **BU** (ブ); **FU** (フ)
Less common **kun** reading: **ayu** (あゆ)

COMMON WORDS AND COMPOUNDS		
歩く	*to walk*	**aru·ku** ある・く
一歩	one + walk = *one step*	**IP·PO** イッ・ポ
歩き回る	walk + rotate = *to ramble about*	**aru·ki mawa·ru** ある・き まわ・る
歩道	walk + road = *sidewalk*	**HO·DŌ** ホ・ドウ
歩行	walk + go = *walking*	**HO·KŌ** ホ・コウ
歩行者	walk + go + individual = *pedestrian*	**HO·KŌ·SHA** ホ・コウ・シャ

SAMPLE SENTENCE

家　　から　　山　　まで　歩きました。

ie   kara   yama   made   aru·kimashita.

house from mountain until   walked

= *(We) walked from the house to the mountain.*

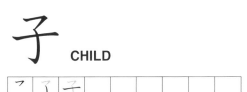

KANJI 56

CHILD

kun-yomi suggestion: "**coat**"

Write your sentence to remember the **on-yomi** and **kun-yomi** readings in the box below.

Meaning
Child. As seen in the final compound below, this character can also be used to suggest something small. No story required.

Less Common Pronunciations
Less common **ON** reading: **SU** (ス)
Less common **kun** reading: none

COMMON WORDS AND COMPOUNDS		
子	*child*	**ko** こ
女子	woman + child = *women's*	**JO·SHI** ジョ・シ
王子	king + child = *prince*	**Ō·JI** オウ・ジ
男子	man + child = *men's*	**DAN·SHI** ダン・シ
子牛	child + cow = *calf*	**ko·ushi** こ・うし
電子	electric + child = *electron*	**DEN·SHI** デン・シ

Common Pronunciations
Common **ON** reading: **SHI** (シ)
Common **kun** reading: **ko** (こ)

Interestingly, both of these readings can at times become voiced (pronounced **JI** and **go**) in the second position, as seen in the third examples of this entry and that of Entry 167. Japanese parents often choose this kanji for a suffix when naming their children (eg. **Aki·ko**); it is read "**SHI**" in the case of males, and "**ko**" when applied to females.

SAMPLE SENTENCE

五月　　に女王と王子が　　米国
GO·GATSU ni JO·Ō to Ō·JI ga BEI·KOKU
　May　　queen prince　　America
へ　　行きました。
e　　i·kimashita.
　　　　went
= *In May, the queen and prince went to America.*

好 LIKE

く	ノ	女	女'	女ᄀ	好			

BUILDING THIS KANJI
Woman 女(16) + Child 子(56) = 好

Meaning
To like/Good/Favorable…nothing but positive feelings are associated with this gentle character!

Remembering this kanji
This is one of those kanji that is so logically constructed as to need no story at all.

Common Pronunciations
Common **ON** reading: **KŌ** (コ ウ)
Common **kun** reading: **su** (す)

The **kun-yomi** is often voiced when in the second position (becoming "**zu**"), as below in examples three and four.

kun-yomi suggestion: "**soon**"

Write your sentence to remember the **on-yomi** and **kun-yomi** readings in the box below.

Less Common Pronunciations
Less common **ON** reading: none
Less common **kun** reading: **kono** (こ の)

COMMON WORDS AND COMPOUNDS		
好き	*like*	**su**·ki す·き
大好き	large + like = *to really like*	DAI **su·ki** ダイ す·き
人好き	person + like = *amiability*	hito **zu·ki** ひと ず·き
話し好き	speak + like = *talkative*	hana·shi **zu·ki** はな·し ず·き
友好	friend + like = *friendship*	YŪ·KŌ ユウ·コウ
同好	same + like = *same tastes*	DŌ·KŌ ドウ·コウ

SAMPLE SENTENCE

山口さん　はあそこ　の　女　の　人
Yama·guchi-san wa asoko no onna no hito
 Yamaguchi-san   over there   woman person
が　大好き　です。
ga DAI su·ki   desu.
   really likes
= *Yamaguchi-san really likes that woman over there.*

KANJI 58

古 OLD

| 一 | 十 | 十 | 古 | 古 | | | |

BUILDING THIS KANJI
Ten (scarecrow) 十 (28) + Mouth (vampire) 口 (8) = 古

Meaning
Old/Ancient/Antique.

Remembering this kanji
Even though **vampires** never die, they do grow OLD and suffer the same deterioration of mental faculties as the rest of us. The **scarecrow** can attest to this; as he lives in a field next to an OLD folks home, he'll often look down to find an elderly **vampire** bravely fastening its gums onto his ankle. It's more of a nuisance for him than anything, of course, but he's always nice enough to show respect for those OLDER by acting scared.

Common Pronunciations
Common **ON** reading: **KO** (コ)
Common **kun** reading: **furu** (ふ る)

Remember that your **on-yomi** keyword here will be different from that used in the preceding entry (for 好).

kun-yomi suggestion: "**who ru**es…"

Create your **on-yomi** keyword and enter it in the table at the back of the book. After that, write your sentence to remember the **on-yomi** and **kun-yomi** readings in the box below.

Less Common Pronunciations
Less common **ON** reading: none
Less common **kun** reading: none

COMMON WORDS AND COMPOUNDS		
古い	*old*	**furu·i** ふ・る・い
中古	middle + old = *secondhand*	**CHŪ·KO** チュウ・コ
最古	most + old = *oldest*	**SAI·KO** サイ・コ
古語	old + words = *archaic word*	**KO·GO** コ・ゴ
古来	old + come = *time honored*	**KO·RAI** コ・ライ
古里	old + hamlet = *the old hometown*	**furu·sato** ふ・る・さと

SAMPLE SENTENCE
山下さん は 中古 の 品をよく
Yama·shita-san wa CHŪ·KO no shina o yoku
Yamashita-san   secondhand   goods   often
買います。
ka·imasu.
   buys
= *Yamashita-san often buys secondhand goods.*

火 **FIRE**

丶	丷	丷	火				

Write your sentence to remember the **on-yomi** and **kun-yomi** readings in the box below.

Meaning

This beautifully simple character encompasses all things to do with fire. No story required, although you can imagine the illustration as a **FIRE person** with a couple of flaming **jelly beans**.

Less Common Pronunciations

Less common **ON** reading: none

Less common **kun** reading: **ho** (ほ)

COMMON WORDS AND COMPOUNDS		
火	*fire*	hi ひ
火元	fire + basis = *origin of a fire*	hi·moto ひ·もと
大火	large + fire = *conflagration*	TAI·**KA** タイ·カ
火山	fire + mountain = *volcano*	**KA**·ZAN カ·ザン
花火	flower + fire = *fireworks*	hana·**bi** はな·び
火曜日	fire + day of the week + sun (day) = *Tuesday*	**KA**·YŌ·bi カ·ヨウ·び
火星	fire + star = *Mars (planet)*	**KA**·SEI カ·セイ

Common Pronunciations

Common **ON** reading: **KA** (カ)
Common **kun** reading: **hi** (ひ)

The **kun-yomi** is always voiced (becomes **bi**) when in the second position, as seen here in example five.

kun-yomi suggestion: "**heat**"

SAMPLE SENTENCE

日 本 に は 火山 が あ り ま す。
NI·HON ni wa KA·ZAN ga   arimasu.
Japan   volcano   are
= *There are volcanoes in Japan.*

COMPONENT #60

RUNNING CHICKEN

KANJI 60

冬 **WINTER**

| ノ | ク | 夂 | 冬 | 冬 | | | |

BUILDING THIS KANJI

Running Chicken 夂 + Jelly Bean 丶 + Jelly Bean 丶 = 冬

Meaning

Winter.

Remembering this kanji

WINTER is such a drab time of year. To add a bit of color to the season, therefore, I enjoy strapping bags of **jelly beans** to **chickens running** in the yard, as the **beans** spill out and make everything more cheerful. It's a mystery to me why more people don't do this; even the grayest WINTER would be tolerable if everyone followed my lead.

Common Pronunciations

Common **ON** reading: **TŌ** (ト ウ)
Common **kun** reading: **fuyu** (ふ ゆ)

kun-yomi suggestion: "**who u**ses…"

Create your **on-yomi** keyword and enter it in the table at the back of the book. After that, write your sentence to remember the **on-yomi** and **kun-yomi** readings in the box below.

Less Common Pronunciations

Less common **ON** reading: none
Less common **kun** reading: none

COMMON WORDS AND COMPOUNDS		
冬	*winter*	**fuyu** ふゆ
冬休み	winter + rest = *winter vacation*	**fuyu** yasu·mi ふゆ やす·み
立冬	stand + winter = *first day of winter*	RIT·**TŌ** リッ·ト ウ
冬物	winter + thing = *winter clothing*	**fuyu**·mono ふゆ·もの
冬空	winter + empty (sky) = *winter sky*	**fuyu**·zora ふゆ·ぞら

SAMPLE SENTENCE

冬 に なる と スイス の 山 は
fuyu ni naru to suisu no yama wa
winter becomes Switzerland mountain
美しい。
utsuku·shii.
beautiful
= *The mountains of Switzerland are beautiful in winter.*

CHAPTER 3 REVIEW EXERCISES

A. Please match the following kanji to their meanings.

1.	高	a.	Few
2.	止	b.	Hundred
3.	古	c.	Basis
4.	百	d.	Tall
5.	南	e.	Winter
6.	京	f.	Left
7.	元	g.	Capital
8.	左	h.	Stop
9.	少	i.	South
10.	冬	j.	Old

B. Please match the following meanings to their kanji, and these to their **on-** or **kun-yomi**.

1.	Like (**kun-yomi**)	a. 歩	1.	**HO** (ホ)
2.	Child	b. 火	2.	**ko** (こ)
3.	Neck	c. 工	3.	**kubi** (くび)
4.	Craft	d. 首	4.	**ka** (か)
5.	Walk	e. 七	5.	**EN** (エン)
6.	See	f. 子	6.	**SHICHI** (シチ)
7.	Fire (**kun-yomi**)	g. 見	7.	**KŌ** (コウ)
8.	Buy	h. 円	8.	**mi** (み)
9.	Circle	i. 好	9.	**hi** (ひ)
10.	Seven	j. 買	10.	**su** (す)

C. Please choose the best answer(s) to the following questions.

1. Which of the following readings apply to the kanji 南?
   a. **NAN** (ナン)
   b. **fuyu** (ふゆ)
   c. **HYAKU** (ヒャク)
   d. **minami** (みなみ)
   e. **hidari** (ひだり)

2. What is the worst thing you can hear someone say from behind while you're standing on a plank of a ship?
   a. 子
   b. 七
   c. 好
   d. 元
   e. 歩

3. Which of the following readings apply to the kanji 高?
   a. **hi** (ひ)
   b. **GETSU** (ゲツ)
   c. **KŌ** (コウ)
   d. **taka** (たか)
   e. **TAI** (タイ)

4. Which of the following readings apply to the kanji 元?
   a. **GEN** (ゲン)
   b. **moto** (もと)
   c. **furu** (ふる)
   d. **GAN** (ガン)
   e. **HAN** (ハン)

5. Which of the following readings apply to the kanji 少?
   a. **KŌ** (コウ)
   b. **SHŌ** (ショウ)
   c. **suko** (すこ)
   d. **suku** (すく)
   e. **to** (と)

D. Please choose the best answer to the following questions.

1. Which is the correct reading of 少し?
   a. **mawa·shi** (ま わ · し)
   b. **suko·shi** (す こ · し)
   c. **de·shi** (で · し)
   d. **suku·shi** (す く · し)

2. Which kanji would precede 口 to form the compound for "volcanic crater"?
   a. 冬
   b. 火
   c. 左
   d. 首
   e. 止

3. Which is the correct reading of 古い?
   a. **furu·i** (ふ る · い)
   b. **ka·i** (か · い)
   c. **yuru·i** (ゆ る · い)
   d. **futo·i** (ふ と · い)

4. Which of the following kanji has the most number of strokes?
   a. 見
   b. 好
   c. 南
   d. 歩
   e. 京

5. Which is the correct reading of 少ない?
   a. **aka·nai** (あ か · な い)
   b. **to·nai** (と · な い)
   c. **aga·nai** (あ が · な い)
   d. **suku·nai** (す く · な い)

E. Please match the following compounds and words to their meanings and pronunciations.

1. 南米 　　a. To really like
2. 中古 　　b. Secondhand
3. 上京 　　c. Semicircle
4. 大火 　　d. South America
5. 半円 　　e. Artificial
6. 中止 　　f. Discontinue
7. 一歩 　　g. Seven hundred
8. 七百 　　h. Come/ Go to Tokyo
9. 人工 　　i. One step
10. 大好き 　j. Conflagration

1. **CHŪ·SHI** (チュウ·シ)
2. **JŌ·KYŌ** (ジョウ· キョウ)
3. **JIN·KŌ** (ジン·コウ)
4. **CHŪ·KO** (チュウ·コ)
5. **IP·PO** (イッ·ポ)
6. **NAN·BEI** (ナン·ベイ)
7. **TAI·KA** (タイ·カ)
8. **DAI su·ki** (ダイ す·き)
9. **HAN·EN** (ハン·エン)
10. **nana· HYAKU** (なな· ヒャク)

Kanji #61—80

水 **WATER**

Meaning
Another gracefully balanced character, this one suggesting water. The "wavy" effect in the illustration will be easier to remember if you imagine the harpoon being pulled upward. No story required.

Common Pronunciations
Common **ON** reading: **SUI** (スイ)
Common **kun** reading: **mizu** (みず)

kun-yomi suggestion: "make **me zoo**m"

Create your **on-yomi** keyword and enter it in the table at the back of the book. After that, write your

sentence to remember the **on-yomi** and **kun-yomi** readings in the box below.

Less Common Pronunciations
Less common **ON** reading: none
Less common **kun** reading: none

COMMON WORDS AND COMPOUNDS		
水	*water*	**mizu** みず
水中	water + middle = *underwater;* *in the water*	**SUI·CHŪ** スイ・チュウ
下水	lower + water = *sewage*	**GE·SUI** ゲ・スイ
水玉	water + jewel = *drop of water*	**mizu·tama** みず・たま
水星	water + star = *Mercury (planet)*	**SUI·SEI** スイ・セイ
水曜日	water + day of the week + sun (day) = *Wednesday*	**SUI·YŌ·bi** スイ・ヨウ・び
水死	water + death = *drowning*	**SUI·SHI** スイ・シ

SAMPLE SENTENCE:
あの ダム には 水 が ありません。
ano damu ni wa mizu ga arimasen.
that dam water isn't
= *There is no water at that dam.*

COMPONENT #62

PINCERS

KANJI 62

安 **EASE**

'	''	宀	灾	安	安		

BUILDING THIS KANJI
Pincers 宀 + Woman 女(16) = 安

Meaning
The general sense is of "ease", "peacefulness," and "stability." An important secondary meaning is "inexpensive." In this regard, the kanji's opposite is "高" (Entry 49).

Remembering this kanji
Pincers have always allowed the legendary **women** of history to lead lives of EASE. Nefertiti and Cleopatra had **pincers** deposit them into cushiony boats on the Nile; Catherine the Great had **pincers** EASE her onto a bed strewn with sable… Even Joan of Arc, after a tiring day on the battlefield, would always have **pincers** set her gently into a bubble bath.

Common Pronunciations
Common **ON** reading: AN (アン)
Common **kun** reading: yasu (やす)

kun-yomi suggestion: "try **a su**it"

Create your **on-yomi** keyword and enter it in the table at the back of the book. After that, write your sentence to remember the **on-yomi** and **kun-yomi** readings in the box below.

Less Common Pronunciations
Less common **ON** reading: none
Less common **kun** reading: none

COMMON WORDS AND COMPOUNDS		
安い	*easy; cheap*	**yasu·i** やす・い
円安	circle (yen) + ease = *weak yen*	**EN·yasu** エン・やす
安心	ease + heart = *peace of mind*	**AN·SHIN** アン・シン
安全	ease + complete = *safety*	**AN·ZEN** アン・ゼン
不安	not + ease = *uneasiness*	**FU·AN** フ・アン
公安	public + ease = *public peace*	**KŌ·AN** コウ・アン

SAMPLE SENTENCE:

安心　　して　下さい。
AN·SHIN　　shite　　kuda·sai.
peace of mind　　do　　　please
= *Please don't worry.*

KANJI 63

力　**STRENGTH**

フ	力						

Meaning

Strength/Power/Force. No story required.

Common Pronunciations

Common **ON** readings: **RYOKU** (リ ョ ク);
RIKI (リ キ)
Common **kun** reading: **chikara** (ち か ら)

RYOKU will be encountered far more often than
RIKI; the **kun-yomi** is a common word on its own.

kun-yomi suggestion: "in my **cheek a ra**t…"

Create your **on-yomi** keywords and enter them in
the table at the back of the book. After that, write
your sentence to remember the **on-yomi** and **kun-
yomi** readings in the box below.

Less Common Pronunciations

Less common **ON** reading: none
Less common **kun** reading: none

COMMON WORDS AND COMPOUNDS		
力	*strength*	**chikara**　ち か ら
全力	complete + strength = *all one's power*	ZEN·**RYOKU**　ゼ ン · リ ョ ク
有力	have + strength = *powerful*	YŪ·**RYOKU**　ユ ウ · リ ョ ク
水力	water + strength = *hydro power*	SUI·**RYOKU**　ス イ · リ ョ ク
火力	fire + strength = *thermal power*	KA·**RYOKU**　カ · リ ョ ク
電力	electric + strength = *electric power*	DEN·**RYOKU**　デ ン · リ ョ ク
力士	strength + gentleman = *sumo wrestler*	**RIKI**·SHI　リ キ · シ

SAMPLE SENTENCE:

中山さん　は　車　のビジネスで
Naka·yama-san wa kuruma no bijinesu de
Nakayama-san　　　　car　　　business
とても　　有力　　な　　人　　です。
totemo　　YŪ·RYOKU　na　　hito　　desu.
very　　　powerful　　　　person　　is
= *In the automotive business, Nakayama-san is
a very powerful person.*

KANJI 64

夏 **SUMMER**

| 一 | 一 | 下 | 下 | 百 | 百 | 百 | 頁 | 頁 |
| 夏 | | | | | | | | |

BUILDING THIS KANJI
One (top of a bun) 一(3) + Self 自(33) +
Running Chicken 夂 = 夏

Meaning
Summer.

Remembering this kanji
When SUMMER rolls around I enjoy throwing parties, but like most farming folk, I don't stand on ceremony. After all, what with it being so darn hot in the SUMMER, the last thing I want to do is cook! So you'd better be prepared if you drop by. I'll give you the **top of a bun**, of course, but you'll be heading straight to the coop after that. "Go catch yourself a **running chicken**," I'll say. "This here's a **self**-serve party."

Common Pronunciations
Common **ON** reading: **KA** (カ)
Common **kun** reading: **natsu** (なつ)

kun-yomi suggestion: "gnat soup"

Write your sentence to remember the **on-yomi** and **kun-yomi** readings in the box below.

Less Common Pronunciations
Less common **ON** reading: **GE** (ゲ)
Less common **kun** reading: none

COMMON WORDS AND COMPOUNDS		
夏	*summer*	**natsu** なつ
夏休み	summer + rest = *summer vacation*	**natsu** yasu·**mi** なつ やす·み
夏物	summer + thing = *summer clothing*	**natsu**·mono なつ·もの
立夏	stand + summer = *first day of summer*	RIK·**KA** リッ·カ

SAMPLE SENTENCE:
この 夏 には 東京 へ 行きます。
kono natsu ni wa TŌ·KYŌ e i·kimasu.
this summer Tokyo go
= *(We'll) be going to Tokyo this summer.*

KANJI 65

千 **THOUSAND**

´	一	千					

BUILDING THIS KANJI
Comet ´ + **Ten (scarecrow)** 十 (28) = 千

Meaning
Thousand. Like the character for "hundred" (Entry 51), this kanji sometimes conveys a general idea of "many".

Remembering this kanji
My favorite story in the "**THOUSAND** and One Nights" is the tale in which a comet on a **THOUSAND**-year journey has a chat with a **scarecrow**.

"What's up?" he asks.

"Nothing much besides my getting sick of this view," answers the **scarecrow**. "I must say, I'd sure love to take a trip like yours."

"Well, why don't you go, then?" says the **comet**, smiling. "Remember: a journey of a **THOUSAND** miles starts with a single step."

"Gee, thanks for that pearl of wisdom," says the scarecrow sarcastically. "In case you haven't noticed, I'm tied to a couple of boards here."

Common Pronunciations
Common **ON** reading: **SEN** (セ ン)
Common **kun** reading: none

As seen with the kanji " 百 ," note how SEN changes phonetically with different numbers, and how **kun-yomi** are used in examples four and seven.

Create your **on-yomi** keyword and enter it in the table at the back of the book. After that, write your sentence to remember the **on-yomi** reading in the box below.

Less Common Pronunciations
Less common **ON** reading: none
Less common **kun** reading: **chi** (ち)

COMMON WORDS AND COMPOUNDS		
千	one thousand	SEN セン
二千	two + thousand = two thousand	NI·SEN ニ·セン
三千	three + thousand = three thousand	SAN·ZEN サン·ゼン
四千	four + thousand = four thousand	yon·SEN よん·セン
五千	five + thousand = five thousand	GO·SEN ゴ·セン
六千	six + thousand = six thousand	ROKU·SEN ロク·セン
七千	seven + thousand = seven thousand	nana·SEN なな·セン
八千	eight + thousand = eight thousand	HAS·SEN ハッ·セン
九千	nine + thousand = nine thousand	KYŪ·SEN キュウ·セン

SAMPLE SENTENCE:

米	は	七千円	なので
kome	**wa**	**nana·SEN·EN**	**na no de**
rice		seven thousand yen	because

安くない。
yasu·kunai.
not cheap

= At seven thousand yen, rice isn't cheap.

COMPONENT #66

GIRAFFE

You will notice this component used extensively in written Japanese, as it appears in almost one hundred kanji.

KANJI 66

 REST

BUILDING THIS KANJI
Giraffe 亻 + Tree 木 (13) = 休

Meaning
Rest.

Remembering this kanji
One of the surprises of my trip to Africa was learning that **giraffes** RESTED in trees. The safari leader mentioned that this was natural behavior. "They prefer baobabs," he said. "The branches are lower, so when the **giraffes** make a running leap at them they can jump higher into the **tree**. But this is not done simply for REST," he then added. "It also serves as an effective way for any **giraffe** to avoid its natural creditors."

Common Pronunciations
Common **ON** reading: **KYŪ** (キュウ)
Common **kun** reading: **yasu** (やす)

kun-yomi suggestion: "try a souffle"

Create your **on-yomi** keyword and enter it in the table at the back of the book. After that, write your sentence to remember the **on-yomi** and **kun-yomi** readings in the box below.

Less Common Pronunciations
Less common **ON** reading: none
Less common **kun** reading: none

COMMON WORDS AND COMPOUNDS		
休む	to rest	yasu·mu やす・む
お休み	"Good night!"	o·yasu·mi お・やす・み
休日	rest + sun (day) = holiday	KYŪ·JITSU キュウ・ジツ
夏休み	summer + rest = summer vacation	natsu yasu·mi なつ やす・み
冬休み	winter + rest = winter vacation	fuyu yasu·mi ふゆ やす・み
休火山	rest + fire + mountain = dormant volcano	KYŪ·KA·ZAN キュウ・カ・ザン

SAMPLE SENTENCE:

山口さん　　　は　　　半日
Yama·guchi-san　　wa　　HAN·NICHI
Yamaguchi-san　　　　　　　half a day
休みました。
yasu·mimashita.
　　rested
= Yamaguchi-san rested for half a day.

KANJI 67

HAND

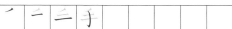

Meaning

Hand. No story required.

Common Pronunciations

Common **ON** reading: **SHU** (シュ)
Common **kun** reading: **te** (て)

The **kun-yomi** is by far the most common reading.

kun-yomi suggestion: "tent"

Write your sentence to remember the **on-yomi** and **kun-yomi** readings in the box below.

Less Common Pronunciations

Less common **ON** reading: none
Less common **kun** reading: **ta** (た)

ta (た) is an extremely rare reading, although it does show up in 下手, a common irregular reading we learned back in Chapter 2. It is presented again below following its companion; the two words are best learned as a pair.

IRREGULAR READINGS		
上手	upper + hand = *to be good at (something)*	JŌ·zu ジョウ・ず
下手	lower + hand = *to be poor at (something)*	he·ta へ・た

COMMON WORDS AND COMPOUNDS		
手	*hand*	te て
右手	right + hand = *right hand*	migi·te みぎ・て
左手	left + hand = *left hand*	hidari·te ひだり・て
手元	hand + basis = *at hand*	te·moto て・もと
手首	hand + neck = *wrist*	te·kubi て・くび
手話	hand + speak = *sign language*	SHU·WA シュ・ワ
空手	empty + hand = *karate*	kara·te から・て

SAMPLE SENTENCE:

あの ピアニスト の 手 は 美しい

ano   pianisuto   no te wa utsuku·shii

that   pianist   hands   beautiful

です ね。

desu   ne.

aren't they

= *That pianist's hands are beautiful, aren't they?*

KANJI 68

本 **MAIN**

一 十 才 木 本

BUILDING THIS KANJI
Tree 木(13) + One (hamburger patty) 一(3) = 本

Meaning
This intriguing character encompasses a range of meanings from "main" to "origin," and is also used to emphasize the idea of "this". When encountered alone, however, it often indicates a book. It is also one of the more common of an infamous group of kanji that Japanese uses for counting, being employed for long, cylindrical objects such as pencils and bottles. The sense of "origin," incidentally, is evident in the compound for Japan itself, the "Land of the Rising Sun."

Remembering this kanji
Despite cultural differences, there is a surprising amount of commonality in the world's **MAIN** myths. The people of Ur, for example, clearly tell Enkidu in the "Epic of Gilgamesh" that the **MAIN** race of people was conceived from a "union between **hamburger patty** and **tree**." Beowulf, too, quotes Norse mythology to explain the **MAIN** purpose of mankind: "Go forth, so that from **patties** will sprout mighty **trees**…" Coincidence? In the **MAIN**, it's unlikely.

Common Pronunciations
Common **ON** reading: **HON** (ホン)
Common **kun** reading: **moto** (もと)

The **kun-yomi** is common in Japanese family and place names; the fifth compound below provides an example. Create your **on-yomi** keyword and enter it in the table at the back of the book. After that, write your sentence to remember the **on-yomi** and **kun-yomi** readings in the box below.

Less Common Pronunciations
Less common **ON** reading: none
Less common **kun** reading: none

COMMON WORDS AND COMPOUNDS		
本	*book*	**HON** ホン
日本	sun + main = *Japan*	**NI·HON** ニ・ホン **NIP·PON** ニッ・ポン
全日本	complete + sun + main = *all Japan*	**ZEN·NI·HON** ゼン・ニ・ホン
日本人	sun + main + person = *a Japanese (person)*	**NI·HON·JIN** ニ・ホン・ジン
山本 さん	mountain + main = *Yamamoto-san*	yama·**moto**·san やま・もと・さん
日本語	sun + main + words = *Japanese (language)*	**NI·HON·GO** ニ・ホン・ゴ
本土	main + earth = *mainland*	**HON·DO** ホン・ド

SAMPLE SENTENCE:

山下さん　は　高い　本　を
Yama·shita-san **wa** **taka·i** **HON** **o**
Yamashita-san　　expensive　book
買いました。
ka·imashita.
　bought
= *Yamashita-san bought an expensive book.*

COMPONENT #69

BEGGAR 匕

KANJI 69

化 **CHANGE**

ノ	イ	イ′	化				

BUILDING THIS KANJI
Giraffe イ + Beggar 匕 = 化

Meaning
Change/Transform. When used as a suffix (as in several of the compounds below), this character expresses a variety of English words ending in "-ification" or "-ization."

Remembering this kanji
Grandpa liked nothing more than to help those down on their luck. But he never gave money. I learned this when I saw him carrying a stuffed **giraffe** down to skid row one day.

"This is for you," he said to a **beggar**, passing him the toy. "A companion to share your woe."

The **beggar** nodded, and after taking his gift started immediately across the street.

"Where are you going?" Grandpa asked.

"This **giraffe** is so wonderful," said the **beggar**, "that I want to show it to all my friends in the pawn shop."

Grandpa smiled. "Now do you understand?" he said to me. "Giving money CHANGES nothing. It is only through stuffed **giraffes** that a **beggar's** life can truly be CHANGED."

Common Pronunciations
Common **ON** reading: **KA** (カ)
Common **kun** reading: none

Write your sentence to remember the **on-yomi** reading in the box below.

Less Common Pronunciations
Less common **ON** reading: **KE** (ケ)
Less common **kun** reading: **ba** (ば)

COMMON WORDS AND COMPOUNDS		
国有化	country + have + change = *nationalization*	KOKU·YŪ·KA コク・ユウ・カ
美化	beautiful + change = *beautification*	BI·KA ビ・カ
化学	change + study = *chemistry*	**KA·GAKU** カ・ガク
気化	spirit + change = *vaporize*	KI·KA キ・カ
電化	electric + change = *electrification*	DEN·KA デン・カ
同化	same + change = *assimilation*	DŌ·KA ドウ・カ

SAMPLE SENTENCE:

山本さん は 化学 が
Yama·moto-san wa KA·GAKU ga
Yamamoto-san   chemistry
大好き です。
DAI su·ki desu.
really likes
= *Yamamoto-san really likes chemistry.*

KANJI 70

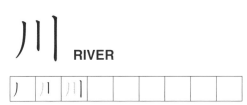 **RIVER**

)	ノ	ノ						

Meaning
River. No story required.

Common Pronunciations
Common **ON** reading: none
Common **kun** reading: **kawa** (か わ)

When appearing as the final character in the names of rivers, this kanji is invariably voiced (becomes "**gawa**").

kun-yomi suggestion: "lac**k a wa**x"

Create your sentence to remember the **kun-yomi** reading in the box below.

Less Common Pronunciations
Less common **ON** reading: **SEN**
Less common **kun** reading: none

COMMON WORDS AND COMPOUNDS		
川	*river*	**kawa** か わ
川上	river + upper = *upstream*	**kawa**·kami か わ·か み
川下	river + lower = *downstream*	**kawa**·shimo か わ·し も
川口	river + mouth = *river mouth*	**kawa**·guchi か わ·ぐ ち
川本さん	river + main = *Kawamoto-san*	**kawa**·moto·san か わ·も と· さ ん

SAMPLE SENTENCE:

山　の　上　に　行く　と　川　が
yama　no　ue　ni　i·ku　to　kawa　ga
mountain　　upper　　go　　river
見えます　か。
mi·emasu　ka.
　can see
= *Can you see the river if you go to the top of the mountain?*

| ノ | イ | イ- | 什 | 付 | 休 | 体 | | |

BUILDING THIS KANJI
Giraffe イ + Main 本 (68) = 体

Meaning
The physical body (of a person or object), as well as secondary ideas of "substance" and "style." Make sure to keep this character distinct in your mind from "休" (Entry 66).

Remembering this kanji
As the **main** part of a **giraffe's** identity is tied to its statuesque BODY, all **giraffes** have a tendency to be vain. This naturally breeds conflict on the savanna. It is a rare wildebeest, for example, who hasn't been left with crippling BODY issues after watching a **giraffe** stride nobly along in the distance. As cats, however, it is the lions who are especially BODY conscious and apt to take a slight personally. Though the **main** part of their diet lies elsewhere, they will attack any **giraffe** who looks down on them.

Common Pronunciations
Common **ON** reading: **TAI** (タイ)
Common **kun** reading: **karada** (からだ)

kun-yomi suggestion: "make a rad ambulance"

Write your sentence to remember the **on-yomi** and **kun-yomi** readings in the box below.

Less Common Pronunciations
Less common **ON** reading: **TEI** (テイ)
Less common **kun** reading: none

COMMON WORDS AND COMPOUNDS		
体	*body*	karada からだ
大体	large + body = *in general*	DAI·TAI ダイ・タイ
全体	complete + body = *the whole*	ZEN·TAI ゼン・タイ
肉体	meat + body = *the body*	NIKU·TAI ニク・タイ
体力	body + strength = *physical strength*	TAI·RYOKU タイ・リョク
自体	self + body = *in itself*	JI·TAI ジ・タイ
団体	group + body = *organization*	DAN·TAI ダン・タイ

SAMPLE SENTENCE:

あの　人　は　すごく　　体力
ano　hito　wa　sugoku　TAI·RYOKU
that　person　　　incredible　physical strength
が　有ります。
ga　a·rimasu.
　　has
= *That person has incredible physical strength.*

COMPONENT #72

SLEEPWALKER

KANJI 72

北 NORTH

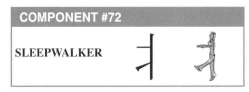

BUILDING THIS KANJI
Sleepwalker 才 + Beggar ヒ = 北

Meaning
North. Note that in the more calligraphic font used above, the second stroke is slightly shortened at the bottom.

Remembering this kanji
Once upon a time, a **sleepwalker** heading NORTH passed a **beggar**. "I'd better follow," thought the **beggar**. "This **sleepwalker** might be on her way to Santa's workshop, and I hear that guy gives away lots of free stuff."

Common Pronunciations
Common **ON** reading: **HOKU** (ホ ク)
Common **kun** reading: **kita** (き た)

As the final example shows, **HOKU** can double up with unvoiced consonant sounds.

kun-yomi suggestion: "**s**ki **ta**x"

Create your **on-yomi** keyword and enter it in the table at the back of the book. After that, write your sentence to remember the **on-yomi** and **kun-yomi** readings in the box below.

Less Common Pronunciations
Less common **ON** reading: none
Less common **kun** reading: none

COMMON WORDS AND COMPOUNDS		
北	*north*	**kita** き た
北米	north + rice (America) = *North America*	**HOKU·BEI** ホ ク・ベ イ
北口	north + mouth = *north exit/entrance*	**kita·guchi** き た・ぐ ち
北東	north + east = *northeast*	**HOKU·TŌ** ホ ク・ト ウ
北西	north + west = *northwest*	**HOKU·SEI** ホ ク・セ イ
北海道	north + sea + road = *Hokkaido*	**HOK·KAI·DŌ** ホ ッ・カ イ・ド ウ

SAMPLE SENTENCE:
北日本　の　冬　はとても美しい。
kita·NI·HON　no　fuyu　wa　totemo　utsuku·shii.
northern Japan　winter　very　beautiful
= *Northern Japan's winter is very beautiful.*

KANJI 73

田

RICE FIELD

| 丨 | 冂 | 冂 | 甲 | 田 | | | |

Meaning

"Rice field," or a "field" in general. No story required.

Common Pronunciations

Common **ON** reading: **DEN** (デン)
Common **kun** reading: **ta** (た)

This kanji is commonly used in Japanese family names; it is often voiced, as in the fourth and fifth examples below, the latter of which has a mix of **on** and **kun-yomi**.

kun-yomi suggestion: "**tack**"

Create your **on-yomi** keyword and enter it in the table at the back of the book. After that, write your sentence to remember the **on-yomi** and **kun-yomi** readings in the box below.

Less Common Pronunciations

Less common **ON** reading: none
Less common **kun** reading: none

Here is a common irregular reading:

IRREGULAR READING		
田舎*	rice field + building = *the countryside*	**inaka** いなか

COMMON WORDS AND COMPOUNDS		
田	*rice field*	**ta** た
水田	water + rice field = *rice paddy*	**SUI·DEN** スイ・デン
田中さん	rice field + middle = *Tanaka-san*	**ta**·naka·san た・なか・さん
山田さん	mountain + rice field = *Yamada-san*	yama·**da**·san やま・だ・さん
本田さん	main + rice field = *Honda-san*	HON·**da**·san ホン・だ・さん

SAMPLE SENTENCE:

水田　　を　見　に　行きました。
SUI·DEN　o　**mi**　ni　**i·kimashita.**
rice paddy　　see　　　　went
= *(She) went to see the rice paddies.*

KANJI 74

男   MAN

丨	冂	冂	田	田	男	男		

BUILDING THIS KANJI
Rice field 田(73) + Strength 力(63) = 男

Meaning
Man/Male.

Remembering this kanji

There is a story from feudal Japan in which a lord asks a group of **MEN** to demonstrate their **strength**. The task he sets them is simple: to lift up as much of a **rice field** as possible. Each **MAN** in the competition does his best, of course, but none save the last can pull up more than an armful of muck. What is this final **MAN'S** secret, you ask? It should be obvious: he was the only one with enough sense to use a bulldozer.

Common Pronunciations

Common **ON** reading: **DAN** (ダン)
Common **kun** reading: otoko (おとこ)

kun-yomi suggestion: "**O! Toe co**ld"

Create your **on-yomi** keyword and enter it in the table at the back of the book. After that, write your sentence to remember the **on-yomi** and **kun-yomi** readings in the box below.

Less Common Pronunciations

Less common **ON** reading: **NAN** (ナン)
Less common **kun** reading: none

COMMON WORDS AND COMPOUNDS		
男	*man*	otoko おとこ
男女	man + woman = *men and women*	DAN·JO ダン・ジョ
男子	man + child = *men's*	DAN·SHI ダン・シ
大男	large + man = *large man*	ō·otoko おお・おとこ
雪男	snow + man = *the abominable snowman*	yuki·otoko ゆき・おとこ

SAMPLE SENTENCE:

あの 男 の 人 は 五千円
ano otoko no hito wa GO·SEN·EN
that man person five thousand yen
を なくした。
o nakushita.
     lost
= *That man lost five thousand yen.*

COMPONENT #75

PIG

KANJI 75

家

HOUSE

| ` | ⼧ | 宀 | 宀 | 宇 | 宇 | 宇 | 家 |
| 家 | | | | | | | |

BUILDING THIS KANJI
Pincers ⼧ + Pig 豕 = 家

Meaning
This character generally imparts some sense of relation to a house or family. When used as a suffix, however, it denotes a person having some degree of skill or interest with respect to the kanji preceding it. The final compound below illustrates this aspect of its meaning.

Remembering this kanji
People told me I was crazy when they learned I was moving from my farm to the metropolis. 'The people are cold there, and you won't make any friends', they all said. Well, I went anyway, and to prove them wrong I got out my **pincers** and hung an enormous **pig** outside my HOUSE in order to welcome people as they walked by. And yet this is the strange thing: despite all the squealing for days on end, nobody visited, and when I told people my HOUSE was the one with the **pincers** and **pig**, they quit talking to me altogether! I guess everyone was right to say folks wouldn't be very friendly, 'cause they sure weren't when it came to my HOUSE.

Common Pronunciations
Common **ON** reading: **KA** (カ)
Common **kun** reading: **ie** (いえ)

kun-yomi suggestion: "Canadian"

Write your sentence to remember the **on-yomi** and **kun-yomi** readings in the box below.

Less Common Pronunciations
Less common **ON** reading: **KE** (ケ)
Less common **kun** reading: **ya** (や)

COMMON WORDS AND COMPOUNDS		
家	house	ie いえ
人家	person + house = dwelling	JIN·KA ジン·カ
売り家	sell + house = "house for sale"	u·ri ie う·り いえ
家具	house + tool = furniture	KA·GU カ·グ
愛鳥家	love + bird + house = bird lover	AI·CHŌ·KA アイ·チョウ·カ

SAMPLE SENTENCE:

本田さん の 家 を 見ました か。
HON·da-san no ie o mi·mashita ka.
Honda-san house see
= *Did you see Honda-san's house?*

東 EAST

BUILDING THIS KANJI
Tree 木(13) + Sun 日(6) = 東

Meaning
East.

Remembering this kanji
Note that the writing order for this kanji does not follow that of the components as listed. This will happen only rarely; the image of a **sun** rising behind a **tree** in the EAST, however, is clearly the logical way to remember this character.

Common Pronunciations
Common **ON** reading: **TŌ** (トウ)
Common **kun** reading: **higashi** (ひがし)

---

kun-yomi suggestion: "he gash easy…"

Write your sentence to remember the **on-yomi** and **kun-yomi** readings in the box below.

Less Common Pronunciations
Less common **ON** reading: none
Less common **kun** reading: none

COMMON WORDS AND COMPOUNDS		
東	east	**higashi** ひがし
東口	east + mouth = *east exit/entrance*	**higashi**·guchi ひがし・ぐち
中東	middle + east = *the Middle East*	CHŪ·TŌ チュウ・トウ
東京	east + capital = *Tokyo*	TŌ·KYŌ トウ・キョウ
南東	south + east = *southeast*	NAN·TŌ ナン・トウ
北北東	north + north + east = *north-northeast*	HOKU·HOKU·TŌ ホク・ホク・トウ

SAMPLE SENTENCE:

東口	の	キオスク	で	本
higashi·guchi	**no**	**kiosuku**	**de**	**HON**
east exit		kiosk		book

を 買いました。
o   ka·imashita.
         bought
= *(I) bought a book at the east exit kiosk.*

KANJI 77

思 THINK

| １ | 冂 | 冂 | 冃 | 田 | 甲 | 思 | 思 | 思 |

BUILDING THIS KANJI
Rice field 田(73) + Heart 心(25) = 思

Meaning
Think.

Remembering this kanji
And so I took the **heart** and buried it in a **rice field**. But soon I began to THINK: What if it rises to the surface? What if a thrifty animal digs it up for food? Horrors! All I could do was THINK...THINK of what I had done, until there was nothing in my head but the beating of that hideous **heart** in the **rice field**. But I know what you THINK: you either THINK I'm mad, or that this story sounds awfully familiar.

Common Pronunciations
Common ON reading: SHI (シ)
Common **kun** reading: omo (おも)

kun-yomi suggestion: "**o, mow**..."

Write your sentence to remember the **on-yomi** and **kun-yomi** readings in the box below.

Less Common Pronunciations
Less common ON reading: none
Less common **kun** reading: none

COMMON WORDS AND COMPOUNDS		
思う	to think	omo·u おも·う
思い出す	think + exit = to remember	omo·i da·su おも·い だ·す
物思い	thing + think = pensiveness	mono omo·i もの おも·い
思い切る	think + cut = to make up one's mind	omo·i ki·ru おも·い き·る
意思	mind + think = (one's) intent	I·SHI イ·シ

SAMPLE SENTENCE:

テーブル の 上 に 四百円
tēburu no ue ni yon·HYAKU·EN
　table　　　above　　four hundred yen
ある と 思います。
aru to omo·imasu.
　is　　　think
= *(I) think there's four hundred yen on the table.*

KANJI 78

耳

EAR

kun-yomi suggestion: "**Me! Me!**"

Create your sentence to remember the **kun-yomi** reading in the box below.

Meaning
Ear. No story required.

Common Pronunciations
Common **ON** reading: none
Common **kun** reading: **mimi** (みみ)

Less Common Pronunciations
Less common **ON** reading: **JI** (ジ)
Less common **kun** reading: none

COMMON WORDS AND COMPOUNDS		
耳	*ear*	mimi みみ
耳元	ear + basis = *close to one's ear*	**mimi**·moto みみ·もと
空耳	empty + ear = *mishearing; feigned deafness*	sora·**mimi** そら·みみ

SAMPLE SENTENCE:

田中さん　の　耳　が　赤い。

Ta·naka-san　no　mimi　ga　aka·i.

Tanaka-san　　　ears　　　red

= *Tanaka-san's ears are red.*

COMPONENT #79

WISHBONES

The various words for father shown below reflect differing levels of familiarity and politeness; most terms used for addressing people in Japan have multiple forms such as these.

kun-yomi suggestion: "**Chichi** Rodriguez"

KANJI 79

父 **FATHER**

Create your **on-yomi** keyword and enter it in the table at the back of the book. After that, write your sentence to remember the **on-yomi** and **kun-yomi** readings in the box below.

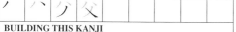

BUILDING THIS KANJI
Eight (volcano) 八(19) + Wishbones メ = 父

Less Common Pronunciations
Less common ON reading: none
Less common kun reading: none

Meaning
Father.

These two irregular readings are extremely common.

IRREGULAR READINGS

お父さん	father = *father*	otōsan おとうさん
伯父さん*	related + father = *uncle*	ojisan おじさん

Remembering this kanji
Jupiter, as FATHER of the gods, can do whatever he wants. Unfortunately, he's not as environmentally conscious as he should be, and often uses the nearest **volcano** to dump **wishbones** and other scraps from his plate. Jupiter's son Vulcan, the god of **volcanoes**, naturally takes exception to this behavior. "So help me, FATHER," he says, "if I wake up with any more **wishbones** on my rug, I might just erupt."

COMMON WORDS AND COMPOUNDS

父	*father*	chichi ちち
父の日	father + sun (day) = *Father's Day*	chichi·no·hi ちち・の・ひ
父母	father + mother = *father and mother*	FU·BO フ・ボ
父親	father + parent = *father*	chichi·oya ちち・おや

SAMPLE SENTENCE:

父　は　ビジネス　で　東京
chichi　wa　bijinesu　de　TŌ·KYŌ
Father　　　business　　　Tokyo
へ　行きました。
e　i·kimashita.
　　went
= *Father went to Tokyo on business.*

Common Pronunciations
Common ON reading: **FU** (フ)
Common kun reading: **chichi** (ちち)

KANJI 80

言　SAY

Meaning
"Saying," and things of a verbal nature. This character, incidentally, will become very familiar; it appears in more than sixty other kanji.

Remembering this kanji

"I vant…to drink…yours…blood." Isn't this what a **vampire** like Dracula always **SAYS**? Sure, you **SAY**, but what's with the bad grammar? Well, give Dracula a break; he's from Transylvania, and English isn't his first language. Notice, by the way, that the second stroke from the top is longer than those above or below it. Also note that in some more calligraphic fonts (such as that used above), the first stroke transforms into our "jelly bean" component.

I VANT
TO DRINK
YOURS
BLOOD

Common Pronunciations
Common **ON** reading: **GEN** (ゲン)
Common **kun** reading: **i** (い)

kun-yomi suggestion: "**eager**"

Write your sentence to remember the **on-yomi** and **kun-yomi** readings in the box below.

Less Common Pronunciations
Less common **ON** reading: **GON** (ゴン)
Less common **kun** reading: **koto** (こと)

The reading **koto** will be encountered primarily in the Japanese term for "word": **koto·ba** (こと·ば), composed of the kanji 言葉 (Say/Leaf *).

COMMON WORDS AND COMPOUNDS		
言う	to say	i·u い·う
言い回し	say + rotate = (turn of) expression	i·i mawa·shi い·い まわ·し
明言	bright + say = declaration	MEI·GEN メイ·ゲン
言語	say + words = language	GEN·GO ゲン·ゴ
言い出す	say + exit = to begin to say	i·i da·su い·い だ·す
言い切る	say + cut = to say definitively	i·i ki·ru い·い き·る

SAMPLE SENTENCE:

川本さん　　　も　　　"はい"　　　と
Kawa·moto-san　**mo**　　**"hai"**　　**to**
Kawamoto-san　also　"yes"
言いました。
i·imashita.
said
= Kawamoto-san also said "yes."

CHAPTER 4 REVIEW EXERCISES

A. Please match the following kanji to their meanings.

1. 父   a. Body

2. 川   b. Hand

3. 安   c. Father

4. 東   d. Thousand

5. 手   e. Main

6. 男   f. Ease

7. 千   g. Man

8. 力   h. East

9. 体   i. Strength

10. 本   j. River

B. Please match the following meanings to their kanji, and these to their **on** or **kun-yomi**.

1. Rest   a. 田   1. **GEN**(ゲン)

2. Change   b. 耳   2. **HOKU**(ホク)

3. North   c. 化   3. **SHI**(シ)

4. House   d. 言   4. **yasu**(やす)
   (**kun-yomi**)

5. Rice field   e. 夏   5. **SUI**(スイ)

6. Think   f. 休   6. **ta**(た)

7. Summer   g. 家   7. **natsu**(なつ)
   (**kun-yomi**)

8. Say   h. 水   8. **ie**(いえ)

9. Water   i. 北   9. **KA**(カ)

10. Ear   j. 思   10. **mimi**(みみ)

C. Please choose the best answer(s) to the following questions.

1. Which of the following readings apply to the kanji 東?
   a. **TŌ**(トウ)
   b. **higashi**(ひがし)
   c. **KA**(カ)
   d. **kita**(きた)
   e. **minami**(みなみ)

2. Which of the following readings apply to the kanji 男?
   a. **onna**(おんな)
   b. **DAN**(ダン)
   c. **otoko**(おとこ)
   d. **KYŪ**(キュウ)
   e. **SUI**(スイ)

3. Which of the following kanji have an **on-yomi** of **KA**(カ)?
   a. 夏
   b. 北
   c. 思
   d. 家
   e. 化

4. What would make a nice gift for a pair of newlyweds?
   a. 手
   b. 体
   c. 耳
   d. 家
   e. 北

5. Which of the following readings apply to the kanji 体?
   a. **SHŌ**(ショウ)
   b. **TAI**(タイ)
   c. **omo**(おも)
   d. **DAI**(ダイ)
   e. **karada**(からだ)

D. Please choose the best answer to the following questions.

1. Which of the following kanji has the most number of strokes?
   a. 東
   b. 男
   c. 言
   d. 思
   e. 体

2. Which is the correct reading of 安い?
   a. **omo·i** (お も·い)
   b. **yasu·i** (や す·い)
   c. **taka·i** (た か·い)
   d. **ō·i** (お お·い)

3. Which is the correct reading of 思う?
   a. **ka·u** (か·う)
   b. **ko·u** (こ·う)
   c. **omo·u** (お も·う)
   d. **o·u** (お·う)

4. Which kanji would precede 力 to form the compound for "physical strength"?
   a. 休
   b. 本
   c. 東
   d. 体
   e. 耳

5. Which is the correct reading of 言う?
   a. **i·u** (い·う)
   b. **o·u** (お·う)
   c. **a·u** (あ·う)
   d. **omo·u** (お も·う)

E. Please match the following compounds and words to their meanings and pronunciations.

1. 大体	a. Close to one's ear	1. **SUI·CHŪ** (スイ・チュウ)
2. 全日本	b. Peace of mind	2. **te·kubi** (て・くび)
3. 北米	c. In general	3. **mimi·moto** (みみ・もと)
4. 耳元	d. Summer vacation	4. **i·i mawa·shi** (い・い まわ・し)
5. 水中	e. Powerful	5. **AN·SHIN** (アン・シン)
6. 有力	f. North America	6. **ZEN·NI·HON** (ゼン・ニ・ホン)
7. 言い回し	g. Wrist	7. **natsu yasu·mi** (なつ やす・み)
8. 夏休み	h. All Japan	8. **HOKU·BEI** (ホク・ベイ)
9. 手首	i. (Turn of) expression	9. **DAI·TAI** (ダイ・タイ)
10. 安心	j. Underwater/ In the water	10. **YŪ·RYOKU** (ユウ・リョク)

Kanji #81—100

KANJI 81

干

DRY

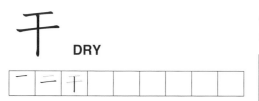

Meaning

Dry/Ebb. This character will not be encountered frequently. It does figure as a component in other more common kanji, however, and because of this is presented here. Take a moment to note the difference between this character and 千 (Entry 65). No story required.

Common Pronunciations

Common **ON** reading: none
Common **kun** readings: **hi** (ひ); **ho** (ほ)

As seen in the third example below, the **kun-yomi** "ho" can become voiced in the second position.

kun-yomi suggestions: "heat"; "hose"

Create your sentence to remember the **kun-yomi** readings in the box below.

Less Common Pronunciations

Less common **ON** reading: **KAN** (カン)
Less common **kun** reading: none

COMMON WORDS AND COMPOUNDS		
干る (intr)	*to dry (on its own)*	**hi**·ru ひ·る
干す (tr)	*to dry (something)*	**ho**·su ほ·す
日干し	sun + dry = *sun-dried*	hi **bo**·shi ひ ぼ·し
干上がる	dry + upper = *to dry up*	**hi** a·garu ひ あ·がる
干物	dry + thing = *dried fish*	**hi**·mono ひ·もの

SAMPLE SENTENCE:

干物　を　買って　下さい。
hi·mono　o　kat·te　kuda·sai.
dried fish　　buy　　please
= *Please buy dried fish.*

KANJI 82

金 **GOLD**

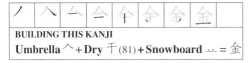

BUILDING THIS KANJI
Umbrella 𠆢 + Dry 干 (81) + Snowboard ㅛ = 金

Meaning
Depending on the context in which it appears, this common character signifies either "gold," "metal," or "money." It clearly means "gold", for instance, when referring to the status of an Olympic champion. When functioning as a component, however, it hints that the kanji involved has some connection to metal in general

Remembering this kanji
Following a quick break with his buddies, the **snowboarder** had another vision. This time, however, the genie was very specific: "Dude, unless this GOLDEN snowboard is kept **dry** at all times, it will immediately turn back into fiberglass. You must, therefore, always use an **umbrella**, even on the gnarliest runs. Should you not keep it **dry**…well, it would still be a decent enough board, it just wouldn't be GOLD anymore. And GOLD is like, really valuable."

Common Pronunciations
Common **ON** reading: **KIN** (キン)
Common **kun** reading: **kane** (かね)

kun-yomi suggestion: "**Khan a**te"

Create your **on-yomi** keyword and enter it in the table at the back of the book. After that, write your sentence to remember the **on-yomi** and **kun-yomi** readings in the box below.

Less Common Pronunciations
Less common **ON** reading: **KON** (コン)
Less common **kun** reading: **kana** (かな)

COMMON WORDS AND COMPOUNDS		
金	gold; metal; money	**KIN** キン
金	metal; money	**kane** かね
金山	gold + mountain = gold mine	**KIN·ZAN** キン・ザン
年金	year + gold (money) = annuity/pension	NEN·**KIN** ネン・キン
金曜日	gold + day of the week + sun (day) = Friday	**KIN**·YŌ·bi キン・ヨウ・び
金星	gold + star = Venus (planet)	**KIN**·SEI キン・セイ

SAMPLE SENTENCE:
内田さん は あまり お金 が ない。
Uchi·da-san wa amari o·kane ga nai.
Uchida-san   not much money   not
= *Uchida-san doesn't have much money.*

語 WORDS

BUILDING THIS KANJI

Say 言 (80) + Five 五 (14) + Mouth (vampire) 口 (8) = 語

Meaning

Words. This kanji will become familiar as the character used to indicate languages; a pair of examples can be seen in the compounds below.

Remembering this kanji

Mark my WORDS: despite what **vampires** everywhere will **say**, you do not want to go to a pentagon party with **five** of them. Their reassuring WORDS of such events being "normal Transylvanian hospitality" are far from the truth.

I VANT
TO DRINK
YOURS
BLOOD

Common Pronunciations

Common **ON** reading: **GO** (ゴ)
Common **kun** reading: **kata** (かた)

Note the importance of long and short vowel sounds in Japanese by looking closely at the second and third examples below. Also note the presence of an irregular reading (上手) in the sample sentence.

kun-yomi suggestion: "**cat a**cne"

Write your sentence to remember the **on-yomi** and **kun-yomi** readings in the box below.

Less Common Pronunciations

Less common **ON** reading: none
Less common **kun** reading: **katari** (かたり)

COMMON WORDS AND COMPOUNDS		
語る	*to talk*	**kata·ru** かた·る
口語	mouth + words = *colloquial language*	**KŌ·GO** コウ·ゴ
古語	old + words = *archaic word*	**KO·GO** コ·ゴ
日本語	sun + main + words = *Japanese (language)*	**NI·HON·GO** ニ·ホン·ゴ
言語	say + words = *language*	**GEN·GO** ゲン·ゴ
英語	English + words = *English (language)*	**EI·GO** エイ·ゴ
語学	words + study = *linguistics*	**GO·GAKU** ゴ·ガク

SAMPLE SENTENCE:

あなたの　日本語　は 上手 ですよ。

anata   no NI·HON·GO wa JŌ·zu desu   yo.

you   Japanese   good at

= *Your Japanese is good!*

KANJI 84

士 GENTLEMAN

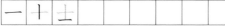

一 十 士

Meaning
The sense is of a gentleman, or of a man who has attained status in a military or academic field. No story required.

Common Pronunciations
Common **ON** reading: **SHI** (シ)
Common **kun** reading: none

Write your sentence to remember the **on-yomi** reading in the box below.

Less Common Pronunciations
Less common **ON** reading: none
Less common **kun** reading: none

COMMON WORDS AND COMPOUNDS		
力士	strength + gentleman = *sumo wrestler*	**RIKI·SHI** リ キ・シ
士気	gentleman + spirit = *morale*	**SHI·KI** シ・キ
工学士	craft + study + gentleman = *Bachelor of Engineering*	**KŌ·GAKU·SHI** コ ウ・ガ ク・シ

SAMPLE SENTENCE:

あの 力士 はとても大きいですよ。
ano RIKI·SHI wa totemo ō·kii desu yo.
that sumo wrestler very large is
= *That sumo wrestler is really large!*

KANJI 85

朝 MORNING

一 十 十 古 古 古 直 卓 朝
朝 朝 朝

BUILDING THIS KANJI
Ten (scarecrow) 十(28) + Early 早(29) + Moon 月 (11) = 朝

Meaning
Morning. A secondary meaning relates to royal dynasties.

Remembering this kanji
As always, each MORNING the **moon** gave a wink to the **scarecrow**. "You're up **early**," he said.

"For godsakes," said the **scarecrow**. "When are you going to get tired of that joke?"

Common Pronunciations

Common **ON** reading: **CHŌ** (チョウ)

Common **kun** reading: **asa** (あさ)

Note the mix of **on** and **kun-yomi** in the final example below.

kun-yomi suggestion: "**Casa**nova"

Create your **on-yomi** keyword and enter it in the table at the back of the book. After that, write your sentence to remember the **on-yomi** and **kun-yomi** readings in the box below.

Less Common Pronunciations

Less common **ON** reading: none

Less common **kun** reading: none

IRREGULAR READING		
今朝	now + morning = *this morning*	kesa けさ

COMMON WORDS AND COMPOUNDS		
朝	*morning*	asa あさ
朝日	morning + sun = *morning sun*	asa·hi あさ・ひ
王朝	king + morning = *dynasty*	Ō·CHŌ オウ・チョウ
早朝	early + morning = *early morning*	SŌ·CHŌ ソウ・チョウ
毎朝	every + morning = *every morning*	MAI·asa マイ・あさ

SAMPLE SENTENCE:

上田さんは　朝　が　大好き　です。

Ue·da-san wa　asa　ga　DAI su·ki desu.

Ueda-san　　morning　　really likes

= *Ueda-san really likes mornings.*

COMPONENT #86

CANDLESTICK HOLDER

KANJI 86

BLUE

BUILDING THIS KANJI

Candlestick Holder 龶 + Moon 月 (11) = 青

Meaning

Blue. Interestingly, this character is also applied to a few objects that Westerners invariably consider green, so prepare yourself to be confronted with blue traffic lights and blue vegetables, amongst other things. As in English, the sense of youth and immaturity is tied up with this idea of "green"; the third compound below provides an example.

Remembering this kanji

Even the **moon** can get depressed, and on those occasions when he's feeling BLUE he doesn't give off his normal amount of light. To cover up for this he'll take out a **candlestick holder**, but as there's nothing in it, his ploy doesn't fool anyone. Luckily for us, he only feels this way once in a BLUE **moon**.

Common Pronunciations

Common **ON** reading: **SEI** (セイ)

Common **kun** reading: **ao** (あお)

kun-yomi suggestion: "**Lao**s"

Create your **on-yomi** keyword and enter it in the table at the back of the book. After that, write your sentence to remember the **on-yomi** and **kun-yomi** readings in the box below.

COMMON WORDS AND COMPOUNDS		
青	*blue; green (noun)*	**ao** あお
青い	*blue; green (adjective)*	**ao·i** あお·い
青春	blue + spring = *youth*	**SEI·SHUN** セイ·シュン
青物	blue + thing = *green vegetables*	**ao·mono** あお·もの
青空	blue + empty (sky) = *blue sky*	**ao·zora** あお·ぞら

Less Common Pronunciations
Less common **ON** reading: **SHŌ** (ショウ)
Less common **kun** reading: none

SAMPLE SENTENCE:

山田さん　の　家　は　青い　です。
Yama·da-san　no　ie　wa　ao·i　desu.
Yamada-san　　　house　　blue
= *Yamada-san's house is blue.*

KANJI 87

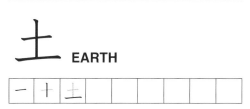

土 **EARTH**

一	十	土						

Meaning
Think of earth here as in "dirt," not the planet on which we live. Take a moment to note the subtle difference between this kanji and "士" (Entry 84); you've developed a practiced eye if you're now able to take such variations into account! No story required.

Common Pronunciations
Common **ON** reading: **DO** (ド)
Common **kun** reading: **tsuchi** (つち)

Note the mixture of **on-** and **kun-yomi** in the second example (and in the last, as expected).

kun-yomi suggestion: "go**t Sioux chee**tahs"

Create your **on-yomi** keyword and enter it in the table at the back of the book. After that, write your sentence to remember the **on-yomi** and **kun-yomi** readings in the box below.

Less Common Pronunciations
Less common **ON** reading: **TO** (ト)
Less common **kun** reading: none

IRREGULAR READING		
土産	earth + produce = *souvenir*	**miyage** みやげ

COMMON WORDS AND COMPOUNDS		
土	*earth*	tsuchi つち
土手	earth + hand = *embankment*	DO·te ド・て
本土	main + earth = *mainland*	HON·DO ホン・ド
土木	earth + tree = *civil engineering*	DO·BOKU ド・ボク
土星	earth + star = *Saturn (planet)*	DO·SEI ド・セイ
土曜日	earth + day of the week + sun (day) = *Saturday*	DO·YŌ·bi ド・ヨウ・び

SAMPLE SENTENCE:

川　の　　土手　　を　上がる　と

kawa no　　DO·te　　o　a·garu　to

river　　embankment　　　　go up

　水田　　　が　　見えます。

　SUI·DEN　　ga　　mi·emasu.

rice paddies　　　　can see

= *If you go up the river embankment, you can see rice paddies.*

COMPONENT #88

FINGER

A ring and a string for a finger. There will be little chance of forgetting this component, incidentally, as it is present in nearly a hundred kanji—most relating in some way to hands and arms.

KANJI 88

掛 **HANG**

ー	丨	扌	扌	扌	扌	挂	挂	挂
掛	掛							

BUILDING THIS KANJI

Finger 扌 + Earth 土(87) + Earth 土(87) + Poor Figure Skater ト = 掛

Meaning

Hang. Note how the last stroke of the bottom "earth" component leads into the next line by being drawn on an upward angle.

Remembering this kanji

Fingers can indicate harsh criticism, especially when it comes to bad figure skating. "HANG up your skates!" people will scream while pointing, making the **bad figure skater** want to hide behind a **couple piles of earth**. Some skaters, apparently, can do nothing but HANG their heads in shame.

Common Pronunciations

Common **ON** reading: none

Common **kun** reading: **ka** (か)

As the final example below shows, this kanji can act similarly to 買う (Entry 50).

kun-yomi suggestion: "**cat**"

There is no **on-yomi** reading for this character. Create your sentence to remember the **kun-yomi** reading in the box below.

COMMON WORDS AND COMPOUNDS		
掛かる (intr)	to hang (by oneself)	**ka·karu** か・かる
掛ける (tr)	to hang (something)	**ka·keru** か・ける
掛金	hang + gold (money) = installment	**kake·KIN** かけ・キン

Less Common Pronunciations
Less common **ON** reading: none
Less common **kun** reading: none

SAMPLE SENTENCE:

シャツ を あそこ に 掛けて 下さい。
shatsu o asoko ni ka·kete kuda·sai.
shirts over there hang please
= *Please hang the shirts over there.*

COMPONENT #89

CHAIR

KANJI 89

TEN THOUSAND

一	フ	万					

BUILDING THIS KANJI
One (top of a bun) 一(3) + Chair 力 = 万

Meaning
Ten thousand. More so than "百" and "千" (Entries 51 and 65), this character can express the general idea of a "countless amount" of something.

Remembering this kanji
The ancient writer Xenophon tells the story of TEN THOUSAND Greek mercenaries marching against Persia in 401 B.C. What is interesting is that each of the TEN THOUSAND carries a lawn **chair**, together with a shield shaped like the **top of a bun**.

Common Pronunciations
Common **ON** reading: **MAN** (マ ン)
Common **kun** reading: none

As we saw for the kanji "百" and "千," note how the numbers four and seven appear with their **kun-yomi**.

Create your **on-yomi** keyword and enter it in the table at the back of the book. After that, write your sentence to remember the **on-yomi** reading in the box below.

Less Common Pronunciations
Less common **ON** reading: **BAN** (バ ン)
Less common **kun** reading: none

BAN shows up in Japan's famous word for "hurrah!", 万歳 (Ten thousand/Annual): **BAN·ZAI** (バ ン・ザ イ)

COMMON WORDS AND COMPOUNDS

一万	one + ten thousand = *ten thousand*	ICHI·MAN イチ・マン
二万	two + ten thousand = *twenty thousand*	NI·MAN ニ・マン
三万	three + ten thousand = *thirty thousand*	SAN·MAN サン・マン
四万	four + ten thousand = *forty thousand*	yon·MAN よん・マン
五万	five + ten thousand = *fifty thousand*	GO·MAN ゴ・マン
六万	six + ten thousand = *sixty thousand*	ROKU·MAN ロク・マン
七万	seven + ten thousand = *seventy thousand*	nana·MAN なな・マン
八万	eight + ten thousand = *eighty thousand*	HACHI·MAN ハチ・マン
九万	nine + ten thousand = *ninety thousand*	KYŪ·MAN キュウ・マン

SAMPLE SENTENCE:

あの	国	の	人口	は
ano	**kuni**	**no**	**JIN·KŌ**	**wa**
that	country		population	

八万人	です。
HACHI·MAN·NIN	**desu.**
eighty thousand people	is

= *That country's population is eighty thousand.*

 RAIN

Meaning

Rain. This wonderfully distinctive character is more easily learned without being broken into components. Because of this, no story is required.

Common Pronunciations

Common **ON** reading: none
Common **kun** readings: **ame** (あめ); **ama** (あま)

The **kun-yomi** "ama" only appears in the first position.

kun-yomi suggestions: "scam age"; "**ama**retto"

Create your sentence to remember the **kun-yomi** readings in the box below.

Less Common Pronunciations

Less common **ON** reading: U (ウ)
Less common **kun** reading: none

The following word can be read with its normal **on-yomi**, but is often heard with the irregular reading pronunciation below.

IRREGULAR READING		
梅雨*	plum tree + rain = *the rainy season*	tsuyu つゆ

COMMON WORDS AND COMPOUNDS		
雨	*rain*	**ame** あめ
雨上がり	rain + upper = *after the rain*	**ame** a·gari あめ あ·がり
大雨	large + rain = *heavy rain*	**ō·ame** おお·あめ
雨空	rain + empty (sky) = *a rainy sky*	**ama**·zora あま·ぞら

SAMPLE SENTENCE:

九月 に は 日本 で 大雨 の
KU·GATSU ni wa NI·HON de ō·ame no
September　　　　Japan　　heavy rain
日 が 多い です。
hi ga ō·i desu.
day　　many
= *In September, Japan has many days with heavy rain.*

KANJI 91

電 ELECTRIC

BUILDING THIS KANJI
Rain 雨 (90) + Sun 日 (6) + Hook ∟ = 電

Meaning
Electric/Electricity.

Remembering this kanji
The atmosphere was **ELECTRIC**: **rain** and **sun** were on a collision course! At the last moment, however, a **hook** was used to hold the **sun** back, saving either it from being extinguished or the **rain** from being evaporated. As the kanji shows, the elements remain in this state even now, so close than an **ELECTRIC** current would have difficulty passing between them.

Common Pronunciations
Common **ON** reading: **DEN** (デン)
Common **kun** reading: none

Write your sentence to remember the **on-yomi** reading in the box below.

Less Common Pronunciations
Less common **ON** reading: none
Less common **kun** reading: none

COMMON WORDS AND COMPOUNDS		
電化	electric + change = *electrification*	**DEN·KA** デン·カ
電力	electric + strength = *electric power*	**DEN·RYOKU** デン·リョク
電子	electric + child = *electron*	**DEN·SHI** デン·シ
電気	electric + spirit = *electricity*	**DEN·KI** デン·キ
電話	electric + speak = *telephone*	**DEN·WA** デン·ワ
電車	electric + car = *(electric) train*	**DEN·SHA** デン·シャ

SAMPLE SENTENCE:

田中さん は 電車 を 下りました。
Ta·naka-san wa DEN·SHA o o·rimashita.
Tanaka-san　　　　train　　　descended
= *Tanaka-san got off the train.*

Component 92

UFO

Make sure you clearly see the difference between this component and the "pincers" 冖.

KANJI 92

売 **SELL**

| 一 | 十 | 士 | 声 | 声 | 売 | 売 | | |

BUILDING THIS KANJI
Gentleman 士(84) + UFO 冖 + Ballet 儿 = 売

Meaning
Sell.

Remembering this kanji
It is common knowledge that the statues of Easter Island relate to the visit of a **UFO**. What is less well known is that the **gentleman** piloting this **UFO** chose to **SELL ballet** gear to the locals. What was the purpose of this? Were the natives to put tutus on the monoliths? Wear the slippers themselves? Given the lack of **ballet** dancers or practice facilities on Easter Island at the time, anthropologists wonder why this **gentleman** didn't **SELL** the locals something more useful.

Common Pronunciations

Common **ON** reading: **BAI** (バイ)
Common **kun** reading: **u** (う)

As the final example below shows, this is another kanji that can function similarly to "買" (Entry 50).

kun-yomi suggestion: "**oo**dles"

Create your **on-yomi** keyword and enter it in the table at the back of the book. After that, write your sentence to remember the **on-yomi** and **kun-yomi** readings in the box below.

Less Common Pronunciations
Less common **ON** reading: none
Less common **kun** reading: none

COMMON WORDS AND COMPOUNDS		
売る	to sell	u·ru う・る
売り歩く	sell + walk = to peddle	u·ri aru·ku う・り ある・く
売春	sell + spring = prostitution	BAI·SHUN バイ・シュン
売り家	sell + house = "house for sale"	u·ri ie う・り いえ
売り切れる	sell + cut = to be sold out	u·ri ki·reru う・り き・れる
売切れ	sell + cut = "sold out"	uri ki·re うり き・れ

SAMPLE SENTENCE:

田口さん は 日本語 の 本 を
Ta·guchi-san wa NI·HON·GO no HON o
Taguchi-san   Japanese   books
売って います。
u·tte   imasu.
sells
= *Taguchi-san sells Japanese books.*

KANJI 93

者 **INDIVIDUAL**

一	十	土	少	耂	者	者	者

BUILDING THIS KANJI
Earth 土(87) + Comet 一 + Sun 日(6) = 者

Meaning
Think of individual in the sense of a human being. The characters in a compound that precede this kanji (it never comes first) define the person.

Remembering this kanji
It's never a good idea to generalize, but let's face it: you can tell a lot about an **INDIVIDUAL** by the way they look. A heap of **earth**, for example, tends to be dirty; it clearly doesn't care about appearances and is thus down to **earth**. **Suns**, on the other hand, are obviously outgoing **INDIVIDUALS** with blazing style. **Comets**, however, have personalities that lie between these extremes (as the kanji shows); with qualities of **earth** and **sun**, each must be considered a separate **INDIVIDUAL**.

Common Pronunciations
Common **ON** reading: **SHA** (シ ャ)
Common **kun** reading: none

Create your **on-yomi** keyword and enter it in the table at the back of the book. After that, write your sentence to remember the **on-yomi** reading in the box below.

Less Common Pronunciations
Less common **ON** reading: none
Less common **kun** reading: **mono** (も の)

COMMON WORDS AND COMPOUNDS		
有力者	have + strength + individual = *powerful person*	YŪ·RYOKU·SHA ユウ·リョク·シャ
前者	before + individual = *the former*	ZEN·SHA ゼン·シャ
後者	after + individual = *the latter*	KŌ·SHA コウ·シャ
学者	study + individual = *scholar*	GAKU·SHA ガク·シャ

SAMPLE SENTENCE:

あ の　国　で 王 子 は　　有力者
ano kuni de Ō·JI wa YŪ·RYOKU·SHA
that country　　prince　　powerful person
です。
desu.
= *The prince is a powerful person in that country.*

KANJI 94

入 **ENTER**

ノ	入					

Meaning
Entering/Putting in. Make sure that you clearly see the difference between this kanji and those for "人" (Entry 2), and "八" (Entry 19). No story required.

Common Pronunciations
Common **ON** reading: **NYŪ** (ニュウ)
Common **kun** readings: **hai** (はい); **i** (い)

It is worth looking carefully at the first three entries below. The word "**hai·ru**" expresses the **intransitive** meaning of the verb "enter" (that is, to enter some type of place); it is rarely used in compounds. "**i·ru**", on the other hand, is most commonly found in compounds, primarily when the other kanji is read with **kun-yomi** (**NYŪ** performs this function when the other kanji is read with **on-yomi**). The word **i·reru** is simply the transitive companion of **hai·ru**.

One last twist is that the kanji can behave on rare occasions like 買; this can be seen in the fourth example.

kun-yomi suggestions: "**high**way"; "ether"

Create your **on-yomi** keyword and enter it in the table at the back of the book. After that, write your sentence to remember the **on-yomi** and **kun-yomi** readings in the box below.

Less Common Pronunciations
Less common **ON** reading: none
Less common **kun** reading: none

COMMON WORDS AND COMPOUNDS		
入る (intr)	*to enter*	**hai**·ru は い・る
入る (intr)	*to enter*	i·ru い・る
入れる (tr)	*to put (something) into*	i·reru い・れ る
入口	enter + mouth = *entrance*	**iri**·guchi い り・ぐ ち
入国	enter + country = *to enter a country*	**NYŪ**·KOKU ニ ュ ウ・コ ク
入金	enter + gold (money) = *payment*	**NYŪ**·KIN ニ ュ ウ・キ ン
買い入れる	buy + enter = *to stock up on*	ka·i i·reru か・い い・れ る

SAMPLE SENTENCE:

お 金 を 入 れ て 下 さ い。
o·kane o i·rete kuda·sai.
money put in please
= *Please insert the money.*

Component 95

COMB

KANJI 95

雪 **SNOW**

BUILDING THIS KANJI
Rain 雨(90) + Comb ヨ = 雪

Meaning
Snow.

Remembering this kanji
I've come in from the **rain** and need to straighten my hair for a date. I do this, of course, but looking down moments later I tremble like a kitten: my **comb** is now covered with dandruff! I start to panic…until realizing that the **rain** had at some point become SNOW.

Common Pronunciations
Common **ON** reading: none
Common **kun** reading: **yuki** (ゆ き)

Note that the sample sentence contains an irregular reading (明 日).

kun-yomi suggestion: "**you kee**p"

Create your sentence to remember the **kun-yomi** reading in the box below.

Less Common Pronunciations
Less common **ON** reading: **SETSU** (セ ツ)
Less common **kun** reading: none

Here are two irregular readings that make use of this character.

IRREGULAR READINGS		
吹雪*	blow + snow = *blizzard*	**fubuki** ふ ぶ き
雪崩*	snow + crumble = *avalanche*	**nadare** な だ れ

COMMON WORDS AND COMPOUNDS		
雪	*snow*	**yuki** ゆ き
雪玉	snow + jewel = *snowball*	**yuki**·dama ゆ き・だ ま
雪女	snow + woman = *snow fairy*	**yuki**·onna ゆ き・お ん な
雪男	snow + man = *the Abominable Snowman*	**yuki**·otoko ゆ き・お と こ
大雪	large + snow = *heavy snow*	**ō·yuki** お お・ゆ き
小雪	small + snow = *light snow*	ko·**yuki** こ・ゆ き

SAMPLE SENTENCE:
テ レ ビ の ニ ュ ー ス に よ る と
terebi no nyūsu ni yoru to
television news according to
明 日 か ら 大 雪 で す。
ashita kara ōyuki desu.
tomorrow from heavy snow
= *According to the TV news, heavy snow will be starting tomorrow.*

KANJI 96

門 **GATE**

Create your **on-yomi** keyword and enter it in the table at the back of the book. After that, write your sentence to remember the **on-yomi** and **kun-yomi** readings in the box below.

Meaning
Gate. No story required.

Common Pronunciations
Common **ON** reading: **MON** (モン)
Common **kun** reading: **kado** (かど)

Note that this kanji is usually read with its **on-yomi** when appearing alone.

kun-yomi suggestion: "**cod o**ver"

Less Common Pronunciations
Less common **ON** reading: none
Less common **kun** reading: none

COMMON WORDS AND COMPOUNDS		
門	gate	**MON** モン
門口	gate + mouth = *front door*	**kado**·guchi かど・ぐち
水門	water + gate = *sluice gate*	**SUI·MON** スイ・モン
校門	school + gate = *school gate*	**KŌ·MON** コウ・モン

SAMPLE SENTENCE:

あそこ の 高い 門 は とても
asoko　no　taka·i　MON　wa　totemo
over there　　　tall　　gate　　　　very
古い です ね。
furu·i　desu　ne.
old
= *That tall gate over there is very old, isn't it?*

KANJI 97

間 **INTERVAL**

BUILDING THIS KANJI
Gate 門 (96) + Sun 日 (6) = 間

Meaning
This character indicates an interval in time or space, and thus incorporates the ideas of "during", "between" and "among". When used with the **kun-yomi** "ma", it can also mean a room.

Remembering this kanji

If the **sun** in this kanji is rising (as every fiber in my being leads me to believe), it will pass, after a short INTERVAL, through that INTERVAL between the **gates**.

Common Pronunciations

Common **ON** reading: **KAN** (カン)
Common **kun** readings: **aida** (あいだ); **ma** (ま)

kun-yomi suggestions: "Idaho;" "map"

Create your **on-yomi** keyword and enter it in the table at the back of the book. After that, write your sentence to remember the **on-yomi** and **kun-yomi** readings in the box below.

Less Common Pronunciations

Less common **ON** reading: **KEN** (ケン)
Less common **kun** reading: none

COMMON WORDS AND COMPOUNDS		
間	*interval*	**aida** あいだ
手間	hand + interval = *labor; trouble*	te·**ma** て・ま
中間	middle + interval = *midway*	CHŪ·**KAN** チュウ・カン
時間	time + interval = *time*	JI·**KAN** ジ・カン
空間	empty + interval = *space*	KŪ·**KAN** クウ・カン

SAMPLE SENTENCE:

アメリカ に いる 間 英語 を
Amerika ni iru aida EI·GO o
America be interval English
話します。
hana·shimasu.
 speak
= *I'll speak English while I'm in America.*

COMPONENT #98

GARBAGE CAN

KANJI 98

出 **EXIT**

BUILDING THIS KANJI
Pole | + Garbage Can ⊔ + Garbage Can ⊔
= 出

Meaning

Leave/Let out. Take care with the stroke order of this character.

Remembering this kanji

All right, so maybe I misunderstood my boss: putting a couple of **garbage cans** on a **pole** and standing at the EXIT of the voting station wasn't the right thing to do. But asking people to put "yes" votes in one **can** and "no" votes in the other…wouldn't anyone have thought that's what she meant by an EXIT poll?

Common Pronunciations

Common **ON** reading: **SHUTSU** (シュツ)
Common **kun** readings: **de** (で); **da** (だ)

Note how the **on-yomi** "doubles up" with an unvoiced consonant sound in the last example below.

kun-yomi suggestions: "**date**"; "**dash**"

Create your **on-yomi** keyword and enter it in the table at the back of the book. After that, write your sentence to remember the **on-yomi** and **kun-yomi** readings in the box below.

COMMON WORDS AND COMPOUNDS		
出る (intr)	to leave	**de**·ru で·る
出す (tr)	to let out	**da**·su だ·す
出かける	to leave (for somewhere)	**de**·kakeru で·かける
思い出す	think + exit = to remember	omo·i **da**·su おも·い だ·す
出口	exit + mouth = exit	**de**·guchi で·ぐち
出国	exit + country = to leave a country	**SHUK**·KOKU シュッ·コク

SAMPLE SENTENCE:

すみません、	出口	は	どこ
sumimasen	**de**·**guchi**	**wa**	**doko**
excuse me	exit		where

です	か。
desu	**ka.**

= *Excuse me, where's the exit?*

Less Common Pronunciations

Less common **ON** reading: **SUI** (スイ)
Less common **kun** reading: none

LIFE

ノ	ー	十	牛	生			

BUILDING THIS KANJI
Jelly Bean ╲ + Candlestick Holder 生 = 生

Meaning

One of the most fascinating characters in the language, this kanji deals with life in all its guises. Along with the ideas of "birth", "production", and "growing", it also incorporates the notions of "pure", "raw", and "fresh", in everything from beer to silk. When used as a suffix, it will often indicate "student".

Remembering this kanji

"Is there a better symbol of **LIFE**," asked Sartre, "than a **jelly bean** stuck to the side of a **candlestick holder**, one that sits there alone and grows brittle with each passing year?"

It's an interesting question. From what I've heard, though, **jelly beans** hold their flavor quite well, even when stuck to **candlestick holders**. So who knows, maybe **LIFE** isn't so bad after all.

Common Pronunciations
Common ON reading: **SEI** (セイ)
Common **kun** readings: **i** (い); **u** (う); **nama** (なま)

In terms of its variety of pronunciations, kanji do not come any more complicated than this. Perhaps it's appropriate, though: life itself can be complicated, so shouldn't the character representing it be as well? Fortunately, the two initial **kun-yomi** are verb stems (as are "**o**" and "**ha**" of the less common **kun-yomi** below), and **nama** appears only in the first position. This will always belong to the ranks of the toughest kanji, however, so allow yourself time to learn it, while not forgetting to enjoy a few of the fifth example below along the way.

kun-yomi suggestions: "**eag**le;" "**oo**dles;" "Viet**nam a**pple"

Write your sentence to remember the **on-yomi** and **kun-yomi** readings in the box below.

Less Common Pronunciations
Less common ON reading: **SHŌ** (ショウ)
Less common **kun** readings: **o** (お); **ha** (は); **ki** (き)

IRREGULAR READING		
芝生*	lawn + life = *lawn*	**shiba·fu** しば・ふ

COMMON WORDS AND COMPOUNDS		
生きる (intr)	*to live*	**i·kiru** い・きる
生かす (tr)	*to give life to*	**i·kasu** い・かす
生まれる (intr)	*to be born*	**u·mareru** う・まれる
生む (tr)	*to give birth to*	**u·mu** う・む
生ビール	life + beer = *draft beer*	**nama·bīru** なま・ビール
人生	person + life = *(human) life*	**JIN·SEI** ジン・セイ
学生	study + life = *student*	**GAKU·SEI** ガク・セイ
先生	precede + life = *teacher*	**SEN·SEI** セン・セイ

SAMPLE SENTENCE:
生 ビール は 好き です か。
nama bīru wa su·ki desu ka.
draft beer like
= *Do you like draft beer?*

 COW

Meaning
Cow/Ox/Bull. Note the difference in stroke order between this character and that of "生" (Entry 99). No story required.

Common Pronunciations
Common ON reading: **GYŪ** (ギュウ)
Common **kun** reading: **ushi** (うし)

kun-yomi suggestion: "**true shee**n"

Create your **on-yomi** keyword and enter it in the table at the back of the book. After that, write your sentence to remember the **on-yomi** and **kun-yomi** readings in the box below.

COMMON WORDS AND COMPOUNDS		
牛	*cow*	**ushi** うし
子牛	child + cow = *calf*	ko·**ushi** こ・うし
水牛	water + cow = *water buffalo*	SUI·**GYŪ** スイ・ギュウ
牛肉	cow + meat = *beef*	**GYŪ**·NIKU ギュウ・ニク
牛馬	cow + horse = *cattle and horses*	**GYŪ**·BA ギュウ・バ

Less Common Pronunciations
Less common **ON** reading: none
Less common **kun** reading: none

SAMPLE SENTENCE:

アフリカ で 水牛 と キリン
Afurika de SUI·GYŪ to kirin
 Africa   water buffalo   giraffe
を 見ました。
o mi·mashita.
              saw
= *(I) saw a water buffalo and a giraffe in Africa.*

CHAPTER 5 REVIEW EXERCISES

A. Please match the following kanji to their meanings.

1. 土   a. Words

2. 士   b. Gentleman

3. 雨   c. Sell

4. 間   d. Exit

5. 売   e. Rain

6. 干   f. Life

7. 生   g. Interval

8. 電   h. Earth

9. 出   i. Electric

10. 語   j. Dry

B. Please match the following meanings to their kanji, and these to their **on** or **kun-yomi**.

1. Hang   a. 者   1. **SHA** (シャ)

2. Snow   b. 牛   2. **MAN** (マン)

3. Individual   c. 青   3. **asa** (あさ)

4. Morning   d. 掛   4. **GYŪ** (ギュウ)

5. Gold   e. 雪   5. **yuki** (ゆき)

6. Gate   f. 入   6. **MON** (モン)

7. Cow   g. 金   7. **ao** (あお)

8. Enter   h. 万   8. **KIN** (キン)

9. Ten thousand i. 門   9. **NYŪ** (ニュウ)

10. Blue   j. 朝   10. **ka** (か)

C. Please choose the best answer(s) to the following questions.

1. Which of the following kanji have an **on-yomi** of **SEI** (セイ)?
    a. 士
    b. 者
    c. 生
    d. 朝
    e. 青

2. Which of the following readings apply to the kanji 出?
a. **da** (だ)
b. **SHUTSU** (シュツ)
c. **MON** (モン)
d. **de** (で)
e. **u** (う)

3. I went to the Himalayas and saw the Abominable ___ Man.
a. 牛
b. 雨
c. 青
d. 土
e. 雪

4. Which of the following kanji have an **on-yomi** of **KAN** (カン)?
a. 士
b. 金
c. 語
d. 間
e. 電

5. Which of the following readings apply to the kanji 生?
a. **de** (で)
b. **i** (い)
c. **kado** (かど)
d. **nama** (なま)
e. **u** (う)

D. Please choose the best answer to the following questions.

1. Which of the following kanji has the most number of strokes?
a. 間
b. 語
c. 掛
d. 朝
e. 電

2. Which is the correct reading of 売る?
a. **de·ru** (で·る)
b. **i·ru** (い·る)
c. **u·ru** (う·る)
d. **kata·ru** (かた·る)

3. Which is the correct reading of 入れる?
a. **ka·reru** (か·れる)
b. **omo·reru** (おも·れる)
c. **kama·reru** (かま·れる)
d. **i·reru** (い·れる)

4. Which answer best captures the meaning of the compound 電化?
a. Toast
b. Electrification
c. Cactus
d. Lawnmower
e. Yogurt

5. Which is the most common reading of 入る when it appears alone (is not part of a compound)?
a. **i·ru** (い·る)
b. **kata·ru** (かた·る)
c. **u·ru** (う·る)
d. **hai·ru** (はい·る)
e. **hi·ru** (ひ·る)

E. Please match the following compounds and words to their meanings and pronunciations.

1. 朝日　a. Entrance　1. **DEN·RYOKU** (デン·リョク)

2. 掛金　b. Snow fairy　2. **DO·te** (ド·て)

3. 口語　c. Midway　3. **KŌ·GO** (コウ·ゴ)

4. 入口　d. Installment　4. **asa·hi** (あさ·ひ)

5. 中間　e. Youth　5. **yuki·onna** (ゆき·おんな)

6. 大雨　f. Morning sun　6. **CHŪ·KAN** (チュウ·カン)

7. 青春　g. Electric power　7. **kake·KIN** (かけ·キン)

8. 電力　h. Colloquial language　8. **ō·ame** (おお·あめ)

9. 雪女　i. Embankment　9. **iri·guchi** (いり·ぐち)

10. 土手　j. Heavy rain　10. **SEI·SHUN** (セイ·シュン)

CUMULATIVE REVIEW EXERCISES FOR

CHAPTER 1 - 5

A. Please match the following kanji to their meanings.

1.	京	a.	Self
2.	北	b.	Summer
3.	玉	c.	Half
4.	自	d.	North
5.	化	e.	Spring
6.	半	f.	Capital
7.	朝	g.	Like
8.	春	h.	Change
9.	好	i.	Jewel
10.	夏	j.	Morning

B. Which kanji does not belong in the group?

1. a. 耳   b. 目   c. 北   d. 手   e. 首
2. a. 土   b. 女   c. 王   d. 男   e. 子
3. a. 川   b. 回   c. 山   d. 木   e. 田
4. a. 木   b. 牛   c. 米   d. 貝   e. 玉
5. a. 子   b. 上   c. 左   d. 右   e. 下
6. a. 二   b. 九   c. 七   d. 工   e. 三
7. a. 万   b. 干   c. 十   d. 千   e. 百
8. a. 川   b. 雪   c. 全   d. 水   e. 雨
9. a. 肉   b. 出   c. 歩   d. 回   e. 入
10. a. 日   b. 月   c. 火   d. 水   e. 木
    f. 金   g. 土   h. 夏

C. Identify the kanji having the most number of strokes.

1. a. 山   b. 日   c. 工   d. 万   e. 女
2. a. 男   b. 貝   c. 回   d. 金   e. 体
3. a. 冬   b. 木   c. 子   d. 五   e. 元
4. a. 言   b. 者   c. 東   d. 南   e. 売
5. a. 早   b. 出   c. 耳   d. 全   e. 見
6. a. 家   b. 雪   c. 買   d. 掛   e. 高
7. a. 夏   b. 歩   c. 首   d. 雨   e. 思
8. a. 家   b. 掛   c. 明   d. 国   e. 青
9. a. 生   b. 本   c. 白   d. 古   e. 肉
10. a. 電   b. 朝   c. 語   d. 間   e. 雪

D. Please list the following kanji in the order indicated (alphabetical).

1. Body / Main / Rest / Rice / Tree
   a. 休   b. 木   c. 本   d. 体   e. 米

2. Dry / Earth / Gentleman / Ten thousand / Thousand
   a. 士   b. 干   c. 千   d. 土   e. 万

3. Cow / Half / Jewel / King / Life
   a. 王   b. 生   c. 牛   d. 玉   e. 半

4. Buy / Eye / See / Self / Shellfish
   a. 自   b. 目   c. 買   d. 貝   e. 見

5. Early / Hundred / Individual / Sun / White
   a. 早   b. 白   c. 日   d. 者   e. 百

6. Capital / Early / Morning / Old / Tall
   a. 高 b. 京 c. 早 d. 朝 e. 古

7. Eight / Enter / Gentleman / Large / Person
   a. 士 b. 人 c. 入 d. 大 e. 八

8. Basis / Hand / Ten thousand / Thousand / Three
   a. 元 b. 万 c. 三 d. 手 e. 千

9. Circle / Ear / Inside / Meat / Moon
   a. 肉 b. 耳 c. 円 d. 内 e. 月

10. Change / Lower / North / Stop / Upper
    a. 下 b. 化 c. 上 d. 北 e. 止

E. Please choose the best answer to the following questions.

1. I went on a nice vacation to the ____.
   a. 日 b. 火 c. 耳 d. 牛 e. 南

2. What is the best thing to take on a desert crossing?
   a. 木 b. 水 c. 火 d. 門 e. 掛

3. I bought some boots and took up ____ climbing.
   a. 米 b. 肉 c. 雨 d. 山 e. 口

4. A country would be run most poorly by a ____.
   a. 王 b. 男 c. 女 d. 牛
   e. All of the preceding

5. The vampire bat flew in and went straight for my ___.
   a. 目 b. 貝 c. 首 d. 手 e. Wallet

F. Please choose the best answer(s) to the following questions.

1. Which of the following are readings for the kanji 木?
   a. **BOKU** (ボク)
   b. **ki** (き)
   c. **SETSU** (セツ)
   d. **haru** (はる)
   e. **MOKU** (モク)

2. Which of the following are readings for the kanji 下?
   a. **shita** (した)
   b. **o** (お)
   c. **kado** (かど)
   d. **kuda** (くだ)
   e. **KA** (カ)
   f. **sa** (さ)
   g. **GE** (ゲ)

3. Which of the following are readings for the kanji 米?
   a. **MAI** (マイ)
   b. **kome** (こめ)
   c. **BEI** (ベイ)
   d. **HOKU** (ホク)
   e. **yuki** (ゆき)

4. Which of the following are readings for the kanji 上?
   a. **kami** (かみ)
   b. **ue** (うえ)
   c. **JŌ** (ジョウ)
   d. **nobo** (のぼ)
   e. **a** (あ)
   f. **ie** (いえ)
   g. **uwa** (うわ)

5. Which of the following are readings for the kanji 生?
   a. **i** (い)
   b. **nama** (なま)
   c. **SEI** (セイ)
   d. **haru** (はる)
   e. **u** (う)

G. Please choose the best answer to the following questions.

1. Which is the correct reading of 歩く?
   a. **haba·ku** (は ば·く)
   b. **aru·ku** (あ る·く)
   c. **fu·ku** (ふ·く)
   d. **kata·ku** (か た·く)

2. Which is the correct reading of 高い?
   a. **taka·i** (た か·い)
   b. **kata·i** (か た·い)
   c. **ara·i** (あ ら·い)
   d. **usu·i** (う す·い)

3. Which is the correct reading of 休む?
   a. **kara·mu** (か ら·む)
   b. **i·mu** (い·む)
   c. **u·mu** (う·む)
   d. **yasu·mu** (や す·む)

4. Which is the correct reading of 入れる?
   a. **de·reru** (で·れ る)
   b. **u·reru** (う·れ る)
   c. **kata·reru** (か た·れ る)
   d. **i·reru** (い·れ る)

5. Which is the correct reading of 二つ?
   a. **mi·tsu** (み·つ)
   b. **futa·tsu** (ふ た·つ)
   c. **hito·tsu** (ひ と·つ)
   d. **u·tsu** (う·つ)

6. Which is the correct reading of 古い?
   a. **taka·i** (た か·い)
   b. **omo·i** (お も·い)
   c. **furu·i** (ふ る·い)
   d. **haya·i** (は や·い)

7. Which is the correct reading of 早い?
   a. **haya·i** (は や·い)
   b. **yasu·i** (や す·い)
   c. **ao·i** (あ お·い)
   d. **furu·i** (ふ る·い)

8. Which is the correct reading of 小さい?
   a. **ka·sai** (か·さ い)
   b. **ko·sai** (こ·さ い)
   c. **chii·sai** (ち い·さ い)
   d. **uru·sai** (う る·さ い)

9. Which is the correct reading of 少ない?
   a. **de·nai** (で·な い)
   b. **suku·nai** (す く·な い)
   c. **taka·nai** (た か·な い)
   d. **kata·nai** (か た·な い)

10. Which is the correct reading of 少し?
    a. **ma·shi** (ま·し)
    b. **saga·shi** (さ が·し)
    c. **u·shi** (う·し)
    d. **suko·shi** (す こ·し)

H. Please match the following compounds and words to their meanings and pronunciations.

1. 東京   a. To stock up on   1. **HON·DO** (ホン·ド)

2. 見上げる   b. To remember   2. **AN·ZEN** (アン·ゼン)

3. 休日   c. Five hundred   3. **TŌ·KYŌ** (トウ·キョウ)

4. 人生   d. Mainland   4. **JŪ·ICHI·GATSU** (ジュウ·イチ·ガツ)

5. 思い出す   e. To look up (to/at) 5. **ka·i i·reru** (か·い い·れ る)

6. 十一月   f. November   6. **JIN·SEI** (ジン·セイ)

7. 五百　　g. To enter a country　　7. **ko·haru** (こ·はる)

8. 下水　　h. Holiday　　8. **GYŪ· NIKU** (ギュウ· ニク)

9. 小春　　i. Safety　　9. **GO· HYAKU** (ゴ·ヒ ャク)

10. 入国　　j. One time　　10. **mi a·geru** (み あ· げる)

11. 安全　　k. Tokyo　　11. **IK·KAI** (イッ· カイ)

12. 牛肉　　l. Indian summer　　12. **omo·i da·su** (おも· い だ· す)

13. 買い入 れる　　m. (Human) Life　　13. **NYŪ· KOKU** (ニュウ· コク)

14. 一回　　n. Sewage　　14. **KYŪ· JITSU** (キュウ· ジツ)

15. 本土　　o. Beef　　15. **GE·SUI** (ゲ·スイ)

Kanji #101—120

KANJI 101

BEAUTIFUL

BUILDING THIS KANJI
Rabbit `ソ` + King 王(23) + Large (sumo wrestler) 大(17) = 美

Meaning
Used for all things beautiful, this character lives up to its name in a visual sense as well. Take care with the stroke order by writing the components as listed.

Remembering this kanji
The Zulu, along with several other tribes in southern Africa, equate **large** size with being BEAUTIFUL. A **king**, therefore, will make good use of the region's **rabbit** population to grow as **large** as possible, through eating incredible amounts of a filling **rabbit** stew. In being read from the top down, the kanji shows this process clearly: **rabbit** goes into **king**… **king** becomes as **large** as a sumo wrestler… **large** is BEAUTIFUL.

Common Pronunciations
Common **ON** reading: **BI** (ビ)
Common **kun** reading: **utsuku** (うつく)

kun-yomi suggestion: "fruits cooling"

Create your **on-yomi** keyword and enter it in the table at the back of the book. After that, write your sentence to remember the **on-yomi** and **kun-yomi** readings in the box below.

Less Common Pronunciations
Less common **ON** reading: none
Less common **kun** reading: none

The following is a very common irregular reading.

IRREGULAR READING		
美味しい	beautiful + taste = *delicious*	**oi·shii** おい・しい

COMMON WORDS AND COMPOUNDS		
美しい	*beautiful*	**utsuku·shii** うつく・しい
美人	beautiful + person = *beautiful woman*	**BI·JIN** ビ・ジン
美化	beautiful + change = *beautification*	**BI·KA** ビ・カ
美学	beautiful + study = *aesthetics*	**BI·GAKU** ビ・ガク

SAMPLE SENTENCE:

山　　の　木　が　美しい　です。

yama　　no　ki　ga　utsuku·shii　desu.

mountain　　trees　　beautiful

= *The trees on the mountain are beautiful.*

COMPONENT #102

DINOSAUR 鳥

KANJI 102

島 **ISLAND**

′	⺁	⺁	户	自	自	鳥	鳥	島
島								

BUILDING THIS KANJI

Dinosaur 鳥 + Mountain 山(1) = 島

Meaning
Island.

Remembering this kanji
OK, so I have this great idea for a movie. It's set on an ISLAND, but what makes this ISLAND interesting is that some **dinosaurs** are still living on one of its **mountains**! It's a blockbuster concept, and though I'm still working out the details, I've already decided on a title: "Jurassic ISLAND".

Common Pronunciations
Common **ON** reading: **TŌ** (ト ウ)
Common **kun** reading: **shima** (し ま)
The **kun-yomi** for this kanji is often voiced when in the final position, as in the second compound below. Note also the voiced reading for 国 in the third example.

kun-yomi suggestion: "**she maps**"

Write your sentence to remember the **on-yomi** and **kun-yomi** readings in the box below.

Less Common Pronunciations
Less common **ON** reading: none
Less common **kun** reading: none

COMMON WORDS AND COMPOUNDS		
島	*island*	**shima** し ま
小島	small + island = *small island*	ko·**jima** こ·じ ま
島国	island + country = *island nation*	**shima**·guni し ま·ぐ に
半島	half + island = *peninsula*	HAN·**TŌ** ハ ン·ト ウ
本島	main + island = *main island*	HON·**TŌ** ホ ン·ト ウ

SAMPLE SENTENCE:

オーストラリア　と　　日本　　は

Ōsutoraria　　　　to　　NI·HON　　wa

Australia　　　　　　　　Japan

島国　　です。

shima·guni　desu.

island nation

= *Australia and Japan are island nations.*

KANJI 103

寸
TINY

一	寸	寸						

Meaning
Tiny.

Remembering this kanji

How TINY, you ask? Well, given that the soccer player in this illustration is life-size...pretty TINY. This kanji, as the lack of compounds below makes clear, will be much more important for us as a component than a character on its own; the tiny soccer player will be used to suggest it in all future stories.

Common Pronunciations

Common **ON** reading: **SUN** (スン)
Common **kun** reading: none

Create your **on-yomi** keyword and enter it in the table at the back of the book. After that, write your sentence to remember the **on-yomi** reading in the box below.

Less Common Pronunciations

Less common **ON** reading: none
Less common **kun** reading: none

COMMON WORDS AND COMPOUNDS		
一寸	one + tiny = *a tiny bit*	**IS·SUN** イッ・スン
寸前	tiny + before = *immediately before*	**SUN·ZEN** スン・ゼン

SAMPLE SENTENCE:

出かける　　　寸前　　　に　高木さん
de·kakeru　　**SUN·ZEN**　　**ni**　**Taka·gi-san**
　　leave　　immediately before　　Takagi-san
を　　見ました。
o　　**mi·mashita.**
　　　　saw

= *I saw Takagi-san just before I left.*

KANJI 104

寺
TEMPLE

一	十	土	士	寺	寺		

BUILDING THIS KANJI
Earth 土(87) + Tiny (soccer player) 寸(103)
= 寺

Meaning
(Buddhist) temple.

Remembering this kanji

Tiny soccer players are always in danger of being pushed around by their opponents. As a result of this, they usually become known as fearless defenders who protect their positions at all costs — treating even the **tiniest** piece of **earth** they occupy like a TEMPLE that must not be defiled. A TEMPLE in which it is permitted to wear cleats, of course.

Common Pronunciations
Common **ON** reading: **JI** (ジ)
Common **kun** reading: **tera** (てら)

The **kun-yomi** becomes voiced when not in the first position, as it does below in the third example. The final compound can also be read by the respective **kun-yomi**: **furu·dera** (ふ・る・でら).

kun-yomi suggestion: "**tear a**pples"

Write your sentence to remember the **on-yomi** and **kun-yomi** readings in the box below.

Less Common Pronunciations
Less common **ON** reading: none
Less common **kun** reading: none

COMMON WORDS AND COMPOUNDS		
寺	*temple*	**tera** てら
寺田 さん	temple + rice field = *Terada-san*	**tera·da·san** てら・だ・さん
山寺	mountain + temple = *mountain temple*	**yama·dera** やま・でら
古寺	old + temple = *old temple*	**KO·JI** コ・ジ

SAMPLE SENTENCE:

山寺　　　 の 古い　 門　 の
yama·dera　　 **no furu·i**　 **MON**　 **no**
mountain temple　　　 old　 gate
下　 で 休みました。
shita　 de　 yasu·mimashita.
under　　　 rested
= *(We) rested under the old gate of the mountain temple.*

先　PRECEDE

ノ 一 ナ 生 先 先

BUILDING THIS KANJI
Jelly Bean ヽ + Earth ⼟(87) + Ballet 儿 = 先

Meaning
This character has a multitude of meanings, all of them derived from the general sense of "preceding", or the idea of an object "ahead" in a literal or figurative way. Depending on the context in which it appears, this kanji can signify the "tip" or "point" of something, the general future (or the specific past, when used as in the third compound), or a destination. It can also refer to people in the sense of "the other party".

Remembering this kanji
Most people are unaware that Tchaikovsky deleted a **jelly bean** character from his **ballet** "The Nutcracker". This **jelly bean** was to always PRECEDE the Sugar Plum Fairy onstage, then be pinned to the **earth** and devoured by her at the end of the work (she by this time having been driven wild with sugar cravings). It was an edgy scene, but fortunately for **ballet** lovers everywhere, Tchaikovsky concluded it was incompatible with what PRECEDED, and decided to remove the **jelly bean** character altogether.

Common Pronunciations

Common **ON** reading: **SEN** (セン)
Common **kun** reading: **saki** (さき)

kun-yomi suggestion: "sack eels". If using your own idea for this **kun-yomi**, keep in mind that Japan's famous rice wine is pronounced **saké** (さけ), and should not be confused with the reading of this character.

Write your sentence to remember the **on-yomi** and **kun-yomi** readings in the box below.

COMMON WORDS AND COMPOUNDS		
先	*precede; point; tip*	saki さき
先生	precede + life = *teacher*	SEN·SEI セン·セイ
先月	precede + moon (month) = *last month*	SEN·GETSU セン·ゲツ
口先	mouth + precede = *lip service*	kuchi·**saki** くち·さき

SAMPLE SENTENCE:

先生　　は　　冬休み　　に
SEN·SEI　**wa**　**fuyu yasu·mi**　**ni**
teacher　　　　　winter vacation
日本アルプス　へ　行きました。
NI·HON arupusu　**e**　**i·kimashita.**
Japanese Alps　　　　　　went
=*(Our) teacher went to the Japanese Alps for winter vacation.*

Less Common Pronunciations

Less common **ON** reading: none
Less common **kun** reading: none

COMPONENT #106

PICNIC TABLE

Admittedly, this is not the most comfortable-looking picnic table.

KANJI 106

開 **OPEN**

BUILDING THIS KANJI
Gate 門(96) + Picnic Table 开 = 開

Meaning

Open. Secondary meanings include "starting", and the idea of "developing" things (in the sense of opening or reclaiming land, for example).

Remembering this kanji

Their picnic thrown into chaos by the sight of Visigoths on the horizon, the partiers ran desperately back to the castle. "OPEN the **gates**!", "OPEN the **gates**!" they yelled to no avail, for nobody on the other side could hear them. It was only when the **picnic table** was used as a battering ram (thus breaking it) that the **gates** finally flew OPEN to let them in.

Common Pronunciations

Common **ON** reading: **KAI** (カイ)
Common **kun** readings: **a** (あ); **hira** (ひら)

As a glance at the first three examples below suggests, this character can be a little tricky. In the general physical sense of "to open", however, **a·ku** (あ·く) and **a·keru** (あ·ける) function as a normal intransitive/transitive verb pair. The word **hira·ku**, on the other hand, is more concerned with a metaphorical or non-physical sense of "opening", and appears primarily in certain expressions (in the "opening", for example, of a conference, of new lands, or of cherry blossoms). Expressing the sense of a shop's front door being open would thus call for the verb **a·ku**, while conveying the idea of opening a business would require **hira·ku**.

In the first position, this kanji invariably takes the **on-yomi**.

kun-yomi suggestions: "**a**ppetite"; "**he ra**pidly"

Write your sentence to remember the **on-yomi** and **kun-yomi** readings in the box below.

Less Common Pronunciations

Less common **ON** reading: none
Less common **kun** reading: none

COMMON WORDS AND COMPOUNDS		
開く (intr)	to be open	**a·ku** あ·く
開ける (tr)	to open (something)	**a·keru** あ·ける
開く (intr/tr)	to open; to develop	**hira·ku** ひら·く
開化	open + change = becoming civilized	**KAI·KA** カイ·カ
開国	open + country = to open up a country	**KAI·KOKU** カイ·コク
開会	open + meet = to open a meeting	**KAI·KAI** カイ·カイ
公開	public + open = open to the public	**KŌ·KAI** コウ·カイ

SAMPLE SENTENCE:

水門　を　開けて　下さい。

SUI·MON　o　**a·kete**　**kuda·sai.**
sluice gate　　　open　　　please

= *Please open the sluice gate.*

COMPONENT #107

GAS STOVE

KANJI 107

鳥 **BIRD**

BUILDING THIS KANJI
Dinosaur 鳥 + Gas Stove 灬 = 鳥

Meaning
Bird.

Remembering this kanji
As recent archaeological evidence has shown, BIRDS were an important part of a **dinosaur's** diet. Numerous cave drawings, in fact, show **dinosaurs** cooking BIRDS over **gas stoves**. This is interesting, for it has led some scholars to theorize that it was the **dinosaurs'** clumsy use of **gas stoves** that led to their extinction. If this is true, it explains nicely how BIRDS have managed to survive to the present day.

Common Pronunciations

Common **ON** reading: **CHŌ** (チ ョ ウ)
Common **kun** reading: **tori** (と り)

kun-yomi suggestion: "lava**tory**"

Write your sentence to remember the **on-yomi** and **kun-yomi** readings in the box below.

COMMON WORDS AND COMPOUNDS		
鳥	*bird*	**tori** と り
白鳥	white + bird = *swan*	HAKU·**CHŌ** ハ ク·チ ョ ウ
小鳥	small + bird = *small bird*	ko·**tori** こ·と り
夜鳥	night + bird = *nocturnal bird*	YA·**CHŌ** ヤ·チ ョ ウ
愛鳥家	love + bird + house = *bird lover*	AI·**CHŌ**·KA ア イ·チ ョ ウ·カ

Less Common Pronunciations

Less common **ON** reading: none
Less common **kun** reading: none

SAMPLE SENTENCE:

あ の　青 い　小 鳥　の　名 前　が
ano　　ao·i　ko·tori　no　na·mae　ga
that　　blue　little bird　　　name
分 か り ま す　か 。
wa·karimasu　ka.
understand
= *Do you know the name of that little blue bird?*

KANJI 108 ·

夕

EVENING

ノ	ク	夕					

Meaning

Evening. At this time of day, our friend the moon is not yet entirely visible through the evening mist. No story required.

Common Pronunciations

Common **ON** reading: none
Common **kun** reading: **yū** (ゆ う)

kun-yomi suggestion: "**u**k**u**lele"

Create your sentence to remember the **kun-yomi** reading in the box below.

Less Common Pronunciations

Less common **ON** reading: **SEKI** (セ キ)
Less common **kun** reading: none

COMMON WORDS AND COMPOUNDS		
夕べ	*evening*	**yū**·be ゆ う·べ
夕日	evening + sun = *setting sun*	**yū**·hi ゆ う·ひ
夕立	evening + stand = *late afternoon (rain) shower*	**yū**·dachi ゆ う·だ ち

SAMPLE SENTENCE:

山　　か ら 見 る　夕 日　が 美 し い 。
yama　　kara mi·ru　yū·hi　ga utsuku·shii.
mountain from　see　setting sun　　beautiful
= *The setting sun is beautiful when seen from the mountain.*

KANJI 109

外 **OUTSIDE**

| ノ | ク | 夕 | 夘 | 外 | | | |

BUILDING THIS KANJI
Evening 夕 (108) + Poor Figure Skater 卜 = 外

Meaning
Outside. The idea of "foreign" or "other" is also present, as the third example below makes clear. The less common readings convey some secondary meanings of removal and disconnection.

Remembering this kanji
There is a very rigid hierarchy in the world of figure skating. When **evening** arrives, for instance, the arenas are often so full that the **poor figure skaters** are forced OUTSIDE. Unfortunately, the frozen puddles on the OUTSIDE parking lot do not provide nearly enough room for jumps.

Common Pronunciations
Common **ON** reading: **GAI** (ガ イ)
Common **kun** reading: **soto** (そ と)

kun-yomi suggestion: "**so to**asty"

Create your **on-yomi** keyword and enter it in the table at the back of the book. After that, write your sentence to remember the **on-yomi** and **kun-yomi** readings in the box below.

Less Common Pronunciations
Less common **ON** reading: **GE** (ゲ)
Less common **kun** readings: **hoka** (ほ か); **hazu** (は ず)

COMMON WORDS AND COMPOUNDS		
外	*outside*	soto そ と
外見	outside + see = *external appearance*	**GAI·KEN** ガ イ · ケ ン
外国人	outside + country + person = *foreigner*	**GAI·KOKU·JIN** ガ イ · コ ク · ジ ン
外出	outside + exit = *going out*	**GAI·SHUTSU** ガ イ · シ ュ ツ
海外	sea + outside = *overseas*	**KAI·GAI** カ イ · ガ イ

SAMPLE SENTENCE:

日本 には 外国人 が 多い。
NI·HON ni wa GAI·KOKU·JIN ga ō·i.
 Japan   foreigners   many
= *There are many foreigners in Japan.*

KANJI 110

TONGUE

BUILDING THIS KANJI
Thousand 千 (65) + Mouth (vampire) 口 (8) = 舌

Meaning
Tongue.

Remembering this kanji
Interesting fact: a survey showed that **Thousand** Island dressing was a favorite amongst **vampires**. "It's very pleasing to the TONGUE," said one, "and it doesn't have any…unfortunate ingredients." Manufacturers of garlic-based dressings, it seems, need to take the TONGUES of **vampires** more into account if they want access to this market segment.

Common Pronunciations
Common **ON** reading: none
Common **kun** reading: **shita** (し た)

kun-yomi suggestion: "**she ta**ps"

Create your sentence to remember the **kun-yomi** reading in the box below.

Less Common Pronunciations
Less common **ON** reading: ZETSU (ゼ ツ)
Less common **kun** reading: none

COMMON WORDS AND COMPOUND		
舌	*tongue*	shita し た

SAMPLE SENTENCE:

Uchi·da-san	**wa**	**shita**	**ni**	**piasu**	**o**
Uchida-san		tongue		piercing	

し ま し た。
shimashita.
    did
= *Uchida-san got her tongue pierced.*

COMPONENT #111

BANANA PEELS

Note to subtle different between this component and the "Wishbones" of Component 79.

BUILDING THIS KANJI
Prison □ + Jelly Bean 丶 + Jelly Bean 丶 + Banana Peels ㄨ = 図

Meaning
Diagram/Drawing. By extension comes the idea of "planning".

KANJI 111

DIAGRAM

Remembering this kanji

"You have to be sly if you're going to break out of this **prison**," my cellmate told me as I settled in. "The guards won't allow us any pens so there's no way to draw up an escape DIAGRAM. That's why I have these." He placed a couple of moldy **jelly beans** and some rotting **banana peels** on my bunk. "These **jelly beans** will be us," he whispered, "and the **banana peels** will represent the guards. It's not much, but we can plan our break using these as a DIAGRAM."

I nodded. My time in **prison**, it seemed, was not only going to be long, but more boring than I could have possibly imagined.

Common Pronunciations

Common **ON** readings: **ZU** (ズ); **TO** (ト)
Common **kun** reading: none

ZU is the more common reading. Note in the second example below how effectively Japanese can express complex English words.

Create your **on-yomi** keywords and enter them in the table at the back of the book. After that, write your sentence to remember the **on-yomi** readings in the box below.

Less Common Pronunciations

Less common **ON** reading: none
Less common **kun** reading: **haka** (は か)

COMMON WORDS AND COMPOUNDS		
図工	diagram + craft = *drawing and manual arts*	ZU·KŌ ズ・コウ
心電図	heart + electric + diagram = *electrocardiogram*	SHIN·DEN·ZU シン・デン・ズ
海図	sea + diagram = *nautical chart*	KAI·ZU カイ・ズ
意図	mind + diagram = *(one's) aim*	I·TO イ・ト

SAMPLE SENTENCE:

心電図　　モニター　を
SHIN·DEN·ZU　　**monitā**　　**o**
electrocardiogram　monitor
見せて　下さい。
mi·sete　　**kuda·sai.**
show　　please
= *Please show me the electrocardiogram monitor.*

KANJI 112

立 **STAND**

Meaning

Stand/Rise. No story required.

Common Pronunciations

Common **ON** reading: **RITSU** (リ ツ)
Common **kun** reading: **ta** (た)

Consistent with other **on-yomi** ending in **TSU** (ツ), **RITSU** "doubles up" with unvoiced consonant sounds that follow it, as the fifth example below demonstrates. It can also act like 買 (Entry 10) and absorb its accompanying hiragana, as the final example shows.

kun-yomi suggestion: "**tax**"

Create your **on-yomi** keyword and enter it in the table at the back of the book. After that, write your sentence to remember the **on-yomi** and **kun-yomi** readings in the box below.

Less Common Pronunciations

Less common **ON** reading: **RYŪ** (リ ュ ウ)
Less common **kun** reading: none

COMMON WORDS AND COMPOUNDS		
立つ (intr)	to stand	ta·tsu た・つ
立てる (tr)	to set up	ta·teru た・てる
自立	self + stand = *independence*	JI·RITSU ジ・リツ
中立	middle + stand = *neutrality*	CHŪ·RITSU チュウ・リツ
立春	stand + spring = *first day of spring*	RIS·SHUN リッ・シュン
立ち入る	stand + enter = *to go into*	ta·chi i·ru た・ち い・る
夕立	evening + stand = *late afternoon (rain) shower*	yū·dachi ゆう・だち

SAMPLE SENTENCE:

女　の　人　が　美しい　　月
onna　no　hito　ga　utsuku·shii　tsuki
woman　　　person　　　beautiful　　moon
の　下　に　立っています。
no　shita　ni　tat·te imasu.
　　under　　　is standing
=*The woman is standing under a beautiful moon.*

KANJI 113

親 PARENT

BUILDING THIS KANJI
Stand 立(112) + Tree 木(13) + See 見(42) = 親

Meaning
"Parent", together with the senses of intimacy and closeness.

Remembering this kanji
When she was young, her PARENTS would often sing the following ditty:

> "**Stand** on a **tree**,
> And what do you **see**?
> Your PARENTS! Your PARENTS!"

It was cute, of course, but they really should have stopped at some point. After all, it wasn't easy for her as a university student having to answer the question "What's up with your PARENTS and that dumb song?"

Common Pronunciations

Common **ON** reading: **SHIN** (シ ン)
Common **kun** reading: **oya** (お や)

kun-yomi suggestion: "**coy a**bout"

Write your sentence to remember the **on-yomi** and **kun-yomi** readings in the box below.

Less Common Pronunciations

Less common **ON** reading: none
Less common **kun** reading: **shita** (し た)

COMMON WORDS AND COMPOUNDS		
親	*parent*	**oya** おや
父親	father + parent = *father*	chichi·**oya** ちち·おや
親子	parent + child = *parent and child*	**oya**·ko おや·こ
肉親	meat + parent = *blood relative*	NIKU·**SHIN** ニク·シン
母親	mother + parent = *mother*	haha·**oya** はは·おや
親切	parent + cut = *kindhearted*	**SHIN**·SETSU シン·セツ

SAMPLE SENTENCE:

中川さん　　の　父親　は　山　が
Naka·gawa-san no chichi·oya wa yama ga
Nakagawa-san　　　　father　　mountain
大好き　です。
DAI su·ki　desu.
really likes
=*Nakagawa-san's father really likes the mountains.*

KANJI 114

星　**STAR**

丨	冂	冖	日	尸	旦	早	星	星

BUILDING THIS KANJI
Sun 日 (6) + **Life** 生 (99) = 星

Meaning
Star.

Remembering this kanji

When the **sun** is shining over your **life**, it's impossible not to feel like a **STAR**. A famous **STAR** like Sirius, mind you, not one of those dim ones nobody cares about.

Common Pronunciations

Common **ON** reading: **SEI** (セイ)
Common **kun** reading: **hoshi** (ほし)

kun-yomi suggestion: "tally **ho, Shee**ba!"

Write your sentence to remember the **on-yomi** and **kun-yomi** readings in the box below.

Less Common Pronunciations

Less common **ON** reading: **SHŌ** (ショウ)
Less common **kun** reading: none

	COMMON WORDS AND COMPOUNDS	
星	*star*	hoshi ほし
水星	water + star = *Mercury (planet)*	SUI·SEI スイ・セイ
金星	gold + star = *Venus (planet)*	KIN·SEI キン・セイ
火星	fire + star = *Mars (planet)*	KA·SEI カ・セイ
木星	tree + star = *Jupiter (planet)*	MOKU·SEI モク・セイ
土星	earth + star = *Saturn (planet)*	DO·SEI ド・セイ

SAMPLE SENTENCE:

あの　明るい　星　は　金星　だ
ano　aka·rui　hoshi　wa　KIN·SEI　da
that　bright　star　　　Venus
と　思います　か。
to　omo·imasu　ka.
　　think
= *Do you think that bright star is Venus?*

CROPS

When this component appears it usually indicates a kanji with some connection to crops and harvesting.

KANJI 115

秋 **AUTUMN**

BUILDING THIS KANJI
Crops 禾 + Fire 火(59) = 秋

Meaning
Autumn.

Remembering this kanji

No need for a long story here, given that the origin of this graceful character is clearly apparent, AUTUMN being the time when the stubble of **crops** was set on **fire** after harvesting.

Common Pronunciations

Common **ON** reading: **SHŪ** (シュウ)
Common **kun** reading: **aki** (あき)

Note the great four-kanji compound in the third example below.

kun-yomi suggestion: "st**ack ea**sily"

Create your **on-yomi** keyword and enter it in the table at the back of the book. After that, write your sentence to remember the **on-yomi** and **kun-yomi** readings in the box below.

Less Common Pronunciations
Less common **ON** reading: none
Less common **kun** reading: none

COMMON WORDS AND COMPOUNDS		
秋	*autumn*	aki あ き
立秋	stand + autumn = *first day of autumn*	RIS·SHŪ リッ·シュウ
春夏 秋冬	spring + summer + autumn + winter = *the four seasons; year round*	SHUN·KA·SHŪ·TŌ シュン·カ· シュウ·トウ
秋空	autumn + empty (sky) = *autumn sky*	aki·zora あ き·ぞ ら
秋分	autumn + part = *autumnal equinox*	SHŪ·BUN シュウ·ブン

SAMPLE SENTENCE:

aki ni wa NI·HON no yama ga utsuku·shii.
autumn   Japan   mountain   beautiful
=*Japan's mountains are beautiful in autumn.*

WHISKEY JUG

It's hard to imagine many whiskey drinkers being happy about the stopper for this jug taking up so much room!

KANJI 116

 WEST

Meaning
West.

Remembering this kanji
Everyone knows there were a lot of alcohol problems in the wild WEST. Fittingly, a drained **whiskey jug** is used to show this.

Common Pronunciations
Common **ON** reading: SEI (セ イ)
Common **kun** reading: nishi (に し)

kun-yomi suggestion: "ho**ney shie**ld"

Write your sentence to remember the **on-yomi** and
kun-yomi readings in the box below.

[   ]

Less Common Pronunciations
Less common **ON** reading: **SAI** (サイ)
Less common **kun** reading: none

COMMON WORDS AND COMPOUNDS		
西	*west*	**nishi** にし
西口	west + mouth = *west exit/entrance*	**nishi**·guchi にし・ぐち
北西	north + west = *northwest*	HOKU·**SEI** ホク・セイ
北北西	north + north + west = *north-northwest*	HOKU·HOKU·**SEI** ホク・ホク・ セイ
南西	south + west = *southwest*	NAN·**SEI** ナン・セイ
南南西	south + south + west = *south-southwest*	NAN·NAN·**SEI** ナン・ナン・ セイ

SAMPLE SENTENCE:

西口	から	出て	父	に
nishi·guchi	**kara**	**de·te**	**chichi**	**ni**
west exit		exit	father	

会いました。
　　a·imashita.
　　　met
=(She) left by the west exit and met her father.

KANJI 117

刀

SWORD

[フ | 刀 | | | | | |]

Meaning
Sword. No story required.

Common Pronunciations
Common **ON** reading: **TŌ** (トウ)
Common **kun** reading: **katana** (かたな)

kun-yomi suggestion: "ma**k**e **a tan a**pple"

Write your sentence to remember the **on-yomi** and
kun-yomi readings in the box below.

[   ]

Less Common Pronunciations
Less common **ON** reading: none
Less common **kun** reading: none

COMMON WORDS AND COMPOUNDS		
刀	sword	**katana** かたな
刀工	sword + craft = *sword maker*	**TŌ·KŌ** トウ·コウ
日本刀	sun + main + sword = *Japanese sword*	**NI·HON·TŌ** ニ·ホン·トウ

SAMPLE SENTENCE:

先月　　東京　で　日本刀　を
SEN·GETSU TŌ·KYŌ de NI·HON·TŌ o
last month　Tokyo　　Japanese sword
買いました。
ka·imashita.
　bought
=*Last month I bought a Japanese sword in Tokyo.*

KANJI 118

 CUT

ー	ヒ	七刀	切				

BUILDING THIS KANJI
Seven 七 (44) + Sword 刀 (117) = 切

Meaning
Cut. When the **kun-yomi** is used as a suffix it can impart a sense of completely finishing something, or acting in a decisive manner. The final compound provides an example.

Remembering this kanji
Seven samurai means **seven swords**, and **seven swords** can mean trouble on the set:

"For the last time," said the director, exasperated, "when I yell 'CUT', it does *not* mean to CUT each other."

Common Pronunciations
Common **ON** reading: **SETSU** (セ ツ)
Common **kun** reading: **ki** (き)

As can be seen in the fourth example, this is another kanji that behaves like 買.

kun-yomi suggestion: "**qui**che"

Create your **on-yomi** keyword and enter it in the table at the back of the book. After that, write your sentence to remember the **on-yomi** and **kun-yomi** readings in the box below.

Less Common Pronunciations
Less common **ON** reading: **SAI** (サ イ)
Less common **kun** reading: none

As the **kun-yomi** of 切 "doubles up" with the kanji following it in this next pair of words, these compounds are best learned as irregular readings.

IRREGULAR READINGS		
切手	cut + hand = *postage stamp*	**kit·te** きっ·て
切符*	cut + symbol = *ticket*	**kip·pu** きっ·プ

COMMON WORDS AND COMPOUNDS

切れる (intr)	to break (by itself)	ki·reru き・れる
切る (tr)	to cut (something)	ki·ru き・る
切り下げる	cut + lower = to devalue	ki·ri sa·geru き・り さ・げる
切下げ	cut + lower = devaluation	kiri sa·ge きり さ・げ
親切	parent + cut = kindhearted	SHIN·SETSU シン・セツ
大切	large + cut = important	TAI·SETSU タイ・セツ
思い切る	think + cut = to make up one's mind	omo·i ki·ru おも・い き・る

SAMPLE SENTENCE:

水力　と　火力　は　大切

SUI·RYOKU to KA·RYOKU wa TAI·SETSU

hydro power　　thermal power　　important

です ね。

desu ne.

= *Hydro and thermal power are important, aren't they?*

SQUIRRELS (ON A BRICK WALL)

隹

Why are they hanging out on a brick wall? 'Cause they're tough, that's why.

Remembering this kanji

Every DAY OF THE WEEK the **squirrels** sit on their brick wall and wait for the **sun** to come up. Once it does, it becomes light enough for each to grab a **comb** and start slicking back his fur in order to look tough. This is always necessary. After all, every DAY OF THE WEEK is a struggle if you're a **squirrel**.

KANJI 119

曜　**DAY OF THE WEEK**

BUILDING THIS KANJI

Sun 日 (6) + Comb ⦀ + Comb ⦀ + Squirrels 隹 = 曜

Meaning

Day of the week.

Common Pronunciations

Common **ON** reading: **YŌ** (ヨ ウ)

Common **kun** reading: none

Remember that the final kanji in each compound below is read with its **kun-yomi** (in voiced form). Create your **on-yomi** keyword and enter it in the table at the back of the book. After that, write your sentence to remember the **on-yomi** reading in the box below.

COMMON WORDS AND COMPOUNDS

日曜日	sun + day of the week + sun (day) = *Sunday*	NICHI·**YŌ**·bi ニチ・ヨウ・び
月曜日	moon + day of the week + sun (day) = *Monday*	GETSU·**YŌ**·bi ゲツ・ヨウ・び
火曜日	fire + day of the week + sun (day) = *Tuesday*	KA·**YŌ**·bi カ・ヨウ・び
水曜日	water + day of the week + sun (day) = *Wednesday*	SUI·**YŌ**·bi スイ・ヨウ・び
木曜日	tree + day of the week + sun (day) = *Thursday*	MOKU·**YŌ**·bi モク・ヨウ・び
金曜日	gold + day of the week + sun (day) = *Friday*	KIN·**YŌ**·bi キン・ヨウ・び
土曜日	earth + day of the week + sun (day) = *Saturday*	DO·**YŌ**·bi ド・ヨウ・び

SAMPLE SENTENCE:

土曜日 に パーティー が あります。

DO·YŌ·bi ni　　pātī　　ga　arimasu.

Saturday　　　　party　　　　　is

=*There's a party on Saturday.*

Less Common Pronunciations

Less common **ON** reading: none
Less common **kun** reading: none

KANJI 120

周 **AROUND**

BUILDING THIS KANJI

Gorilla 冂 + **Earth** 土(87) + **Mouth (vampire)** 口(8) = 周

Meaning

"Around", as in the sense of a lap or circuit.

Remembering this kanji

If a **gorilla** and **vampire** show up at your local square dance, you'd best be gettin' outta their way. Reason being that they'll spin AROUND and AROUND, tramplin' the **earth** and anything else that gets between 'em. Yup, there's no gettin' AROUND it: they ain't exactly graceful.

Common Pronunciations

Common **ON** reading: **SHŪ** (シュウ)
Common **kun** reading: none

Write your sentence to remember the **on-yomi** reading in the box below.

	COMMON WORDS AND COMPOUNDS	
円周	circle + around = *circumference*	EN·**SHŪ** エン・シュウ
周回	around + rotate = *going around*	**SHŪ**·KAI シュウ・カイ
一周	one + around = *once around*	IS·**SHŪ** イッ・シュウ

SAMPLE SENTENCE:

寺田さん　　は　　ニュージーランド
Tera·da-san　　**wa**　　　　**Nyūjīrando**
Terada-san　　　　　　　　New Zealand
を　　　　一周　　しました。
o　　　**IS·SHŪ**　　**shimashita.**
　　　　once around　　did
=*Terada-san did a circuit of New Zealand.*

Less Common Pronunciations

Less common **ON** reading: none
Less common **kun** reading: none

CHAPTER 6 REVIEW EXERCISES

A. Please match the following kanji to their meanings.

1. 立   a. Bird

2. 星   b. Autumn

3. 切   c. Star

4. 鳥   d. Temple

5. 秋   e. Outside

6. 外   f. Stand

7. 美   g. Cut

8. 先   h. West

9. 寺   i. Beautiful

10. 西   j. Precede

B. Please match the following meanings to their kanji, and these to their **on** or **kun-yomi**.

1. Island   a. 刀   1. **ZU** (ズ)

2. Parent   b. 図   2. **oya** (おや)

3. Day of the week   c. 寸   3. **SHŪ** (シュウ)

4. Tiny   d. 夕   4. **shita** (した)

5. Sword   e. 開   5. **katana** (かたな)

6. Around   f. 親   6. **YŌ** (ヨウ)

7. Evening   g. 舌   7. **shima** (しま)

8. Open   h. 曜   8. **yū** (ゆう)

9. Tongue   i. 島   9. **a** (あ)

10. Diagram   j. 周   10. **SUN** (スン)

C. Please choose the best answer(s) to the following questions.

1. Which of the following readings apply to the kanji 鳥?
   a. **AI** (アイ)
   b. **tori** (とり)
   c. **hoshi** (ほし)
   d. **SHŪ** (シュウ)
   e. **CHŌ** (チョウ)

2. Which of the following readings apply to the kanji 星?
   a. **SEI** (セイ)
   b. **soto** (そと)
   c. **BUN** (ブン)
   d. **hoshi** (ほし)
   e. **ZU** (ズ)

3. Which of the following presents the greatest danger to a newly-washed car?
   a. 夕
   b. 星
   c. 鳥
   d. 外
   e. 舌

4. Which of the following readings apply to the kanji 秋?
   a. **BI** (ビ)
   b. **a** (あ)
   c. **tera** (てら)
   d. **SHŪ** (シュウ)
   e. **aki** (あき)

5. Which of the following readings apply to the kanji 先?
   a. **saki** (さき)
   b. **YŌ** (ヨウ)
   c. **SEN** (セン)
   d. **yū** (ゆう)
   e. **JI** (ジ)

D. Please choose the best answer(s) to the following questions.

1. Which is the correct reading of 美しい?
    a. **ara·shii** (あら・しい)
    b. **tama·shii** (たま・しい)
    c. **mawa·shii** (まわ・しい)
    d. **utsuku·shii** (うつく・しい)

2. Which answer best captures the meaning of the compound 月曜日?
    a. Sunday
    b. Thursday
    c. Monday
    d. Saturday
    e. All of the preceding

3. Which of the following kanji has the most number of strokes?
    a. 開
    b. 鳥
    c. 美
    d. 秋
    e. 星

4. Which is the correct reading of 立つ?
    a. **ta·tsu** (た・つ)
    b. **u·tsu** (う・つ)
    c. **ma·tsu** (ま・つ)
    d. **ka·tsu** (か・つ)

5. Which are the correct readings of 開く? (There are two possible answers.)
    a. **o·ku** (お・く)
    b. **a·ku** (あ・く)
    c. **ama·ku** (あま・く)
    d. **hira·ku** (ひら・く)

E. Please match the following compounds and words to their meanings and pronunciations.

1. 木曜日　a. Setting sun
2. 自立　b. Mars (planet)
3. 親切　c. Beautiful woman
4. 先生　d. Independence
5. 西口　e. Foreigner
6. 火星　f. Peninsula
7. 夕日　g. Thursday
8. 外国人　h. Kindhearted
9. 半島　i. West exit/entrance
10. 美人　j. Teacher

1. **SHIN·SETSU** (シン・セツ)
2. **HAN·TŌ** (ハン・トウ)
3. **MOKU·YŌ·bi** (モク・ヨウ・び)
4. **yū·hi** (ゆう・ひ)
5. **nishi·guchi** (にし・ぐち)
6. **KA·SEI** (カ・セイ)
7. **SEN·SEI** (セン・セイ)
8. **GAI·KOKU·JIN** (ガイ・コク・ジン)
9. **BI·JIN** (ビ・ジン)
10. **JI·RITSU** (ジ・リツ)

Kanji #121—140

KANJI 121

読 READ

| ` | 一 | 二 | 言 | 言 | 言 | 言 | 言 | 言 |
| 計 | 評 | 読 | 読 | 読 | | | | |

BUILDING THIS KANJI
Say 言 (80) + Sell 売 (92) = 読

Meaning
Read.

Remembering this kanji
The sales manager rose to address her staff. It was time for the **READING**.

"And lo, **I say** unto you who **sell**," she intoned. "**READ** carefully the customer's face. **READ** their gestures and clothes. But **READ** not, **I say**, our price protection guarantee; this let them **READ** for themselves."

Common Pronunciations
Common **ON** reading: **DOKU** (ド ク)
Common **kun** reading: **yo** (よ)

kun-yomi suggestion: "**yoga**"

Create your **on-yomi** keyword and enter it in the table at the back of the book. After that, write your sentence to remember the **on-yomi** and **kun-yomi** readings in the box below.

Less Common Pronunciations
Less common **ON** readings: **TOKU** (ト ク); **TŌ** (ト ウ)
Less common **kun** reading: none

COMMON WORDS AND COMPOUNDS		
読む	to read	yo·mu よ·む
読み切る	read + cut = to finish reading	yo·mi ki·ru よ·み き·る
読者	read + individual = reader	**DOKU**·SHA ド ク·シャ
読み物	read + thing = reading matter	yo·mi mono よ·み もの
多読家	many + read + house = well-read person	TA·**DOKU**·KA タ·ド ク·カ

SAMPLE SENTENCE:
この 古い 本 を 読んでいますか。
kono furu·i HON o yo·nde imasu ka.
this old book are reading
= *Are you reading this old book?*

KANJI 122

道 **ROAD**

| ` | ` | ニ | �丷 | 宀 | 宀 | 芉 | 首 | 首 | |
| 首 | 首 | 道 | 道 | | | | | | |

BUILDING THIS KANJI
Neck 首 (54) + Seal 辶 = 道

Meaning
Road/Way. This interesting kanji can signify both a physical road and a spiritual "path". In this latter sense it is often translated as "the way".

Remembering this kanji
Being so poor growing up, we had to use our imaginations when it came time for fun. That's why it was so lucky for us when the **seal** washed up on the beach that day; once some yellow lines were painted down the back of its **neck**, we had ourselves a nice ROAD on which to race our toys. And did we ever get good mileage out of that ROAD! We played on it for ages, and only quit using it when our wheels started getting stuck.

Common Pronunciations
Common **ON** reading: **DŌ** (ド ウ)
Common **kun** reading: **michi** (み ち)
kun-yomi suggestion: "give **me chee**se"

Create your **on-yomi** keyword and enter it in the table at the back of the book. After that, write your sentence to remember the **on-yomi** and **kun-yomi** readings in the box below.

Less Common Pronunciations
Less common **ON** reading: **TŌ** (ト ウ)
Less common **kun** reading: none

TŌ is extremely rare, although it is found in a common word formed by the characters "God" and "Road" to indicate the Japanese religion Shinto (神道): **SHIN·TŌ** (シ ン · ト ウ).

COMMON WORDS AND COMPOUNDS		
道	*road; way*	**michi** み ち
小道	small + road = *path*	ko·**michi** こ · み ち
水道	water + road = *water supply system*	SUI·DŌ ス イ · ド ウ
下水道	lower + water + road = *sewer system*	GE·SUI·DŌ ゲ · ス イ · ド ウ
歩道	walk + road = *sidewalk*	HO·DŌ ホ · ド ウ
国道	country + road = *national highway*	KOKU·DŌ コ ク · ド ウ

SAMPLE SENTENCE:

あ の　国　に　は　安全　な
ano　kuni　ni　wa　AN·ZEN　na
that　country　　　　safe
水道水　が　ありません。
SUI·DŌ·SUI　ga　arimasen.
tap water　　　　isn't
=*There is no safe tap water in that country.*

KANJI 123

天 HEAVEN

| 一 | 一 | 𠂉 | 天 | | | | |

BUILDING THIS KANJI

One (top of a bun) 一(3) + Large (sumo wrestler) 大(17) = 天

Meaning

Heaven/The heavens. This character can indicate both the spiritual sense of heaven as well as the more down to earth notions of sky and air.

Remembering this kanji

The Japanese believe that **sumo wrestlers** in HEAVEN live in mansions built of food. The ceilings of these are made from the **tops of buns** that exude various types of mustards and sauces when they leak. Such living conditions must truly be HEAVEN for a **sumo wrestler**.

Common Pronunciations

Common **ON** reading: **TEN** (テン)
Common **kun** reading: none

Note how the **on-yomi** for "country" (国) is voiced in the first example below. One more curiosity occurs in the fourth compound; in this word, note how 天 changes the **on-yomi** of "king" from Ō (オ ウ) to **NŌ** (ノ ウ) in order to make the pronunciation smoother. This type of phonetic change is extremely rare. Note that the sample sentence contains an irregular reading (明 日).

Create your **on-yomi** keyword and enter it in the table at the back of the book. After that, write your sentence to remember the **on-yomi** reading in the box below.

Less Common Pronunciations

Less common **ON** reading: none
Less common **kun** readings: **ame** (あ め); **ama** (あ ま)

COMMON WORDS AND COMPOUNDS		
天国	heaven + country = *heaven*	**TEN·GOKU** テン・ゴク
天下	heaven + lower = *the whole land*	**TEN·KA** テン・カ
天体	heaven + body = *heavenly body*	**TEN·TAI** テン・タイ
天王星	heaven + king + star = *Uranus (planet)*	**TEN·NŌ·SEI** テン・ノ ウ・ セ イ
天気	heaven + spirit = *the weather*	**TEN·KI** テン・キ

SAMPLE SENTENCE:

明日 の 天気 は 雨 だ そ う で す。

ashita no TEN·KI wa ame da sō desu.
tomorrow   weather   rain   seems
=*It seems the weather will be rainy tomorrow.*

KANJI 124

分 PART

ノ	八	分	分				

BUILDING THIS KANJI
Eight (volcano) 八(19) + Sword 刀(117) = 分

Meaning
This important character suggests the ideas of "dividing" and "portion". It appears in a wide range of words, but the sense of division is always present in some way; the first example below, for instance, can be thought of as "parting" the unknown to arrive at understanding

Remembering this kanji
Modern scientists may scoff at the notion, but a lot of people still believe that **volcanoes** show how the underground dwellers made their way to the surface. By PARTING the rock and magma with **swords** on the way up, it is thought, they created the **volcanoes** we have today. Though the kanji clearly shows a **sword** beneath the missing PART of a **volcano**, it is impossible to verify this theory until the underground dwellers themselves shed more light on their past.

Common Pronunciations
Common **ON** reading: **BUN** (ブン)
Common **kun** reading: **wa** (わ)

kun-yomi suggestion: "**wa**tch"

Create your **on-yomi** keyword and enter it in the table at the back of the book. After that, write your sentence to remember the **on-yomi** and **kun-yomi** readings in the box below.

Less Common Pronunciations
Less common **ON** readings: **FUN** (フン);
BU (ブ)
Less common **kun** reading: none

As these readings are both used following numbers, it is important to know the context in which each is employed. **FUN** relates to minutes (of time or arc), as in the example 五分 **GO·FUN** (ゴ·フン): five minutes. **BU** deals with percentages and rates; 五分 in this sense would be pronounced **GO·BU** (ゴ·ブ), and mean either five (or fifty) percent. It merits learning the words for minutes as irregular readings, as they will be needed for telling time.

Note also that 大分 **DAI·BUN** (ダイ·ブン), one of many Japanese words expressing the idea of "much" or "very", is often pronounced **DAI·BU** (ダイ·ブ).

COMMON WORDS AND COMPOUNDS		
分かる (intr)	*to understand*	**wa**·karu わ·かる
分ける (tr)	*to part; to divide*	**wa**·keru わ·ける
自分	self + part = *oneself*	**JI·BUN** ジ·ブン
半分	half + part = *half*	**HAN·BUN** ハン·ブン
春分	spring + part = *vernal equinox*	**SHUN·BUN** シュン·ブン
秋分	autumn + part = *autumnal equinox*	**SHŪ·BUN** シュウ·ブン

SAMPLE SENTENCE:

日本語　が　分かります　か。
NI·HON·GO **ga** **wa·karimasu** **ka.**
　Japanese　　　　　　understand
= *Do you understand Japanese?*

COMPONENT #125

STOOPING

Labor Code regulations require the following disclaimer be inserted: "This is not an appropriate method of lifting heavy objects."

KANJI 125

物 **THING**

BUILDING THIS KANJI
Cow 牛 (100) + **Stooping** 勹 = 物

Meaning
Thing/Object. Note that the writing order for "cow" differs when it is used as a component; slanting the final stroke upward makes for a smoother transition to the next part of the character.

Remembering this kanji
"What's that THING?" asked a guy **stooping** next to a **cow**.
  "That's my tail," said the **cow**, irritated.
  "And what's that THING?"
  "It's a hoof, OK? Everyone knows it's a hoof."
  "And what about those THINGS?"
  "What?! How dare you **stoop** so low as to question me about my udder!"

  Though THINGS had started out well, relations between **cows** and tourists had slowly become strained.

Common Pronunciations
Common **ON** reading: **BUTSU** (ブツ)
Common **kun** reading: **mono** (もの)

Pronunciation-wise, this is a tough kanji to pin down; both readings are found extensively, and there are no easy rules to fall back on as to when each is used in compounds. This is a character that has to be taken on a word-for-word basis.

kun-yomi suggestion: "**moan o**ver"

Create your **on-yomi** keyword and enter it in the table at the back of the book. After that, write your sentence to remember the **on-yomi** and **kun-yomi** readings in the box below.

Less Common Pronunciations
Less common **ON** reading: **MOTSU** (モツ)
Less common **kun** reading: none

COMMON WORDS AND COMPOUNDS		
物	*thing*	**mono** もの
買い物	buy + thing = *shopping*	ka·i **mono** か·い もの
読み物	read + thing = *reading matter*	yo·mi **mono** よ·み もの
人物	person + thing = *one's character*	**JIN·BUTSU** ジン·ブツ
見物	see + thing = *sightseeing*	**KEN·BUTSU** ケン·ブツ
物体	thing + body = *an object*	**BUT·TAI** ブッ·タイ

SAMPLE SENTENCE:

本田さん は どんな 人物
Hon·da-san wa donna JIN·BUTSU
Honda-san   what kind of   character
です か。
desu ka.
= *What kind of person is Honda-san?*

KANJI 126

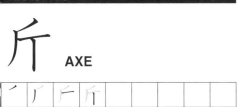

AXE

´	⁄	⼂	斤					

Meaning
Axe. Though rarely encountered on its own, this character serves as a component in several important kanji (an example being Entry 127). No story required.

Common Pronunciations
Common **ON** reading: **KIN** (キン)
Common **kun** reading: none

Write your sentence to remember the **on-yomi** reading in the box below.

Less Common Pronunciations
Less common **ON** reading: none
Less common **kun** reading: none

COMMON WORDS AND COMPOUND		
斤	*axe*	**KIN** キン

SAMPLE SENTENCE:

"斤" が 読めます か。
"KIN" ga yo·memasu ka.
KIN can read
= *Can you read "*斤*"?*

KANJI 127

NEW

´	一	亠	立	立	辛	产	亲
新	新	新	新				

BUILDING THIS KANJI
Stand 立(112) + Tree 木(13) + Axe 斤(126)
= 新

Meaning
New.

Remembering this kanji
Standing in the **tree**, I felt safe from the **axe**-wielding maniac.

  "Come on down," he said. "I'll give you my **axe**."

  I thought about this for a moment and realized I needed to split some wood behind the barn. "Is it **NEW**?" I asked warily.

  "Brand **NEW**," he said. "I just got it."

  "What's that stuff on the blade, then?"

  "Oh, that? That's from the wrapper. Trust me, it's totally **NEW**."

  "Well, OK then," I said, climbing down from the **tree**. "I suppose you can't hurt me if you don't have your **axe**."

Common Pronunciations

Common **ON** reading: **SHIN** (シ ン)
Common **kun** reading: **atara** (あ た ら)

kun-yomi suggestion: "**at a raffle**"

Write your sentence to remember the **on-yomi** and **kun-yomi** readings in the box below.

COMMON WORDS AND COMPOUNDS		
新しい	*new*	**atara**·shii あ た ら・し い
一新	one + new = *complete renewal*	**IS·SHIN** イ ッ・シ ン
新月	new + moon = *new moon*	**SHIN·GETSU** シ ン・ゲ ツ
新星	new + star = *nova*	**SHIN·SEI** シ ン・セ イ
最新	most + new = *newest*	**SAI·SHIN** サ イ・シ ン

Less Common Pronunciations

Less common **ON** reading: none
Less common **kun** readings: **ara** (あ ら);
nii (に い)

SAMPLE SENTENCE:

新しい　　日本刀　を　買いました。
atara·shii　　NI·HON·TŌ　o　ka·imashita.
new　　Japanese sword　　bought
= *(I) bought a new Japanese sword.*

COMPONENT #128

WREATH

This component figures prominently in characters related to grasses and plants.

KANJI 128

花 **FLOWER**

一	＋	＋＋	⺡	⺘	花	花		

BUILDING THIS KANJI
Wreath ⁺⁺ + **Change** 化(69) = 花

Meaning
Flower.

Remembering this kanji

Crowned with a **wreath**, Caesar strode into Rome.

"Everything has **changed**," whispered a senator. "Look how the masses throw FLOWERS! It bodes ill."

"Perhaps," said another, slowly, "but the FLOWERS in that **wreath** – be they sweet smelling roses – will also **change**, and become as these that are now trampled underfoot."

Common Pronunciations

Common **ON** reading: **KA** (カ)
Common **kun** reading: **hana** (は な)

As the second example below shows, **hana** can become voiced when not in the first position. Also note the interesting juxtaposition of characters in the fourth and fifth examples as well as the irregular reading (上手) used in the sample sentence.

kun-yomi suggestion: "**Han a**mulet"

Write your sentence to remember the **on-yomi** and **kun-yomi** readings in the box below.

COMMON WORDS AND COMPOUNDS		
花	*flower*	**hana** はな
生け花	life + flower = *flower arrangement*	i·ke **bana** い·け ばな
花見	flower + see = *cherry blossom viewing*	**hana**·mi はな·み
花火	flower + fire = *fireworks*	**hana**·bi はな·び
火花	fire + flower = *sparks*	hi·**bana** ひ·ばな
開花	open + flower = *bloom*	KAI·**KA** カイ·カ

Less Common Pronunciations
Less common **ON** reading: none
Less common **kun** reading: none

SAMPLE SENTENCE:

西田さん は 生け花 が 上手ですね。

Nishi·da san wa i·ke bana ga JŌ·zu desu ne.

Nishida-san   ikebana   good at

= *Nishida-san is good at ikebana isn't (she)?*

NAME

ノ	ク	ク	ク	名	名		

BUILDING THIS KANJI
Evening 夕 (108) + Mouth (vampire) 口 (8)
= 名

Meaning
Name. By extension, this kanji also includes the ideas of "reputation" and "fame".

Remembering this kanji
Dracula, of course, is a **vampire** whose **NAME** is synonymous with **evening**. This is the real reason he comes out only then; his **NAME** and reputation would suffer, after all, if someone were to spot him at a coffee shop in broad daylight.

Common Pronunciations
Common **ON** reading: **MEI** (メイ)
Common **kun** reading: **na** (な)

kun-yomi suggestion: "**na**pkin"

Write your sentence to remember the **on-yomi** and **kun-yomi** readings in the box below.

Less Common Pronunciations
Less common **ON** reading: **MYŌ** (ミョウ)
Less common **kun** reading: none

COMMON WORDS AND COMPOUNDS		
名高い	name + tall = *renowned*	**na** daka·i な だか・い
有名	have + name = *famous*	**YŪ·MEI** ユウ・メイ
名山	name + mountain = *famous mountain*	**MEI·ZAN** メイ・ザン
名物	name + thing = *famous regional product*	**MEI·**BUTSU メイ・ブツ
名前	name + before = *name*	**na·**mae な・まえ

SAMPLE SENTENCE:

日本　の　　　名山　　　の　一つ　を
NI·HON no   MEI·ZAN   no hito·tsu o
　Japan   famous mountains   one
見ました　か。
mi·mashita ka.
　seen
= *Have you seen one of Japan's famous mountains?*

MOTHER

L	乃	勾	囚	母			

Meaning
Mother. No story required.

Common Pronunciations
Common **ON** reading: **BO** (ボ)
Common **kun** reading: **haha** (はは)

As with the kanji for father (Entry 79), the variety of words for mother shown below reflect different levels of familiarity and politeness.

kun-yomi suggestion: "**Ha! Ha!**"

Create your **on-yomi** keyword and enter it in the table at the back of the book. After that, write your sentence to remember the **on-yomi** and **kun-yomi** readings in the box below.

Less Common Pronunciations
Less common **ON** reading: none
Less common **kun** reading: none

These two irregular readings correspond to those we learned earlier for "father".

IRREGULAR READINGS

お母さん	mother	okāsan おかあさん
伯母 さん*	related + mother = aunt	obasan おばさん

COMMON WORDS AND COMPOUNDS

母	mother	haha はは
母親	mother + parent = mother	haha·oya はは・おや
母国語	mother + country + words = mother tongue	BO·KOKU·GO ボ・コク・ゴ
母の日	mother + sun (day) = Mother's Day	haha·no·hi はは・の・ひ
父母	father + mother = father and mother	FU·BO フ・ボ

SAMPLE SENTENCE:

新しい　先生　の　母国語　は
atara·shii SEN·SEI no BO·KOKU·GO wa
new　　　teacher　　　　mother tongue
英語　です。
EI·GO　desu.
English
= *The new teacher's mother tongue is English.*

COMPONENT #131

BROKEN CRUTCH

Although this component appears to have three strokes, it is actually written with two; this is shown in the following kanji.

KANJI 131

  PRIVATE

BUILDING THIS KANJI
Crops 禾 + Broken Crutch 厶 = 私

Meaning
Private. This character is also used for the first person singular, "I".

Remembering this kanji

Nobody could figure out what was going on with the **crops**. The oats were acting wilder than ever, and rumor had it that gangs of wheat were causing trouble amongst the barley. PRIVATELY we began to worry about the harvest, especially when stalks of rye began showing up with bruises and **broken crutches**. Several of us tried to ask the **crops** what was going on, but nobody got very far. "What happens between us **crops** is none of your business," they always replied. "It's PRIVATE, you got that? PRIVATE!"

Common Pronunciations

Common **ON** reading: **SHI** (シ)
Common **kun** reading: **watashi** (わたし)

kun-yomi suggestion: "**what a sheer**"

Write your sentence to remember the **on-yomi** and **kun-yomi** readings in the box below.

COMMON WORDS AND COMPOUNDS		
私	*I*	watashi わたし
私有	private + have = *privately owned*	**SHI·YŪ** シ·ユウ
私道	private + road = *private road*	**SHI·DŌ** シ·ドウ
私物	private + thing = *private property*	**SHI·BUTSU** シ·ブツ
私学	private + study = *private school*	**SHI·GAKU** シ·ガク

Less Common Pronunciations

Less common **ON** reading: none
Less common **kun** reading: **watakushi** (わた くし)

SAMPLE SENTENCE:

私　は　本　を　読んでいます。

watashi wa HON o yo·nde imasu.
I book reading
= *I'm reading a book.*

夜 NIGHT

BUILDING THIS KANJI

Police ⼇ + Giraffe 亻 + Evening 夕 (108) + Comet 一 = 夜

Meaning

Night. Make sure to write this character in the order given.

Remembering this kanji

After a long day policing the savanna, the **ranger** went to her local watering hole for a drink. Surprisingly, the **giraffes** were already there, and seemed well on the way to making a NIGHT of it.

"It's safe to come here the moment a **comet** is visible in the **evening**," said one, slurring over a gin and tonic. "That means it's NIGHT, and dark enough so that nothing can hunt."

"I wouldn't be so sure about that," said the **ranger**. "The leopards I just passed on the way over didn't look like they were coming here for a NIGHTCAP."

Common Pronunciations

Common **ON** reading: **YA** (ヤ)
Common **kun** reading: **yoru** (よる); **yo** (よ)

yoru is only used when this kanji appears alone; **yo** and **YA** are distributed evenly through compounds.

kun-yomi suggestions: "**you're oo**zing"; "**yo**gurt"

Create your **on-yomi** keyword and enter it in the table at the back of the book. After that, write your sentence to remember the **on-yomi** and **kun-yomi** readings in the box below.

COMMON WORDS AND COMPOUNDS		
夜	*night*	**yoru** よる
夜中	night + middle = *middle of the night*	**yo·naka** よ・なか
夜明け	night + bright = *dawn*	**yo a·ke** よ あ・け
月夜	moon + night = *moonlit night*	**tsuki·yo** つき・よ
夜間	night + interval = *night time*	**YA·KAN** ヤ・カン

Less Common Pronunciations

Less common **ON** reading: none
Less common **kun** reading: none

SAMPLE SENTENCE:

夜明け に 家 を 出ました。

yo a·ke   ni   ie   o   de·mashita.
   dawn   house   exit

= *I left the house at dawn.*

COMPONENT #133

CHISEL

KANJI 133

前 **BEFORE**

BUILDING THIS KANJI
Snowboard 丷 + Moon 月 (11) + Chisel 刂
= 前

Meaning
Before/Front. It is worth comparing the compounds below to those for "先" (Entry 105) to get a sense of the subtle differences between these two characters.

Remembering this kanji
We all know that a waxing **moon** comes BEFORE a full **moon**, but how many know where the expression "waxing **moon**" originated? It's an interesting story, in that the **moon** used to work at a **snowboard** shop long BEFORE he took his place in the sky. Using a **chisel**, he would wax the **snowboards** as carefully as possible, trying not to let the **chisel** slip and add yet another crater to his face. He was, by all accounts, a conscientious worker, one who always reminded customers to prep their boards BEFORE they hit the slopes.

Common Pronunciations
Common **ON** reading: **ZEN** (ゼン)
Common **kun** reading: **mae** (まえ)

kun-yomi suggestion: "llama ate"

Write your sentence to remember the **on-yomi** and **kun-yomi** readings in the box below.

COMMON WORDS AND COMPOUNDS		
前	*before*	mae まえ
名前	name + before = *name*	na·**mae** な・まえ
手前	hand + before = *this side of*	te·**mae** て・まえ
前半	before + half = *first half*	**ZEN**·HAN ゼン・ハン
前者	before + individual = *the former*	**ZEN**·SHA ゼン・シャ
午前	noon + before = *A.M.; morning*	GO·**ZEN** ゴ・ゼン

Less Common Pronunciations
Less common **ON** reading: none
Less common **kun** reading: none

SAMPLE SENTENCE:

門	の	前	に	美しい	花
MON	**no**	**mae**	**ni**	**utsuku·shii**	**hana**
gate		before		beautiful	flower

が あります。
ga   arimasu.
　　　are
= *There are beautiful flowers in front of the gate.*

KANJI 134

MANY

BUILDING THIS KANJI
Evening 夕 (108) + **Evening** 夕 (108) = 多

Meaning
Many/Much.

Remembering this kanji
Evening after **evening**, MANY **evenings** ago, something happened…to MANY.

Common Pronunciations
Common **ON** reading: **TA** (タ)
Common **kun** reading: **ō** (おお)

kun-yomi suggestion: "oboe"

Create your **on-yomi** keyword and enter it in the table at the back of the book. After that, write your sentence to remember the **on-yomi** and **kun-yomi** readings in the box below.

Less Common Pronunciations
Less common **ON** reading: none
Less common **kun** reading: none

COMMON WORDS AND COMPOUNDS		
多い	*many*	**ō**·i おお・い
多少	many + few = *more or less*	**TA**·**SHŌ** タ・ショウ
多分	many + part = *perhaps*	**TA**·**BUN** タ・ブン
多大	many + large = *great quantity*	**TA**·**DAI** タ・ダイ
多読家	many + read + house = *well-read person*	**TA**·**DOKU**·**KA** タ・ドク・カ

SAMPLE SENTENCE:

この　国　には　お金　が　大好き　な
kono　kuni　ni wa　o kane　ga　DAI su·ki　na
this　country　　　money　　really like

人　が　多い。
hito　ga　ō·i.
person　　many

= *In this country, there are a lot of people who really like money.*

KANJI 135

持 **HOLD**

BUILDING THIS KANJI
Finger 扌 + Temple 寺(104) = 持

Meaning
Hold/Possess.

Remembering this kanji
I saw a **finger** emerge from a **temple** I was passing one day. "HOLD me," came a shaky voice from behind a curtain.
　For some reason, I decided not to.

Common Pronunciations
Common **ON** reading: none
Common **kun** reading: **mo** (も)

As the fourth example below shows, this kanji can act like 買.

kun-yomi suggestion: "**mocha**"

Create your sentence to remember the **kun-yomi** reading in the box below.

Less Common Pronunciations
Less common **ON** reading: **JI** (ジ)
Less common **kun** reading: none

COMMON WORDS AND COMPOUNDS		
持つ	*to hold*	**mo·tsu** も・つ
金持ち	gold + hold = *rich person*	kane **mo·chi** かね も・ち
持ち上げる	hold + upper = *to lift up*	**mo·chi a·geru** も・ち あ・げる
持物	hold + thing = *one's belongings*	**mochi·mono** もち・もの
気持ち	spirit + hold = *feeling*	KI **mo·chi** キ も・ち

SAMPLE SENTENCE:

雪男　　　　は　田中さん
yuki·otoko　　wa　Tanaka-san
The Abominable Snowman　　Tanaka-san
を　持ち上げました。
o　mo·chi a·gemashita.
　　　lifted up

= *The Abominable Snowman lifted up Tanaka-san.*

COMPONENT #136

PITCHFORK

Fittingly for a pitchfork, this component will always be stabbing through at least one other line in the kanji. The next entry provides an example.

KANJI 136

WRITE

ㄱ	⼆	⺕	⺕	⺕	⼟	書	書	書
書								

BUILDING THIS KANJI
Pitchfork ⺕ + Two ⼆(4) + Pole | + Sun ⽇ (6) = 書

Meaning
Write. This character has to do with all matters related to writing, and can suggest such things as books, notes, documents, and calligraphy, amongst others.

Remembering this kanji
Even if you dip them in ink, it is simply not possible to WRITE the Japanese kanji for "**two**" using a **pitchfork** (it makes a triple line) or a **pole** (a single line). Using the **sun** is even worse; it burns the paper and is thus unsuitable for any kind of WRITING.

Common Pronunciations
Common **ON** reading: SHO (ショ)
Common **kun** reading: ka (か)

The third and fifth examples below show how this kanji can act like 買. Be aware that the **kun-yomi** is always voiced when it appears in the second position, as it is in the final compound.

kun-yomi suggestion: "**ca**lendar"

Create your **on-yomi** keyword and enter it in the table at the back of the book. After that, write your sentence to remember the **on-yomi** and **kun-yomi** readings in the box below.

Less Common Pronunciations
Less common **ON** reading: none
Less common **kun** reading: none

COMMON WORDS AND COMPOUNDS		
書く	*to write*	**ka**·ku か・く
書き入れる	write + enter = *to write in*	**ka**·ki i·reru か・き い・れる
書入れ	write + enter = *an entry*	**kaki** i·re か き い・れ
書道	write + road = *calligraphy*	**SHO**·DŌ ショ・ドウ
前書	before + write = *preface*	mae·**gaki** まえ・がき

SAMPLE SENTENCE:

お名前 を こちら へ 書いて 下さい。

o na·mae   o   kochira   e   ka·ite   kuda·sai.
  name   here   write   please
= *Please write your name here.*

音 **SOUND**

'	一	丷	立	立	音	音	音	音

BUILDING THIS KANJI
Stand 立(112) + **Sun** 日(6) = 音

Meaning
Sound.

Remembering this kanji
Crackling, sizzling, hissing…it's easy, unfortunately, to imagine the **SOUNDS** that would be
produced if someone were **standing** on the **sun**.

Common Pronunciations
Common **ON** reading: **ON** (オン)
Common **kun** reading: **oto** (おと)

Although it is a mixture of **on-** and **kun-yomi**, the
second example below is probably very familiar to you by now. Note also how the meaning

of the same compound changes in the example
following this, when both kanji are read with their
on-yomi.

kun-yomi suggestion: "gua**no to**ast"

Create your **on-yomi** keyword and enter it in the
table at the back of the book. After that, write your
sentence to remember the **on-yomi** and **kun-yomi**
readings in the box below.

Less Common Pronunciations
Less common **ON** reading: **IN** (イン)
Less common **kun** reading: **ne** (ね)

COMMON WORDS AND COMPOUNDS		
音	sound	**oto** おと
音読み	sound + read = the **on-yomi**	**ON** yo·mi オン よ·み
音読	sound + read = *reading aloud*	**ON·DOKU** オン·ドク
物音	thing + sound = *a noise*	mono·**oto** もの·おと
足音	leg + sound = *sound of footsteps*	**ashi·oto** あし·おと

SAMPLE SENTENCE:

あれ は　水　の　音　だ　と　思います。

are   wa   mizu   no   oto   da   to   omo·imasu.
that   water   sound   think
= *(I) think that's the sound of water.*

COMPONENT #138

SPY

As with the broken crutch in ム, the bottom of this component is written with two strokes, not three.

KANJI 138

会 **MEET**

BUILDING THIS KANJI
Umbrella 𠆢 + Spy 云 = 会

Meaning
Meet/Meeting. When found at the end of compounds, this kanji often expresses English words such as "society", "association" and "party".

Remembering this kanji
"What's with the **umbrella**?" she asked on MEETING the **spy**, looking around nervously.
 "What do you mean?"
 "What do I mean!? The weather's perfect, so why in the world are you under an **umbrella**? Everyone's staring at us!"
 "That's enough!" interrupted the **spy**. "You obviously don't know the rules; if you MEET a **spy**, you MEET under an **umbrella**. Everyone knows it's more stylish that way."

Common Pronunciations
Common **ON** reading: **KAI** (カイ)
Common **kun** reading: **a** (あ)

kun-yomi suggestion: "ambassador"

Write your sentence to remember the **on-yomi** and **kun-yomi** readings in the box below.

Less Common Pronunciations
Less common **ON** reading: **E** (エ)
Less common **kun** reading: none

COMMON WORDS AND COMPOUNDS		
会う	to meet	a·u あ·う
会見	meet + see = *interview*	KAI·KEN カイ·ケン
大会	large + meet = *convention; tournament*	TAI·KAI タイ·カイ
開会	open + meet = *to open a meeting*	KAI·KAI カイ·カイ
入会金	enter + meet + gold (money) = *enrollment fee*	NYŪ·KAI·KIN ニュウ·カイ·キン

SAMPLE SENTENCE:

米国大会 は 九月 に
BEI·KOKU·TAI·KAI wa KU·GATSU ni
 U.S. tournament September
あります か。
 arimasu ka.
  is
= *Is the U.S. tournament in September?*

聞 **HEAR**

BUILDING THIS KANJI
Gate 門 (96) + Ear 耳 (78) = 聞

Meaning
Hear/Ask. Like "早" (Entry 29), this is another kanji with two unrelated and distinct meanings.

Remembering this kanji
I pressed my **ear** against the **gate**.
"What do you HEAR?" she asked.
"'HEAR ye', 'HEAR ye'," I answered.
"How can I?" she said. "You're in my way."
"No," I said. "I HEAR 'HEAR ye…' oh, forget it."

Common Pronunciations
Common **ON** reading: **BUN** (ブン)
Common **kun** reading: **ki** (き)

Only the **kun-yomi** appears in the first position.

kun-yomi suggestion: "**key**note address"

Write your sentence to remember the **on-yomi** and **kun-yomi** readings in the box below.

Less Common Pronunciations
Less common **ON** reading: **MON** (モン)
Less common **kun** reading: none

COMMON WORDS AND COMPOUNDS		
聞こえる (intr)	*to be heard*	**ki**·koeru き・こえる
聞く (tr)	*to hear; to ask*	**ki**·ku き・く
聞き出す	hear + exit = *to find out about*	**ki**·ki da·su き・き だ・す
聞き入れる	hear + enter = *to comply with*	**ki**·ki i·reru き・き い・れる
新聞	new + hear = *newspaper*	**SHIN·BUN** シン・ブン
見聞	see + hear = *information*	**KEN·BUN** ケン・ブン

SAMPLE SENTENCE:

夜中　　　に　物音　を
yo·naka　　ni　mono·oto　o
middle of the night　　sound
聞きました。
　ki·kimashita.
　heard
= *(She) heard a sound in the middle of the night.*

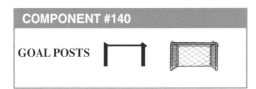

COMPONENT #140

GOAL POSTS

KANJI 140

央 CENTER

BUILDING THIS KANJI
Goal Posts 冂 + Large (sumo wrestler)
大(17) = 央

Meaning
Center. Other than the first example (and words derived from it), this kanji is rarely used.

Remembering this kanji
You put a **sumo wrestler** dead CENTER between the **goal posts**, and chances are your team will give up fewer goals. Your opponent, quite simply, will never hit the CENTER of the net.

Common Pronunciations
Common **ON** reading: Ō (オウ)
Common **kun** reading: none

Write your sentence to remember the **on-yomi** reading in the box below.

Less Common Pronunciations
Less common **ON** reading: none
Less common **kun** reading: none

COMMON WORDS AND COMPOUNDS		
中央	middle + center = *center*	CHŪ·Ō チュウ·オウ
中央口	middle + center + mouth = *central exit/entrance*	CHŪ·Ō·guchi チュウ· オウ·ぐち

SAMPLE SENTENCE:

中央口　　で　秋山さん　を
CHŪ·Ō·guchi　de　Aki·yama-san　o
central entrance　　Akiyama-san
見ました。
mi·mashita.
　saw
= *(He) saw Akiyama-san at the central entrance.*

CHAPTER 7 REVIEW EXERCISES

A. Please match the following kanji to their meanings.

1.	多	a.	Many
2.	物	b.	Mother
3.	音	c.	Heaven
4.	天	d.	Read
5.	花	e.	Write
6.	書	f.	Thing
7.	読	g.	Hear
8.	私	h.	Flower
9.	母	i.	Private
10.	聞	j.	Sound

B. Please match the following meanings to their kanji, and these to their **on** or **kun-yomi**.

1.	New	a.	会	1.	**Ō**(オウ)
2.	Hold	b.	前	2.	**wa**(わ)
3.	Center	c.	新	3.	**KIN**(キン)
4.	Road	d.	分	4.	**mo**(も)
5.	Meet	e.	夜	5.	**SHIN**(シン)
6.	Axe	f.	央	6.	**yoru**(よる)
7.	Before	g.	名	7.	**a**(あ)
8.	Part	h.	持	8.	**MEI**(メイ)
9.	Name	i.	道	9.	**mae**(まえ)
10.	Night	j.	斤	10.	**DŌ**(ドウ)

C. Please choose the best answer(s) to the following questions.

1. Which of the following kanji have an **on-yomi** of **BUN**(ブン)?
   a. 読
   b. 聞
   c. 分
   d. 母
   e. 物

2. Which of the following readings apply to the kanji 多?
   a. **TA**(タ)
   b. **hana**(はな)
   c. **DŌ**(ドウ)
   d. **michi**(みち)
   e. **ō**(おお)

3. Which of the following readings apply to the kanji 花?
   a. **YA**(ヤ)
   b. **na**(な)
   c. **hana**(はな)
   d. **KA**(カ)
   e. **ON**(オン)

4. I planted a beautiful ___ in a corner of my garden.
   a. 斤
   b. 母
   c. 道
   d. 花
   e. 音

5. Which of the following readings apply to the kanji 物?
   a. **mono**(もの)
   b. **SHŌ**(ショウ)
   c. **SHITSU**(シツ)
   d. **na**(な)
   e. **BUTSU**(ブツ)

D. Please choose the best answer(s) to the following questions.

1. Which is the correct reading of 聞く ?
   a. **yu·ku** (ゆ・く)
   b. **ki·ku** (き・く)
   c. **a·ku** (あ・く)
   d. **ka·ku** (か・く)

2. Which is the correct reading of 読む?
   a. **o·mu** (お・む)
   b. **ka·mu** (か・む)
   c. **u·mu** (う・む)
   d. **yo·mu** (よ・む)

3. Which of the following kanji has the most
   number of strokes?
   a. 前
   b. 物
   c. 書
   d. 夜
   e. 持

4. Which is the correct reading of 書く ?
   a. **ka·ku** (か・く)
   b. **ama·ku** (あま・く)
   c. **ki·ku** (き・く)
   d. **shi·ku** (し・く)

5. Which is the correct reading of 新しい?
   a. **atara·shii** (あたら・しい)
   b. **mawa·shii** (まわ・しい)
   c. **utsuku·shii** (うつく・しい)
   d. **ara·shii** (あら・しい)

E. Please match the following compounds and
words to their meanings and pronunciations.

1. 金持ち   a. National   1. **i·ke bana**
                 highway   (い・け ばな)

2. 新聞   b. An entry   2. **ka·i mono**
                                       (か・い もの)

3. 生け花   c. Oneself   3. **na·mae**
                                       (な・まえ)

4. 国道   d. Center   4. **kane mo·chi**
                                       (かね も・ち)

5. 自分   e. Flower   5. **JI·BUN**
                 arrangement   (ジ・ブン)

6. 書入れ   f. Name   6. **NYŪ·**
                                       KAI·KIN
                                       (ニュウ・
                                       カイ・キン)

7. 名前   g. Newspaper 7.   **KOKU·DŌ**
                                       (コク・ドウ)

8. 中央   h. Enrollment 8.   **kaki i·re**
                 fee   (かき い・れ)

9. 買い物   i. Rich   9. **SHIN·BUN**
                 person   (シン・ブン)

10. 入会金   j. Shopping   10. **CHŪ·Ō**
                                       (チュウ・
                                       オウ)

Kanji #141—160

KANJI 141

 NEAR

BUILDING THIS KANJI
Axe 斤 (126) + Seal 辶 = 近

Meaning
Near. The sense of "recent" is also incorporated.

Remembering this kanji
Brandishing an **axe**, the **seal** came NEARER and NEARER the waiter's station.

"Don't come NEAR me!" I screamed.

"You ever gonna slip me farmed salmon again?" he said threateningly.

I shouldn't have tried to be sneaky; any **seal** would have known that farmed salmon didn't taste NEARLY as good as wild.

Common Pronunciations
Common **ON** reading: **KIN** (キン)
Common **kun** reading: **chika** (ちか)

kun-yomi suggestion: "**chica**"

Write your sentence to remember the **on-yomi** and **kun-yomi** readings in the box below.

Less Common Pronunciations
Less common **ON** reading: none
Less common **kun** reading: none

COMMON WORDS AND COMPOUNDS		
近い	near	**chika**·i ち か・い
近づく	to approach	**chika**·zuku ち か・づ く
近道	near + road = *shortcut*	**chika**·michi ち か・み ち
近親	near + parent = *close relative*	**KIN**·SHIN キ ン・シ ン
最近	most + near = *recently*	SAI·**KIN** サ イ・キ ン

SAMPLE SENTENCE:

新しい　家　は　川　の　近く　に
atara·shii　ie　wa　kawa　no　chika·ku　ni
new　　house　　river　　near

あります。
arimasu.
is

= *The new house is near a river.*

COMPONENT #142

HAMMER

失 **LOSE**

BUILDING THIS KANJI
Hammer � + Large (sumo wrestler) 大(17)
= 失

Meaning
Lose, in the sense of "mislay". This character often conveys a hint of failure and error, so guard against becoming depressed on seeing it.

Remembering this kanji
LOSING one's belt is obviously the worst thing that can happen to a **sumo wrestler**. Should this occur, the **wrestler** is to strike himself repeatedly with a **hammer** to atone for LOSING face.

Common Pronunciations
Common **ON** reading: **SHITSU** (シ ツ)
Common **kun** reading: **ushina** (う し な)

kun-yomi suggestion: "**ooh, she na**pped"

Create your **on-yomi** keyword and enter it in the table at the back of the book. After that, write your sentence to remember the **on-yomi** and **kun-yomi** readings in the box below.

Less Common Pronunciations
Less common **ON** reading: none
Less common **kun** reading: none

COMMON WORDS AND COMPOUNDS		
失う	*to lose*	**ushina·u** うしな・う
見失う	see + lose = *to lose sight of*	mi **ushina·u** みうしな・う
失言	lose + say = *slip of the tongue*	**SHITSU·GEN** シ ツ・ゲン

SAMPLE SENTENCE:

大会　で　　失言　　しました。
TAI·KAI de SHITSU·GEN shimashita.
convention　slip of the tongue　did
= *(I) made a slip of the tongue at the convention.*

KANJI 143

弓 **BOW**

Meaning
Bow (the partner to an arrow).

Remembering this kanji
It's a shame about this **BOW** having been run over by a tractor.

Common Pronunciations
Common **ON** reading: **KYŪ** (キュウ)
Common **kun** reading: **yumi** (ゆみ)

kun-yomi suggestion: "**you, me** and…"

Write your sentence to remember the **on-yomi** and **kun-yomi** readings in the box below.

Less Common Pronunciations
Less common **ON** reading: none
Less common **kun** reading: none

COMMON WORDS AND COMPOUNDS		
弓	*bow*	yumi ゆみ
弓道	bow + road = *(Japanese) archery*	**KYŪ·DŌ** キュウ・ドウ

SAMPLE SENTENCE:

前田さん は 古い 弓 と 美しい
Mae·da·san wa furu·i yumi to utsuku·shii
Maeda-san　　　　old　bow　　　beautiful
日本刀　　　を 買いました。
NI·HON·TŌ　o　ka·imashita.
Japanese sword　　　bought
= *Maeda-san bought an old bow and a beautiful Japanese sword.*

COMPONENT #144

SADDLE 馬

KANJI 144

馬 **HORSE**

丨	厂	冂	干	馬	馬	馬	馬
馬							

BUILDING THIS KANJI
Saddle 馬 + Gas Stove ⺣ = 馬

Meaning
Horse.

Remembering this kanji

I was devastated when Trigger slipped his **saddle** and bolted off with another HORSE. I waited for him to return, naturally, but it was all in vain: he had left for greener pastures. In the end I hurled his **saddle** onto a **gas stove**; it was hateful to me now, and I didn't want anything to remind me of how fickle a HORSE could be.

Common Pronunciations

Common **ON** reading: **BA** (バ)
Common **kun** reading: **uma** (うま)

kun-yomi suggestion: "**zoom a**round"

Create your **on-yomi** keyword and enter it in the table at the back of the book. After that, write your sentence to remember the **on-yomi** and **kun-yomi** readings in the box below.

Less Common Pronunciations

Less common **ON** reading: none
Less common **kun** reading: **ma** (ま)

COMMON WORDS AND COMPOUNDS		
馬	*horse*	**uma** うま
子馬	child + horse = *colt; pony*	ko·**uma** こ・うま
牛馬	cow + horse = *cows and horses*	GYŪ·**BA** ギュウ・バ
馬具	horse + tool = *harness*	**BA**·GU バ・グ

SAMPLE SENTENCE:

馬	と	牛	の	どちら	が	好き
uma	**to**	**ushi**	**no**	**dochira**	**ga**	**su·ki**
horse		cow		which		like

です か。
desu ka.
= *Which do you like, horses or cows?*

 WEEK

)	刀	刀	冂	用	用	用	周	周
周	週							

BUILDING THIS KANJI
Around 周(120) + Seal 辶 = 週

Meaning
Week.

Remembering this kanji

"It's the same routine every WEEK here at the aquarium," said the **seal**, shrugging. "I swim **around** and **around** 'cause there's nothing else to do."

I nodded. Digging up stories for my magazine "**Seal WEEKLY**", it seemed, was going to be harder than I had thought.

Common Pronunciations
Common **ON** reading: **SHŪ** (シュウ)
Common **kun** reading: none

Write your sentence to remember the **on-yomi** reading in the box below.

Less Common Pronunciations
Less common **ON** reading: none
Less common **kun** reading: none

COMMON WORDS AND COMPOUNDS		
週間	week + interval = *week*	**SHŪ·KAN** シュウ・カン
一週間	one + week + interval = *one week*	**IS·SHŪ·KAN** イッ・シュウ・カン
二週間	two + week + interval = *two weeks*	**NI·SHŪ·KAN** ニ・シュウ・カン
週日	week + sun (day) = *weekday*	**SHŪ·JITSU** シュウ・ジツ
先週	precede + week = *last week*	**SEN·SHŪ** セン・シュウ
来週	come + week = *next week*	**RAI·SHŪ** ライ・シュウ

SAMPLE SENTENCE:

月曜日　から　二週間　の
GETSU·YŌ·bi　kara　NI·SHŪ·KAN　no
Monday　from　two weeks
夏休み　　です
natsu yasu·mi　desu.
summer vacation
= *There's a two-week summer vacation from Monday.*

KANJI 146

PULL

¬	⁊	弓	引				

BUILDING THIS KANJI
Bow 弓 (143) + Pole | = 引

Meaning
Pull. This character also conveys the idea of "attraction" (best seen in the fourth example) and the senses of receding and withdrawing. You will notice it frequently on signs; it indicates "pull" on doors, and "discount" when used with numbers.

Remembering this kanji
A **bow** obviously needs to be **PULLED** in order to work effectively as a weapon, and the same is true for a **pole**. How so? Well, a catapult is basically a **pole**, and if you think about it, the sound "PULL" is actually found in "catapult".

Common Pronunciations
Common **ON** reading: **IN** (イン)
Common **kun** reading: **hi** (ひ)

As seen in the third example, this is another kanji that can act like 買. The **kun-yomi** can also become voiced in the second position, as happens in the fifth compound.

kun-yomi suggestion: "**hea**ve"

Create your **on-yomi** keyword and enter it in the table at the back of the book. After that, write your sentence to remember the **on-yomi** and **kun-yomi** readings in the box below.

COMMON WORDS AND COMPOUNDS		
引く	*to pull*	**hi**·ku ひ・く
引き 出す	pull + exit = *to withdraw* *(something)*	**hi**·**ki** da·su ひ・き だ・す
引出し	pull + exit = *a withdrawal;* *a drawer*	**hiki** da·shi ひき だ・し
引力	pull + strength = *gravitation*	**IN**·RYOKU イン・リョク
万引き	ten thousand + pull = *shoplifter*	**MAN** bi·ki マン び・き
引き受 ける	pull + receive = *to undertake*	**hi**·**ki** u·keru ひ・き う・ける
引き 上げる	pull + upper = *to pull up*	**hi**·**ki** a·geru ひ・き あ・げる

SAMPLE SENTENCE:

やっと 牛 を 川 から
yatto ushi o kawa kara
finally cow river from
引き上げました。
hi·ki a·gemashita.
pulled up
= *(We) finally pulled the cow from the river.*

Less Common Pronunciations
Less common **ON** reading: none
Less common **kun** reading: none

SECOND

BUILDING THIS KANJI
Crops 禾 + Few 少 (45) = 秒

Meaning
Second (of time or arc).

Remembering this kanji
"When **crops** are **few**," said the aid worker, "SECONDS count. Food needs to be rushed in, as the population will be growing weaker SECOND by SECOND."

Common Pronunciations
Common **ON** reading: **BYŌ** (ビョウ)
Common **kun** reading: none

Note that the sample sentence contains one of the less common **on-yomi** for "分" (Entry 124) in the compound "十五分".

Create your **on-yomi** keyword and enter it in the table at the back of the book. After that, write your sentence to remember the **on-yomi** reading in the box below.

Less Common Pronunciations
Less common **ON** reading: none
Less common **kun** reading: none

COMMON WORDS AND COMPOUNDS		
一秒	one + second = *one second*	ICHI·**BYŌ** イチ·ビョウ
五秒	five + second = *five seconds*	GO·**BYŌ** ゴ·ビョウ
秒読み	second + read = *countdown*	**BYŌ** yo·mi ビョウ よ·み

SAMPLE SENTENCE:

十五分　　二十秒 かかりました。
JŪ·GO·FUN　NI·JŪ·BYŌ kakarimashita.
fifteen minutes twenty seconds   took
= *It took fifteen minutes and twenty seconds.*

SHELL

Meaning
Shell. This is another character that rarely appears on its own. Like similar kanji we have encountered, however, it proves valuable as a component.

Remembering this kanji
This is another kanji to which we will give an external meaning – in this case, a fly swatter. Why a fly swatter? Well, you'll need one if you ever go down to the seashore to get SHELLS; flies are all over them at low tide.

Common Pronunciations
Common **ON** reading: **KŌ** (コウ)
Common **kun** reading: none

Write your sentence to remember the **on-yomi** reading in the box below.

Less Common Pronunciations
Less common **ON** reading: **KAN** (カン)
Less common **kun** reading: none

COMMON WORDS AND COMPOUND		
手の甲	hand + shell = *back of the hand*	te·no·**KŌ** て·の·コウ

SAMPLE SENTENCE:

上田さん は　手の甲　が かゆい。
Ue·da-san wa te·no·KŌ ga kayui.
Ueda-san   back of the hand   itchy
= *The back of Ueda-san's hand is itchy.*

COMPONENT #149

SKI JUMP

KANJI 149

気 **SPIRIT**

BUILDING THIS KANJI
Hammer ⌐ + One (hamburger patty) 一 (3) +
Ski Jump ⌐ + Banana Peels メ = 気

Meaning
This fascinating character encompasses a range
of meanings, including the ideas of "spirit",
"air", "feeling", and "mood". It is worth spending some time getting to know this kanji; it is
found in many common words and expressions.

Remembering this kanji
I wanted to be a **ski-jumper**, but the national
team crushed my SPIRIT when they left me off
the squad. Oddly, it wasn't long after this that I
grew to dislike everything about the sport, and
began sabotaging all the facilities I could find.
My method was simple: use a **hammer** to drive
hamburger patties into the **ski jump** so that the
athletes would be thrown off course, and leave
banana peels on the side so that the spectators
would slip. Isn't it strange what happens when
the SPIRIT moves you?

Common Pronunciations
Common **ON** reading: **KI** (キ)
Common **kun** reading: none

The sample sentence is an extremely common
greeting/question in Japanese. Create your
on-yomi keyword and enter it in the table at the
back of the book. After that, write your sentence to
remember the **on-yomi** reading in the box below.

Less Common Pronunciations
Less common **ON** reading: **KE** (ケ)
Less common **kun** reading: none

COMMON WORDS AND COMPOUNDS		
気	*spirit*	**KI** キ
元気	basis + spirit = *high spirits*	GEN·**KI** ゲン・キ
人気	person + spirit = *popularity*	NIN·**KI** ニン・キ
電気	electric + spirit = *electricity*	DEN·**KI** デン・キ
天気	heaven + spirit = *the weather*	TEN·**KI** テン・キ
気持ち	spirit + hold = *feeling*	**KI** mo·chi キ も·ち

SAMPLE SENTENCE:

元気 です か。
GEN·KI desu ka.
high spirits
= *How are you?*

KANJI 150

時 TIME

丨	冂	日	日	日一	日ˡ	昨一	昨二	時
時								

BUILDING THIS KANJI
Sun 日 (6) + Temple 寺 (104) = 時

Meaning
Time. This character will become familiar to you through its use in the hours of the day (the third and fourth compounds below are examples).

Remembering this kanji
The Incas developed a remarkable system of measuring TIME. The **sun temple** at Machu Picchu was of great importance in this respect, for it marked the exact TIME of the solstices.

Common Pronunciations
Common **ON** reading: JI (ジ)
Common **kun** reading: toki (と き)

Note how the final half of the second compound becomes voiced; this is an occasional feature of repeated compounds.

kun-yomi suggestion: "**stoke ee**ls"

Write your sentence to remember the **on-yomi** and **kun-yomi** readings in the box below.

Less Common Pronunciations
Less common **ON** reading: none
Less common **kun** reading: none

This irregular reading is very common.

IRREGULAR READING		
時計	time + measure = *watch; clock*	**to·KEI** と・ケイ

COMMON WORDS AND COMPOUNDS		
時	*time*	**toki** と き
時々	time + time = *sometimes*	**toki·doki** と き・ど き
四時	four + time = *four o'clock*	**yo·JI** よ・ジ
九時半	nine + time + half = *nine-thirty*	**KU·JI·HAN** ク・ジ・ハン
同時	same + time = *simultaneous*	**DŌ·JI** ド ウ・ジ

SAMPLE SENTENCE:

八時半　　に　　東口　　の
HACHI·JI·HAN ni higashi·guchi no
　eight-thirty　　east entrance
近く　で　会いましょう。
chika·ku de　　a·imashō.
　near　　　　 let's meet
= *Let's meet near the east entrance at eight-thirty.*

KANJI 151

話 **SPEAK**

`	一	二	三	三	言	言	言
計	訐	話	話				

BUILDING THIS KANJI
Say 言 (80) + Tongue 舌 (110) = 話

Meaning
Speak, along with the ideas of conversations and stories.

Remembering this kanji
"SPEAK freely."

"Though it is on the tip of my **tongue**, pharaoh, I dare not **say** it."

"Then I order you: SPEAK!"

I shriveled inwardly, knowing I would have to **say** it to avoid a **tongue**-lashing, or worse. "All right," I answered, shaking, "if you must know then, yes, it's true: those pants *do* tend to make you look big in the hips."

Pharaoh approached me with his headgear swaying menacingly. "I **say** to you this," he warned. "You will lose that **tongue** should you SPEAK of this further."

Common Pronunciations
Common **ON** reading: **WA** (ワ)
Common **kun** readings: **hanashi** (はなし); **hana** (はな)

As in the final example below, the **kun-yomi** for this kanji is always voiced in the second position.

kun-yomi suggestions: "**Hannah shi**elded"; "**Han a**mbassador"

Create your **on-yomi** keyword and enter it in the table at the back of the book. After that, write your sentence to remember the **on-yomi** and **kun-yomi** readings in the box below.

Less Common Pronunciations
Less common **ON** reading: none
Less common **kun** reading: none

COMMON WORDS AND COMPOUNDS		
話	story	**hanashi** はなし
話す	to speak	**hana·su** はな・す
話し好き	speak + like = talkative	**hana·shi zu·ki** はな・し ず・き
電話	electric + speak = telephone	**DEN·WA** デン・ワ
会話	meet + speak = conversation	**KAI·WA** カイ・ワ
立ち話	stand + speak = chatting while standing	ta·chi **banashi** た・ち ばなし

SAMPLE SENTENCE:

田中さん は フランス語 を 上手 に
Tana·ka-san wa Furansu·GO o JO·zu ni
Tanaka-san French well
話せます。
hana·semasu.
can speak
= *Tanaka-san can speak French well.*

KANJI 152

英 **ENGLISH**

BUILDING THIS KANJI
Wreath 艹 + Center 央(140) = 英

Meaning
Although a secondary meaning relates to "brilliance", this character will be far more familiar to you through its connection with all things English.

Remembering this kanji
To the ENGLISH, there can be only one object at the **center** of a **wreath**: the ENGLISH rose.

Common Pronunciations
Common **ON** reading: **EI** (エイ)
Common **kun** reading: none

Create your **on-yomi** keyword and enter it in the table at the back of the book. After that, write your sentence to remember the **on-yomi** reading in the box below.

Less Common Pronunciations
Less common **ON** reading: none
Less common **kun** reading: none

COMMON WORDS AND COMPOUNDS		
英語	English + words = *English (language)*	**EI·GO** エイ・ゴ
英国	English + country = *England*	**EI·KOKU** エイ・コク
英会話	English + meet + speak = *English conversation*	**EI·KAI·WA** エイ・カイ・ワ
日英	sun + English = *Japan and England*	**NICHI·EI** ニチ・エイ

SAMPLE SENTENCE:

英会話 は 日本 で
EI·KAI·WA **wa** **NI·HON** **de**
English conversation Japan
人気 が あります。
NIN·KI **ga** **arimasu.**
popular is
= *English conversation is popular in Japan.*

KANJI 153

訓 **INSTRUCTION**

BUILDING THIS KANJI
Say 言 (80) + River 川(70) = 訓

Meaning
Instruction. This kanji tends to give a more serious or spiritual sense of teaching to the compounds in which it appears.

Remembering this kanji

INSTRUCTION for **rivers**: "All right everyone, listen carefully to what I **say**. What you want to do is head for the ocean; that means going downhill. Also, keep up a good pace or you'll either turn into a swamp or one of those **rivers** without a current that everyone laughs at. Oh, and don't be afraid to overflow your banks now and then; if anyone asks what's going on, just **say** "that's what **rivers** are supposed to do". Follow these INSTRUCTIONS and you'll be fine."

Common Pronunciations
Common **ON** reading: **KUN** (クン)
Common **kun** reading: none

The first compound below presents another reading with which you may have become familiar. Now create your **on-yomi** keyword and enter it in the table at the back of the book. After that, write your sentence to remember the **on-yomi** reading in the box below.

Less Common Pronunciations
Less common **ON** reading: none
Less common **kun** reading: none

COMMON WORDS AND COMPOUNDS		
訓読み	instruction + read = *the **kun-yomi***	**KUN** yo·mi クン よ·み
訓話	instruction + speak = *moral discourse*	**KUN·WA** クン·ワ

SAMPLE SENTENCE:

これ を 訓読み で 読んで 下さい。
kore o KUN yo·mi de yo·nde kuda·sai.
this   kun-yomi   read   please
= *Please read this with kun-yomi.*

 PUSH

BUILDING THIS KANJI
Finger 扌 + Shell (Fly swatter) 甲 (148) = 押

Meaning
"Push", together with the ideas of "suppression" and "restraint". This kanji also serves as the partner to "引" (Entry 146) on door signs.

Remembering this kanji
OK, then, your **fingers** are now gripping the **fly swatter**. Excellent. The next step is simple: in order to kill the fly, PUSH the **fly swatter** away from you with a PUSHING motion.

Common Pronunciations
Common **ON** reading: none
Common **kun** reading: **o** (お)

As indicated by the last two examples below, this is another kanji that often shows up in the manner of 買.

kun-yomi suggestion: "orangutan"

Create your sentence to remember the **kun-yomi** reading in the box below.

Less Common Pronunciations
Less common **ON** reading: Ō (オウ)
Less common **kun** reading: none

COMMON WORDS AND COMPOUNDS		
押す	*to push*	o·su お·す
押し出す	push + exit = *to push out*	o·shi da·su お·し だ·す
押し上げる	push + upper = *to push up*	o·shi a·geru お·し あ·げる
押し開ける	push + open = *to push open*	o·shi a·keru お·し あ·ける
押入れ	push + enter = *closet*	**oshi** i·re おし い·れ
押売	push + sell = *high-pressure sales*	**oshi**·uri おし·うり

SAMPLE SENTENCE:

押入れ の 中 に 物 が 少ない。
oshi i·re no naka ni mono ga suku·nai.
　closet　　middle　　things　　few
= *There aren't many things in the closet.*

COMPONENT #155

WHIRLING DERVISH 　中　

KANJI 155

 年 **YEAR**

BUILDING THIS KANJI
Hammer ⸜ + Whirling Dervish 中 = 年

Meaning
Year.

Remembering this kanji
One of the events at the track and field championships is starting to become controversial: the **hammer** toss. Why? Simply because a **whirling dervish** wins it every YEAR. Athletes unable to whirl as quickly have complained that the **dervishes** have an unfair advantage. YEAR after YEAR of winning, it seems, can bring YEAR after YEAR of envy.

Common Pronunciations
Common **ON** reading: **NEN** (ネン)
Common **kun** reading: **toshi** (とし)

kun-yomi suggestion: "lotto sheet"

Create your **on-yomi** keyword and enter it in the table at the back of the book. After that, write your sentence to remember the **on-yomi** and **kun-yomi** readings in the box below.

Less Common Pronunciations
Less common **ON** reading: none
Less common **kun** reading: none

<table>
<tr><td colspan="3">COMMON WORDS AND COMPOUNDS</td></tr>
<tr><td>年</td><td>year</td><td>toshi
とし</td></tr>
<tr><td>年上</td><td>year + upper
= older</td><td>toshi·ue
とし·うえ</td></tr>
<tr><td>年下</td><td>year + lower
= younger</td><td>toshi·shita
とし·した</td></tr>
<tr><td>新年</td><td>new + year
= the New Year</td><td>SHIN·NEN
シン·ネン</td></tr>
<tr><td>中年</td><td>middle + year
= middle age</td><td>CHŪ·NEN
チュウ·ネン</td></tr>
<tr><td>一年生</td><td>one + year + life
= first-year student</td><td>ICHI·NEN·SEI
イチ·ネン·セイ</td></tr>
</table>

SAMPLE SENTENCE:

青木さん　は　　　三年生　　　です。
Ao·ki-san　wa　SAN·NEN·SEI　　desu.
Aoki-san　　　　third-year student
= *Aoki-san is a third-year student.*

KANJI 156

来 **COME**

BUILDING THIS KANJI
One (hamburger patty) 一(3) + Rice 米(32)
= 来

Meaning
Come. As the final four compounds below make clear, the related meaning of "next" is also included.

Remembering this kanji
"COME on, everyone, dig in!"

I didn't want to be rude, but a **hamburger patty** on a pile of uncooked **rice**? COME on! Not to mention the noise we all made as we crunched our way through the grains… Really, it was enough to make me wish I hadn't COME to the **patty** and **rice** festival at all.

Common Pronunciations
Common **ON** reading: **RAI** (ライ)
Common **kun** reading: **ku** (く)

This character is infamous for being one of only two irregular verbs in Japanese, but whereas "to do" (為る) is rarely presented with its kanji (it is now universally written in **hiragana**), "to come" still is. What this means for us is that the character can be read variously as "**ku**" (く), "**ki**" (き) or "**ko**" (こ), depending on which tense of the verb is being used. The sample sentence offers an example of the polite past tense. Note, however, an important exception in the second compound below (an extremely common word); when following the kanji "出", 来 is always read "**ki**". Lucky for us there are only two odd verbs in Japanese!

kun-yomi suggestion: "**cool**"

Create your **on-yomi** keyword and enter it in the table at the back of the book. After that, write your sentence to remember the **on-yomi** and **kun-yomi** readings in the box below.

This reading applies to only a pair of words: **ki·tasu** (来たす) "to be forthcoming", and **ki·taru** (来たる) "coming". This latter word is used as an adjective.

COMMON WORDS AND COMPOUNDS		
来る	*to come*	ku·ru く・る
出来る	exit + come = *to be able to*	de ki·ru で き・る
来週	come + week = *next week*	**RAI·SHŪ** ライ・シュウ
来月	come + moon = *next month*	**RAI·GETSU** ライ・ゲツ
来年	come + year = *next year*	**RAI·NEN** ライ・ネン
来春	come + spring = *next spring*	**RAI·SHUN** ライ・シュン

SAMPLE SENTENCE:

先生　　は　　一週間　　前　　に
SEN·SEI　wa　IS·SHŪ·KAN　mae　ni
teacher　　　one week　　before
来ました。
ki·mashita.
came
= *The teacher came a week ago.*

Less Common Pronunciations
Less common **ON** reading: none
Less common **kun** reading: **ki** (き)

COMPONENT #157

CLAW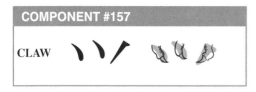

KANJI 157

学 **STUDY**

BUILDING THIS KANJI
Claw ⺍ + UFO ⼍ + Child 子(56) = 学

Meaning
This character appears in words related to study and learning. When used as a suffix, it is often equivalent to the English "-ology". The final compound offers such an example.

Remembering this kanji
"I don't want to STUDY," the **child** said. "You can't make me."

"Oh, really?" the teacher replied. "Don't you know what happens to a **child** who doesn't STUDY? A **UFO** flies down to get them."

"Is that so?" said the **child**, now sauntering to the blackboard. "And when the **UFO** arrives, will my screams be like this? Like **claws** scraping down a blackboard?"

"No! Don't do that!"

"Then what happens if I refuse to STUDY?"

"Nothing! You become very successful!"

So it was true, then, thought the other students: there really was no need to STUDY.

Common Pronunciations
Common **ON** reading: **GAKU** (ガク)
Common **kun** reading: **mana** (まな)

kun-yomi suggestion: "**man a**nswer"

Create your **on-yomi** keyword and enter it in the table at the back of the book. After that, write your sentence to remember the **on-yomi** and **kun-yomi** readings in the box below.

Less Common Pronunciations
Less common **ON** reading: none
Less common **kun** reading: none

COMMON WORDS AND COMPOUNDS		
学ぶ	to study	**mana**·bu まな·ぶ
大学	large + study = university	DAI·**GAKU** ダイ·ガク
学生	study + life = student	**GAKU**·SEI ガク·セイ
休学	rest + study = absence from school	KYŪ·**GAKU** キュウ·ガク
語学	words + study = linguistics	GO·**GAKU** ゴ·ガク
生物学	life + thing + study = biology	SEI·BUTSU·**GAKU** セイ·ブツ·ガク

SAMPLE SENTENCE:
この 家 には　 大学生　 が 多い。
kono ie   ni wa DAI·GAKU·SEI ga   ō·i.
 this house   university students   many
= *There are many university students in this house.*

KANJI 158

意 MIND

`	一	宀	立	立	产	音	音	音
音	意	意	意					

BUILDING THIS KANJI
Sound 音 (137) + Heart 心 (25) = 意

Meaning
Mind/Thought. This abstract character appears in many compounds conveying the ideas of "will", "intention" and "opinion", etc.

Remembering this kanji

Juliet : Take me in your arms, Romeo.

Romeo : My darling.

Juliet : The **sound** of your **heart**…it fills my **MIND**.

Romeo : Sorry, what's that?

Juliet : My **MIND**, it's filled with the **sound** of your **heart**.

Romeo : Oh…um…that's great.

Juliet : What do you mean "that's great"?
(stepping Is that the best you can do? Doesn't
back) this moment inspire anything more eloquent than that?

Romeo : Hey look, I've got a lot on my **MIND**, OK? Finals are coming up, I've got an important stag hunt this weekend, my cousin's wedding is just around the corner…oh, never **MIND**.

Common Pronunciations
Common **ON** reading: **I** (イ)
Common **kun** reading: none

Create your **on-yomi** keyword and enter it in the table at the back of the book. After that, write your sentence to remember the **on-yomi** reading in the box below.

Less Common Pronunciations
Less common **ON** reading: none
Less common **kun** reading: none

COMMON WORDS AND COMPOUNDS		
意思	mind + think = (one's) intent	I·SHI イ・シ
意図	mind + diagram = (one's) aim	I·TO イ・ト
意外	mind + outside = unforeseen	I·GAI イ・ガイ
意見	mind + see = opinion	I·KEN イ・ケン
意気	mind + spirit = morale	I·KI イ・キ
注意	pour + mind = attention	CHŪ·I チュウ・イ

SAMPLE SENTENCE:
あなた の 意見 が 分かりません。
anata   no I·KEN ga   wa·karimasen.
you   opinion   don't understand
= *I don't understand your opinion.*

KANJI 159

又 **AGAIN**

フ	又						

Meaning

Again/Also. Though this character will rarely be encountered on its own (indeed, it is often written in **hiragana**), it does serve as a component in several important kanji. Like other characters we have encountered of this type, we will assign a meaning with a more immediate visual connection: an ironing board.

Remembering this kanji

"Do it AGAIN," ordered the headmistress. AGAIN and AGAIN I brought out the **ironing board**; AGAIN and AGAIN I failed to get rid of the wrinkles.

Common Pronunciations

Common **ON** reading: none
Common **kun** reading: **mata** (また)

kun-yomi suggestion: "**mat a**ctivity"

Note how the second kanji in the final example below is voiced. The pronunciation of "来なか った" in the sample sentence, incidentally, is the informal past tense reading of "来". There is no **on-yomi** reading for this character. Create your sentence to remember the **kun-yomi** reading in the box below.

Less Common Pronunciations

Less common **ON** reading: none
Less common **kun** reading: none

COMMON WORDS AND COMPOUNDS		
又	*again*	**mata** また
又々	again + again = *once again*	**mata·mata** また・また
又聞き	again + hear = *hearsay*	**mata·giki** また・ぎき

SAMPLE SENTENCE:

北川さん　は　又　来なかったよ。

Kita·gawa-san wa mata   ko·nakatta yo.
Kitagawa-san   again   didn't come
= *Kitagawa-san didn't come again!*

COMPONENT #160

ANTEATER 小

KANJI 160

赤 **RED**

BUILDING THIS KANJI
Earth 土 (87) + Anteater 小 = 赤

Meaning
Red.

Remembering this kanji
It's pretty obvious what this **anteater** is doing: looking for RED ants in the RED, RED **earth**.

Common Pronunciations
Common **ON** reading: SEKI (セキ)
Common **kun** reading: aka (あか)

kun-yomi suggestion: "stack apples"

Create your **on-yomi** keyword and enter it in the table at the back of the book. After that, write your sentence to remember the **on-yomi** and **kun-yomi** readings in the box below.

Less Common Pronunciations
Less common **ON** reading: SHAKU (シャク)
Less common **kun** reading: none

COMMON WORDS AND COMPOUNDS		
赤	red (noun)	aka あか
赤い	red (adjective)	aka·i あか·い
赤ちゃん	baby	aka·chan あか·ちゃん
赤道	red + road = equator	SEKI·DŌ セキ·ドウ

SAMPLE SENTENCE:

あの 赤い 花 は 美しい です ね。
ano aka·i hana wa utsuku·shii desu ne.
that red flower beautiful isn't it
= *That red flower is beautiful, isn't it?*

CHAPTER 8 REVIEW EXERCISES

A. Please match the following kanji to their meanings.

1. 又   a. Horse

2. 話   b. Again

3. 馬   c. Shell

4. 赤   d. Speak

5. 近   e. Push

6. 訓   f. Pull

7. 引   g. Near

8. 甲   h. Study

9. 押   i. Red

10. 学   j. Instruction

B. Please match the following meanings to their kanji, and these to their **on** or **kun-yomi**.

1. Time   a. 失   1. **toshi** (とし)

2. Year   b. 年   2. **EI** (エイ)

3. Bow   c. 気   3. **SHŪ** (シュウ)

4. Mind   d. 秒   4. **I** (イ)

5. Spirit   e. 来   5. **ushina** (うしな)

6. Come   f. 弓   6. **BYŌ** (ビョウ)

7. Lose   g. 英   7. **RAI** (ライ)

8. Week   h. 意   8. **KI** (キ)

9. Second   i. 週   9. **yumi** (ゆみ)

10. English j. 時   10. **toki** (とき)

C. Please choose the best answer(s) to the following questions.

1. Which of the following readings apply to the kanji 赤?
   a. **KAN** (カン)
   b. **aka** (あか)
   c. **ON** (オン)
   d. **o** (お)
   e. **SEKI** (セキ)

2. I wasn't popular on my tug-of-war team because I always liked to ___.
   a. 秒
   b. 赤
   c. 近
   d. 押
   e. 年

3. Which of the following readings apply to the kanji 馬?
   a. **BA** (バ)
   b. **NEN** (ネン)
   c. **uma** (うま)
   d. **KI** (キ)
   e. **hana** (はな)

4. Which of the following readings apply to the kanji 近?
   a. **TA** (タ)
   b. **toki** (とき)
   c. **hi** (ひ)
   d. **chika** (ちか)
   e. **KIN** (キン)

5. Which of the following readings apply to the kanji 話?
   a. **hana** (はな)
   b. **YŪ** (ユウ)
   c. **hanashi** (はなし)
   d. **WA** (ワ)
   e. **mi** (み)

D. Please choose the best answer(s) to the following questions.

1. Which is the correct reading of 引く?
   a. **o·ku** (お・く)
   b. **ki·ku** (き・く)
   c. **yu·ku** (ゆ・く)
   d. **hi·ku** (ひ・く)

2. Which is the correct reading of 学ぶ?
   a. **a·bu** (あ・ぶ)
   b. **mana·bu** (ま な・ぶ)
   c. **kara·bu** (か ら・ぶ)
   d. **yo·bu** (よ・ぶ)

3. Which of the following kanji has the most number of strokes?
   a. 週
   b. 馬
   c. 訓
   d. 時
   e. 秒

4. Which is the correct reading of 押す?
   a. **o·su** (お・す)
   b. **ama·su** (あ ま・す)
   c. **ko·su** (こ・す)
   d. **hi·su** (ひ・す)

5. Which kanji would come next in the following series: 日....週....月....?
   a. 秒
   b. 来
   c. 年
   d. 弓
   e. 引

E. Please match the following compounds and words to their meanings and pronunciations.

1. 週間   a. English (language)   1. **o·shi da·su** (お・し だ・す)

2. 生物学   b. Week   2. **MAN bi·ki** (マ ン び・き)

3. 英語   c. Conversation   3. **SEI· BUTSU· GAKU** (セイ・ ブ ツ・ ガ ク)

4. 押し出す   d. Four o'clock   4. **KAI·WA** (カ イ・ワ)

5. 来年   e. Feeling   5. **SHŪ·KAN** (シュ ウ・ カ ン)

6. 四時   f. To push out   6. **RAI·NEN** (ライ・ネ ン)

7. 赤道   g. Equator   7. **KI mo·chi** (キ も・ち)

8. 万引き   h. Biology   8. **SEKI·DŌ** (セ キ・ ド ウ)

9. 会話   i. Shoplifter   9. **EI·GO** (エ イ・ゴ)

10. 気持ち   j. Next year   10. **yo·JI** (よ・ジ)

Kanji #161—180

KANJI 161

公 **PUBLIC**

ノ	八	厶	公			

BUILDING THIS KANJI
Eight (volcano) 八(19) + Broken Crutch 厶
= 公

Meaning
Public. In many instances, this character serves as the opposite to "私" (Entry 131).

Remembering this kanji
The eruption of a **volcano** is a very PUBLIC event, but nobody suffers more than those on **crutches** who are blown off their feet. After all, if you're hobbling along with **broken crutches** as a result of this, you might as well carry a sign that announces "Stay Away: I'm Really Unlucky". It's a very PUBLIC humiliation.

Common Pronunciations
Common **ON** reading: **KŌ** (コ ウ)
Common **kun** reading: none

Write your sentence to remember the **on-yomi** reading in the box below.

Less Common Pronunciations
Less common **ON** reading: **KU** (ク)
Less common **kun** reading: **ōyake** (おおやけ)

COMMON WORDS AND COMPOUNDS		
公有	public + have = *publicly owned*	**KŌ·YŪ** コウ·ユウ
公安	public + ease = *public peace*	**KŌ·AN** コウ·アン
公開	public + open = *open to the public*	**KŌ·KAI** コウ·カイ
公金	public + gold (money) = *public funds*	**KŌ·KIN** コウ·キン
公道	public + road = *public road*	**KŌ·DŌ** コウ·ドウ
公会	public + meet = *public meeting*	**KŌ·KAI** コウ·カイ

SAMPLE SENTENCE:
ここ は 公道 です。
koko wa KŌ·DŌ desu.
 this public road
= *This is a public road.*

KANJI 162

巾 **CLOTH**

Ⅰ	冂	巾					

BUILDING THIS KANJI
Gorilla 冂 + Pole Ⅰ = 巾

Meaning
Cloth, rag. As the lack of compounds below indicates, this character will prove to be of more use to us as a component in other kanji.

Remembering this kanji
And so the **gorilla** won the **pole**-vaulting competition and was given a CLOTH as a prize. Why a CLOTH? Well, a medal or trophy was judged to be of no use at all to a **gorilla**, whereas a CLOTH, at the very least, could be used to wipe the **pole**.

Common Pronunciations
Common **ON** reading: **KIN** (キン)
Common **kun** reading: none

Write your sentence to remember the **on-yomi** reading in the box below.

Less Common Pronunciations
Less common **ON** reading: none
Less common **kun** reading: **haba** (はば)

COMMON WORDS AND COMPOUNDS		
巾	*cloth, rag*	KIN キン
巾着	cloth + wear = *pouch (for coins, etc.)*	KIN·CHAKU キン・チャク

SAMPLE SENTENCE:

あそこ　に　　　巾着　　　を　掛けて
asoko　**ni**　**KIN·CHAKU**　**o**　**ka·kete**
over there　　　pouch　　　　　　hang
下さい。
kuda·sai
　please
= *Please hang the pouch over there.*

KANJI 163

市 **CITY**

'	一	亠	巾	市			

BUILDING THIS KANJI
Police 亠 + Cloth 巾 (162) = 市

Meaning
City. A secondary meaning relates to "market"; in this sense the character can refer to anything from a simple fair to the idea of a general "business" market. This will be the first of four kanji in Chapter 9 connected with groups of people living in a defined area; moving from larger to smaller units will provide a sense of their relative sizes.

Remembering this kanji

One of the **policeman** grabbed a **cloth**. "All right, guys," he said, "you all heard what the captain said: let's get out there and clean up this CITY!" Numamura could only sigh as he watched his officers hurriedly picking up **cloths**. The CITY crime sweep, it seemed, was already off to a rocky start.

Common Pronunciations

Common **ON** reading: **SHI** (シ)
Common **kun** reading: none

Write your sentence to remember the **on-yomi** reading in the box below.

Less Common Pronunciations

Less common **ON** reading: none
Less common **kun** reading: **ichi** (い ち)

This **kun-yomi** occurs in compounds when the kanji carries its secondary meaning of "market" or "fair".

COMMON WORDS AND COMPOUNDS		
市	city	**SHI** シ
市内	city + inside = *within the city*	**SHI·NAI** シ・ナイ
市外	city + outside = *outside the city*	**SHI·GAI** シ・ガイ
市立	city + stand = *municipal*	**SHI·RITSU** シ・リツ
市有	city + have = *city-owned*	**SHI·YŪ** シ・ユウ

SAMPLE SENTENCE:

夜　は　一人　で　市内　を
yoru wa　hito·ri　de　SHI·NAI　o
night　one person　　within the city

歩かないで　下さい。
aru·kanaide　kuda·sai.
don't walk　　please

= *Please don't walk alone at night in the city.*

主　**PRIMARY**

BUILDING THIS KANJI
Jelly Bean 丶 + King 王(23) = 主

Meaning

This character conveys a sense of importance and authority; it is used in this vein with both concrete objects and abstract ideas. Note the difference between this kanji and that for "Jewel" in Entry 24 (玉).

Remembering this kanji

The PRIMARY reason a **king** puts a **jelly bean** on his head is to learn from the reaction it generates amongst his subjects. If no one dares tell him it's there, the **king** knows he is ruling PRIMARILY by fear. If it is pointed out to him with a smile, however, he knows he is viewed PRIMARILY with kindness.

Common Pronunciations

Common **ON** reading: **SHU** (シュ)
Common **kun** reading: **nushi** (ぬし)

kun-yomi suggestion: "**new shears**"

Write your sentence to remember the **on-yomi** and **kun-yomi** readings in the box below.

Less Common Pronunciations

Less common **ON** reading: **SU** (ス)
Less common **kun** reading: **omo** (おも)

COMMON WORDS AND COMPOUNDS		
主力	primary + strength = *main force*	SHU·RYOKU シュ・リョク
主人公	primary + person + public = *main character*	SHU·JIN·KŌ シュ・ジン・コウ
売主	sell + primary = *seller*	uri·**nushi** うり・ぬし
持主	hold + primary = *owner*	mochi·**nushi** もち・ぬし

SAMPLE SENTENCE:

主人公　は　有名　な
SHU·JIN·KŌ wa YŪ·MEI na
main character　　　famous
美人　　　　です。
BI·JIN　　　　desu.
beautiful woman
= *The main character is a famously beautiful woman.*

KANJI 165

丁

BLOCK

Meaning

The main sense is of a city "block", although more obscure meanings can range from "pages" to "polite". This is a quirky character that shows up often as a component in other kanji.

Remembering this kanji

Let's face it: this looks like a capital "T", so best think of it as an overhead view of a "T" junction marking the intersection of **BLOCKS**.

Common Pronunciations

Common **ON** reading: **CHŌ** (チョウ)
Common **kun** reading: none

Write your sentence to remember the **on-yomi** reading in the box below.

Less Common Pronunciations

Less common **ON** reading: **TEI** (テイ)

Less common **kun** reading: none

COMMON WORDS AND COMPOUNDS		
丁目	block + eye = *city block area*	**CHŌ**·me チョウ·め
二丁目	two + block + eye = *City Block 2*	**NI**·**CHŌ**·me ニ·チョウ·め
四丁目	four + block + eye = *City Block 4*	yon·**CHŌ**·me よん·チョウ·め

SAMPLE SENTENCE:

私　　の　新しい　　家　　は

watashi　no　atara·shii　ie　wa

my　　　　　new　　house

五丁目　　に　あります。

GO·CHŌ·me　ni　arimasu.

City Block 5　　　　　　is

= *My new house is in City Block 5.*

KANJI 166

 友 FRIEND

一 ナ 方 友

BUILDING THIS KANJI

Superhero ナ + Again (ironing board) 又 (159) = 友

Meaning

Friend. The first two strokes are written in the same order as Entry 48 ("左").

Remembering this kanji

"I just think you're taking me for granted as a FRIEND," said the **superhero**.

"What do you mean? All I asked you to do was pick up an **ironing board** for me. That's something any FRIEND would do."

"Yeah, but I mean…it's embarrassing to fly with an **ironing board**. I look ridiculous."

"You need to quit worrying about the opinions of others. And don't make that face; I'm telling you this as a FRIEND."

Common Pronunciations

Common **ON** reading: **YŪ** (ユウ)

Common **kun** reading: **tomo** (とも)

kun-yomi suggestion: "lot**to mo**ment"

Write your sentence to remember the **on-yomi** and **kun-yomi** readings in the box below.

Less Common Pronunciations

Less common **ON** reading: none

Less common **kun** reading: none

COMMON WORDS AND COMPOUNDS		
友	*friend*	**tomo** とも
友人	friend + person = *friend*	**YŪ**·**JIN** ユウ·ジン
友好	friend + like = *friendship*	**YŪ**·**KŌ** ユウ·コウ

SAMPLE SENTENCE:

西山さん　の　友人　は　　南米

Nishi·yama-san　no　YŪ·JIN wa　NAN·BEI

Nishiyama-san　　friend　　South America

から　来ました。

kara　ki·mashita.

from　　came

= *Nishiyama-san's friend came from South America*

KANJI 167

 GROUP

BUILDING THIS KANJI
Prison 囗 + Tiny (soccer player) 寸(103) = 団

Meaning
Group. Good luck making sense of the third example below!

Remembering this kanji
When they first arrive in **prison**, **tiny** soccer players will always huddle together in a GROUP. This behavior draws the attention of the regular cons, and a GROUP of them will soon approach the newcomers with welcoming smiles.

Common Pronunciations
Common **ON** reading: **DAN** (ダ ン)
Common **kun** reading: none

Write your sentence to remember the **on-yomi** reading in the box below.

Less Common Pronunciations
Less common **ON** reading: **TON** (ト ン)
Less common **kun** reading: none

TON is found only in the well-known Japanese word for bedding: **FU·TON** (フ・ト ン), composed of the kanji 布団 (Spread* + Group).

COMMON WORDS AND COMPOUNDS		
一団	one + group = *a group*	**ICHI·DAN** イ チ・ダ ン
団体	group + body = *organization*	**DAN·TAI** ダ ン・タ イ
団子	group + child = *dumpling*	**DAN·go** ダ ン・ご
入団	enter + group = *joining (a group)*	**NYŪ·DAN** ニ ュ ウ・ダ ン

SAMPLE SENTENCE:

内田さん は 団子 が 好き です。
Uchi·da-san wa DAN·go ga su·ki desu.
Uchida-san   dumplings   likes
= *Uchida-san likes dumplings.*

COMPONENT #168

ROWER

KANJI 168

BUILDING THIS KANJI
Hammer ⼀ + Rower 毋 = 毎

Meaning
Every.

 EVERY

Remembering this kanji

"How long you been a **rower**?"

"A while. I was on the crew that took Caesar to North Africa. You?"

"Just started."

"Well, all you have to remember is this: when the **hammer** comes down, you row. EVERY minute of EVERY hour of EVERY boring day. Not that I'm bitter, though. Like EVERY other guy here, all I want is a little variety in the beat."

Common Pronunciations

Common **ON** reading: **MAI** (マイ)

Common **kun** reading: none

Note the mix of readings in the last three examples. Write your sentence to remember the **on-yomi** reading in the box below.

Less Common Pronunciations

Less common **ON** reading: none

Less common **kun** reading: **goto** (ごと)

COMMON WORDS AND COMPOUNDS		
毎日	every + sun (day) = *daily*	**MAI**·NICHI マイ・ニチ
毎週	every + week = *weekly*	**MAI**·SHŪ マイ・シュウ
毎月	every + moon (month) = *monthly*	**MAI**·tsuki マイ・つき
毎年	every + year = *yearly*	**MAI**·toshi マイ・とし
毎朝	every + morning = *every morning*	**MAI**·asa マイ・あさ

SAMPLE SENTENCE:

私	は	毎朝	父	と
watashi	**wa**	**MAI·asa**	**chichi**	**to**
I		every morning	my father	

話	を	します。
hanashi	**o**	**shimasu.**
speak		

= *I speak with my father every morning.*

COMPONENT #169

WEIGHTLIFTER 穴

KANJI 169

空 **EMPTY**

'	'	宀	宀	穴	空	空	空

BUILDING THIS KANJI

Weightlifter 穴 + **Craft** 工(47) = 空

Meaning

Empty/Sky. As in English, "empty" can incorporate suggestions of uselessness and futility.

Remembering this kanji

Like a lot of students, I became a **weightlifter** at college and practiced my **craft** well. First up were EMPTY cans – I could curl a lot of those. Next came EMPTY bottles, followed by EMPTY kegs. It was only later that I realized how EMPTY the **craft** of **weightlifting** beer really was.

Common Pronunciations

Common **ON** reading: **KŪ** (ク ウ)
Common **kun** readings: **sora** (そ ら); **kara** (か ら)

This kanji takes a bit of work, although **KŪ** is by far the most common reading in compounds. **sora**, as shown in the first example, means "sky"; it becomes voiced in the second position (as in the compound following). **kara** occasionally appears in first position with a meaning of "empty", and is a reading you will no doubt be familiar with from the third example.

kun-yomi suggestions: "**soar a**lbatross"; "**cara**mba"

Create your **on-yomi** keyword and enter it in the table at the back of the book. After that, write your sentence to remember the **on-yomi** and **kun-yomi** readings in the box below.

Less Common Pronunciations

Less common **ON** reading: none
Less common **kun** reading: **a** (あ)

This reading is used to make the verbs 空く and 空ける (**a·ku** and **a·keru**). Meaning "to open", these can be thought of as interchangeable with the more common 開く and 開ける (also **a·ku** and **a·keru**) from Entry 106. A few nouns, however, make use of this kanji exclusively: 空 き缶*(**a·ki KAN**) "an empty can", and 空き瓶* (**a·ki BIN**) "an empty bottle", are two examples.

COMMON WORDS AND COMPOUNDS		
空	*sky*	**sora** そら
青空	blue + empty (sky) = *blue sky*	**ao·zora** あお・ぞら
空手	empty + hand = *karate*	**kara·te** から・て
空間	empty + interval = *space*	**KŪ·KAN** ク ウ・カ ン
空気	empty + spirit = *air*	**KŪ·KI** ク ウ・キ

SAMPLE SENTENCE:

朝 の 空 は きれい です よ。
asa   no   sora   wa   kirei   desu   yo.
morning   sky   lovely
= *The morning sky is lovely!*

町 **TOWN**

| 一 | 冂 | 冂 | 田 | 田 | 田 | 町 | 町 | | |

BUILDING THIS KANJI
Rice Field 田 (73) + Block 丁 (165) = 町

Meaning
Town. One size smaller than a city is the town, making this the second of our four kanji related to people living in defined locations. This character can also refer on occasion to a "street" or an "alley".

Remembering this kanji
"TOWN! TOWN!"

Strong and clear it resounded over the **rice fields**. From **block** to **block** it was heard in the neighborhoods.

"TOWN! TOWN!"

In all honesty, though, nobody could really see the point of the TOWN crier.

Common Pronunciations
Common **ON** reading: **CHŌ** (チョウ)
Common **kun** reading: **machi** (まち)

Write your sentence to remember the **on-yomi** and **kun-yomi** readings in the box below.

Less Common Pronunciations
Less common **ON** reading: none
Less common **kun** reading: none

COMMON WORDS AND COMPOUNDS		
町	town	**machi** まち
町内	town + inside = *in the town*	**CHŌ·NAI** チョウ·ナイ
町立	town + stand = *established by the town*	**CHŌ·RITSU** チョウ·リツ
町会	town + meet = *town assembly*	**CHŌ·KAI** チョウ·カイ

SAMPLE SENTENCE:

この　町　の　ラーメン　は　有名
kono　machi　no　rāmen　wa　YŪ·MEI
this　town　　　ramen　　　famous
です。
desu.
= *This town's ramen is famous.*

犬 **DOG**

| 一 | ナ | 大 | 犬 | | | | |

BUILDING THIS KANJI
Large (sumo wrestler) 大 (17) + Jelly Bean ヽ
= 犬

Meaning
Dog.

Remembering this kanji
Only a **jelly bean** dangled next to his head could make a **sumo wrestler** jump up like a **DOG**.

Common Pronunciations
Common **ON** reading: **KEN** (ケン)
Common **kun** reading: **inu** (いぬ)

kun-yomi suggestion: "**enu**merate"

Write your sentence to remember the **on-yomi** and **kun-yomi** readings in the box below.

Less Common Pronunciations
Less common **ON** reading: none
Less common **kun** reading: none

COMMON WORDS AND COMPOUNDS		
犬	*dog*	**inu** いぬ
子犬	child + dog = *puppy*	ko·**inu** こ·いぬ
秋田犬	autumn + rice field + dog = *an Akita dog*	aki·ta·**KEN** あき·た·ケン
愛犬	love + dog = *pet dog*	AI·**KEN** アイ·ケン
愛犬家	love + dog + house = *dog lover*	AI·**KEN**·KA アイ·ケン·カ

SAMPLE SENTENCE:

古川さん　が　子犬　を　買いました
Furu·kawa-san ga ko·inu o ka·imashita.
  Furukawa-san   puppy   bought
= *Furukawa-san bought a puppy.*

KANJI 172

死 **DEATH**

BUILDING THIS KANJI
One (top of a bun) 一 (3) + **Evening** 夕 (108) + **Beggar** ヒ = 死

Meaning
Death.

Remembering this kanji
"So how did DEATH arrive for you?" she asked the **beggar**.

  "It was weird," he said. "I was begging on my usual corner when I noticed it starting to get dark. "Is it **evening** already?" I wondered. I looked up to check, but realized I was mistaken, that what I had thought was **evening** was actually the **top of a bun** settling over me. Now, you would have thought I'd be scared by this, but I wasn't; the bun was really warm and smelled great, and for the first time in ages I didn't feel hungry. I wasn't afraid of DEATH at all."

Common Pronunciations
Common **ON** reading: **SHI** (シ)
Common **kun** reading: **shi** (し)

It is a welcome event when both types of reading for a kanji are identical like this; truly, death can sometimes be kind!

kun-yomi suggestion: "**sheet**"

Write your sentence to remember the **on-yomi** and **kun-yomi** readings in the box below.

COMMON WORDS AND COMPOUNDS		
死ぬ	to die	**shi**·nu し・ぬ
水死	water + death = *drowning*	**SUI**·**SHI** スイ・シ
死体	death + body = *dead body*	**SHI**·TAI シ・タイ
死火山	death + fire + mountain = *extinct volcano*	**SHI**·KA·ZAN シ・カ・ザン

SAMPLE SENTENCE:

私　　の　好きな　馬　は
watashi　no　su·ki　na　uma　wa
　my　　　like　　horse
五年前　　　に　死にました。
GO·NEN·mae　　ni　　shi·nimashita.
five years ago　　　　died
= *My horse that I liked died five years ago.*

Less Common Pronunciations
Less common **ON** reading: none
Less common **kun** reading: none

RAZOR

KANJI 173

行 **GO**

BUILDING THIS KANJI
Razor 彳 + One (hamburger patty) 一 (3) +
Block 丁 (165) = 行

Meaning
"Go" is the primary meaning of this character, along with related ideas of "carrying out" or "doing". Far less common is the secondary sense of a "stroke" or "line" of text.

Remembering this kanji
When the **razor** moved into our neighborhood, no one in the **block** knew quite what to do. "How can it fit in with us?" I asked my wife. "**GO** and invite it to our **block** party," she said. I didn't want to do this, of course, but this turned out to be a great idea, for the **razor** was a big hit when it came time to prepare the **hamburger patties** that day. Shaving each one perfectly, it soon had everyone cheering "**GO! GO! GO!**" as it worked faster and faster. "You know something, honey?" I said to my wife. "Looks like the **razor's** going to fit in well with our **block** after all. You were right telling me to **GO** and invite it here."

Common Pronunciations
Common **ON** reading: **KŌ** (コウ)
Common **kun** readings: **i** (い); **yu** (ゆ)

his is another character for our rogues' gallery f troublesome kanji, and one that merits added ttention from the outset. For the general sense of ie verb "to go", **i·ku** (い・く) is the choice; **yu·ku** ゆ・く) is employed far less often and is of most se in a few specific compounds (such as in the econd example), or as a suffix meaning "bound or" (as in the third). It can also act like 買, albeit trangely in that on rare occasions it will incorpo- te **yuku** as opposed to **yuki**. This is seen in the vell-known compound **yuku·e·FU·MEI** (ゆ く・ え・フ・メ イ) 行方不明: "Missing", built from ie two words "whereabouts" (Go/Direction) and unclear" (Not/Bright).

un-yomi suggestions: "Egypt"; "Unicorn"

Vrite your sentence to remember the **on-yomi** and **un-yomi** readings in the box below.

.ess Common Pronunciations

.ess common **ON** readings: **GYŌ** (ギ ョ ウ); N (ア ン)

.ess common **kun** reading: **okona** (お こ な)

GYŌ is found primarily in compounds relating to this kanji's secondary meaning of "line" or "stroke". Note the irregular compound used at the beginning of the sample sentence (今日); we encountered this word back in Entry 6 (日).

COMMON WORDS AND COMPOUNDS		
行く	*to go*	**i·ku** い・く
行き先	go + precede = *destination*	**yu·ki saki** ゆ・き さき
東京行き	east + capital + go = *bound for Tokyo*	**TŌ·KYŌ yu·ki** ト ウ・キ ョ ウ ゆ・き
夜行	night + go = *night travel*	**YA·KŌ** ヤ・コ ウ
歩行	walk + go = *walking*	**HO·KŌ** ホ・コ ウ
歩行者	walk + go + individual = *pedestrian*	**HO·KŌ·SHA** ホ・コ ウ・シ ャ

SAMPLE SENTENCE:

今日　は　　歩行者　　が　　多い。
kyō　wa　HO·KŌ·SHA　ga　　ō·i.
today　　　　pedestrians　　　many
= *There are many pedestrians today.*

取 **TAKE**

BUILDING THIS KANJI
Ear 耳 (78) + **Again (ironing board)** 又 (159)
= 取

Meaning
Take.

Remembering this kanji

The **ear** was nervous.

"Um…I was wondering…" he said to the **ironing board**, "if, uh…"

"Yes?"

"If I could, uh…you know, TAKE you…"

"TAKE me where?"

"TAKE you on a…stroll or something."

The **ironing board** smiled, and for the first time noticed the **ear's** wrinkles; she understood now that he needed her.

"That would be nice," she said. "I'd love for you to TAKE me out."

Common Pronunciations
Common **ON** reading: none
Common **kun** reading: **to** (と)

As the second example below shows, this kanji acts like 買. It can also become voiced in the second position, as shown here in the final compound.

kun-yomi suggestion: "**to**ll"

Create your sentence to remember the **kun-yomi** reading in the box below.

	COMMON WORDS AND COMPOUNDS	
取る	*to take*	**to·ru** と・る
取引	take + pull = *transactions*	**tori·hiki** とり・ひき
取り上 げる	take + upper = *to pick up*	**to·ri a·geru** と・り あ・げる
取り入 れる	take + enter = *to take in*	**to·ri i·reru** と・り い・れる
取り出 す	take + exit = *to take out*	**to·ri da·su** と・り だ・す
気取る	spirit + take = *to put on airs*	**KI do·ru** キ ど・る

SAMPLE SENTENCE:

赤とうがらし を 取り出して 下さい。
aka·tōgarashi   o   to·ri da·shite   kuda·sai.
red peppers   take out   please
= *Please take out the red peppers.*

Less Common Pronunciations
Less common **ON** reading: **SHU** (シュ)
Less common **kun** reading: none

村 **VILLAGE**

一	十	才	木	木'	村	村	

BUILDING THIS KANJI
Tree 木(13) + Tiny (soccer player) 寸(103)
= 村

Meaning
Village. Here we have the third of our four "community" kanji. Keep in mind that this character implies something smaller than a city or town.

Remembering this kanji
As the population of our **VILLAGE** is **tiny**, the **tiny** soccer players have no one to play with. A suggestion that they use **trees** for opponents, however, was dismissed by everyone. This was hardly surprising given that it was proposed by the **VILLAGE** idiot.

Common Pronunciations
Common **ON** reading: **SON** (ソン)
Common **kun** reading: **mura** (むら)

Note that the reading for "人" in the second example is voiced.

kun-yomi suggestion: "**moor a**longside"

Create your **on-yomi** keyword and enter it in the table at the back of the book. After that, write your sentence to remember the **on-yomi** and **kun-yomi** readings in the box below.

COMMON WORDS AND COMPOUNDS		
村	*village*	**mura** むら
村人	village + person = *villager*	**mura·bito** むら・びと
山村	mountain + village = *mountain village*	**SAN·SON** サン・ソン

SAMPLE SENTENCE:

村人　は　小道　に立っています。
mura·bito wa　ko·michi ni　　ta·tte imasu.
 villager　　　path　　　　　　is standing
= *A villager is standing in the path.*

Less Common Pronunciations
Less common **ON** reading: none
Less common **kun** reading: none

CHARACTER

BUILDING THIS KANJI
Pincers ⼧ + Child 子(56) = 字

Meaning
"Character", in the sense of a Chinese character or letter of an alphabet.

Remembering this kanji
There are various ways of teaching Japanese CHARACTERS to a **child**, but a controversial method in days gone by involved the use of **pincers**. In it, a set of pincers would be suspended menacingly over a **child** practicing kanji. Should a mistake be made with any CHARACTER, the **pincers** would…well, best not describe what happened. Learning CHARACTERS today, quite simply, is a lot less stressful.

Common Pronunciations
Common **ON** reading: **JI** (ジ)
Common **kun** reading: none

Note that the reading for "引" is voiced in the final example.

Write your sentence to remember the **on-yomi** reading in the box below.

Less Common Pronunciations
Less common **ON** reading: none
Less common **kun** reading: **aza** (あざ)

COMMON WORDS AND COMPOUNDS		
十字	ten + character = *a cross*	**JŪ·JI** ジュウ・ジ
赤十字	red + ten + character = *the Red Cross*	**SEKI·JŪ·JI** セキ・ジュウ・ジ
字引	character + pull = *dictionary*	**JI·biki** ジ・びき

SAMPLE SENTENCE:

多く　の　国　で　は　赤十字　は
ō·ku　no　kuni　de　wa　SEKI·JŪ·JI wa
many　　country　　　　　　Red Cross
大切　です。
TAI·SETSU　desu.
 important
= *The Red Cross is important in many countries.*

COMPONENT #177

SEESAW

KANJI 177

具 TOOL

丨	冂	冂	冃	目	且	具	具	具

BUILDING THIS KANJI
Eye (Cyclops) 目 (15) + Seesaw 六 = 具

Meaning
Tool/Equipment.

Remembering this kanji

I once got on a **seesaw** with a **Cyclops** and soon found myself stuck in the air. As he was in no hurry to let me down I had to endure watching him eat his lunch as I sat there dangling, which was unpleasant given his manners. Instead of cutlery, he used the only TOOL he had – his club – to do everything from spread butter to roll up pasta. That being said, though, it did work well as a cheese grater, so I suppose he had a point in describing it as a multi-purpose TOOL.

Common Pronunciations
Common **ON** reading: **GU** (グ)
Common **kun** reading: none

Create your **on-yomi** keyword and enter it in the table at the back of the book. After that, write your sentence to remember the **on-yomi** reading in the box below.

Less Common Pronunciations
Less common **ON** reading: none
Less common **kun** reading: none

COMMON WORDS AND COMPOUNDS		
道具	road + tool = *tool*	DŌ·GU ド ウ・グ
家具	house + tool = *furniture*	KA·GU カ・グ
具体	tool + body = *definite; concrete*	GU·TAI グ・タ イ
馬具	horse + tool = *harness*	BA·GU バ・グ

SAMPLE SENTENCE:

山下先生　は　新しい　家具　を
Yama·shita-sensei　wa　atara·shii　KA·GU　o
(teacher) Yamashita　　　new　　furniture
買いました。
ka·imashita.
bought
= *Yamashita-sensei bought new furniture.*

COMPONENT #178

SPLASH

This important component usually indicates a character having some connection to water. It will be encountered frequently, being present in more than one hundred of the general-use kanji.

KANJI 178

注 POUR

BUILDING THIS KANJI
Splash 氵 + Primary 主(164) = 注

Meaning
Pour. In addition to the literal meaning, there is often an implied sense of "directing" something (a gaze or one's attention, for instance) toward an object.

Remembering this kanji
This is how I was taught to POUR:
   "When you POUR, your **primary** objective is not to let anything **splash** out. POUR carefully, but POUR confidently. **Splashes** are the **primary** indication that someone does not know how to POUR properly."

Common Pronunciations
Common **ON** reading: **CHŪ** (チュウ)
Common **kun** reading: **soso** (そそ)

kun-yomi suggestion: "**so-so**"

Write your sentence to remember the **on-yomi** and **kun-yomi** readings in the box below.

Less Common Pronunciations
Less common **ON** reading: none
Less common **kun** reading: none

COMMON WORDS AND COMPOUNDS		
注ぐ	*to pour*	soso·gu そそ·ぐ
注意	pour + mind = *attention*	CHŪ·I チュウ·イ
注水	pour + water = *watering*	CHŪ·SUI チュウ·スイ
注入	pour + enter = *infusion*	CHŪ·NYŪ チュウ·ニュウ
注目	pour + eye = *notice*	CHŪ·MOKU チュウ·モク

SAMPLE SENTENCE:
犬 に 注意 して 下さい。
inu ni CHŪ·I shite kuda·sai.
dog attention do please
= *Watch out for the dog.*

KANJI 179

口口 **GOODS**

ヽ	冖	口	口	口口	口口	口口	口口	品

BUILDING THIS KANJI
Mouth (vampire) 口 (8) + Mouth (vampire) 口
(8) + Mouth (vampire) 口 (8) = 品

Meaning
This character expresses the idea of "goods"
or "articles" in the majority of compounds in
which it appears. It can occasionally have the
more abstract notion of "refinement"; the fourth
and fifth examples below illustrate this aspect
of its meaning.

Remembering this kanji
You can imagine the GOODS a trio of **vampires**
might have: capes, coffins, hair gel, teeth whit-
eners, blood pudding…all manner of GOODS,
really.

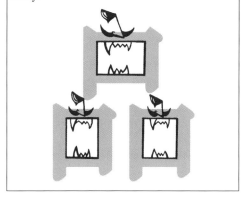

Common Pronunciations
Common **ON** reading: **HIN** (ヒ ン)
Common **kun** reading: **shina** (し な)

Note how the second character in example three
below has become voiced.

kun-yomi suggestion: "**she na**bbed"

Create your **on-yomi** keyword and enter it in the
table at the back of the book. After that, write your
sentence to remember the **on-yomi** and **kun-yomi**
readings in the box below.

Less Common Pronunciations
Less common **ON** reading: none
Less common **kun** reading: none

COMMON WORDS AND COMPOUNDS		
品	*goods*	**shina** し な
品物	goods + thing = *merchandise*	**shina·mono** し な・も の
品切れ	goods + cut = *"out of stock"*	**shina** gi·re し な ぎ・れ
上品	upper + goods = *elegant*	**JŌ·HIN** ジョ ウ・ヒ ン
下品	lower + goods = *vulgar*	**GE·HIN** ゲ・ヒ ン
中古品	middle + old + goods = *secondhand goods*	**CHŪ·KO·HIN** チュ ウ・コ・ヒ ン

SAMPLE SENTENCE:

下品 な 人 です ね。
GE·HIN na hito desu ne.
vulgar   person is
= *(He's) a vulgar person, isn't he?*

里 HAMLET

| 一 | 冂 | 冃 | 日 | 甲 | 甲 | 里 | | |

BUILDING THIS KANJI
Shell (Fly swatter) 甲 (148) + Two 二 (4) = 里

Meaning
Hamlet. Here we have the fourth and smallest of our populated units. This character can also signify the countryside in general; not surprisingly, given how small a settlement this kanji implies.

Remembering this kanji
When Hamlet came to our HAMLET, me 'n the other resident were pretty darn excited; the guy was the prince of Denmark, after all. Unfortunately, with only **two** of us in the HAMLET we only had **two fly swatters**, and what with all the flies buzzin' everywhere, I wasn't in any mood to lend him mine. Anyway, rumor has it he told folks back in Elsinore that he didn't much care for our HAMLET. Which strikes me as kind of ironic.

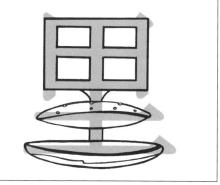

Common Pronunciations
Common **ON** reading: none
Common **kun** reading: **sato** (さ と)
The final compound below reminds us once again that this reading of "人" is always voiced when it appears in the second position

kun-yomi suggestion: "**sat o**penly"

Create your sentence to remember the **kun-yomi** reading in the box below.

Less Common Pronunciations
Less common **ON** reading: **RI** (リ)
Less common **kun** readings: none

COMMON WORDS AND COMPOUNDS		
里	*hamlet*	**sato** さと
古里	old + hamlet = *the old hometown*	furu·**sato** ふる・さと
里人	hamlet + person = *country folk*	**sato**·bito さと・びと

SAMPLE SENTENCE:

先週 は 古里 へ 行きました。
SEN·SHŪ wa furu·sato e i·kimashita.
last week   old hometown   went
= *Last week I went to my old hometown.*

CHAPTER 9 REVIEW EXERCISES

A. Please match the following kanji to their meanings.

1. 丁   a. Hamlet

2. 死   b. Death

3. 村   c. Take

4. 行   d. Pour

5. 主   e. Goods

6. 取   f. Village

7. 友   g. Block

8. 注   h. Primary

9. 品   i. Friend

10. 里   j. Go

B. Please match the following meanings to their kanji, and these to their **on** or **kun-yomi**.

1.	Dog	a. 犬	1.	**KŌ**(コウ)
2.	Cloth	b. 巾	2.	**KIN**(キン)
3.	Group	c. 公	3.	**kara**(から)
4.	Every	d. 町	4.	**MAI**(マイ)
5.	Public	e. 具	5.	**GU**(グ)
6.	Character	f. 市	6.	**SHI**(シ)
7.	City	g. 毎	7.	**machi**(まち)
8.	Tool	h. 字	8.	**inu**(いぬ)
9.	Empty	i. 団	9.	**DAN**(ダン)
10.	Town	j. 空	10.	**JI**(ジ)

C. Please choose the best answer(s) to the following questions.

1. Which of the following readings apply to the kanji 村?
   a. **mura**(むら)
   b. **CHŌ**(チョウ)
   c. **SON**(ソン)
   d. **machi**(まち)
   e. **SHI**(シ)

2. Which of the following readings apply to the kanji 友?
   a. **sato**(さと)
   b. **YŪ**(ユウ)
   c. **YŌ**(ヨウ)
   d. **minato**(みなと)
   e. **tomo**(とも)

3. Which of the following readings apply to the kanji 品?
   a. **SHŪ**(シュウ)
   b. **shina**(しな)
   c. **hana**(はな)
   d. **HIN**(ヒン)
   e. **IN**(イン)

4. It became really hot that day, and I needed to wipe my face with a ___.
   a. 犬
   b. 友
   c. 巾
   d. 具
   e. 注

5. Which of the following readings apply to the kanji 行?
   a. **i**(い)
   b. **KŌ**(コウ)
   c. **yu**(ゆ)
   d. **to**(と)
   e. **KA**(カ)

D. Please choose the best answer(s) to the following questions.

1. Which kanji would come next in the following series: 市....町....村....?
   a. 行
   b. 丁
   c. 空
   d. 里
   e. 具

2. Which is the correct reading of 死ぬ?
   a. **shi·nu** (し·ぬ)
   b. **a·nu** (あ·ぬ)
   c. **chi·nu** (ち·ぬ)
   d. **u·nu** (う·ぬ)

3. Which of the following kanji has the most number of strokes?
   a. 具
   b. 品
   c. 取
   d. 里
   e. 注

4. Which is the correct reading of 注ぐ?
   a. **ama·gu** (あ ま·ぐ)
   b. **shi·gu** (し·ぐ)
   c. **soso·gu** (そ そ·ぐ)
   d. **o·gu** (お·ぐ)

5. Which is the correct reading of 取る?
   a. **mawa·ru** (ま わ·る)
   b. **shi·ru** (し·る)
   c. **hi·ru** (ひ·る)
   d. **to·ru** (と·る)

E. Please match the following compounds and words to their meanings and pronunciations.

1. 取り上げる	a. Daily	1. **CHŌ·KAI** (チョウ·カイ)
2. 注意	b. Drowning	2. **KA·GU** (カ·グ)
3. 家具	c. Blue sky	3. **CHŪ·I** (チュウ·イ)
4. 青空	d. Attention	4. **shina·mono** (しな·もの)
5. 毎日	e. Organization	5. **MAI·NICHI** (マイ·ニチ)
6. 主人公	f. Town assembly	6. **DAN·TAI** (ダン·タイ)
7. 品物	g. Furniture	7. **SUI·SHI** (スイ·シ)
8. 団体	h. Merchandise	8. **to·ri a·geru** (と·り あ·げる)
9. 町会	i. Main character	9. **SHU·JIN·KŌ** (シュ·ジン·コウ)
10. 水死	j. To pick up	10. **ao·zora** (あお·ぞら)

Kanji #181—200

KANJI 181

 GROVE

BUILDING THIS KANJI
Tree 木(13) + Tree 木(13) = 林

Meaning
Grove.

Remembering this kanji
No story needed, as it's easy to see how this character could stand for a small group of trees!

Common Pronunciations
Common **ON** reading: **RIN** (リ ン)
Common **kun** reading: **hayashi** (は や し)

As the common Japanese family name in the second example below shows, this reading becomes voiced when not in the first position.

kun-yomi suggestion: "**high ash e**vent"

Create your **on-yomi** keyword and enter it in the table at the back of the book. After that, write your sentence to remember the **on-yomi** and **kun-yomi** readings in the box below.

Less Common Pronunciations
Less common **ON** reading: none
Less common **kun** reading: none

COMMON WORDS AND COMPOUNDS		
林	*grove*	**hayashi** は や し
小林 さん	small + grove = *Kobayashi-san*	ko·**bayashi**·san こ·ば や し·さ ん
林道	grove + road = *woodland trail;* *road*	**RIN**·DŌ リ ン·ド ウ
人工林	person + craft + grove = *planted forest*	JIN·KŌ·**RIN** ジ ン·コ ウ·リ ン
公有林	public + have + grove = *public woodland*	KŌ·YŪ·**RIN** コ ウ·ユ ウ·リ ン

SAMPLE SENTENCE:

あ の　国　に　は　　公有林　　が
ano　kuni　ni　wa　KŌ·YŪ·RIN　ga
that　country　　　　public woodland
少ない。
suku·nai.
　few
= *That country has little public woodland.*

KANJI 182

 FOREST

| 一 | 十 | ナ | 木 | 木 | 木 | 木 | 木 | 森 |
| 森 | 森 | 森 | | | | | | |

BUILDING THIS KANJI
Tree 木(13) + Grove 林(181) = 森

Meaning
Forest.

Remembering this kanji
Another wonderfully simple character! You've probably guessed that this kanji implies a larger area of trees than that of the preceding entry.

Common Pronunciations
Common **ON** reading: **SHIN** (シン)
Common **kun** reading: **mori** (もり)

kun-yomi suggestion: "Nemo realized"

Write your sentence to remember the **on-yomi** and **kun-yomi** readings in the box below.

Less Common Pronunciations
Less common **ON** reading: none
Less common **kun** reading: none

COMMON WORDS AND COMPOUNDS		
森	*forest*	**mori** もり
森林	forest + grove = *forests*	**SHIN·RIN** シン・リン
森林学	forest + grove + study = *forestry*	**SHIN·RIN·GAKU** シン・リン・ガク

SAMPLE SENTENCE:

森 に 入る 時 は 注意 して
mori ni hai·ru toki wa CHŪ·I shite
forest   enter time   attention do
下さい。
kuda·sai.
 please
= *Please be careful when going into the forest.*

KANJI 183

 DAWN

丨	冂	日	日	旦			

BUILDING THIS KANJI
Sun 日 (6) + One (bottom of a bun) 一(3) = 旦

Meaning
Dawn. You will see this character figure more prominently as a component in other kanji than on its own.

Remembering this kanji

When the rays of the **sun** hit the **bottom of a bun**, it's DAWN.

Common Pronunciations

Common **ON** reading: **TAN** (タ ン)

Common **kun** reading: none

Create your **on-yomi** keyword and enter it in the table at the back of the book. After that, write your sentence to remember the **on-yomi** reading in the box below.

Less Common Pronunciations

Less common **ON** reading: **DAN** (ダ ン)

Less common **kun** reading: none

COMMON WORDS AND COMPOUNDS		
一旦	one + dawn = *once*	IT·**TAN** イッ・タン
元旦	basis + dawn = *New Year's Day*	GAN·**TAN** ガン・タン

SAMPLE SENTENCE:

元旦　　に　お寺　へ　行きました。

GAN·TAN　ni　o·tera　e　i·kimashita

New Year's Day　　temple　　　　went

= *(I) went to a temple on New Year's Day.*

黒 BLACK

ヽ	冂	⿱	日	甲	里	里	里	黒
黒	黒							

BUILDING THIS KANJI

Hamlet 里 (180) + Gas Stove 灬 = 黒

Meaning

Black.

Remembering this kanji

The introduction of **gas stoves** was problematic for our **hamlet**; nobody was sure how to cook with them, and a lot of food was burnt beyond recognition. The inevitable result was that **BLACK** smoke drifted everywhere, covering the landscape and **hamlet** with soot. Residents began to grumble. "We should go back to the old ways," some said, "because these **gas stoves** are nothing but trouble. It was a **BLACK** day when they arrived here".

Common Pronunciations

Common **ON** reading: **KOKU** (コ ク)

Common **kun** reading: **kuro** (く ろ)

With the exception of the third example, the **kun-yomi** is always voiced in the second position (as it appears in the fourth compound).

kun-yomi suggestion: "**coo ro**sily"

Write your sentence to remember the **on-yomi** and **kun-yomi** readings in the box below.

COMMON WORDS AND COMPOUNDS		
黒	*black (noun)*	**kuro** く ろ
黒い	*black (adjective)*	**kuro·i** く ろ・い
白黒	white + black = *black-and-white*	shiro·**kuro** し ろ・く ろ
赤黒い	red + black = *dark red*	aka **guro·i** あ か ぐ ろ・い
黒人	black + person = *a black person*	**KOKU·JIN** コ ク・ジ ン

Less Common Pronunciations
Less common **ON** reading: none
Less common **kun** reading: none

SAMPLE SENTENCE:

こ の 黒い 馬 は 美しい で す ね。

kono kuro·i uma wa utsuku·shii desu ne.
this   black horse   beautiful isn't it
= *This black horse is beautiful, isn't it?*

交 **MIX**

'	一	六	六	亣	交		

BUILDING THIS KANJI
Police ⼇ + Father 父(79) = 交

Meaning
This character conveys a general sense of things mixing in both physical and figurative ways ("associating" with people or "exchanging" words are examples of the latter).

Remembering this kanji
My **father** was a **police** officer who enjoyed throwing MIXERS. Such occasions would always draw an interesting MIX of ranks: corporals, constables, inspectors…they all attended. My **father**, however, would not let anyone else MIX the drinks. "The last thing you want," he said to me, "is a MIX-up with all these guns around."

Common Pronunciations
Common **ON** reading: **KŌ** (コ ウ)
Common **kun** reading: **ma** (ま)

kun-yomi suggestion: "**ma**tch"

Write your sentence to remember the **on-yomi** and **kun-yomi** readings in the box below.

Less Common Pronunciations
Less common **ON** reading: none
Less common **kun** readings: **maji** (ま じ); **ka** (か)

COMMON WORDS AND COMPOUNDS		
交ざる (intr)	*to mingle*	**ma·zaru** ま・ざ る
交ぜる (tr)	*to mix (something)*	**ma·zeru** ま・ぜ る
外交	outside + mix = *foreign policy*	**GAI·KŌ** ガ イ・コ ウ

SAMPLE SENTENCE:

あの	国	の	外交	が
ano	kuni	no	**GAI·KŌ**	ga
that	country		foreign policy	

分かりません。
wa·karimasen.
don't understand
= *(I) don't understand that country's foreign policy.*

NOT

| 一 | フ | 不 | 不 | | | | |

Meaning
Expressing the idea of "not" or "un-", this is an important negating prefix in Japanese.

Remembering this kanji
What is this, you ask? Well, it's **NOT** a superhero, it's **NOT** a giraffe, and it's **NOT** a figure skater. It's just…**NOT** like anything, really.

Common Pronunciations
Common **ON** reading: **FU** (フ)
Common **kun** reading: none

Note how this kanji can function as a prefix with complete words, as it does below in the final

example [the base compound for this word (親切) was presented in Entry 118].

Write your sentence to remember the **on-yomi** reading in the box below.

Less Common Pronunciations
Less common **ON** reading: **BU** (ブ)
Less common **kun** readings: none

COMMON WORDS AND COMPOUNDS		
不意	not + mind = *unexpectedly*	**FU·I** フ・イ
不安	not + ease = *uneasy*	**FU·AN** フ・アン
不明	not + bright = *unclear*	**FU·MEI** フ・メイ
不死	not + death = *immortal*	**FU·SHI** フ・シ
不親切	not + parent + cut = *unkind*	**FU·SHIN·SETSU** フ・シン・セツ

SAMPLE SENTENCE:

小林さん　の　意図　は　不明　です。
Ko·bayashi·san no I·TO wa FU·MEI desu.
Kobayashi-san   aim   unclear
= *Kobayashi-san's aim is unclear.*

COMPONENT #187

FRUSTRATION

As will be seen in the following entry, this component is written with three strokes.

KANJI 187

後 **AFTER**

BUILDING THIS KANJI
Razor 彳 + Frustration 厶 + Running Chicken 夂 = 後

Meaning
After/Later/Behind. These meanings apply to the ideas of both physical location and time.

Remembering this kanji
A butcher's lament:

   "Am I **frustrated**? Yeah, I'm **frustrated**. I just spent an hour chasing **AFTER** a **running chicken** with a **razor**. Why? 'Cause a customer wanted shaved chicken, that's why! And then **AFTER** I got it for them, they complained about the taste of the **AFTER** shave!"

Common Pronunciations
Common **ON** readings: **KŌ** (コウ); **GO** (ゴ)
Common **kun** readings: **ato** (あと); **ushi** (うし)

This can be a tough character to master, but is not as fearsome as might be expected given its many readings. Look for **KŌ** in the first position; **ato** and **ushi·ro** (this reading is always accompanied by **ro**) appear far less frequently here, and **GO** pops up in only a few words. In second position, moreover, the reading will invariably be **GO**.

   It is worth having another look at the compounds for " 前 " in Chapter 7 (Entry 133), to see how the fourth, fifth and sixth examples given there "pair up" with the three below.

kun-yomi suggestions: "**at O**klahoma"; "**Ooh, she**…"

Write your sentence to remember the **on-yomi** and **kun-yomi** readings in the box below.

Less Common Pronunciations
Less common **ON** reading: none
Less common **kun** readings: **nochi** (のち); **oku** (おく)

COMMON WORDS AND COMPOUNDS		
後	*after*	**ato** あと
後ろ	*behind*	**ushi·ro** うし·ろ
後年	after + year = *in later years*	**KŌ·NEN** コウ·ネン
後半	after + half = *second half*	**KŌ·HAN** コウ·ハン
後者	after + individual = *the latter*	**KŌ·SHA** コウ·シャ
午後	noon + after = *P.M.; afternoon*	**GO·GO** ゴ·ゴ

SAMPLE SENTENCE:

後 で 友人 と 東京 へ 行きます。
ato de YŪ·JIN to TŌ·KYŌ e   i·kimasu.
after   friend with Tokyo   go
= *Afterward, I'll go to Tokyo with a friend.*

最 MOST

| 一 | 冂 | 曱 | 日 | 旦 | 旱 | 昻 | 昺 | 冣 |
| 冣 | 最 | 最 | | | | | | |

BUILDING THIS KANJI
Sun 日 (6) + Take 取 (174) = 最

Meaning
Most. Note how the first stroke of "ear" has been lengthened.

Remembering this kanji
So the ear was finally able to **take** the ironing board on a date, and luckily for him it turned out to be the MOST wonderful, MOST picturesque day. Not to mention the MOST romantic, too, for when the **sun** grew overly hot, the ear stretched himself out so that the ironing board would be shaded. He really was a MOST chivalrous ear when it came to **taking** care of a date.

Common Pronunciations
Common **ON** reading: **SAI** (サイ)
Common **kun** reading: none

Create your **on-yomi** keyword and enter it in the table at the back of the book. After that, write your sentence to remember the **on-yomi**.

Less Common Pronunciations
Less common **ON** reading: none
Less common **kun** readings: **motto** (もっと);
mo (も)

COMMON WORDS AND COMPOUNDS		
最小	most + small = *smallest*	**SAI·SHŌ** サイ・ショウ
最少	most + few = *fewest*	**SAI·SHŌ** サイ・ショウ
最高	most + tall = *highest; the best*	**SAI·KŌ** サイ・コウ
最古	most + old = *oldest*	**SAI·KO** サイ・コ
最新	most + new = *newest*	**SAI·SHIN** サイ・シン
最後	most + after = *the last*	**SAI·GO** サイ・ゴ

SAMPLE SENTENCE:

この 天気 は 最高 です よ。
kono TEN·KI wa SAI·KŌ desu yo.
this weather the best is
= *This weather is fantastic!*

KANJI 189

太 FAT

| 一 | ナ | 大 | 太 | | | | |

BUILDING THIS KANJI
Large (sumo wrestler) 大 (17) + **Jelly Bean** 丶
= 太

Meaning
Fat/Thick. Note the difference between this character and "犬" (Entry 171).

Remembering this kanji

This is what happens when a **sumo wrestler** gets too FAT: try as he might, he can't even bend down to pick up a **jelly bean** lying between his feet.

Common Pronunciations

Common **ON** reading: **TAI** (タイ)

Common **kun** reading: **futo** (ふと)

kun-yomi suggestion: "**who to**ld"

Write your sentence to remember the **on-yomi** and **kun-yomi** readings in the box below.

Less Common Pronunciations

Less common **ON** reading: **TA** (タ)

Less common **kun** reading: none

COMMON WORDS AND COMPOUNDS		
太い	*fat; thick*	**futo·i** ふと・い
太る	*to grow fat*	**futo·ru** ふと・る
太子	fat + child = *crown prince*	**TAI·SHI** タイ・シ

SAMPLE SENTENCE:

私　　は　　　冬休み　　に　とても
watashi　wa　　fuyu yasu·mi　ni　totemo
　I　　　　　　winter vacation　　really
太った。
futo·tta.
grew fat
= *I really put on weight during winter vacation.*

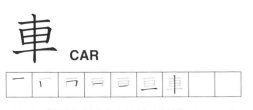

CAR

Meaning

Car. As the compounds below indicate, this character can also refer to a wide range of other vehicles. No story required.

Common Pronunciations

Common **ON** reading: **SHA** (シャ)

Common **kun** reading: **kuruma** (くるま)

kun-yomi suggestion: "**coo rheuma**tism"

Write your sentence to remember the **on-yomi** and **kun-yomi** readings in the box below.

Less Common Pronunciations

Less common **ON** reading: none

Less common **kun** reading: none

COMMON WORDS AND COMPOUNDS		
車	car; vehicle	**kuruma** くるま
電車	electric + car = *(electric) train*	**DEN·SHA** デン・シャ
空車	empty + car = *(taxi) "for hire"*	**KŪ·SHA** クウ・シャ
車内	car + inside = *inside the car*	**SHA·NAI** シャ・ナイ
中古車	middle + old + car = *used car*	**CHŪ·KO·SHA** チュウ・コ・シャ

SAMPLE SENTENCE:

中村さん　　は　　　中古車　　を
Naka·mura-san　　wa　　CHŪ·KO·SHA　　o
Nakamura-san　　　　　　used car
買いました。
ka·imashita.
　bought
= *Nakamura-san bought a used car.*

COMPONENT #191

STROLLER

KANJI 191

受　RECEIVE

BUILDING THIS KANJI
Stroller 丆 + UFO ⌐ + Again (ironing
board) 又 (159) = 受

Meaning
Receive/Accept. This interesting character
encompasses a wide range of meanings having
to do with the idea of reception; "taking" an
exam, "undergoing" an operation, or "suffering"
injuries are several examples.

Remembering this kanji
The **ironing board** longed to have a miniature
ironing board in the worst way, but still hadn't
RECEIVED the adoption papers. As the wait
dragged on, she began to have visions of a **UFO**
descending with a **stroller** on top of it: "We have
your **ironing board**," a voice would announce,
"will you RECEIVE it?". "I will RECEIVE it,
yes" she always answered, "I will".

Common Pronunciations
Common **ON** reading: **JU** (ジュ)
Common **kun** reading: **u** (う)

The third and fourth examples below show this to be another kanji sharing the pronunciation characteristics of 買.

kun-yomi suggestion: "**oo**long tea"

Create your **on-yomi** keyword and enter it in the table at the back of the book. After that, write your sentence to remember the **on-yomi** and **kun-yomi** readings in the box below.

Less Common Pronunciations
Less common **ON** reading: none
Less common **kun** reading: none

COMMON WORDS AND COMPOUNDS		
受ける	to receive; to accept	**u**·keru う・ける
受け 取る	receive + take = to receive	**u**·ke to·ru う・け と・る
受取	receive + take = receipt	**uke**·tori うけ・とり
受取人	receive + take + person = recipient	**uke**·tori·NIN うけ・とり・ ニン
引き受 ける	pull + receive = to undertake	hi·ki **u**·keru ひ・き う・ける
受注	receive + pour = receipt of an order	JU·CHŪ ジュ・チュウ

SAMPLE SENTENCE:

田中さん　は　新しい　本　を
Ta·naka-san wa atara·shii HON o
Tanaka-san   new   book
受け取りました。
u·ke to·rimashita.
　　　received
= *Tanaka-san received a new book.*

凶
EVIL

BUILDING THIS KANJI
Banana Peels メ + Garbage Can 凵 = 凶

Meaning
Take care: this unpleasant character relates exclusively to evil and misfortune.

Remembering this kanji
EVIL comes in all forms. Environmentalists, for example, regard **banana peels** in a **garbage can** as EVIL, as this is a telltale sign of someone being uninterested in composting.

Common Pronunciations
Common **ON** reading: KYŌ (キョウ)
Common **kun** reading: none

Write your sentence to remember the **on-yomi** reading in the box below.

Less Common Pronunciations
Less common **ON** reading: none
Less common **kun** reading: none

COMMON WORDS AND COMPOUNDS		
凶年	evil + year = *a bad year*	**KYŌ**·NEN キョウ・ネン
凶行	evil + go = *violence*	**KYŌ**·KŌ キョウ・コウ

SAMPLE SENTENCE:

凶年　　だ　そう　です。
KYŌ·NEN da　sō　desu.
　bad year　　　seems
= *Apparently it's a bad year.*

KANJI 193

 SEA

BUILDING THIS KANJI
Splash 氵 + Every 毎 (168) = 海

Meaning
Sea.

Remembering this kanji
Q. Which SEA **splashes every** shoreline in the Caribbean?
A. a) The SEA of Confusion?
　b) The SEA of Tranquility?
　c) The Caribbean SEA?

Common Pronunciations
Common **ON** reading: **KAI** (カイ)
Common **kun** reading: **umi** (うみ)

Recall that the fourth example below was presented early in Chapter 2; we've come a long way since then!

kun-yomi suggestion: "**ooh, me!**"

Write your sentence to remember the **on-yomi** and **kun-yomi** readings in the box below.

Less Common Pronunciations
Less common **ON** reading: none
Less common **kun** reading: none

COMMON WORDS AND COMPOUNDS		
海	*sea*	**umi** うみ
海水	sea + water = *sea water*	**KAI**·SUI カイ・スイ
海図	sea + diagram = *nautical chart*	**KAI**·ZU カイ・ズ
海王星	sea + king + star = *Neptune (planet)*	**KAI**·Ō·SEI カイ・オウ・セイ
北海道	north + sea + road = *Hokkaido*	HOK·**KAI**·DŌ ホッ・カイ・ドウ

SAMPLE SENTENCE:

夏休み　　に　　北海道　　へ
natsu yasu·mi　ni　HOK·KAI·DŌ　e
summer vacation　　　Hokkaido
行きました。
i·kimashita.
　went
= *(We) went to Hokkaido for summer vacation.*

校 SCHOOL

一	十	才	木	木'	术	杧	柊	校
校								

BUILDING THIS KANJI
Tree 木(13) + Mix 交(185) = 校

Meaning
School. A secondary meaning related to "proof-reading" shows up in only a few compounds.

Remembering this kanji
When **trees** attend SCHOOL, they are often required to **mix** with other species. This can be problematic; maple **trees** refuse to take exams with evergreens, for example, and thus drag down test scores for the SCHOOL as a whole. This, as we know, is a traditional source of tension; when it comes to SCHOOL, some argue, coniferous and deciduous **trees** simply cannot **mix**.

Common Pronunciations
Common **ON** reading: KŌ (コ ウ)
Common **kun** reading: none

Note how "学" in the second example "doubles up" with 校 , and how this remains constant in the other compounds in which this word occurs.

Write your sentence to remember the **on-yomi** reading in the box below.

Less Common Pronunciations
Less common **ON** reading: none
Less common **kun** reading: none

COMMON WORDS AND COMPOUNDS		
校外	school + outside = *off-campus*	KŌ·GAI コウ·ガイ
学校	study + school = *school*	GAK·KŌ ガッ·コウ
小学校	small + study + school = *elementary school*	SHŌ·GAK·KŌ ショウ·ガッ· コウ
中学校	middle + study + school = *junior high school*	CHŪ·GAK·KŌ チュウ·ガッ· コウ
高校	tall + school = *high school*	KŌ·KŌ コウ·コウ
女学校	woman + study + school = *girls' school*	JO·GAK·KŌ ジョ·ガッ· コウ

SAMPLE SENTENCE:

あの	女	の	子	は	高校
ano	**onna**	**no**	**ko**	**wa**	**KŌ·KŌ**
that	woman		child		high school

二年生	です。
NI·NEN·SEI	**desu.**
second year student	

= *That girl is a second-year high school student.*

KANJI 195

LEG

| 丶 | 冂 | 口 | 严 | 早 | 尸 | 足 | | |

BUILDING THIS KANJI
Mouth (vampire) 口 (8) + **Good Figure Skater**
卜 + **Person** 人 (2) = 足

Meaning
Confusingly for English speakers, this character can signify both "leg" and "foot". A secondary meaning relates to the sense of "suffice".

Remembering this kanji
Even a **good figure skater** can mess up on occasion, and the kanji here provides an example of this happening. The steps are easy to follow: 1. **Vampire** flies onto **good figure skater**; 2. Figure skater is distracted, lands awkwardly on the **person** skating with her (this takes place during a pairs competition); 3. Said **person** breaks LEG.

Common Pronunciations
Common **ON** reading: **SOKU** (ソ ク)
Common **kun** reading: **ashi** (あ し)

Note that "取" is voiced in the fouth example.
kun-yomi suggestion: "**ash ea**ting"

Create your **on-yomi** keyword and enter it in the table at the back of the book. After that, write your sentence to remember the **on-yomi** and **kun-yomi** readings in the box below.

Less Common Pronunciations
Less common **ON** reading: none
Less common **kun** reading: **ta** (た)

IRREGULAR READING		
裸足*	naked + leg = *barefoot*	**hadashi** は だ し

COMMON WORDS AND COMPOUNDS		
足	*leg; foot*	**ashi** あ し
足首	leg + neck = *ankle*	**ashi**·kubi あ し・く び
足音	leg + sound = *sound of footsteps*	**ashi**·oto あ し・お と
足取り	leg + take = *one's gait*	**ashi** do·ri あ し ど・り
土足	earth + leg = *with shoes on*	DO·**SOKU** ド・ソ ク
足元 注意	leg + basis + pour + mind = *"watch your step"*	**ashi**·moto·CHŪ·I あ し・も と・ チ ュ ウ・イ

SAMPLE SENTENCE:

足音		を	聞きました	か。
ashi·oto		**o**	**ki·kimashita**	**ka.**
sound of footsteps			heard	

= *Did you hear footsteps?*

COMPONENT #196

TRIPOD

KANJI 196

糸 **THREAD**

⟨	∠	幺	幺	糸	糸		

BUILDING THIS KANJI
Frustration 幺 + Tripod ⺌ = 糸

Meaning
Thread. You will become very familiar with this character over time; it appears as a component in more than sixty other kanji.

Remembering this kanji
If you want to get a sense of **frustration**, try doing anything with a **tripod** made out of THREAD. The moment you use it with a camera, the THREAD collapses and ruins your shot. As a support for painting, though, it's even worse: the **tripod** falls over and leaves a bunch of THREAD stuck in your masterpiece.

Common Pronunciations
Common **ON** reading: none
Common **kun** reading: **ito** (いと)

Note that " ロ " is voiced in the second example.

kun-yomi suggestion: "**eat o**nly"

From this point on, the "create your own" reminders will only be presented for those kanji that feature new **on-yomi**. The absence of this reminder and blank box will indicate that you have already created an **on-yomi** keyword for that reading. In such instances, try to recall your keyword without having to look it up in the table at the back of the book.

Less Common Pronunciations
Less common **ON** reading: **SHI** (シ)
Less common **kun** reading: none

COMMON WORDS AND COMPOUNDS		
糸	*thread*	**ito** いと
糸口	thread + mouth = *beginning; clue*	**ito**·guchi いと・ぐち

SAMPLE SENTENCE:

青い　糸　が あります　か。
ao·i　**ito**　**ga**　**arimasu**　**ka.**
blue　thread　　　is
= *Is there any blue thread?*

KANJI 197

同 **SAME**

		⎵	冂	冂	冋	同		

BUILDING THIS KANJI
Gorilla 冂 + One (hamburger patty) 一 (3) +
Mouth (vampire) ロ (8) = 同

Meaning
Same.

Remembering this kanji

As a vegetarian, a **gorilla's** diet is always the SAME: fruits, nuts and berries. A **vampire**, too, is only interested in having the SAME meal over and over: the blood of living creatures. It should come as no surprise, therefore, that a **gorilla** and **vampire** will react the SAME way if a **hamburger patty** is placed between them – neither will want it.

Less Common Pronunciations

Less common **ON** reading: none
Less common **kun** reading: none

COMMON WORDS AND COMPOUNDS		
同じ	*same*	ona·ji おな・じ
同意	same + mind = *agreement*	DŌ·I ド ウ・イ
同一	same + one = *identical*	DŌ·ITSU ド ウ・イ ツ
同時	same + time = *simultaneous*	DŌ·JI ド ウ・ジ
同化	same + change = *assimilation*	DŌ·KA ド ウ・カ
同行者	same + go + individual = *traveling companion*	DŌ·KŌ·SHA ド ウ・コ ウ・シャ

Common Pronunciations

Common **ON** reading: **DŌ** (ド ウ)
Common **kun** reading: **ona** (お な)

Remember that **ona** (お な) differs from **onna** (お ん な), a reading for "女" in Entry 16.

kun-yomi suggestion: "**o, na**sty!"

SAMPLE SENTENCE:

私　と　中村さん　は　　同時
watashi　to　Naka·mura-san　wa　　DŌ·JI
　I　　Nakamura-san　　simultaneous
に　来ました。
ni　ki·mashita.
　　came
= *Nakamura-san and I arrived at the same time.*

KANJI 198

NOON

ノ	′	′	午				

BUILDING THIS KANJI
Hammer ′ + Ten (scarecrow) 十(28) = 午

Meaning
Noon.

Remembering this kanji

Everyone feels sorry for a **scarecrow** at NOON, as NOON is when the heat starts to pound on him like a **hammer**.

Common Pronunciations

Common **ON** reading: **GO** (ゴ)
Common **kun** reading: none

Less Common Pronunciations

Less common **ON** reading: none
Less common **kun** reading: none

COMMON WORDS AND COMPOUNDS		
午前	noon + before = A.M.; morning	**GO·ZEN** ゴ・ゼン
午後	noon + after = P.M.; afternoon	**GO·GO** ゴ・ゴ
午前中	noon + before + middle = all morning	**GO·ZEN·CHŪ** ゴ・ゼン・チュウ

SAMPLE SENTENCE:

SAMPLE SENTENCE:

午前　　　　八時　　に　　高校　　へ
GO·ZEN　HACHI·JI　ni　KŌ·KŌ　e
A.M.　　eight o'clock　　high school
行きます。
i·kimasu.
　　go
= I go to high school at 8 A.M.

KANJI 199

 LOVE

BUILDING THIS KANJI
Stroller ⼌ + **UFO** ⼍ + **Heart** 心(25) +
Running Chicken 夂 = 愛

Meaning
Love. After an entry for "evil", space had to be made for this character!

Remembering this kanji
LOVE, as we know, is profound, and the components in this kanji all have a connection to its secrets. A **stroller** can be filled through LOVE, a **UFO** is as mysterious as LOVE, a **heart** is the symbol of LOVE, and a **running chicken**...well, a **running chicken** has clearly been set free by someone who LOVES chickens.

Common Pronunciations
Common **ON** reading: **AI** (アイ)
Common **kun** reading: none

Create your **on-yomi** keyword and enter it in the table at the back of the book. After that, write your sentence to remember the **on-yomi** reading in the box below.

Less Common Pronunciations
Less common **ON** reading: none
Less common **kun** reading: none

The following is a very common irregular reading.

IRREGULAR READING		
可愛い	possible + love = cute	**KA·WAI·i** カ・ワイ・い

COMMON WORDS AND COMPOUNDS		
愛好	love + like = love; like	**AI·KŌ** アイ・コウ
愛犬	love + dog = pet dog	**AI·KEN** アイ・ケン
愛犬家	love + dog + house = dog lover	**AI·KEN·KA** アイ・ケン・カ
愛鳥家	love + bird + house = bird lover	**AI·CHŌ·KA** アイ・チョウ・カ
愛国心	love + country + heart = patriotism	**AI·KOKU·SHIN** アイ・コク・シン

SAMPLE SENTENCE:

本田さん　は　愛鳥家　として　有名
Hon·da-san　wa　AI·CHŌ·KA　toshite　YŪ·MEI
Honda-san　　bird lover　　as　　famous
です。
desu.
= Honda-san is famous as a bird lover.

SEPARATE

BUILDING THIS KANJI
Police ⼇ + Evil 凶(192) + Gorilla 冂 +
Broken Crutch 厶 + Squirrels 隹 = 離

Meaning
Separate/Leave. This is one the most compli-
cated-looking of all the kanji, but as you are
now familiar with each its components, even
a ferocious character like this can be tackled
with confidence.

Remembering this kanji
A warning: *never* try to SEPARATE the
squirrels, as they will offer violent resist-
ance should you try. The **police** once made
an effort, of course, but the **squirrels**
SEPARATED them from their weapons and
committed an act of such unspeakable **evil** that
it cannot be related here. The **police** then sent in
a **gorilla** to do their dirty work, but as the **broken
crutch** indicates, this maneuver failed miser-
ably as well. In the end, everyone was forced
to agree that it was best not to SEPARATE the
squirrels at all.

Common Pronunciations
Common **ON** reading: **RI** (リ)
Common **kun** reading: **hana** (はな)
Note how the reading of this character has become
voiced in the third compound.

kun-yomi suggestions: "**Han a**mulet"

Create your **on-yomi** keyword and enter it in the
table at the back of the book. After that, write your
sentence to remember the **on-yomi** and **kun-yomi**
readings in the box below.

Less Common Pronunciations
Less common **ON** reading: none
Less common **kun** reading: none

COMMON WORDS AND COMPOUNDS		
離れる (intr)	to separate; to leave	**hana**·reru はな·れる
離す (tr)	to separate (something)	**hana**·su はな·す
離れ 離れ	separate + separate = *scattered; separated*	**hana**·re **bana**·re はな·れ ばな·れ
切り 離す	cut + separate = *to cut off*	ki·ri **hana**·su き·り はな·す
分離	part + separate = *separation*	**BUN·RI** ブン·リ
離村	separate + village = *rural exodus*	**RI·SON** リ·ソン

SAMPLE SENTENCE:

山   で その   親子   は
yama   de   sono   oya·ko   wa
mountain   that   parent and child
離れ離れ   に なってしまいました。
hana·re bana·re   ni   natte shimaimashita.
  separated   ended up
= *That parent and child ended up getting separated on the mountain.*

CHAPTER 10 REVIEW EXERCISES

A. Please match the following kanji to their meanings.

1. 旦   a. Separate

2. 午   b. After

3. 交   c. Sea

4. 後   d. Same

5. 海   e. Mix

6. 太   f. Black

7. 離   g. Receive

8. 受   h. Dawn

9. 黒   i. Noon

10. 同   j. Fat

B. Please match the following meanings to their
kanji, and these to their **on** or **kun-yomi**.

1. Not   a. 林   1. **SAI** (サイ)

2. School   b. 最   2. **ashi** (あし)

3. Grove   c. 足   3. **KŌ** (コウ)

4. Car   d. 不   4. **mori** (もり)

5. Love   e. 凶   5. **AI** (アイ)

6. Leg   f. 糸   6. **hayashi** (はやし)

7. Forest   g. 車   7. **KYŌ** (キョウ)

8. Evil   h. 愛   8. **ito** (いと)

9. Most   i. 森   9. **FU** (フ)

10. Thread   j. 校   10. **kuruma** (くるま)

C. Please choose the best answer(s) to the following questions.

1. Which of the following readings apply to
   the kanji 離?
   a. **YŪ** (ユウ)
   b. **mori** (もり)
   c. **RYŌ** (リョウ)
   d. **hana** (はな)
   e. **RI** (リ)

2. Which of the following readings apply to
   the kanji 太?
   a. **futo** (ふと)
   b. **DAI** (ダイ)
   c. **inu** (いぬ)
   d. **TAI** (タイ)
   e. **ō** (おお)

3. I was going to win the marathon, but got a
   massive cramp in my _____.
   a. 旦
   b. 車
   c. 森
   d. 愛
   e. 足

4. Which of the following readings apply to
   the kanji 海?
   a. **mizu** (みず)
   b. **umi** (うみ)
   c. **KAI** (カイ)
   d. **kawa** (かわ)
   e. **KŌ** (コウ)

5. Which of the following readings apply to
   the kanji 後?
   a. **ushi** (うし)
   b. **KŌ** (コウ)
   c. **SHŌ** (ショウ)
   d. **ato** (あと)
   e. **GO** (ゴ)

D. Please choose the best answer(s) to the following questions.

1. . Which is the correct reading of 交ぜる?
   a. **ora·zeru**（おら・ぜる）
   b. **ko·zeru**（こ・ぜる）
   c. **ma·zeru**（ま・ぜる）
   d. **a·zeru**（あ・ぜる）

2. Which is the correct reading of 同じ?
   a. **ona·ji**（おな・じ）
   b. **ara·ji**（あら・じ）
   c. **aka·ji**（あか・じ）
   d. **u·ji**（う・じ）

3. Which of the following kanji has the most number of strokes?
   a. 後
   b. 森
   c. 最
   d. 愛
   e. 黒

4. Which is the correct reading of 受ける?
   a. **a·keru**（あ・ける）
   b. **u·keru**（う・ける）
   c. **tata·keru**（たた・ける）
   d. **oda·keru**（おだ・ける）

5. Which is the correct reading of 黒い?
   a. **shiro·i**（しろ・い）
   b. **ao·i**（あお・い）
   c. **aka·i**（あか・い）
   d. **kuro·i**（くろ・い）

E. Please match the following compounds and words to their meanings and pronunciations.

1. 分離   a. Smallest

2. 赤黒い   b. To undertake

3. 同意   c. Afternoon

4. 海王星   d. Unclear

5. 引き受ける   e. Agreement

6. 最小   f. High school

7. 足首   g. Neptune (planet)

8. 不明   h. Dark red

9. 午後   i. Separation

10. 高校   j. Ankle

1. **DŌ·I**（ドウ・イ）

2. **ashi·kubi**（あし・くび）

3. **KAI·Ō·SEI**（カイ・オウ・セイ）

4. **GO·GO**（ゴ・ゴ）

5. **KŌ·KŌ**（コウ・コウ）

6. **SAI·SHŌ**（サイ・ショウ）

7. **BUN·RI**（ブン・リ）

8. **hi·ki u·keru**（ひ・き う・ける）

9. **FU·MEI**（フ・メイ）

10. **aka guro·i**（あか ぐろ・い）

CUMULATIVE REVIEW EXERCISES FOR
CHAPTERS 1 - 10

A. Please match the following kanji to their meanings.

1.	家	a.	Electric
2.	干	b.	Country
3.	先	c.	Mother
4.	母	d.	Spirit
5.	空	e.	Dry
6.	国	f.	House
7.	太	g.	Precede
8.	有	h.	Fat
9.	電	i.	Empty
10.	気	j.	Have

B. Which kanji does not belong in the group?

1. a. 日　b. 週　c. 年　d. 首　e. 秒
2. a. 赤　b. 外　c. 青　d. 白　e. 黒
3. a. 春　b. 秋　c. 注　d. 冬　e. 夏
4. a. 市　b. 里　c. 高　d. 町　e. 村
5. a. 金　b. 馬　c. 牛　d. 鳥　e. 犬
6. a. 東　b. 南　c. 西　d. 北　e. 干
7. a. 舌　b. 売　c. 目　d. 足　e. 耳
8. a. 鳥　b. 午　c. 夕　d. 朝　e. 夜
9. a. 車　b. 寺　c. 門　d. 花　e. 道
10. a. 美　b. 好　c. 愛　d. 天　e. 凶

C. Identify the kanji having the most number of strokes.

1. a. 出　b. 主　c. 右　d. 央　e. 百
2. a. 車　b. 学　c. 持　d. 押　e. 周
3. a. 道　b. 週　c. 島　d. 黒　e. 校
4. a. 字　b. 図　c. 来　d. 英　e. 糸
5. a. 秋　b. 思　c. 書　d. 品　e. 前
6. a. 森　b. 鳥　c. 開　d. 新　e. 朝
7. a. 年　b. 私　c. 気　d. 甲　e. 母
8. a. 注　b. 夜　c. 音　d. 訓　e. 具
9. a. 掛　b. 時　c. 雪　d. 海　e. 最
10. a. 親　b. 離　c. 読　d. 語　e. 一

D. Please list the following kanji in the order indicated (alphabetical).

1. Dog / Fat / Heaven / Large / Lose
   a. 大　b. 犬　c. 太　d. 天　e. 失

2. Come / Half / Mix / Rice / Tree
   a. 来　b. 米　c. 木　d. 半　e. 交

3. Block / Dry / Noon / Not / Thousand
   a. 午　b. 干　c. 丁　d. 不　e. 千

4. Father / Heaven / Mix / School / Stand
   a. 天　b. 交　c. 父　d. 校　e. 立

5. Complete / Jewel / King / Pour / Primary
   a. 主　b. 注　c. 玉　d. 王　e. 全

6. Basis / Meet / Part / Public / Same
   a. 同　b. 公　c. 分　d. 会　e. 元

7. Precede / Read / Receive / Red / Sell
   a. 受   b. 売   c. 先   d. 読   e. 赤

8. Mind / New / Parent / Sound / Stand
   a. 親   b. 新   c. 音   d. 意   e. 立

9. Character / City / Ease / House / Study
   a. 学   b. 字   c. 安   d. 家   e. 市

10. Buy / Neck / Road / Shellfish / Tool
    a. 具   b. 道   c. 首   d. 買   e. 貝

E. Please choose the best answer to the following questions.

1. I often see monks when I walk past that ___.
   a. 星   b. 馬   c. 足   d. 電   e. 寺

2. The samurai made a menacing gesture with his ___.
   a. 花   b. 車   c. 刀   d. 川   e. 牛

3. What is the worst thing to find waiting for you on your doorstep?
   a. 金   b. 品   c. 親   d. 鳥   e. 死

4. Romeo was troubled. How could he demonstrate his ___ for Juliet?
   a. 凶   b. 太   c. 具   d. 愛   e. 田

5. It's so quiet and peaceful in the middle of this ___!
   a. 森   b. 犬   c. 月   d. 肉   e. 火

F. Please choose the best answer(s) to the following questions.

1. As 小 is to 大, 少 is to ___.
   a. 多   b. 人   c. 名   d. 外   e. 主

2. As 読 is to 書, 押 is to ___.
   a. 有   b. 交   c. 買   d. 引   e. 休

3. As 内 is to 外, 私 is to ___.
   a. 毎   b. 公   c. 不   d. 元   e. 取

4. As 上 is to 下, 前 is to ___.
   a. 本   b. 生   c. 最   d. 山   e. 後

5. As 林 is to 森, 好 is to ___.
   a. 赤   b. 愛   c. 心   d. 先   e. 図

G. Please choose the best answer to the following questions.

1. Which is the correct reading of 行く?
   a. **a·ku** (あ・く)
   b. **i·ku** (い・く)
   c. **fu·ku** (ふ・く)
   d. **ta·ku** (た・く)

2. Which is the correct reading of 切る?
   a. **tabe·ru** (た べ・る)
   b. **ino·ru** (い の・る)
   c. **a·ru** (あ・る)
   d. **ki·ru** (き・る)

3. Which is the correct reading of 会う?
   a. **a·u** (あ・う)
   b. **o·u** (お・う)
   c. **muka·u** (む か・う)
   d. **i·u** (い・う)

4. Which is the correct reading of 近い?
   a. **chika·i** (ち か・い)
   b. **ao·i** (あ お・い)
   c. **kata·i** (か た・い)
   d. **aka·i** (あ か・い)

5. Which is the correct reading of 話す?
   a. **wata·su** (わ た・す)
   b. **furu·su** (ふ る・す)
   c. **hana·su** (は な・す)
   d. **ta·su** (た・す)

6. Which is the correct reading of 赤い?
   a. **furu·i** (ふ る・い)
   b. **taka·i** (た か・い)
   c. **ō·i** (お お・い)
   d. **aka·i** (あ か・い)

7. Which is the correct reading of 少し?
   a. **suko·shi** (すこ・し)
   b. **haya·shi** (はや・し)
   c. **ara·shi** (あら・し)
   d. **hana·shi** (はな・し)

8. Which is the correct reading of 古い?
   a. **kuro·i** (くろ・い)
   b. **shiro·i** (しろ・い)
   c. **furu·i** (ふる・い)
   d. **usu·i** (うす・い)

9. Which is the correct reading of 聞く?
   a. **hi·ku** (ひ・く)
   b. **ki·ku** (き・く)
   c. **a·ku** (あ・く)
   d. **ara·ku** (あら・く)

10. Which is the correct reading of 押す?
    a. **hana·su** (はな・す)
    b. **u·su** (う・す)
    c. **ama·su** (あま・す)
    d. **o·su** (お・す)

H. Please match the following compounds and words to their meanings and pronunciations.

1. 有名   a. Exit   1. **TA·DOKU·KA** (タ・ド ク・カ)

2. 多読家 b. Talkative 2. **NYŪ·KAI·KIN** (ニュ ウ・カイ・キン)

3. 出口   c. Famous 3. **BI·KA** (ビ・カ)

4. 同行者 d. The four seasons 4. **ta·chi i·ru** (た・ち い・る)

5. 書き入れる e. "Watch Your Step" 5. **ka·ki i·reru** (か・き い・れる)

6. 午前   f. Traveling companion 6. **GAI·KŌ** (ガイ・コウ)

7. 立ち入る   g. Patriotism   7. **GO·ZEN** (ゴ・ゼン)

8. 春夏秋冬   h. Well-read person   8. **YŪ·MEI** (ユウ・メイ)

9. 美化   i. Beautification   9. **hana·shi zu·ki** (はな・しず・き)

10. 足元注意   j. Fireworks   10. **hana·bi** (はな・び)

11. 外交   k. Morning (a.m.)   11. **de·guchi** (で・ぐち)

12. 愛国心   l. Enrollment fee   12. **SHUN·KA· SHŪ·TO** (シュン・カ・シュ ウ・トウ)

13. 話し好き   m. To go into   13. **AI· KOKU· SHIN** (アイ・コク・シン)

14. 入会金   n. Foreign policy   14. **DŌ·KŌ· SHA** (ドウ・コウ・シャ)

15. 花火   o. To write in   15. **ashi· moto· CHŪ·I** (あし・もと・チュウ・イ)

Kanji #201—225

KANJI 201

 TRUST

BUILDING THIS KANJI
Giraffe 亻 + Say 言 (80) + = 信

Meaning
Trust. As can be seen in the final entry of the "Common Words and Compounds" section below, a secondary meaning relates to the ideas of messages and correspondence. This will be the first entry, incidentally, for which there is no sample sentence. In its place, a short passage of written Japanese in the chapter review section will enable you to better test your comprehension skills.

Remembering this kanji
Can you **TRUST** what a **giraffe says**? Well, my neighbor's a **giraffe**, and here's what he said yesterday: "**TRUST** me, I won't chew on your new shrubs", "**TRUST** me, I'll have your lawn-mower back next week", "**TRUST** me, I'll give you that money soon."

I sure as heck hope you can **TRUST** what a **giraffe says**.

Common Pronunciations
Common **ON** reading: **SHIN** (シ ン)
Common **kun** reading: none

Less Common Pronunciations
Less common **ON** reading: none
Less common **kun** reading: none

COMMON WORDS AND COMPOUNDS		
信じる	*believe*	**SHIN**·jiru シン・じる
自信	self + trust = *self confidence*	**JI·SHIN** ジ・シン
信号	trust + title = *signal*	**SHIN**·GŌ シン・ゴウ
通信	passage + trust = *correspondence*	TSŪ·**SHIN** ツウ・シン

KANJI 202

文 **LITERATURE**

'	一	ゲ	文					

BUILDING THIS KANJI
Police ⼇ + Wishbones メ = 文

Common Pronunciations
Common **ON** reading: **BUN** (ブン);**MON** (モン)
Common **kun** reading: none
BUN is the far more common reading.

Less Common Pronunciations
Less common **ON** reading: none
Less common **kun** reading: **fumi** (ふみ)

IRREGULAR READING		
文字	literature + character = *character/letter (of an alphabet)*	MO·JI モ·ジ

COMMON WORDS AND COMPOUNDS		
文化	literature + change = *culture*	BUN·KA ブン·カ
文明	literature + bright = *civilization*	BUN·MEI ブン·メイ
注文	pour + literature = *order; request*	CHŪ·MON チュウ·モン
天文学	heaven + literature + study = *astronomy*	TEN·MON·GAKU テン·モン·ガク

Meaning
This character relates to writing and composition, from grand literary works to sentences and individual letters.

Remembering this kanji
Crime (as symbolized by the **police** hat) and cooking (as symbolized by the **wishbones**) have always been popular topics in LITERATURE. So why, then, is my novel about a **policeman's** desperate search for a missing **wishbone** not considered high LITERATURE?

KANJI 203

進 **ADVANCE**

'	⼁	ｲ	ｲ'	ｲ亠	ｲ十	隹	隹	｀隹
³隹	進							

BUILDING THIS KANJI
Squirrels 隹 + Seal ⻌ = 進

Meaning
Advance, along with the idea of progressing in a figurative sense.

Remembering this kanji
Criticize if you want, but my opinion is this: **squirrels** and **seals** have yet to ADVANCE. They have not invented the wheel, are unable to use cutlery, and their communication skills remain minimal. And don't tell me that **squirrels** ADVANCE with whiskers twitching and **seals** ADVANCE by bellying over beaches; such statements in no way ADVANCE this discussion.

Common Pronunciations
Common **ON** reading: **SHIN** (シン)
Common **kun** reading: **susu** (すす)

kun-yomi suggestion: "Sue! Sue!"

This is the last time a suggestion will be given for a **kun-yomi**. Using your **on-yomi** keyword and the **kun-yomi** suggestion above, write your sentence to remember these readings in the box below.

Less Common Pronunciations
Less common **ON** reading: **JIN** (ジン)
Less common **kun** reading: none

COMMON WORDS AND COMPOUNDS		
進む (intr)	*advance; progress*	**susu·mu** すす・む
進める (tr)	*lead; promote (something)*	**susu·meru** すす・める
進行	advance + go = *advance; proceed*	**SHIN·KŌ** シン・コウ
先進国	precede + advance + country = *developed nation*	SEN·**SHIN**·KOKU セン・シン・コク

KANJI 204

 SAKÉ

`	ˋ	⠆	✓	⠆	氵	汀	沂	洒	洒	酒
酒										

BUILDING THIS KANJI
Splash 氵 + Whiskey Jug 酉 = 酒

Meaning
This kanji can refer to Japan's famous rice wine specifically, as well as to alcoholic drinks in general.

Remembering this kanji
"Hey you, gimme a **splash** out of that there **whiskey jug**," the grizzled prospector said with a scowl. Fearing trouble, the bartender quickly set out a shot glass, but had it slapped away the moment it was filled.
  "What in tarnation!" the oldtimer yelled. "This is SAKÉ! If I'm havin' SAKÉ, I want it in a dainty cup on a lacquered tray!"

Common Pronunciations
Common **ON** reading: **SHU** (シュ)
Common **kun** reading: **saké** (さけ); **saka** (さか)

Saké and saka are always voiced (becoming zaka and zaké) when they appear outside of first position. Using your **on-yomi** keyword for シュ and your ideas for words or sounds that approximate the two **kun-yomi**, write your sentence to remember the **on-yomi** and **kun-yomi** readings in the box below.

Less Common Pronunciations
Less common **ON** reading: none
Less common **kun** reading: none

COMMON WORDS AND COMPOUNDS		
酒	*saké; liquor*	**saké** さけ
日本酒	Japan + saké = *(Japanese) saké*	NI·HON·**SHU** ニ・ホン・シュ
酒屋	saké + roof = *liquor store*	**saka·ya** さか・や
飲酒	drink + saké = *to drink alcohol*	**IN·SHU** イン・シュ

COMPONENT #205

FLAG

KANJI 205

DOOR

一	フ	�_コ	戸				

BUILDING THIS KANJI
One (top of a bun) 一 (3) + Flag 尸 = 戸

Meaning
Door. This kanji is also used as a counter for buildings and houses.

Remembering this kanji
Let's assume you've moved into an apartment that has no DOOR. What would be better in its place, the **top of a bun**, or a **flag**? I can't help feeling that the **top of a bun** wouldn't do a very good job, as it would tear easily off the hinges and leave sesame seeds on the carpet whenever you moved it. A **flag** would be better, offering more privacy and having the added advantage of being shaped like a DOOR.

Common Pronunciations
Common **ON** reading: KO (コ)
Common **kun** reading: to (と)

The **kun-yomi** is almost always voiced when not in first position; the third compound below offers an example. The only instance where the **on-yomi** becomes voiced is shown in the final compound.

After creating a keyword to remember the **kun-yomi**, write your sentence to remember the **on-yomi** and **kun-yomi** readings in the box below.

Less Common Pronunciations
Less common **ON** reading: none
Less common **kun** reading: none

COMMON WORDS AND COMPOUNDS		
戸	*door*	**to** と
戸外	door + outside = *outdoors; open air*	**KO·GAI** コ・ガイ
雨戸	rain + door = *sliding door; shutter*	ama·**do** あま・ど
泣き 上戸	cry + upper + door = *a weepy drunk*	na·ki JŌ·**GO** な・き ジョウ・ゴ

KANJI 206

MATTER

一	丶	ㄇ	彐	写	写	写	事

BUILDING THIS KANJI
One (hamburger patty) 一 (3) + Mouth (vampire)
口 (8) + Pitchfork ㅋ + Harpoon 亅 = 事

Meaning
A matter. This is an important kanji that appears in a number of common words.

Remembering this kanji

"What's the MATTER honey?" she asked, concerned. "You haven't even touched your **hamburger patty**."

"Nothing's the MATTER dear," said the **vampire**.

"I don't believe you. Something's definitely the MATTER."

"OK, maybe there is. I'm just starting to suspect that you don't understand me very well. I mean, really, a **hamburger patty**? I can't have that in my diet. And the **pitchfork** you gave me yesterday? As much as I'd like to help out around the farm, I can't be out there pitching hay in broad daylight. And do I even have to go into the **harpoon** you gave me for my birthday? I wouldn't go after my victims with that as a MATTER of principle."

Common Pronunciations

Common **ON** reading: **JI** (ジ)
Common **kun** readings: **koto** (こ と)

The **kun-yomi** is always voiced when not in first position, as shown in the final compound below (an extremely common word composed of a mix of on and **kun-yomi**).

After creating a kun-yomi keyword, write your sentence to remember the **on-yomi** and **kun-yomi** readings in the box below.

Less Common Pronunciations

Less common **ON** reading: **ZU** (ズ)
Less common **kun** reading: none

COMMON WORDS AND COMPOUNDS		
事	*matter*	**koto** こ と
工事	craft + matter = *construction work*	**KŌ·JI** コ ウ · ジ
大事	large + matter = *serious/important matter*	**DAI·JI** ダ イ · ジ
仕事	serve + matter = *job; work*	**SHI·goto** シ · ご と

WAIT

BUILDING THIS KANJI
Razor 彳 + **Temple** 寺 (104) = 待

Meaning

Wait. A secondary meaning relates to the sense of how someone or something is treated or handled.

Remembering this kanji
"WAIT! WAIT!"

Once more the **razor** was drawn away from the girl's head. "Look," the **temple** priestess sighed, "if you wish to be one of us your hair must be shaved off."

She nodded and tried to steel herself, but as soon as the **razor** approached her scalp, she broke down as before: "WAIT! WAIT!"

"I may be wrong," one of the other initiates whispered, "but something tells me this might not be the right career choice for Rapunzel."

Common Pronunciations
Common **ON** reading: **TAI** (タイ)
Common **kun** reading: **ma** (ま)

As the final compound shows, this is another common verb that can "absorb" its hiragana accompaniment in the manner of 買.

After creating a **kun-yomi** keyword, write your sentence to remember the **on-yomi** and **kun-yomi** readings in the box below.

Less Common Pronunciations
Less common **ON** reading: none
Less common **kun** reading: none

COMMON WORDS AND COMPOUNDS		
待つ	wait	**ma**·tsu ま·つ
ちょっと待って	Just a moment!	chotto **ma**·tte ちょっと ま·って
期待	period + wait = *expectation*	**KI·TAI** キ·タイ
待合室	wait + match + room = *waiting room*	**machi**·ai·SHITSU まち·あい·シツ

KANJI 208

兄 **ELDER BROTHER**

丿	冂	口	尸	兄			

BUILDING THIS KANJI
Mouth (vampire) 口 (8) + Ballet 儿 = 兄

Meaning
Elder brother.

Remembering this kanji
Q. Why is an **ELDER BROTHER** more likely to attend a **vampire ballet**?

A. A **vampire ballet** has to take place long after nightfall, which is past the bedtimes of an **ELDER BROTHER'S** siblings.

Common Pronunciations
Common **ON** reading: **KEI** (ケイ)
Common **kun** reading: **ani** (あに)

Create your **on-yomi** keyword and enter it in the table at the back of the book. Then, after creating your **kun-yomi** keyword, write your sentence to remember the **on-yomi** and **kun-yomi** readings in the box below.

IRREGULAR READING		
お兄さん	*elder brother*	o·nii·san お・にい・さん

This is a more polite form of address.

COMMON WORDS AND COMPOUNDS		
兄	*elder brother*	ani あに
父兄会	father + elder brother + meet = *parents' association*	FU·KEI·KAI フ・ケイ・カイ

Less Common Pronunciations
Less common **ON** reading: **KYŌ** (キョウ)
Less common **kun** reading: none

FORKLIFT   └

県   PREFECTURE

BUILDING THIS KANJI
Eye (Cyclops) 目 (15) + Forklift └ + Tripod 小 = 県

Meaning
Prefecture.

Remembering this kanji
The **Cyclops** paused a moment. "I'm attempting to uncover the essence of the Japanese **forklift**," he said finally, folding up his **tripod**. This or that PREFECTURE has its own variation; **forklifts** in Aomori PREFECTURE, for example, are slightly smaller due to the frigid climate, while those in Okinawa PREFECTURE tend to have a tanned complexion. I'm wandering from PREFECTURE to PREFECTURE with my trusty **tripod** so that I can capture these subtleties. You obviously need a good eye to do this."

Common Pronunciations
Common **ON** reading: **KEN** (ケン)
Common **kun** reading: none

Less Common Pronunciations
Less common **ON** reading: none
Less common **kun** readings: none

COMMON WORDS AND COMPOUNDS		
県	*prefecture*	KEN ケン
県立	prefecture + stand = *prefectural*	KEN·RITSU ケン・リツ
山口県	mountain + mouth + prefecture = *Yamaguchi prefecture*	yama·guchi·KEN やま・ぐち・ケン
愛知県	love + know + prefecture = *Aichi prefecture*	AI·CHI·KEN アイ・チ・ケン

KANJI 210

BACK

BUILDING THIS KANJI
North 北(72) + Moon 月(11) = 背

Meaning
The 'back' of someone or something. This character is commonly used to refer to a person's height, but also has a secondary meaning related to disobedience or betrayal (think of "turning one's back" on someone).

Remembering this kanji
With his BACK against the wall of our igloo, the ancient one would tell tales of the **north**, of an age when the **moon** trod over the tundra. "We often hunted, the **moon** and I," he said, "sitting BACK to BACK so that crafty musk-ox could not surprise us. But the **moon** eventually left, turning his BACK on the ways of the **north** so that he could take his place in the sky."

Common Pronunciations
Common **ON** reading: **HAI** (ハイ)
Common **kun** reading: **se** (せ); **sei** (せい)

This kanji takes a bit of work to pin down. **sei** refers only to one's height, and appears in very few words. **se** and **HAI** are more common, but whereas **se** refers primarily to the 'back' of someone or something, **HAI** not only incorporates this meaning, but also the sense of betrayal mentioned above. Both **kun-yomi** can become voiced when not in first position.

Create your **on-yomi** keyword and enter it in the table at the back of the book. After that, create your **kun-yomi** keywords and write your sentence to remember the **on-yomi** and **kun-yomi** readings in the box below.

Less Common Pronunciations
Less common **ON** reading: none
Less common **kun** reading: **somu** (そむ)

COMMON WORDS AND COMPOUND		
背	*back*	**se** せ
背	*one's height*	**sei** せい
背中	back + middle = *one's back*	**se**·naka せ·なか
背後	back + after = *back; rear*	**HAI**·GO ハイ·ゴ

KANJI 211

晴

CLEAR

BUILDING THIS KANJI
Sun 日 (6) + Blue 青 (86) = 晴

Meaning
Clear, as in weather.

Remembering this kanji
"Hmm…**sun** and **blue** sky. Unless I miss my guess, we got us some CLEAR weather here."

Common Pronunciations
Common **ON** readings: **SEI** (セ イ)
Common **kun** reading: **ha** (は)

The **kun-yomi** becomes voiced when not in first position, as it does in the second example below.

Less Common Pronunciations
Less common **ON** reading: none
Less common **kun** reading: none

COMMON WORDS AND COMPOUNDS		
晴れ	*clear skies*	**ha·**re は·れ
秋晴れ	autumn + clear = *fine autumn weather*	aki **ba·**re あ き ば·れ
晴天	clear + heaven = *fine weather*	**SEI·**TEN セ イ·テ ン

COMPONENT #212

SURFER

KANJI 212

走 **RUN**

一	十	土	丰	走	赱	走	

BUILDING THIS KANJI
Ten (scarecrow) 十(28) + Surfer 疋 = 走

Meaning
Run.

Remembering this kanji
I was really upset when those cool **surfer** dudes showed up at my local beach. "**RUN** along, **scarecrow**," they said, "us **surfers** are taking over here. You don't belong around our rippling abs and easygoing ways."

Well, I thought, I may have a saggy physique and be a bit uptight, but I'm not going to **RUN** anywhere. Which isn't surprising, I suppose, given that I really am a **scarecrow**.

Common Pronunciations
Common **ON** reading: **SŌ** (ソ ウ)
Common **kun** reading: **hashi** (は し)

The **kun-yomi** becomes voiced when not in first position, as it is in the third example below.

Less Common Pronunciations
Less common **ON** reading: none
Less common **kun** reading: none

COMMON WORDS AND COMPOUNDS		
走る	*run*	**hashi·**ru は し·る
走り 回る	run + rotate = *run around*	**hashi·**ri mawa·ru は し·り まわ·る
口走る	mouth + run = *blurt out*	kuchi **bashi·**ru く ち ばし·る
走行 時間	run + go + time + interval = *travel time*	**SŌ·**KŌ·JI·KAN ソ ウ·コ ウ·ジ·カ ン

洗 **WASH**

BUILDING THIS KANJI
Splash 氵 + Precede 先 (105) = 洗

Meaning
Wash.

Remembering this kanji
OK, so you've showered and thus had a **WASH**.
Well done. But what exactly does it mean to
WASH? According to physicists, when the
process is slowed down sufficiently, a **WASH** is
nothing more than a set of **splashes** – one **splash**
precedes another **splash**, which **precedes** another
splash, and so on. When linked, these isolated
splashes form what is known as a **WASH**.

Common Pronunciations
Common **ON** reading: **SEN** (セン)
Common **kun** reading: **ara** (あら)

Less Common Pronunciations
Less common **ON** reading: none
Less common **kun** reading: none

COMMON WORDS AND COMPOUNDS		
洗う	*wash*	**ara·u** あら・う
お手洗い	hand + wash = *washroom;* *lavatory*	o·te **ara·i** お・て あら・い
洗車	wash + car = *car wash*	**SEN·SHA** セン・シャ
皿洗い	dish + wash = *dishwashing*	sara **ara·i** さら あら・い

己 **ONESELF**

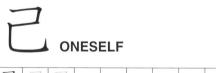

Meaning
Oneself. Though close in meaning to " 自 "
("self", from Entry 33), this character is much
less common—you are only likely to encounter
it in the two compounds shown below. It does,
however, show up frequently as a component in
other kanji, so as we have done with other such
characters (" 寸 ", " 又 ", etc.) we will assign it
an external meaning having a more immediate
visual connection: "whip".

Remembering this kanji

A **whip** is an excellent symbol for ONESELF, as it can be used to **whip** ONESELF into a frenzy or **whip** ONESELF into shape. And, as any hardcore medieval sinner will tell you, nothing beats a **whip** when it comes time to literally **whip** ONESELF.

Common Pronunciations

Common **ON** reading: **KO** (コ)
Common **kun** reading: none

Less Common Pronunciations

Less common **ON** reading: **KI** (キ)
Less common **kun** reading: **onore** (おのれ)

COMMON WORDS AND COMPOUNDS		
自己	self + oneself = *oneself*	JI·KO ジ·コ
利己的	profit + oneself + target = *selfish; egoistic*	RI·KO·TEKI リ·コ·テキ

KANJI 215

 ROLL

一	厂	冂	亘	亘	車	車	車	転
転	転							

BUILDING THIS KANJI
Car 車(190) + Spy 云 = 転

Meaning

Roll, tumble. This character can also imply a sense of change or transition when it appears in certain compounds.

Remembering this kanji

I grew nervous as I watched the **car** ROLL up. "Get in," said the **spy**. I did as told, and asked him to let me ROLL a cigarette. He looked at me warily. "All right," he said at last, "but ROLL down the window. I don't want you smelling up my **car**."

Common Pronunciations

Common **ON** reading: **TEN** (テン)
Common **kun** reading: **koro** (ころ)

Note the interesting difference between the two intransitive verbs below.

Less Common Pronunciations

Less common **ON** reading: none
Less common **kun** reading: none

COMMON WORDS AND COMPOUNDS		
転ぶ (intr)	*roll; tumble (by accident)*	**koro**·bu ころ·ぶ
転がる (intr)	*roll; tumble (on purpose)*	**koro**·garu ころ·がる
転がす (tr)	*to roll (something)*	**koro**·gasu ころ·がす
自転車	self + roll + car = *bicycle*	JI·TEN·SHA ジ·テン·シャ

COMPONENT #216

FIRECRACKER

KANJI 216

楽 **MUSIC**

| ´ | l | 冂 | 白 | 白 | ﾞ白 | 泊 | 泊´ | 泊ﾞ |
| 泊 | 楽 | 楽 | 楽 | | | | | |

BUILDING THIS KANJI
White 白 (7) + Firecracker 氵 + 木 (13) = 楽

Meaning
This beautiful character can mean two things: music, or a sense of comfort and pleasure.

Remembering this kanji
The **white** bark of the birch **tree** had great significance for the elders, as the **firecracker** noises it made when burning were believed to be MUSIC sent from the beyond. Indeed, the distinctive patterns on the trunk of this **white tree** are still thought to represent the notations of this other-worldly MUSIC.

Common Pronunciations
Common **ON** readings: **GAKU** (ガク);
RAKU (ラク)
Common **kun** reading: **tano** (たの)

GAKU is used when the compound relates to music, **RAKU** when referring to pleasure and comfort.

After entering your **on-yomi** keyword for ラク in the table at the back of the book and creating a **kun-yomi** keyword, write your sentence to remember the **on-yomi** and **kun-yomi** readings in the box below.

Less Common Pronunciations
Less common **ON** reading: none
Less common **kun** reading: none

COMMON WORDS AND COMPOUNDS		
楽しい	*fun*	tano·shii たの・しい
音楽	sound + music = *music*	ON·GAKU オン・ガク
楽団	music + group = *band; orchestra*	GAKU·DAN ガク・ダン
楽園	music (pleasure) + garden = *paradise*	RAKU·EN ラク・エン

KANJI 217

理 **REASON**

| ー | l | 干 | 王 | 圵 | 坧 | 玡 | 珇 | 理 |
| 理 | 理 | | | | | | | |

BUILDING THIS KANJI
King 王 (23) + Hamlet 里 (180) = 理

Meaning
The idea of 'reason'. This is an important character that appears in many common words.

Remembering this kanji

"What REASON did the **king** have for visiting such a humble **hamlet**?" she asked me.

"A very important REASON," I answered, playing it cool.

"Well, what was it? No one can come up with any REASON why he went there."

I smiled knowingly, paused for effect, then told her in a hushed tone.

"That's a really dumb REASON," she said.

Common Pronunciations

Common **ON** reading: **RI** (リ)

Common **kun** reading: none

Less Common Pronunciations

Less common **ON** reading: none

Less common **kun** reading: none

COMMON WORDS AND COMPOUNDS		
心理学	heart + reason + study = *psychology*	SHIN·**RI**·GAKU シン・リ・ガク
理由	reason + cause = *reason; cause*	**RI**·YŪ リ・ユウ
無理	without + reason = *unreasonable; impossible*	MU·**RI** ム・リ
代理	substitute + reason = *representation; proxy*	DAI·**RI** ダイ・リ

KANJI 218

ORDER

一	⺊	勹	勹	乊	丷	釆	釆	番
番	番	番						

BUILDING THIS KANJI

Comet 𠂉 + Rice 米 (32) + Rice field 田 (73) = 番

Meaning

This kanji can appear in a variety of seemingly unrelated compounds, but there will usually be some sense of 'order' present, from the order of a person's turn in line, to the order of numbers, to the keeping of order by overseeing something.

Remembering this kanji

There is an ORDER to everything, as the ORDER of building this kanji demonstrates: a **comet** passes above **rice**, which can only grow out of a **rice field**.

Common Pronunciations

Common **ON** reading: **BAN** (バン)

Common **kun** reading: none

Create your **on-yomi** keyword and enter it in the table at the back of the book. After that, write your sentence to remember the **on-yomi** reading in the box below.

Less Common Pronunciations

Less common **ON** reading: none

Less common **kun** reading: none

COMMON WORDS AND COMPOUNDS		
一番	one + order = *number one; the best*	ICHI·**BAN** イチ・バン
交番	mix + order = *police box/stand*	KŌ·**BAN** コウ・バン
番号	order + title = *number*	**BAN**·GŌ バン・ゴウ
番組	order + association = *(television, etc.) program*	**BAN**·gumi バン・ぐみ

KANJI 219

両 **BOTH**

一 厂 匚 币 両 両

BUILDING THIS KANJI
One (top of a bun) 一(3) + Gorilla 冂 +
Mountain 山(1) = 両

Meaning
Both. This kanji is also used as a counter for such
vehicles as railway cars and carriages.

Remembering this kanji
"That's enough! BOTH of you!" said the **gorilla**,
placing herself between the **top of the bun** and
the **mountain**. "Can't you understand that I'm
fond of you BOTH? That BOTH of you are
important to me?" Sighing, she turned at last to
the **top of the bun**. "I'm sorry," she said. "You're
delicious, but you have to realize that I'll always
be a **mountain gorilla**."

Common Pronunciations
Common **ON** reading: **RYŌ** (リ ョ ウ)
Common **kun** reading: none

Create your **on-yomi** keyword and enter it in the
table at the back of the book. After that, write
your sentence to remember the **on-yomi** reading
in the box below.

Less Common Pronunciations
Less common **ON** reading: none
Less common **kun** reading: none

COMMON WORDS AND COMPOUNDS		
両親	both + parent = *parents*	**RYŌ**·SHIN リ ョ ウ・シン
両者	both + individual = *both people*	**RYŌ**·SHA リ ョ ウ・シャ
両面	both + mask = *both sides*	**RYŌ**·MEN リ ョ ウ・メン

COMPONENT #220

GHOST 七

This is the first in a 'family' of five components
that you will meet in this book. Each one that
follows will be built on the one preceding it
through the addition of an extra stroke.

KANJI 220

ｱ ニ 尸 尸 民

BUILDING THIS KANJI
Flag 尸 + Ghost 七 = 民

Meaning
People. This is the only character in the 2,136
general-use kanji in which the flag component
is bent.

民 **PEOPLE**

Remembering this kanji

"PEOPLE, PEOPLE, listen!" yelled the **ghost**. "I'm claiming this land for… Oh, come on, PEOPLE!"

"Give it up," said another **ghost**. "PEOPLE can't tell we're here. And anyway, that **ghost flag** is so flimsy the staff's already bent."

Common Pronunciations

Common **ON** reading: **MIN** (ミ ン)
Common **kun** reading: none

Create your **on-yomi** keyword and enter it in the table at the back of the book. After that, write your sentence to remember the **on-yomi** reading in the box below.

Less Common Pronunciations

Less common **ON** reading: none
Less common **kun** reading: **tami** (た み)

COMMON WORDS AND COMPOUNDS		
市民	city + people = *citizen*	SHI·MIN シ・ミ ン
国民	country + people = *the people (of a nation)*	KOKU·MIN コ ク・ミ ン
民主	people + primary = *democratic*	MIN·SHU ミ ン・シ ュ
住民	reside + people = *residents; inhabitants*	JŪ·MIN ジ ュ ウ・ミ ン

質 **QUALITY**

、	／	／	斤	斤ʼ	斤ʼ	斤ʼ	斦	斦
斦	質	質	質	質	質			

BUILDING THIS KANJI
Axe 斤 (126) + Axe 斤 (126) + Shellfish 貝 (21) = 質

Meaning

The quality or intrinsic nature of something. A secondary meaning, curiously, relates to pawning and pawnshops.

Remembering this kanji

"How's the QUALITY of these **shellfish**?" she asked the merchant.

"Fantastic! You couldn't break 'em apart with a **couple of axes**."

"Uh…that's not what I meant."

"Oh. Well then, what kind of weird QUALITY are you looking for?"

Common Pronunciations

Common **ON** reading: **SHITSU** (シ ツ), **SHICHI** (シ チ)
Common **kun** reading: none

SHITSU is the most common reading, and is used when this kanji relates to the idea of quality. **SHICHI** is used with respect to pawnshops and pawned objects; the third compound below (note the mixture of on and **kun-yomi**) provides an example and is the only time this reading becomes voiced.

Less Common Pronunciations
Less common **ON** readings: **CHI** (チ)
Less common **kun** reading: none

COMMON WORDS AND COMPOUNDS		
本質	main + quality = *essence*	HON·**SHITSU** ホン・シツ
体質	body + quality = *(physical) constitution*	TAI·**SHITSU** タイ・シツ
人質	person + quality (pawn) = *hostage*	hito·**JICHI** ひと・ジチ
質問	quality + question = *question*	**SHITSU**·MON シツ・モン

KANJI 222

正 **PROPER**

一 丁 下 〒 正

BUILDING THIS KANJI
One (top of a bun) 一 (3) + Stop 止 (43) = 正

Meaning
Proper. This versatile kanji can convey a sense of 'formality', as well as the ideas of what is correct or just, etc.

Remembering this kanji
Using the **top of a bun** will not help you **stop** in a PROPER way, as it will quickly crumble under stress. No, it's far more PROPER to have PROPER brakes.

Common Pronunciations
Common **ON** reading: **SEI** (セイ);
SHŌ (ショウ)
Common **kun** reading: **tada** (ただ)

SEI is the more common of the **on-yomi**. **tada** appears in only the first example below.

Less Common Pronunciations
Less common **ON** reading: none
Less common **kun** reading: **masa** (まさ)

COMMON WORDS AND COMPOUNDS		
正しい	*proper; correct*	**tada**·shii ただ・しい
正午	proper + noon = *noon*	**SHŌ**·GO ショウ・ゴ
正式	proper + type = *formal; official*	**SEI**·SHIKI セイ・シキ

KANJI 223

方 **DIRECTION**

| ' | 一 | 丁 | 方 | | | | |

BUILDING THIS KANJI
Police 宀 + Chair 力 = 方

Meaning

This commonly-used kanji has to do with direction. It can refer to both physical directions as well as to the idea of directions as a method for doing something. In this latter sense it attaches to verb stems and can be translated as "how to …"; the final compound below provides an example. Ensure that you can clearly see the difference between this kanji and that for "ten thousand" (万), from Entry 89.

Remembering this kanji

"What with all the budget cutbacks," said the **police** chief, "we've needed to do things a little differently around here. Instead of interrogations, for example, we just spin this swivel **chair** in front of a bunch of suspects; whichever **DIRECTION** it points in tells us who the criminal is. We believe we're taking **police** work in an innovative **DIRECTION**."

Common Pronunciations

Common **ON** reading: **HŌ** (ホ ウ)
Common **kun** reading: **kata** (か た)

Note that **kata** can become voiced when not in first position. When the kanji is attached to verb stems in the sense of "how to…", though (as in the final example), it is always read **kata**.

Create your **on-yomi** keyword and enter it in the table at the back of the book. Then, after creating your **kun-yomi** keyword, write your sentence to remember the **on-yomi** and **kun-yomi** readings in the box below.

Less Common Pronunciations

Less common **ON** reading: none
Less common **kun** reading: none

IRREGULAR READING

Recall the following irregular reading from Entry 173, constructed from the words "whereabouts" and "unclear". Remember also that the first kanji has an unusual reading as well (**yuku** as opposed to **yuki**):

行方不明	go + direction + not + bright = "Missing"	yuku·e·FU·MEI ゆ く・え・フ・メ イ

COMMON WORDS AND COMPOUNDS		
一方	one + direction *one side; on the other hand*	IP·PŌ イ ッ・ポ ウ
地方	ground + direction = *district; region*	CHI·HŌ チ・ホ ウ
方法	direction + law = *method; way*	HŌ·HŌ ホ ウ・ホ ウ
作り方	make + direction = *how to make (something)*	tsuku·ri·kata つ く・り・か た

COMPONENT #224

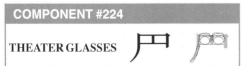

THEATER GLASSES 尸凹

KANJI 224

声

VOICE

| 一 | 十 | 士 | 声 | 声 | 声 | 声 | | |

BUILDING THIS KANJI
Gentleman 士(84) + Theater Glasses 尸凹 = 声

Meaning
Voice.

Remembering this kanji

"Sssh! Keep your VOICE down!"

The **gentleman** with the **theater glasses** was growing irritable. "Please, miss," the **gentleman** said once more, "your VOICE. I can't concentrate on the performance."

"Look," she said. "In case you haven't noticed, I'm a beer vendor at a baseball game. I *have* to raise my VOICE."

Common Pronunciations
Common **ON** reading: **SEI** (セイ)
Common **kun** reading: **koe** (こえ)

With the exception of the second compound below, the **kun-yomi** is always voiced when not in first position (as in the third compound). It is worth noting that when 一 is read with its **kun-yomi** of ひと, no kanji following it ever becomes voiced.

Less Common Pronunciations
Less common **ON** reading: **SHŌ** (ショウ)
Less common **kun** reading: **kowa** (こわ)

COMMON WORDS AND COMPOUNDS		
声	*voice*	koe こえ
一声	one + voice = *a voice; a cry*	hito·koe ひと·こえ
大声	large + voice = *a loud voice*	ō·goe おお·ごえ
声明	voice + bright = *declaration; proclamation*	SEI·MEI セイ·メイ

KANJI 225

住

RESIDE

| ノ | イ | 亻 | 仁 | 住 | 住 | 住 | | |

BUILDING THIS KANJI
Giraffe 亻 + Primary 主(164) = 住

Meaning
Reside.

Remembering this kanji

"As real estate marketers, we need to understand the **giraffe**, in particular his **primary** motive in choosing where to RESIDE. I believe they need to:

a) RESIDE in wide open spaces,
b) RESIDE where there's fine grazing, and
c) RESIDE where it's safe.

For their **primary** residence, therefore, I suggest we tell our **giraffe** clients to RESIDE in that subdivision on the savanna."

Common Pronunciations

Common **ON** reading: JŪ (ジュウ)
Common **kun** reading: su (す)

The **kun-yomi** is voiced when not in first position.

Less Common Pronunciations

Less common **ON** reading: none
Less common **kun** reading: none

COMMON WORDS AND COMPOUNDS		
住む	reside; live	**su**·mu す·む
住民	reside + people = residents	**JŪ**·MIN ジュウ·ミン
住所	reside + location = address	**JŪ**·SHO ジュウ·ショ

CHAPTER 11 REVIEW EXERCISES

A. Please match the following kanji to their meanings.

1.	声	a.	Wait
2.	待	b.	Proper
3.	民	c.	Run
4.	酒	d.	Literature
5.	正	e.	Voice
6.	文	f.	Elder brother
7.	清	g.	Music
8.	走	h.	Clear
9.	楽	i.	Saké
10.	兄	j.	People

B. Please match the following meanings to their kanji, and these to their **on** or **kun-yomi**.

1.	Advance (kun-yomi)	a. 理	1.	su (す)
2.	Trust	b. 県	2.	susu (すす)
3.	Reside	c. 進	3.	koto (こと)
4.	Wash	d. 両	4.	SEN (セン)
5.	Direction	e. 事	5.	koro (ころ)
6.	Reason	f. 信	6.	HŌ (ホウ)
7.	Matter	g. 洗	7.	RYŌ (リョウ)
8.	Prefecture	h. 住	8.	KEN (ケン)

9.	Both	i. 転	9.	**SHIN** (シン)
10.	Roll	j. 方	10.	**RI** (リ)

C. Please choose the best answer(s) to the following questions.

1. Which is the correct reading of 走る?
   a. **ha**·ru (は·る)
   b. **hashi**·ru (はし·る)
   c. **u**·ru (う·る)
   d. **shi**·ru (し·る)

2. Which of the following readings apply to the kanji 正?
   a. **a** (あ)
   b. **SEI** (セイ)
   c. **SHŌ** (ショウ)
   d. **tada** (ただ)
   e. **HŌ** (ホウ)

3. Which of the following kanji has the most number of strokes?
   a. 背
   b. 番
   c. 進
   d. 質
   e. 転

4. I was trapped in a burning house, but managed to open a(n) ___ and get out.
   a. 兄
   b. 背
   c. 戸
   d. 酒
   e. 声

5. Which is the correct reading of 洗う?
   a. **ara·u** (あ ら・う)
   b. **ka·u** (か・う)
   c. **uba·u** (う ば・う)
   d. **chiga·u** (ち が・う)

D. Please match the following compounds to their meanings and pronunciations.

1. 雨戸   a. Sliding door/   1. **ICHI·BAN**
             Shutter   (イ チ・
                                       バ ン)

2. 県立   b. Oneself   2. **ō·goe** (お お・
                                       ご え)

3. 人質   c. Noon   3. **SHŌ·GO**
                                       (シ ョ ウ・ゴ)

4. 大声   d. One's back   4. **se·naka** (せ・
                                       な か)

5. 正午   e. Prefectural   5. **KEN·RITSU**
                                       (ケ ン・リ ツ)

6. 一番   f. The best   6. **JI·KO** (ジ・コ)

7. 自己   g. Hostage   7. **BUN·MEI**
                                       (ブ ン・メ イ)

8. 音楽   h. Music   8. **ama·do**
                                       (あ ま・ど)

9. 背中   i. Civilization   9. **ON·GAKU**
                                       (オ ン・ガ ク)

10. 文明   j. Loud voice   10. **hito·JICHI**
                                       (ひ と・ジ チ)

E. Please read the passage below and answer the questions that follow.

私は午前九時に兄を見た。。。

"お兄さん、ちょっと待って、"
と声をかけた。"どこへ行くのですか"と聞きました。
"大学です。両親と大学の門の前で会います。"
"車で行くのですか。"
"いいえ。自転車で。"

1. At what time did I see my older brother?
2. Where is he going?
3. Who is he going to meet?
4. Where will he meet them?
5. How will he get there?

Kanji #226—250

KANJI 226

付 **ATTACH**

BUILDING THIS KANJI
Giraffe 亻 + Tiny (soccer player) 寸 (103) = 付

Meaning
Attach, in both physical and figurative senses. It's worth learning this kanji well, as it conveys the meanings of many English words—from 'setting' something on fire to 'turning on' a light or an electrical device.

Remembering this kanji
Let's be honest: a **giraffe** doesn't have arms, so it could never ATTACH anything to a **tiny soccer player**. To be fair, though, a **tiny soccer player** couldn't ATTACH much to a **giraffe** either; the moment he tried to ATTACH a leash or a poster, for example, the **giraffe** would simply bolt off.

Common Pronunciations
Common **ON** reading: **FU** (フ)
Common **kun** reading: **tsu** (つ)

Knowing when the **kun-yomi** becomes voiced in second position is a bit tricky, but as this kanji appears in many common words, it pays to spend some extra time with it. In general the reading in second position will be **tsu**, and it always is when this kanji is preceded by another kanji that is read with its verb stem: 見付ける (mi **tsu**·keru / み つ·ける: 'to find') is one example, as 'mi' is the stem of the verb 見る. It is only when the preceding reading does *not* form a verb with its kanji that 付 will sometimes become voiced as **zu**: 気付く (KI **zu**·ku / キ づ·く: 'to notice') and 名付ける (na **zu**·keru / な づ·ける: 'to name') are examples of this, as 気 and 名 do not form standalone verbs with **KI** and **na** in the way 見 does with **mi**. This character can also act like 買 in absorbing its hiragana ending when forming nouns (as shown in the final example below).

Less Common Pronunciations
Less common **ON** reading: none
Less common **kun** reading: none

COMMON WORDS AND COMPOUND		
付く (intr)	*be attached; stick to*	**tsu**·ku つ·く
付ける (tr)	*attach; put on*	**tsu**·keru つ·ける
付近	attach + near = *neighborhood; nearby*	**FU·KIN** フ·キン
受付	receive + attach = *receipt; reception desk*	uke·**tsuke** うけ·つけ

軽 LIGHT

一	一	戸	戸	戸	豆	車	車	軽
軽	軽	軽						

BUILDING THIS KANJI
Car 車 (190) + **Again(ironing board)** 又 (159) + **Earth** 土 (87) = 軽

Meaning
Light, in terms of weight or feeling.

Remembering this kanji
She was all about being LIGHT. Her **car**? A LIGHT-duty pickup. Her **ironing board**? Used with a LIGHT touch from the iron. Her way of patting down **earth**? You've probably guessed: LIGHTLY.

Common Pronunciations
Common **ON** reading: **KEI** (ケ イ)
Common **kun** reading: **karu** (か る)

The **kun-yomi** is voiced when not in first position, as seen in the second and third compounds (the latter a mix of on and **kun-yomi**).

Less Common Pronunciations
Less common **ON** reading: none
Less common **kun** readings: **karo** (か ろ)

COMMON WORDS AND COMPOUNDS		
軽い	*light*	**karu**·i か る・い
手軽	hand + light = *simple; easy*	te·**garu** て・が る
気軽	spirit + light = *lighthearted*	**KI**·garu キ・が る
軽食	light + eat = *light meal; snack*	**KEI**·SHOKU ケ イ・シ ョ ク

弔 MOURN

ㄱ	弓	弓	弔					

BUILDING THIS KANJI
Bow 弓 (143) + **Pole** | = 弔

Meaning
Mourn.

Remembering this kanji
If you want to write the character for 'pull' (引), don't scrunch it up and write 弔. It'll mean you've made a mistake, and that will make you MOURN.

Common Pronunciations
Common **ON** reading: **CHO** (チョウ)
Common **kun** reading: none

Less Common Pronunciations
Less common **ON** reading: none
Less common **kun** readings: **tomura** (とむら)

COMMON WORDS AND COMPOUNDS		
弔意	mourn + mind = *condolence*	**CHŌ·I** チョウ·イ
弔文	mourn + literature = *funeral address*	**CHŌ·BUN** チョウ·ブン
弔問	mourn + question = *sympathy call*	**CHŌ·MON** チョウ·モン

 CRY

`	`	`	`	`	`	`	`	

BUILDING THIS KANJI
Splash 氵 + Stand 立(112) = 泣

Meaning
Cry.

Remembering this kanji
"For **CRYING** out loud, don't **CRY** like that! I told you you'd get a **splash** if you continued to **stand** next to that puddle."

Common Pronunciations
Common **ON** reading: none
Common **kun** reading: **na** (な)

Less Common Pronunciations
Less common **ON** reading: **KYŪ** (キュウ)
Less common **kun** readings: none

COMMON WORDS AND COMPOUNDS		
泣く	*cry*	**na·ku** な·く
泣き出す	cry + exit = *burst out crying*	**na·ki da·su** な·き だ·す
泣き声	cry + voice = *tearful voice*	**na·ki goe** な·き ご·え
泣き虫	cry + insect = *crybaby*	**na·ki mushī** な·き むし

FROG

Note that the long vertical line and bottom leftmost line are written as one stroke.

 SILVER

BUILDING THIS KANJI
Metal 金(82) + Frog 艮 = 銀

Meaning
Silver. Recall from Entry 82 that when the character for gold functions as a component in other kanji, it means 'metal' in general.

Remembering this kanji

"Congratulations! You won the SILVER!"
"Oh, big deal. It's just a hunk of **metal** to me. Nobody cares who gets the SILVER."
"What are you talking about? This 'metal' means you're the runner-up. SILVER's great!"
"Maybe for you. But I'm a **frog**, and you can't imagine what it's like for a **frog** to be beaten by a toad."

Common Pronunciations

Common **ON** reading: **GIN** (ギン)
Common **kun** reading: none

Create your **on-yomi** keyword and enter it in the table at the back of the book. After that, write your sentence to remember the **on-yomi** reading in the box below.

Less Common Pronunciations

Less common **ON** reading: none
Less common **kun** readings: none

COMMON WORDS AND COMPOUNDS		
銀	*silver*	**GIN** ギン
銀行	silver + go = *bank*	**GIN·KŌ** ギン・コウ
銀世界	silver + society + world = *snow-covered scene*	**GIN·SE·KAI** ギン・セ・カイ

問 **QUESTION**

	冂	冂	冂	門	門	門	門	門
問	問							

BUILDING THIS KANJI
Gate 門(96) + Mouth (vampire) 口(8) = 問

Meaning

Question, inquiry. In some words (the second compound below is an example), this kanji can convey the sense of 'problem'.

Remembering this kanji

As both of the components making up this character have now been encountered numerous times, this will be our first kanji presented without an illustration. The absence of a drawing will aid you in progressing to the next stage of kanji recognition—identifying a character on its own.

"I have a QUESTION, ma'am."
"What is it, Jeeves?"
"There's someone at the **gate**. A **vampire**, I believe, who wishes to ask you a QUESTION. What should I do?"
"Well, let him in."
"Are you sure that's wise?"
"How dare you QUESTION me!"

Common Pronunciations

Common **ON** reading: **MON** (モン)
Common **kun** reading: **to** (と)

Less Common Pronunciations

Less common **ON** reading: none
Less common **kun** readings: none

IRREGULAR READING		
問屋	question + roof = *wholesale dealer*	**ton**·ya と ん・や

COMMON WORDS AND COMPOUNDS		
質問	quality + question = *question*	SHITSU·**MON** シ ツ・モ ン
問題	question + topic = *problem; issue*	**MON**·DAI モ ン・ダ イ
問い合 わせる	question + match = *inquire; apply to*	**to**·i a·waseru と・い あ·わ せ る

KANJI 232

 DARK

丨	冂	日	日	日'	日⁻	日ㄶ	日ㄫ	暗
暗	暗	暗	暗					

BUILDING THIS KANJI
Sun 日 (6) + Sound 音 (137) = 暗

Meaning
Dark, with its various implications.

Remembering this kanji
A DARK thought: If we ever heard the **sun** make a **sound**, it would probably be the **sound** of the **sun** exploding. Boy, would it ever be DARK after that happened.

Common Pronunciations

Common **ON** reading: **AN** (ア ン)
Common **kun** reading: **kura** (く ら)

Less Common Pronunciations

Less common **ON** reading: none
Less common **kun** readings: none

COMMON WORDS AND COMPOUNDS		
暗い	*dark*	**kura**·i く ら・い
暗黒	dark + black = *darkness; blackness*	**AN**·KOKU ア ン・コ ク
暗記	dark + note = *memorization*	**AN**·KI ア ン・キ

KANJI 233

 PICTURE

乀	乑	幺	彳	糸	糸	糽	絉	絵
絵	絵	絵						

BUILDING THIS KANJI
Thread 糸 (196) + Meet 会 (138) = 絵

Meaning
Picture.

Remembering this kanji
"OK, this **thread** is to **meet** this **thread**, and that **thread** is to **meet** that **thread**. Do you notice the PICTURE emerging? Still no? Well, what kind of quilters are you? You're just going to have to PICTURE it, then."

Common Pronunciations
Common **ON** reading: **E** (エ)
Common **kun** reading: none

Create your **on-yomi** keyword and enter it in the table at the back of the book. After that, write your sentence to remember the **on-yomi** reading in the box below.

```
┌─────────────────────────────────┐
│                                 │
│                                 │
│                                 │
└─────────────────────────────────┘
```

Less Common Pronunciations
Less common **ON** reading: **KAI** (カイ)
Less common **kun** readings: none

This reading appears in only one compound. The word, however, is commonly used: 絵画 (**KAI·GA** / カイ·ガ) "pictures and paintings", composed of, naturally enough, the kanji for "picture" and "painting" (Entry 251).

COMMON WORDS AND COMPOUNDS		
絵	*picture*	**E** エ
絵本	picture + main (book) = *picture book*	**E·HON** エ·ホン

COMPONENT #234

COAT RACK

KANJI 234

SURNAME

BUILDING THIS KANJI
Coat Rack 匚 + Ghost 𠂉 = 氏

Meaning
Surname. This kanji can also mean 'clan' in some instances, as well as convey a more official-sounding form of "Mr." when it is attached to a family name (as in the final compound below).

Remembering this kanji
"Allow me to put that on the **coat rack**, sir."
"Thank you."
"I'll also need to sign you in. Your SURNAME?"
"Host."
"Ah, I recognize that SURNAME. Mr. **G. Host**, I presume?"

Common Pronunciations
Common **ON** reading: **SHI** (シ)
Common **kun** reading: none

Less Common Pronunciations
Less common **ON** reading: none
Less common **kun** readings: **uji** (うじ)

COMMON WORDS AND COMPOUNDS		
氏名	surname + name = *one's full name*	**SHI·MEI** シ·メイ
中村氏	middle + village + surname = *Mr. Nakamura*	naka·mura·**SHI** なか·むら·シ

KANJI 235

YOUNG

BUILDING THIS KANJI
Wreath 艹 + Right 右 (35) = 若

Meaning
Young.

Remembering this kanji
The ancient Olympics celebrated the accomplishments of those who were **YOUNG**. A **wreath** was presented to a **YOUNG** champion, with the runner-up (who was also **YOUNG**) given the position of honor to his **right**.

Common Pronunciations
Common **ON** reading: none
Common **kun** reading: **waka** (わか)

Note that the second compound uses the less common pronunciation of 者.

Less Common Pronunciations
Less common **ON** reading: **JAKU** (ジャク); **NYAKU** (ニャク)
Less common **kun** readings: none

IRREGULAR READING		
若人	young + person = *young person*	**wakō·do** わこう・ど

COMMON WORDS AND COMPOUNDS		
若い	*young*	**waka·i** わか・い
若者	young + individual = *young person*	**waka·mono** わか・もの
若々しい	young + young = *youthful*	**waka·waka·shii** わか・わか・しい

由 **CAUSE**

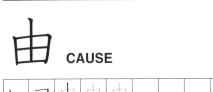

This is written in the same order as the kanji for "rice field" (Entry 73), but with the third stroke lengthened.

Meaning
Cause, reason.

Remembering this kanji
"Oh-oh, he's let his **rice field** grow over its border. What would **CAUSE** him to be so negligent?"

"Who can tell with that guy? This is going to **CAUSE** trouble, though."

Common Pronunciations
Common **ON** reading: **YU** (ユ); **YŪ** (ユウ)
Common **kun** reading: none

This character only appears in roughly ten Japanese compounds, which makes the large number of readings for it seem extreme. The examples below, however, are all very common.

Create your **on-yomi** keyword for ユ and enter it in the table at the back of the book. After that, write your sentence to remember the **on-yomi** readings in the box below.

Less Common Pronunciations
Less common **ON** reading: **YUI** (ユイ)
Less common **kun** readings: **yoshi** (よし)

COMMON WORDS AND COMPOUNDS		
由来	cause + come = *origin*	**YU·RAI** ユ・ライ
自由	self + cause = *freedom*	**JI·YŪ** ジ・ユウ
理由	reason + cause = *reason*	**RI·YŪ** リ・ユウ

KANJI 237

申

DECLARE

BUILDING THIS KANJI
Sun 日(6) + Pole ｜ = 申

Ensure that you are able to see the difference between this kanji and the preceding entry for 由, as well as between these two and the character for "shell" (甲), our "fly swatter" from Entry 148.

Meaning
Declare, in the sense of a more humble way to say the verb "say".

Common Pronunciations
Common **ON** reading: **SHIN** (シ ン)
Common **kun** reading: **mō** (も う)

Less Common Pronunciations
Less common **ON** reading: none
Less common **kun** readings: none

COMMON WORDS AND COMPOUNDS		
申す	say (humble form)	**mō**·su も う・す
申し 上げる	declare + upper = inform; tell (humble form)	**mō**·shi a·geru も う・し あ・げ る
内申	inside + declare = confidential report	NAI·**SHIN** ナ イ・シ ン

Remembering this kanji
"Anything to DECLARE?"
"Yes. I have a sun on a **pole**."
"Well, I DECLARE! I'm afraid I'll have to confiscate that, sir; we can't have an extra **sun** in this solar system."

COMPONENT #238

SUITCASE 西

BUILDING THIS KANJI
Suitcase 西 + Woman 女(16) = 要

KANJI 238

要

Meaning
Essential, necessary.

Remembering this kanji

The **suitcase** of any **woman** taking a trip will be packed with what is ESSENTIAL: important documents, business suits (if needed), guide books and maps, for instance. That's a lot of stuff, making a sturdy **suitcase** pretty much ESSENTIAL.

Common Pronunciations

Common **ON** reading: **YŌ** (ヨ ウ)
Common **kun** reading: **i** (い)

Less Common Pronunciations

Less common **ON** reading: none
Less common **kun** readings: none

COMMON WORDS AND COMPOUNDS		
要る	*need; be needed*	**i·ru** い・る
要する	*require; need*	**YŌ·suru** ヨ ウ・する
必要	certain + essential = *essential; necessary*	**HITSU·YŌ** ヒ ツ・ヨ ウ
重要	heavy + essential = *importance*	**JU·YŌ** ジ ュ ウ・ヨ ウ

KANJI 239

 REACH

BUILDING THIS KANJI
One (top of a bun) 一(3) + **Broken crutch** ム + **Earth** 土(87) = 至

Meaning
Reach, in the sense of 'arrive at' or 'extend to'.

Remembering this kanji
"Must...REACH...the condiments," she gasped.

  You wonder why she's let the situation REACH this stage. The **top of the bun** is where she's left it, of course, but with her **broken crutch** littering the **earth** it might as well be miles away. And yet somehow she much REACH that spot...

Common Pronunciations
Common **ON** reading: **SHI** (シ)
Common **kun** reading: **ita** (い た)

The second compound below is the only word in which the **on-yomi** becomes voiced.

Less Common Pronunciations
Less common **ON** reading: none
Less common **kun** readings: none

COMMON WORDS AND COMPOUNDS		
至る	*reach; extend*	**ita·ru** い た・る
冬至	winter + reach = *winter solstice*	**TŌ·JI** ト ウ・ジ
至る所	reach + location = *everywhere*	**ita·ru tokoro** い た・る と こ ろ
至急	reach + hasten = *urgent*	**SHI·KYŪ** シ・キ ュ ウ

比 COMPARE

BUILDING THIS KANJI
Beggar ヒ + Beggar ヒ = 比

Meaning
Compare. The sense of 'ratio' is also present in a few compounds.

Remembering this kanji
Let's COMPARE these beggars. COMPARE the arms: the ones of the first are held level (and written left to right)! COMPARE the postures: one sits on his calves! Isn't it exciting to COMPARE them?

Common Pronunciations
Common **ON** reading: **HI** (ヒ)
Common **kun** reading: **kura** (く ら)

Create your **on-yomi** keyword and enter it in the table at the back of the book. After that, write your sentence to remember the **on-yomi** and **kun-yomi** readings in the box below.

Less Common Pronunciations
Less common **ON** reading: none
Less common **kun** readings: none

COMMON WORDS AND COMPOUNDS		
比べる	compare	**kura**·beru く ら·べる
背比べ	back + compare = compare heights	sei **kura**·be せ い く ら·べ
見比べる	see + compare = comparison	mi **kura**·beru み く ら·べる
対比	versus + compare = contrast; compare	TAI·HI タ イ·ヒ

計 MEASURE

BUILDING THIS KANJI
Say 言 (80) + Ten (scarecrow) 十 (28) = 計

Meaning
To measure, estimate.

Remembering this kanji
What can you **say** to a **scarecrow** to get the MEASURE of him as a comedian? I'd suggest "What are you doing?", for when I said that to a **scarecrow** once he answered me with "Oh, I'm just posing like this because my tailor's about to MEASURE me for a jacket."

Common Pronunciations
Common **ON** reading: **KEI** (ケ イ)
Common **kun** reading: **haka** (は か)

Don't forget that the reading of 時 in the third compound is irregular.

Less Common Pronunciations
Less common **ON** reading: none
Less common **kun** readings: none

COMMON WORDS AND COMPOUNDS		
計る	*measure; estimate*	**haka**·ru は か・る
会計	meet + measure = *accounts; accounting*	KAI·**KEI** カイ・ケイ
時計	time + measure = *watch; clock*	to·**KEI** と・ケイ
温度計	warm + degree + measure = *thermometer*	ON·DO·**KEI** オン・ド・ケイ

KANJI 242

LOCATION

一 ｱ ㄊ 尸 尸′ 厉 所 所

BUILDING THIS KANJI
Door 戸 (205) + Axe 斤 (126) = 所

Meaning
Location.

Remembering this kanji
Panicking, she crouches behind the bathroom **door** with a baseball bat. Is it a safe LOCA-TION? Unfortunately no, for all too soon he is there, and the **axe** chops through the door... Don't worry though, this is just a scene from a B-movie filmed on LOCATION.

Common Pronunciations
Common **ON** reading: **SHO** (ショ)
Common **kun** reading: **tokoro** (と こ ろ)

We'll need to bring out our work gloves for this one. In first position, **SHO** is by far the more common reading; it's after this, however, that

things can get confusing. In second position, the **kun-yomi** is always voiced, with the exception of only a few words in which this kanji is preceded by a verb in its "ru" form (such as 至る所, the third example in Entry 239). The **on-yomi**, by contrast is almost never voiced in second position; the only time you are likely to encounter it voiced here is in the second example below. In the third position and beyond, however, there is no way to predict on first encountering a compound whether or not the **on-yomi** is voiced (the **kun-yomi** never appears after second position). Since **SHO** and **JO** occur equally here, you may wish to associate your **on-yomi** keyword with each of these compounds as you learn them. In other words, if you can link your keyword for **SHO** to "power station" (発電所: HATSU·DEN·**SHO** / ハツ・デン・ショ) from the kanji for "discharge", "electric" and "location", it will help you to remember that 所 is unvoiced here.

Less Common Pronunciations
Less common **ON** reading: none
Less common **kun** readings: none

COMMON WORDS AND COMPOUNDS		
所	*location; place*	**tokoro** と こ ろ
近所	near + location = *neighborhood; vicinity*	KIN·**JO** キン・ジョ
台所	platform + location = *kitchen*	DAI·**dokoro** ダイ・どころ
場所	place + location = *place*	ba·**SHO** ば・ショ

COMPONENT #243

MACHINE GUNS

KANJI 243

第 **NO. (NUMBER)**

ノ	ﾉ	⺦	⺮	⺮一	⺮ヽ	⺮ケ	⺮ゲ	笌
第	第							

BUILDING THIS KANJI
Machine Guns ⺮ + Mourn 弔(228) + Comet
一 = 第

Meaning
This kanji is usually used as a prefix for numbers, much as English uses 'No.' or '#'. In a few compounds it can also mean 'exam'.

Remembering this kanji
Due to the classified nature of this document, all NO.'s have been removed.

Case NO. xxxx:

Machine guns (serial NO.'s xxxx and xxxx) were employed to shoot down the **comet**. Those firing said **machine guns** (personnel NO.'s xxxx and xxxx) did not survive the **comet**'s impact. We **mourn** their passing.

Agent NO. xxxx

Common Pronunciations
Common **ON** reading: **DAI** (ダイ)
Common **kun** reading: none
Recall that 'ease' plus 'complete' in the second compound below gives us 'safety'.

Less Common Pronunciations
Less common **ON** reading: none
Less common **kun** readings: none

COMMON WORDS AND COMPOUNDS		
第一	*No. 1*	**DAI**·ICHI ダイ・イチ
安全 第一	safety + No. + one = *"safety first"*	AN·ZEN·**DAI**·ICHI アン・ゼン・ダイ・イチ
次第	next + No. = *order;* *circumstances*	SHI·**DAI** シ・ダイ

KANJI 244

旨 **GIST**

ﾉ	ヒ	ヒ	旨	旨	旨			

BUILDING THIS KANJI
Beggar ヒ + Sun 日(6) = 旨

Meaning
Gist. Though rarely encountered on its own, this kanji figures in other more common characters.

Remembering this kanji

"Look, I'm in a big hurry. Just give me the GIST of it."

"The GIST? Well…a **beggar** sat on the **sun**, I guess."

"Really? Hmm... It would seem, then, that the GIST isn't enough to explain this."

Common Pronunciations

Common **ON** reading: none

Common **kun** reading: **mune** (むね)

Less Common Pronunciations

Less common **ON** reading: **SHI** (シ)

Less common **kun** readings: none

	COMMON WORDS AND COMPOUNDS	
旨	*gist; meaning*	**mune** むね

KANJI 245

WEAR

`	ˊ	一	丷	芏	羊	羊	着
着	着	着					

BUILDING THIS KANJI

Rabbit `ˊ + **King** 王(23) + **Comet** 宀 + **Eye (Cyclops)** 目(15) = 着

Meaning

This important kanji has two main meanings: to wear, and to arrive. It may help to think that, in a sense, a person "wears" their surroundings when they arrive at a place. This kanji, in fact, consistently has this idea of things coming together in certain ways.

Remembering this kanji

A rabbit on a **king**? Well sure, if he wants to WEAR a **rabbit** fur collar. A **comet** on a **Cyclops**? Not unless he's found some pajamas with **comets** on them. Because let's not kid ourselves: **kings** WEAR sable robes, and a **Cyclops** always seems to WEAR that smelly toga-like outfit.

Common Pronunciations

Common **ON** reading: **CHAKU** (チャク)

Common **kun** reading: **ki** (き); **tsu** (つ)

As the famous word in the third example makes clear, **ki** is used when this kanji refers to wearing clothes; it is always voiced in second and third position. **tsu** is used in the sense of "arrive", and is never voiced in second position. **CHAKU** is the most common of these readings and has the overarching meaning of things coming together.

Create your **on-yomi** keyword and enter it in the table at the back of the book. Then, after creating your **kun-yomi** keywords, write your sentence to remember the **on-yomi** and **kun-yomi** readings in the box below.

Less Common Pronunciations

Less common **ON** reading: **JAKU** (ジャク)

Less common **kun** readings: none

COMMON WORDS AND COMPOUNDS		
着る	*wear*	**ki·ru** き・る
着く	*arrive*	**tsu·ku** つ・く
着物	wear + thing = *kimono*	**ki·mono** き・もの
接着	join + thing = *adhesion*	**SET·CHAKU** セッ・チャク

COMPONENT #246

LITTLE RED RIDING HOOD

Hey, your arms would be a bit long too if you were carrying a basket like this all day.

KANJI 246

欠 **LACK**

BUILDING THIS KANJI
Little Red Riding Hood 亠 + **Person** 人 (2)
= 欠

Meaning
Lack.

Remembering this kanji

"Hey, there goes **Little Red Riding Hood**."
"She's a strange **person**, isn't she?"
"How so?"
"She seems to **LACK** common sense. Look at how she traipses around everywhere with that basket."
"Well if she **LACKS** anything, it's good judgment. That hairy guy she's chatting with over there looks an awful lot like a wolf."

Common Pronunciations
Common **ON** reading: **KETSU** (ケ ツ)
Common **kun** reading: **ka** (か)

Create your **on-yomi** keyword and enter it in the table at the back of the book. Then, after creating your **kun-yomi** keyword, write your sentence to remember the **on-yomi** and **kun-yomi** readings in the box below.

Less Common Pronunciations
Less common **ON** reading: none
Less common **kun** readings: none

COMMON WORDS AND COMPOUNDS		
欠く	*lack*	**ka·ku** か・く
欠点	lack + point = *defect; shortcoming*	**KET·TEN** ケッ・テン
欠員	lack + member = *vacancy; post*	**KETSU·IN** ケツ・イン

KANJI 247

示 **SHOW**

BUILDING THIS KANJI
Two 二 (4) + **Small** 小 (20) = 示

Meaning
To show.

Remembering this kanji

"Psst! Hey you **two**, I wanna **SHOW** you something."

"What is it?"

"These. Look how **small** they are. And I've only got **two**."

"Are you crazy? You can't **SHOW** stuff like that!"

Common Pronunciations

Common **ON** reading: **JI** (ジ)

Common **kun** reading: **shime** (しめ)

Less Common Pronunciations

Less common **ON** reading: **SHI** (シ)

Less common **kun** readings: none

COMMON WORDS AND COMPOUNDS		
示す	*show*	**shime·su** しめ·す
暗示	dark + show = *hint*	**AN·JI** アン·ジ
指示	finger + show = *indication; direction*	**SHI·JI** シ·ジ
展示	display + show = *display; exhibition*	**TEN·JI** テン·ジ

仕   SERVE

BUILDING THIS KANJI

Giraffe イ + Gentleman 土(84) = 仕

Meaning

Serve, work.

Remembering this kanji

It would not **SERVE** to have a **giraffe SERVE** a **gentleman**; its hoofs would clatter noisily over the floor of the **gentleman's** club and make any **gentleman** look up in annoyance. No, it simply would not **SERVE**.

Common Pronunciations

Common **ON** reading: **SHI** (シ)

Common **kun** reading: none

This kanji is unusual in that its **on-yomi** almost always forms compounds with the **kun-yomi** of other characters, as in the examples below.

Less Common Pronunciations

Less common **ON** reading: **JI** (ジ)

Less common **kun** readings: **tsuka** (つか)

COMMON WORDS AND COMPOUNDS		
仕方	serve + direction = *way; method*	**SHI·kata** シ·かた
仕事	serve + matter = *job; work*	**SHI·goto** シ·ごと
仕切り	serve + cut = *partition; dividing line*	**SHI·ki·ri** シ·き·り
仕上げる	serve + upper = *finish; complete*	**SHI a·geru** シ あ·げる

POGO STICK   甫 甫

BUILDING THIS KANJI

Pogo Stick 甫 + Two 二(4) = 重

Meaning

Heavy, in both the literal and the figurative sense.

重   HEAVY

Remembering this kanji

"A single **pogo stick** wasn't enough. We had to get her **two**."
"Why?"
"Well, she's a bit…HEAVY."

Common Pronunciations

Common **ON** reading: **JŪ** (ジュウ)
Common **kun** reading: **omo** (おも)

JŪ is by far the more common reading.

Less Common Pronunciations

Less common **ON** reading: **CHŌ** (チョウ)
Less common **kun** readings: **kasa** (かさ); **e** (え)

COMMON WORDS AND COMPOUNDS		
重い	*heavy*	omo·i おも·い
重大	heavy + large = *important; grave*	JŪ·DAI ジュウ·ダイ
重要	heavy + essential = *important; essential*	JŪ·YŌ ジュウ·ヨウ

 MATCH

BUILDING THIS KANJI
Umbrella 𠆢 + One (hamburger patty) 一 (3)
+ Mouth (vampire) 口 (8) = 合

Meaning

Match, combine. This is a kanji you will encounter frequently, as it forms many compound verbs (such as in the third example) that suggest some kind of reciprocal action between people or things. These words are often translated into English with the phrase "each other": 押し合う (o·shi **a**·u / お·し あ·う) "to push each other", is one example. As they can be confused, make sure you clearly see the difference between this kanji and that of 'same' (同), from Entry 197.

Remembering this kanji

The centuries-old fingerprints on the **umbrella**? A MATCH!
The fang marks on the **hamburger patty**? Another MATCH!
Yup, it looked like we'd be able to MATCH the **vampire** to the crime scenes of the **umbrella** vendor *and* the butcher.

Common Pronunciations

Common **ON** reading: **GŌ** (ゴウ)
Common **kun** reading: **a** (あ)

This is another tough kanji when it comes to knowing which reading should be used in compounds. **GŌ** is the most common choice in first position, but both it and **a** occur frequently in second. This kanji can also act like 買 in absorbing its hiragana accompaniment in certain compounds.

Create your **on-yomi** keyword and enter it in the table at the back of the book. Then, after creating your **kun-yomi** keyword, write your sentence to remember the **on-yomi** and **kun-yomi** readings in the box below.

Less Common Pronunciations

Less common **ON** reading: **GA-** (ガッ);
KA- (カッ)

Less common **kun** readings: none

These two readings only occur in a few words, and always "double up" with the **on-yomi** of the kanji that follows them (as the small katakana " ッ " indicates). The compound 合宿 (**GAS·SHUKU** / ガッ・シュク) "to lodge together", from the kanji "match" and "lodging" is an example. When the time comes to memorize these **on-yomi** you can do one of two things: come up with new keywords for each (incorporating some way to account for their pronunciation being "clipped"),

or simply use your existing keywords for **GATSU** and **KATSU** (you will create one for this latter **on-yomi** in Entry 300) while remembering that they always change phonetically like this.

COMMON WORDS AND COMPOUNDS		
合う (intr)	match; fit	**a·u** あ・う
合わせる (tr)	put together; combine	**a·waseru** あ・わせる
話し合う	speak + match = discuss; talk	hana·shi **a·u** はな・し あ・う
合意	match + mind = mutual agreement	**GŌ·I** ゴウ・イ

CHAPTER 12 REVIEW EXERCISES

A. Please match the following kanji to their meanings.

1. 第
2. 旨
3. 由
4. 軽
5. 銀
6. 合
7. 欠
8. 至
9. 若
10. 計

a. Young
b. Match
c. Silver
d. Reach
e. Light
f. No.
g. Cause
h. Measure
i. Lack
j. Gist

B. Please match the following meanings to their kanji, and these to their **on** or **kun-yomi**.

1. Attach
2. Surname
3. Location
4. Heavy
   (kun-yomi)
5. Picture
6. Mourn
7. Cry
8. Declare
9. Show
   (kun-yomi)
10. Compare

a. 所
b. 氏
c. 申
d. 比
e. 絵
f. 付
g. 泣
h. 重
i. 弔
j. 示

1. **omo** (おも)
2. **CHŌ** (チョウ)
3. **tokoro** (ところ)
4. **na** (な)
5. **kura** (くら)
6. **SHIN** (シン)
7. **tsu** (つ)
8. **E** (エ)
9. **SHI** (シ)
10. **shime** (しめ)

C. Please choose the best answer(s) to the following questions.

1. Which of the following readings apply to the kanji 着?
a. **tsu** (つ)
b. **CHAKU** (チャク)
c. **SHŌ** (ショウ)
d. **ko** (こ)
e. **ki** (き)

2. He hit his thumb with a hammer, but acted tough and didn't ___ .
a. 至 b. 欠 c. 付 d. 泣 e. 計

3. Which is the correct reading of 思い付く ?
a. **omo·i zu·ku** (おも・い づ・く)
b. **omo·i tsu·ku** (おも・い つ・く)

4. Which of the following kanji has the most number of strokes?
a. 絵 b. 計 c. 要 d. 第 e. 問

5. Which is the correct reading of 軽い?
a. **karu·i** (かる・い)
b. **maru·i** (まる・い)
c. **shiro·i** (しろ・い)
d. **kura·i** (くら・い)

D. Please match the following compounds to their meanings and pronunciations.

1. 銀行   a. Job / Work   1. **ki·mono** (き·もの)

2. 質問   b. Winter solstice   2. **JI·YŪ** (ジ·ユウ)

3. 時計   c. Important   3. **TŌ·JI** (トウ·ジ)

4. 重要   d. Hint   4. **AN·JI** (アン·ジ)

5. 着物   e. Bank   5. **JŪ·YŌ** (ジュウ·ヨウ)

6. 冬至   f. Question   6. **to·KEI** (と·ケイ)

7. 自由   g. Freedom   7. **GIN·KŌ** (ギン·コウ)

8. 仕事   h. Kimono   8. **SHI·goto** (シ·ごと)

9. 合意   i. Mutual agreement   9. **SHITSU·MON** (シツ·モン)

10. 暗示   j. Watch/ Clock   10. **GŌ·I** (ゴウ·イ)

E. Please read the passage below and answer the questions that follow.

金本さんは銀行で受付の仕事をしています。銀行付近に住んでいて、毎朝歩いて十分で着きます。本日正午に重要な会見があります。

1. Where does Kanemoto-san work?
2. What job does she do?
3. How long does it take her to walk to work?
4. What is happening at work today?
5. What time will it happen?

Kanji #251—280

PAINTING

BUILDING THIS KANJI
One (top of a bun) 一(3) + **Cause** 由(236) +
Garbage Can 凵 = 画

Meaning
This character relates primarily to painting. A secondary meaning has to do with kanji strokes (think of how they are "painted" in calligraphy) and things being drawn up, from dividing lines to plans.

Remembering this kanji
Did you realize that the **top of a bun** was the underlying **cause** of DaVinci's Mona Lisa being created? A recently discovered interview unravels the mystery.

"I was broke back then," DaVinci said, "as nobody wanted my PAINTINGS. But one day I was digging through a **garbage can** for food, and saw the **top of a bun**. It was magnificent, and I thought that if I could reproduce the curve of that bun top in a smile…well, I'd have a PAINTING I could really be proud of."

Common Pronunciations
Common **ON** reading: **GA** (ガ); **KAKU** (カク)
Common **kun** reading: none

GA is the reading used when this kanji refers to painting, **KAKU** when it refers to such things as kanji strokes and plans. Recall from Entry 75 how 家 can refer to a skilled person when used as a suffix (as it is in the first compound below).

Create your **on-yomi** keywords and enter them in the table at the back of the book. After that, write your sentence to remember the **on-yomi** readings in the box below.

Less Common Pronunciations
Less common **ON** reading: none
Less common **kun** readings: none

COMMON WORDS AND COMPOUNDS		
画家	painting + house = *painter; artist*	**GA·KA** ガ・カ
計画	measure + painting = *plan; scheme*	**KEI·KAKU** ケイ・カク
映画	reflect + painting = *movie*	**EI·GA** エイ・ガ

POSSIBLE

BUILDING THIS KANJI
One (top of a bun) 一 (3) + Mouth (vampire)
口 (8) + Harpoon 亅 = 可

Meaning
Possible. It's important to learn the proper stroke order of this kanji so as not to confuse it with similar-looking characters we will meet in the future.

Remembering this kanji
"Listen guys, you're not locked into doing these jobs. Anything is POSSIBLE."
"Yeah, right. I'm the **top of a bun**. What else could I do?"
"Why not let yourself go stale and become a Frisbee? That's POSSIBLE. And you, **vampire**: it's POSSIBLE for you to be a night watchman. And don't tell me, **harpoon**, that you couldn't find something as a javelin; you know darn well that's POSSIBLE.

Common Pronunciations
Common **ON** reading: **KA** (カ)
Common **kun** reading: none

Recall from Entry 199 that the reading for 愛 is irregular in the first compound below.

Less Common Pronunciations
Less common **ON** reading: none
Less common **kun** readings: none

COMMON WORDS AND COMPOUNDS		
可愛い	possible + love = *cute*	**KA**·WAI·i カ·ワイ·い
不可欠	not + possible + lack = *indispensable*	FU·**KA**·KETSU フ·カ·ケツ
可動	possible + move = *movable; mobile*	**KA**·DŌ カ·ドウ

WHITTLING

BUILDING THIS KANJI
Whittling 衤 + Declare 申 (237) = 神

Meaning
God.

 GOD

Remembering this kanji

"The **whittling** is done: I **declare** the birth of the universe."

So spoke GOD.

Common Pronunciations

Common **ON** reading: **SHIN** (シン); **JIN** (ジン)
Common **kun** reading: **kami** (か み)

SHIN is by far the most common of these readings, although the others do show up in some important words. Recall that this kanji popped up in the "Less Common Pronunciations" section of 道 (Entry 122).

Less Common Pronunciations

Less common **ON** reading: none
Less common **kun** readings: **kan** (か ん);
kō (こ う)

COMMON WORDS AND COMPOUNDS		
神	God	**kami** か み
神話	God + speak = *myth; mythology*	**SHIN·WA** シン・ワ
神社	God + company = *Shinto shrine*	**JIN·JA** ジン・ジャ

KANJI 254

亡 PERISH

¹	一	亡					

BUILDING THIS KANJI
Police 亠 + Forklift 乚 = 亡

Meaning

Perish, die.

Remembering this kanji

"The load must have been too great," said the **policewoman**, laying her hat over the **forklift**. "It's always tragic when a **forklift** PERISHES," said her partner. "Especially when it has to PERISH on duty."

Common Pronunciations

Common **ON** reading: **BŌ** (ボ ウ)
Common **kun** reading: **na** (な)

Create your **on-yomi** keyword and enter it in the table at the back of the book. Then, after creating your **kun-yomi** keyword, write your sentence to remember the **on-yomi** and **kun-yomi** readings in the box below.

Less Common Pronunciations

Less common **ON** reading: none MŌ (モ ウ)
Less common **kun** readings: **horo** (ほ ろ)

COMMON WORDS AND COMPOUNDS		
亡くなる	*die; pass away*	**na·**kunaru な・く なる
死亡	death + perish = *death*	**SHI·BŌ** シ・ボウ

KANJI 255

占 **OCCUPY**

BUILDING THIS KANJI
Good Figure Skater ⌐ + Mouth (vampire)
口 (8) = 占

Meaning
This character appears in only a few words (although it figures prominently in the makeup of several more common kanji), but has two meanings that are oddly unrelated: "occupy" and "fortune telling".

Remembering this kanji
A **good figure skater** always wants to OCCUPY the top of the podium. In a sense, this is like a **vampire** striving to OCCUPY the best coffin.

Common Pronunciations
Common **ON** reading: **SEN** (セ ン)
Common **kun** reading: **urana** (う ら な)

Less Common Pronunciations
Less common **ON** reading: none
Less common **kun** readings: **shi** (し)

COMMON WORDS AND COMPOUNDS		
占 う	*tell fortunes*	**urana·u** うらな·う
占 有	occupy + have = *occupy*	**SEN·YŪ** セン·ユウ

COMPONENT #256

STRAW

KANJI 256

世 **SOCIETY**

BUILDING THIS KANJI
Straw ⌗ + Forklift └ = 世

Meaning
This interesting kanji encompasses the idea of society. It finds expression in such terms as 'the age', 'the times' and 'the era'.

Remembering this kanji

Marx, on SOCIETY:

SOCIETY is conflict. Some elements are content to siphon from SOCIETY what they will (the so-called "**straws**"), while others strive to raise it to a higher plane (those whom I have termed "**forklifts**").

Common Pronunciations
Common **ON** reading: **SE** (セ); **SEI** (セ イ)
Common **kun** reading: none

SE is the overwhelming choice in first position, **SEI** in second. Note the second compound below: this is one of only two words in which 間 carries its less common **on-yomi** of **KEN** (ケ ン). The other compound, incidentally, means 'humanity', and sees the reading voiced: 人間 NIN·GEN (ニ ン·ゲン), from the kanji 'person' and 'interval'.

Create your **on-yomi** keyword for SE (セ) and enter it in the table at the back of the book. Then, write your sentence to remember the **on-yomi** readings in the box below.

COMMON WORDS AND COMPOUNDS		
世話	society + speak = *help; service*	**SE·WA** セ・ワ
世間	society + interval = *society; life*	**SE·KEN** セ・ケン
中世	middle + society = *the Middle Ages*	CHŪ·**SEI** チュウ・セイ

Less Common Pronunciations
Less common **ON** reading: none
Less common **kun** readings: **yo** (よ)

KANJI 257

定 FIXED

'	''	宀	宀	宁	宇	宇	定

BUILDING THIS KANJI
Pincers 宀 + Surfer 疋 = 定

Meaning
Fixed in time or place. Regular, definite.

Remembering this kanji
The **pincers** were carefully lowered, and another novice **surfer** was FIXED onto his board. "Yeah, it's risky," said one of the laid-off surfing instructors, "but the management of that surf school is really FIXED on reducing expenses."

Common Pronunciations
Common **ON** reading: **TEI** (テイ)
Common **kun** reading: **sada** (さだ)

Create your **on-yomi** keyword and enter it in the table at the back of the book. Then write your sentence to remember the **on-yomi** and **kun-yomi** readings in the box below.

Less Common Pronunciations
Less common **ON** reading: **JŌ** (ジョウ)
Less common **kun** readings: none

COMMON WORDS AND COMPOUNDS		
定まる (intr)	*to be fixed / determined*	**sada**·maru さだ・まる
定める (tr)	*to decide; determine*	**sada**·meru さだ・める
安定	ease + fixed = *stability*	AN·**TEI** アン・テイ
定食	fixed + eat = *set meal*	**TEI**·SHOKU テイ・ショク

KANJI 258

'	'	幺	糸	糸	糸	紀	紅	紙
紙								

紙 PAPER

BUILDING THIS KANJI
Thread 糸 (196) + Surname 氏 (234) = 紙

Meaning
Paper.

Remembering this kanji
"PAPER runs like a **thread** through your family,"
he said, bringing out a dusty roll of PAPER.
"Just look at this **surname**: that was your great
uncle, a PAPER manufacturer. And follow the
thread to this **surname** here: your grandfather,
a PAPER miller. So do you understand? Your
PAPER obsession is nothing to worry about."

Common Pronunciations
Common **ON** reading: **SHI** (シ)
Common **kun** reading: **kami** (か み)

The **kun-yomi** is almost always voiced when
not in first position (as it appears in the second
compound below).

Less Common Pronunciations
Less common **ON** reading: none
Less common **kun** readings: none

COMMON WORDS AND COMPOUNDS		
紙	*paper*	**kami** か み
手紙	hand + paper = *letter*	te·**gami** て・が み
和紙	harmony (Japan) + paper = *Japanese paper*	WA·**SHI** ワ・シ

采 **APPEARANCE**

BUILDING THIS KANJI
Stroller � + Tree 木(13) = 采

Meaning
Appearance, the look of something.

Remembering this kanji
"I can't believe it, the **stroller** landed on top of
a **tree**!"
"Yes, he really is the best at **stroller** toss. His
gaze, his bearing - everything in his APPEAR-
ANCE suggests it."

Common Pronunciations
Common **ON** reading: **SAI** (サ イ)
Common **kun** reading: none

Less Common Pronunciations
Less common **ON** reading: none
Less common **kun** readings: none

COMMON WORDS AND COMPOUNDS		
采	*Appearance*	**SAI** サ イ
風采	wind + appearance = *appearance; bearing*	FŪ·**SAI** フ ウ・サ イ

KANJI 260

軍 **ARMY**

BUILDING THIS KANJI
UFO ⼍ + Car 車(190) = 軍

Meaning
Army, military.

Remembering this kanji
"Look at their **ARMY**," sneered one of the aliens in the **UFO**. They still have **cars**!"
"Don't underestimate their **ARMY** because of that," said another. "I tried to drive a **car** once, and never could figure out how to use the clutch."

Common Pronunciations
Common **ON** reading: **GUN** (グ ン)
Common **kun** reading: none

Create your **on-yomi** keyword and enter it in the table at the back of the book. After that, write your sentence to remember the **on-yomi** reading in the box below.

Less Common Pronunciations
Less common **ON** reading: none
Less common **kun** readings: none

COMMON WORDS AND COMPOUNDS		
軍人	army + person = *military person; soldier*	**GUN·JIN** グン・ジン
海軍	sea + army = *navy*	KAI·**GUN** カイ・グン
空軍	empty (sky) + army = *air force*	KŪ·**GUN** クウ・グン

KANJI 261

 ELDER SISTER

BUILDING THIS KANJI
Woman 女(16) + City 市 (163) = 姉

Meaning
Elder sister.

Remembering this kanji
"Why does Charlotte always get to visit the **city**?" they asked, pouting.
"Because she's your **ELDER SISTER**, that's why."
"That's right," said Charlotte. "I'm your **ELDER SISTER**, which means that I'm a **woman**, and you're still babies."
Even if she was their **ELDER SISTER**, there was no need for Charlotte to be so mean to the other Brontë girls.

Common Pronunciations
Common **ON** reading: **SHI** (シ)
Common **kun** reading: **ane** (あ ね)

Less Common Pronunciations
Less common **ON** reading: none
Less common **kun** readings: none

IRREGULAR READING		
お姉さん	*elder sister*	o·nē·san お・ねえ・さん

COMMON WORDS AND COMPOUNDS		
姉	*elder sister*	ane あね
姉妹	elder sister + younger sister = *sister (city/company, etc.)*	SHI·MAI シ・マイ
姉妹 都市	sister + metropolis + city = *sister city*	SHI·MAI·TO·SHI シ・マイ・ト・シ

As we saw with a similar word for 兄, this is a more polite form of address.

羊
SHEEP

Meaning
Sheep. No story required.

Common Pronunciations
Common **ON** reading: none
Common **kun** reading: **hitsuji** (ひつぎ)

Less Common Pronunciations
Less common **ON** reading: **YŌ** (ヨウ)
Less common **kun** readings: none

COMMON WORDS AND COMPOUNDS		
羊	*sheep*	hitsuji ひつじ
子羊	child + sheep = *lamb*	ko·hitsuji こ・ひつじ

MERGING

介
INTERVENE

BUILDING THIS KANJI
Umbrella 𠆢 + Merging 刂 = 介

Meaning
Intervene, mediate.

Remembering this kanji
So you've noticed that your teenaged daughter is sharing an **umbrella** with her boyfriend, and that they've started **merging**. There's no need to INTERVENE; they're just sheltering from the weather.

Common Pronunciations

Common **ON** reading: **KAI** (カ イ)
Common **kun** reading: none

Less Common Pronunciations

Less common **ON** reading: none
Less common **kun** readings: none

COMMON WORDS AND COMPOUNDS		
介入	intervene + enter = *intervention*	**KAI**·NYŪ カイ・ニュウ
不介入	not + intervene + enter = *nonintervention*	FU·**KAI**·NYŪ フ・カイ・ニュウ

 PLATFORM

BUILDING THIS KANJI
Broken Crutch ム + Mouth (vampire) 口 (8)
= 台

Meaning
This kanji relates to objects that tend to be flat and elevated (think of such things as tables, stands, flatlands and stages, etc.) It's also used as a counter for machinery and vehicles.

Remembering this kanji
It had always been a struggle for the **vampire** to blend in at his local disco. So then given he was on **crutches**, why had he taken his moves onto the raised PLATFORM? It was hardly a surprise that he would have an accident and end up with a **broken crutch**, what with his already shaky footing and the ridiculous PLATFORM shoes he'd put on.

Common Pronunciations

Common **ON** reading: **DAI** (ダ イ); **TAI** (タ イ)
Common **kun** reading: none

DAI is the far more common reading. Note the mix of on and **kun-yomi** in the first compound below.

Less Common Pronunciations

Less common **ON** reading: none
Less common **kun** readings: none

COMMON WORDS AND COMPOUNDS		
台所	platform + location = *kitchen*	**DAI**·dokoro ダイ・どころ
天文台	heaven + literature + platform = *astronomical observatory*	TEN·MON·**DAI** テン・モン・ダイ
台風	platform + wind = *typhoon*	**TAI**·FŪ タイ・フウ

 HASTEN

Meaning
Hasten, and the sense of things being urgent or sudden.

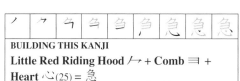

BUILDING THIS KANJI
Little Red Riding Hood ⼄ + Comb 彐 +
Heart 心 (25) = 急

Remembering this kanji

"I must HASTEN home," said **Little Red Riding Hood**, HASTENING to run a **comb** through her curly locks.

"Yes, by all means HASTEN," said the surgeon, "but please remember your **heart** condition."

Common Pronunciations

Common **ON** reading: **KYŪ** (キュウ)
Common **kun** reading: **iso** (いそ)

Less Common Pronunciations

Less common **ON** reading: none
Less common **kun** readings: none

	COMMON WORDS AND COMPOUNDS		
急ぐ		hasten; go quickly	iso·gu いそ·ぐ
急変		hasten + alter = *sudden change*	KYŪ·HEN キュウ·ヘン
急降下		hasten + descend + lower = *nose dive*	KYŪ·KŌ·KA キュウ·コウ·カ

KANJI 266

 STATE

'	ﾉ	小	州	州	州			

BUILDING THIS KANJI
Jelly Beans (3 of them) ﾉ + **River** 川(70) = 州

Meaning

The political subdivision of a 'state' or 'province'.

Remembering this kanji

This is another of those rare characters we will learn (recall the kanji for "east" (東) from Entry 76) whose stroke order does not follow that of the components as listed above.

"Which STATE are we in?" asked the tourist, squinting at his map.

"A STATE is an arbitrary political subdivision," answered the philosopher. "They drift away, having as much permanence as a trio of **jelly beans** cast into a **river**."

Common Pronunciations

Common **ON** reading: **SHŪ** (シュウ)
Common **kun** reading: none

With the two compounds below you are now able to read the names of Japan's four main islands – the other two being Hokkaido and Shikoku: 北海道 (HOK·KAI·DŌ_/ホッ·カイ·ドウ), 四国 (SHI·KOKU/シ·コク).

Less Common Pronunciations

Less common **ON** reading: none
Less common **kun** readings: **su** (す)

	COMMON WORDS AND COMPOUNDS	
本州	main + state = *Honshu*	HON·SHŪ ホン·シュウ
九州	nine + state = *Kyushu*	KYŪ·SHŪ キュウ·シュウ

KANJI 267

辛 **SPICY**

| ' | 一 | 亠 | 立 | 立 | 立 | 辛 | |

BUILDING THIS KANJI
Stand 立(112) + Ten (scarecrow) 十(28) = 辛

Meaning
Spicy, pungent. By extension, this kanji is also used in some compounds to express the ideas of hardship and trials.

Remembering this kanji
She could do nothing but **stand** over the **scarecrow** in disbelief, the curry dinner she had made still in her oven mitts. "But…your dating profile said you were fond of SPICY food," she stammered.

"I'm sorry, but you must have confused me with someone else. I'm a **scarecrow**; I'm not into anything, SPICY or otherwise."

Common Pronunciations
Common **ON** reading: none
Common **kun** reading: **kara** (か ら)

Less Common Pronunciations
Less common **ON** reading: **SHIN** (シ ン)
Less common **kun** readings: none

COMMON WORDS AND COMPOUNDS		
辛い	*spicy; hot*	**kara·i** から・い
辛口	spicy + mouth = *dry* (saké / wine)	**kara·kuchi** から・くち

COMPONENT #268

FERN

KANJI 268

服 **CLOTHES**

| ノ | 月 | 月 | 月 | 月 | 服 | 服 | 服 |

BUILDING THIS KANJI
Moon 月(11) + Fern 卩 + Again (ironing board) 又(159) = 服

Meaning
Clothes. One secondary meaning relates to the ideas of 'obey' and 'submission', while another, curiously, has to do with a 'dose' of something (the second compound offers an example).

Remembering this kanji

It's interesting how CLOTHES are important to some and not to others. The **moon**, for instance, has trouble finding his size, so doesn't care much about CLOTHES. **Ferns**, though, grow in damp climates, and because of this insist on having CLOTHES that are waterproof and breathable. And an **ironing board**? Well, an **ironing board** is obsessed with CLOTHES, isn't it?

Common Pronunciations

Common **ON** reading: **FUKU** (フ ク)
Common **kun** reading: none

Recall from Entry 157 that the first two kanji in the final compound mean 'student' when taken together.

Create your **on-yomi** keyword and enter it in the table at the back of the book. After that, write your sentence to remember the **on-yomi** reading in the box below.

Less Common Pronunciations

Less common **ON** reading: none
Less common **kun** readings: none

COMMON WORDS AND COMPOUNDS		
服	*clothes*	**FUKU** フク
一服	one + clothes (dose) = *a dose; a smoke;* *a rest*	**IP·PUKU** イッ・プク
学生服	student + clothes = *school uniform*	GAKU·SEI·**FUKU** ガク・セイ・フク

KANJI 269

LUCKY

一	十	士	吉	吉	吉		

BUILDING THIS KANJI
Gentleman 士(84) + Mouth (vampire) 口(8) = 吉

Meaning
Lucky, fortunate.

Remembering this kanji

"It would seem, kind **gentleman**," hissed the **vampire** as he drew off, "that today is your LUCKY day."
"LUCKY indeed," said the **gentleman**. "But do allow me to apologize for having garlic breath."

Common Pronunciations

Common **ON** reading: **KICHI** (キチ);
KITSU (キツ)
Common **kun** reading: none

This is another of those quirky kanji that have multiple common readings and only a few compounds.

Create your **on-yomi** keywords and enter them in the table at the back of the book. After that, write your sentence to remember the **on-yomi** readings in the box below.

Less Common Pronunciations

Less common **ON** reading: none
Less common **kun** readings: none

COMMON WORDS AND COMPOUNDS		
吉日	lucky + sun (day) = *lucky day*	**KICHI·JITSU** キチ・ジツ
不吉	not + lucky = *unlucky*	**FU·KITSU** フ・キツ

KANJI 270

用 **UTILIZE**

ノ	丿	刀	月	用			

BUILDING THIS KANJI
Moon 月 (11) + **Pole** │ = 用

Meaning
Utilize. This important kanji also has the sense of a person's 'business' or 'errands'. It is often translated as "for" when used as the last character in a compound (illustrated by the final example below).

Remembering this kanji
"I don't understand why the **moon** has a **pole**. What could he UTILIZE it for?"
"He could UTILIZE it for **pole** vaulting, he could UTILIZE it for rafting…he could UTILIZE it for lots of stuff."

Common Pronunciations
Common **ON** reading: **YŌ** (ヨウ)
Common **kun** reading: none

Note the unusual reading for 心 in the second example; it is extremely rare for this kanji to become voiced like this.

Less Common Pronunciations
Less common **ON** reading: none
Less common **kun** readings: **mochi** (もち)

COMMON WORDS AND COMPOUNDS		
用事	utilize + matter = *business; things to be done*	YŌ·JI ヨウ・ジ
用心	utilize + heart = *caution; care*	YŌ·JIN ヨウ・ジン
男子用	man + child + utilize = *for men; men's*	DAN·SHI·YŌ ダン・シ・ヨウ

COMPONENT #271

ICE HOCKEY

KANJI 271

次 **NEXT**

`	丷	冫	沪	汐	次		

BUILDING THIS KANJI
Ice Hockey 冫 + **Lack** 欠 (246) = 次

Meaning
Next, following.

Remembering this kanji
So you want to have a game of **ice hockey**? Well, it looks as though you **lack** some items. First get some skates and sticks. NEXT, get a puck. NEXT, helmets. NEXT, an arena, and NEXT a couple of teams.

Common Pronunciations

Common **ON** reading: **JI** (ジ)

Common **kun** reading: **tsu** (つ); **tsugi** (つぎ)

JI is the most common of these readings. **tsu** is found only as the verb in the second example below.

Less Common Pronunciations

Less common **ON** reading: **SHI** (シ)

Less common **kun** readings: none

This reading is found in only one word, 次第, which we met earlier as the last compound for 第 in Entry 243.

COMMON WORDS AND COMPOUNDS		
次	*next*	tsugi 次
次ぐ	*come after; follow*	tsu·gu つ・ぐ
目次	eye + next = *table of contents*	MOKU·JI モ ク・ジ

低 LOW

BUILDING THIS KANJI

Giraffe イ + Surname 氏(234) + One (hamburger patty) 一(3) = 低

Meaning

Low.

Remembering this kanji

"LOW! LOW! LOW!" the crowd roared.

"Come on, Mrs. Zebra," said the trainer, holding out a **hamburger patty**.

"LOW! LOW! LOW!"

"Look at the tasty **hamburger patty**…"

The **giraffe** could take it no longer. "What kind of crazy zoo is this?" she yelled. "My **surname** is **Giraffe**, and **hamburger patties** aren't in my diet. But even if they were, I wouldn't LOWER myself to do a limbo dance to get one."

Common Pronunciations

Common **ON** reading: **TEI** (テイ)

Common **kun** reading: **hiku** (ひく)

Less Common Pronunciations

Less common **ON** reading: none

Less common **kun** readings: none

COMMON WORDS AND COMPOUNDS		
低い	*low*	hiku·i ひく・い
低下	low + lower = *lowering; decline*	TEI·KA テイ・カ
低速	low + fast = *low speed*	TEI·SOKU テイ・ソ ク

KANJI 273

 FILIAL PIETY

BUILDING THIS KANJI
Earth 土(87) + Comet 一 + Child 子(56) = 孝

Meaning
Filial piety, obedience to one's parents.

Remembering this kanji
She was a **child** of the **earth**, and was famed for her FILIAL PIETY. She tended the **earth** carefully, raking it with great affection and sprinkling it gently. It was rumored that a **comet** had once flashed between her and the **earth**, but that even then she had not been distracted. I'm totally serious: the **child** had that much FILIAL PIETY.

Common Pronunciations
Common **ON** reading: **KO** (コ ウ)
Common **kun** reading: none

Note the mix of **on** and **kun-yomi** in the two sample compounds.

Less Common Pronunciations
Less common **ON** reading: none
Less common **kun** readings: none

COMMON WORDS AND COMPOUNDS		
親孝行	parent + filial piety + go = *filial piety*	oya·**KŌ**·KŌ おや・コウ・コウ
親不孝	parent + not + filial piety = *lack of filial piety*	oya·FU·**KŌ** おや・フ・コウ

COMPONENT #274

ZOMBIE

KANJI 274

茶 **TEA**

BUILDING THIS KANJI
Wreath 艹 + Umbrella 𠆢 + Zombie 朩 = 茶

Meaning
Tea.

Remembering this kanji
Zombies, I feel, get a bad rap. Why? Well, with no lust for glory, they shun any **wreath** given them. And the idea of a **zombie** using an **umbrella**? It wouldn't happen in a hurricane! TEA, however, finds favor. As one **zombie** told me: "Oh sure, I may rampage as one of the undead, but that doesn't mean I don't enjoy a spot of TEA in the afternoon".

Common Pronunciations
Common **ON** reading: **CHA** (チ ャ)
Common **kun** reading: none

Create your **on-yomi** keyword and enter it in the table at the back of the book. After that, write

your sentence to remember the **on-yomi** reading in the box below.

(blank box)

Less Common Pronunciations
Less common **ON** reading: **SA** (サ)
Less common **kun** readings: none

Though not common, this reading does show up in the Japanese word for 'tea ceremony' (茶道:

SA·DŌ / サ·ドウ), composed of the kanji 'tea' and 'road' (in this instance, better translated as the 'way').

COMMON WORDS AND COMPOUNDS		
茶	*tea*	**CHA** チャ
茶色	tea + color = *brown*	**CHA**·iro チャ·いろ
茶室	tea + room = *tea room*	**CHA·SHITSU** チャ·シツ

利 **PROFIT**

BUILDING THIS KANJI
Crops 禾 + **Chisel** 刂 = 利

Meaning
Profit, advantage.

Remembering this kanji
"Buck up, farmer," he told himself. "Nobody said it would be easy making a **PROFIT**, so grab that **chisel** and get every last grain out of those **crops**."

He'd expected it to be tough, but still...how had he made so much more **PROFIT** as a sculptor?

Common Pronunciations
Common **ON** reading: **RI** (リ)
Common **kun** reading: **ki** (き)

Less Common Pronunciations
Less common **ON** reading: none
Less common **kun** readings: none

COMMON WORDS AND COMPOUNDS		
利く	*take effect; work*	**ki**·ku き·く
利子	profit + child = *interest (on money)*	**RI·SHI** リ·シ
利口	profit + mouth = *smart; clever*	**RI·KŌ** リ·コウ

未 **NOT YET**

BUILDING THIS KANJI
One (hamburger patty) 一(3) + **Tree** 木(13) = 未

Meaning
Not yet. This kanji is invariably used as the first in a compound to indicate something incomplete or unfinished.

Remembering this kanji

Because they are so visually similar, we will be learning this character together with that of the next entry in order to focus on how to tell them apart. It would also be wise at this point to review the stroke order of 本 ("Main" from Entry 68), to see clearly how it differs from the present kanji.

"Have you girls seen the **hamburger patty tree**?"
"NOT YET!" they said excitedly.
"Well," he chuckled, "here it is. Look at that cute little **hamburger patty** growing at the top."
"Can we pick it?"
"NOT YET," he cautioned. "It's NOT YET ready."

Common Pronunciations

Common **ON** reading: **MI** (ミ)
Common **kun** reading: none

Create your **on-yomi** keyword and enter it in the table at the back of the book. After that, write your sentence to remember the **on-yomi** reading in the box below.

Less Common Pronunciations

Less common **ON** reading: none
Less common **kun** readings: none

COMMON WORDS AND COMPOUNDS		
未来	not yet + come = *future; future tense*	**MI·RAI** ミ・ライ
未定	not yet + fixed = *undecided; pending*	**MI·TEI** ミ・テイ
未開発	not yet + open + discharge = *undeveloped*	**MI·KAI·HATSU** ミ・カイ・ハツ

末 **END**

BUILDING THIS KANJI
One (hamburger patty) 一(3) + Tree 木(13)
= 末

Meaning
The "end" of things, in space as well as time.

Remembering this kanji

Were you able to quickly spot the difference between this kanji and that of the preceding entry? The story and illustration, hopefully, will help in remembering that the top stroke here is longer than that of 未.

"Here's another **hamburger patty tree**," he said. "Notice how the **hamburger patty** here is fully formed; it's even grown past the END of the **tree** tips."
"Oh, I wish this wasn't the END of the tour," said one of the girls.
"So do I," he murmured, "but we have to realize that to everything there is an END."

Common Pronunciations
Common **ON** reading: **MATSU** (マ ツ)
Common **kun** reading: none

Create your **on-yomi** keyword and enter it in the table at the back of the book. After that, write your sentence to remember the **on-yomi** reading in the box below.

Less Common Pronunciations
Less common **ON** reading: **BATSU** (バ ツ)
Less common **kun** readings: **sue** (す え)

COMMON WORDS AND COMPOUNDS		
週末	week + end = *weekend*	SHŪ·MATSU シュウ·マツ
年末	year + end = *end of the year*	NEN·MATSU ネン·マツ
末期	end + period = *last stage*	MAK·KI マッ·キ

COMPONENT #278

SCISSORS   十

KANJI 278

斗   **DIPPER**

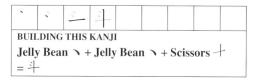

BUILDING THIS KANJI
Jelly Bean ヽ + Jelly Bean ヽ + Scissors 十 = 斗

Meaning
Dipper.

Remembering this kanji
This is another uncommon character that will be encountered far more often as a component in other kanji. It is most easily remembered through the compound below.

This kanji makes it obvious how inadequately **jelly beans** could be gathered with **scissors**. Even a couple of **jelly beans** — like the ones that have slipped through the **scissors** here — could be picked up much more easily with a **DIPPER**.

Common Pronunciations
Common **ON** reading: **TO** (ト)
Common **kun** reading: none

Less Common Pronunciations
Less common **ON** reading: none
Less common **kun** readings: none

COMMON WORDS AND COMPOUNDS		
北斗 七星	north + dipper + seven + star = *the Big Dipper*	HOKU·TO·SHICHI·SEI ホク·ト·シチ·セイ

KANJI 279

PLAY

BUILDING THIS KANJI

Direction 方 (223) + Hammer 宀 + Child 子 (56) + Seal 辶 = 遊

Meaning

Make sure to have fun with this kanji, as it's all about play and amusement. The combination of the 'direction' character and 'hammer' component, incidentally, will show up often in other kanji.

Remembering this kanji

Give the **child** of a **seal** hunter a **hammer** and he'll look in every **direction** for a **seal** to PLAY with. But what about the **seal**? Well, the **seal** will glance in various **directions** too, only a lot more nervously. Because let's be honest, if you're a **seal** and you spot that **child** coming at you with a **hammer**, the last thing you'll want to do is PLAY with him.

Common Pronunciations

Common **ON** reading: **YŪ** (ユウ)
Common **kun** reading: **aso** (あそ)

Less Common Pronunciations

Less common **ON** reading: **YU** (ユ)
Less common **kun** readings: none

COMMON WORDS AND COMPOUNDS		
遊ぶ	*play*	**aso**·bu あそ·ぶ
遊泳	play + swim = *swimming*	**YŪ**·EI ユウ·エイ
遊園地	play + garden + ground = *amusement park; playground*	**YŪ**·EN·CHI ユウ·エン·チ

KANJI 280

BEAN

BUILDING THIS KANJI

One (top of a bun) 一 (3) + Mouth (vampire) 口 (8) + Snowboard 丷 = 豆

Meaning

Bean.

Remembering this kanji

If everyone were crazy about BEANS:

a) BEANS, instead of sesame seeds, would be put on the **top of a bun**.

b) **Vampires** could lure their victims with a promise of BEANS.

c) Those who liked to **snowboard** would rather be knee-deep in BEANS than fresh powder.

Common Pronunciations

Common **ON** reading: none
Common **kun** reading: **mame** (まめ)

Less Common Pronunciations

Less common **ON** reading: **ZU** (ズ); **TŌ** (ト ウ)
Less common **kun** readings: none

ZU appears only in the word for 'soybean' 大豆 (DAI·**ZU** / ダ イ・ズ) made from the kanji for 'large' and 'bean'. **TŌ** is the pronunciation when this kanji shows up in the famous Japanese word 'tofu' 豆腐* (**TŌ**·FU / ト ウ・フ), formed from the kanji 'bean' and 'rot' (the latter character does not appear in this book).

COMMON WORDS AND COMPOUNDS		
豆	*bean*	**mame** まめ

CHAPTER 13 REVIEW EXERCISES

A. Please match the following kanji to their meanings.

1.	神	a.	Bean
2.	利	b.	Next
3.	羊	c.	Sheep
4.	紙	d.	Tea
5.	茶	e.	God
6.	遊	f.	Hasten
7.	急	g.	Paper
8.	世	h.	Play
9.	次	i.	Society
10.	豆	j.	Profit

B. Please match the following meanings to their kanji, and these to their **on** or **kun-yomi**.

1.	Army	a. 画	1.	**FUKU** (フク)
2.	Painting	b. 末	2.	**na** (な)
3.	State	c. 定	3.	**MATSU** (マツ)
4.	Elder sister	d. 軍	4.	**GUN** (グン)
5.	Clothes	e. 姉	5.	**SHŪ** (シュウ)
6.	Fixed	f. 未	6.	**MI** (ミ)
7.	End	g. 服	7.	**ane** (あね)
8.	Perish	h. 辛	8.	**sada** (さだ)
9.	Spicy	i. 州	9.	**GA** (ガ)
10.	Not yet	j. 亡	10.	**kara** (から)

C. Please choose the best answer(s) to the following questions.

1. Which is the correct reading of 低い?
   a. **waka·i** (わか・い)
   b. **hiku·i** (ひく・い)
   c. **ara·i** (あら・い)
   d. **kuro·i** (くろ・い)

2. That falling grand piano just missed you! You're sure ___ .
   a. 辛   b. 台   c. 豆   d. 吉   e. 采

3. Which of the following readings apply to the kanji 神?
   a. **JIN** (ジン)   b. **karu** (かる)
   c. **SHI** (シ)   d. **kami** (かみ)
   e. **SHIN** (シン)

4. Which of the following kanji has the most number of strokes?
   a. 画   b. 服   c. 急   d. 定   e. 姉

5. Which of the following readings apply to the kanji 世?
   a. **SHŪ** (シュウ) b. **SEI** (セイ)
   c. **SEN** (セン) d. **SE** (セ) e. **SHIN** (シン)

D. Please match the following compounds to their meanings and pronunciations.

1.	介入	a. Smart/ Clever	1.	**SHI·BŌ** (シ・ボウ)
2.	用心	b. Kitchen	2.	**HOKU·TO· SHICHI·SEI** (ホク・ト・ シチ・セイ)
3.	利口	c. The Big Dipper	3.	**DAI·dokoro** (ダイ・どころ)
4.	台所	d. Myth / Mythology	4.	**SHIN·WA** (シン・ワ)
5.	死亡	e. Occupy	5.	**KAI·NYŪ** (カイ・ニュウ)
6.	吉日	f. Death	6.	**KICHI·JITSU** (キチ・ジツ)
7.	神話	g. Society / Life	7.	**RI·KŌ** (リ・コウ)
8.	占有	h. Intervention	8.	**SE·KEN** (セ・ケン)
9.	世間	i. Lucky day	9.	**YŌ·JIN** (ヨウ・ジン)
10.	北斗 七星	j. Caution / Care	10.	**SEN·YŪ** (セン・ユウ)

E. Please read the passage below and answer the questions that follow.

姉は茶道が大好きです。週末九州で有名な茶道の大会が有ります。だから土曜日に電車で行くつもりです。

1. What does this elder sister really like?
2. When is there a famous convention taking place?
3. Where will this happen?
4. On which day will she go there?
5. How will she travel?

Kanji #281—305

KANJI 281

屋 ROOF

BUILDING THIS KANJI
Flag 尸 + Reach 至 (239) = 屋

Meaning
Roof. When this kanji is the final character in a compound, it will often mean a 'shop' when referring to a building, or a 'dealer' when referring to a person.

Remembering this kanji
If you're able to grab a **flag** by simply making a **reach** for it, there's a decent chance you're on a ROOF.

Common Pronunciations
Common **ON** reading: **OKU** (オ ク)
Common **kun** reading: **ya** (や)

ya is by far the more common reading, and is invariably used when this kanji appears in the final position of a compound. There is often a mixture of **on** and **kun-yomi** in such words (as in the final two examples below).

Create your **on-yomi** keyword and enter it in the table at the back of the book. Then, after creating your **kun-yomi** keyword, write your sentence to remember the **on-yomi** and **kun-yomi** readings in the box below.

Less Common Pronunciations
Less common **ON** reading: none
Less common **kun** readings: none

COMMON WORDS AND COMPOUNDS		
屋上	roof + upper = *rooftop*	OKU·JŌ オ ク · ジョ ウ
本屋	main (book) + roof = *bookstore*	HON·ya ホン · や
料理屋	fee + reason + roof = *restaurant*	RYŌ·RI·ya リョ ウ · リ · や

KANJI 282

 各 EACH

| ノ | ク | 夂 | 夂 | 各 | 各 | | | |

BUILDING THIS KANJI
Running Chicken 夂 + Mouth (vampire) 口
(8) = 各

Meaning
Each.

Remembering this kanji
EACH **running chicken** behaved differently in the presence of the **vampire**. EACH was running scared, of course, but some zigged while others zagged. Oh well, it was up to EACH to get away, and EACH had their own strategy for doing so.

Common Pronunciations
Common **ON** reading: **KAKU** (カ ク)
Common **kun** reading: none

Less Common Pronunciations
Less common **ON** reading: none
Less common **kun** readings: **onoono**
(おのおの)

COMMON WORDS AND COMPOUNDS		
各人	each + person = *each person*	**KAKU·JIN** カ ク・ジ ン
各地	each + ground = *each area*	**KAKU·CHI** カ ク・チ

COMPONENT #283

SCRATCHES

KANJI 283

形 FORM

| 一 | 二 | 干 | 开 | 形 | 形 | 形 | | |

BUILDING THIS KANJI
Picnic Table 开 + Scratches 彡 = 形

Meaning
Form, shape, appearance.

Remembering this kanji
"Hard to tell. It had a weird FORM, though."
"What kind of FORM?"
"A hunched FORM."
She knelt down to examine the broken **picnic table** and noticed a trio of **scratches**. Could it have been done by the picnic-loving three-toed sloth? Perhaps, but a FORM alone wasn't much to go on…

Common Pronunciations
Common **ON** reading: **KEI** (ケ イ)
Common **kun** reading: **katachi** (か た ち);
kata (か た)

These readings can seem a bit confusing at first, but **katachi** is the choice when this kanji appears on its own; it such a case it means 'form' or 'shape'. In compounds, look for **KEI** in first position (with a notable exception being the second example below), and a split between **KEI** and **kata** after that, keeping in mind that **kata** is almost always voiced in such instances.

Less Common Pronunciations
Less common ON reading: **GYŌ** (ギョウ)
Less common **kun** readings: none

This is a very uncommon reading that you are only likely to meet in the word for 'doll', 人形 (NIN·GYŌ / ニン·ギョウ) from the kanji for 'person' and 'form'.

COMMON WORDS AND COMPOUNDS		
形	*form; shape*	**katachi** かたち
形見	form + see = *memento; keepsake*	**kata·mi** かた·み
手形	hand + form = *bill; draft; note*	te·gata て·がた
形成	form + become = *formation*	**KEI·SEI** ケイ·セイ

COMPONENT #284

BOWING

KANJI 284

的 **TARGET**

BUILDING THIS KANJI
White 白(7) + Bowing ク + Jelly Bean ＼ = 的

Meaning
Target. This is an important character that is used as a suffix to express such ideas as the English equivalent of '-istic' in words such as 'artistic'. If you spend some time getting to know this kanji, you will quickly notice your vocabulary growing in sophistication.

Remembering this kanji
"What are you watching?" she asked.
He adjusted the binoculars. "I'm not sure. There's a little **white** object, and a guy's **bowing** over it...now he's hit it so high into the sky that it doesn't look any bigger than a **jelly bean**! Oh hang on...it seems he was aiming at a TARGET of some sort."
"Really?" she said. "I wonder what that TARGET could be?"

It would seem, apparently, that not everyone living next to a golf course understands the game.

Common Pronunciations
Common ON reading: **TEKI** (テキ)
Common **kun** reading: none

Recall from Entry 202 that 'literature' plus 'change' in the second example below means 'culture', and from Entry 177 that 'tool' plus 'body' in the third example means 'definite; concrete'.

Create your **on-yomi** keyword and enter it in the table at the back of the book. After that, write

your sentence to remember the **on-yomi** reading in the box below.

COMMON WORDS AND COMPOUNDS		
目的	eye + target = *purpose; aim*	MOKU·**TEKI** モク·テキ
文化的	culture + target = *cultural*	BUN·KA·**TEKI** ブン·カ·テキ
具体的	definite + target = *definite; specific; concrete*	GU·TAI·**TEKI** グ·タイ·テキ

Less Common Pronunciations
Less common **ON** reading: none
Less common **kun** readings: **mato** (まと)

BUILDING THIS KANJI
Hammer ⺊ + **Large (sumo wrestler)** 大(17) = 矢

Meaning
Arrow. As these are the same two components used to make the kanji for "Lose" (Entry 142), ensure that you able to tell them apart (the respective illustrations and stories should help).

Remembering this kanji
I tried to shoot an apple off a **sumo wrestler** with an **ARROW**, but it would always be eaten before the **ARROW** made it there. A **hammer** on his head worked better, even if it was hard for him to balance it and the **ARROW** never stuck in.

Common Pronunciations
Common **ON** reading: none
Common **kun** reading: **ya** (や)

Less Common Pronunciations
Less common **ON** reading: **SHI** (シ)
Less common **kun** readings: none

COMMON WORDS AND COMPOUNDS		
矢	*arrow*	**ya** や
弓矢	bow + arrow = *bow and arrow*	yumi·**ya** ゆみ·や

KANJI 286

BUILDING THIS KANJI
Rice Field 田(73) + **Intervene** 介(263) = 界

Meaning
World, circles (in the sense of 'financial circles' or 'scientific circles', etc).

Remembering this kanji

Who cares if you've got your own **rice field**? There'll always be others wanting to **intervene** in it; that's how it is in this **WORLD**.

Common Pronunciations

Common **ON** reading: **KAI** (カ イ)
Common **kun** reading: none

Less Common Pronunciations

Less common **ON** reading: none
Less common **kun** readings: none

COMMON WORDS AND COMPOUNDS		
世界	society + world = *the world*	**SE·KAI** セ・カイ
業界	business + world = *the business world*	**GYO·KAI** ギョウ・カイ
自然界	self + nature + world = *the world of nature*	**SHI·ZEN·KAI** シ・ゼン・カイ

COMPONENT #287

CLIFF

KANJI 287

反 **AGAINST**

一	厂	万	反				

BUILDING THIS KANJI
Cliff 厂 + **Again (ironing board)** 又 (159) = 反

Meaning

Against, anti-.

Remembering this kanji

I tumbled down a **cliff** once and hurt myself. Stupid, arrogant **cliff**, soaring over everything else! I'm AGAINST cliffs. Another day I went into my closet and was struck by my **ironing board**. Grrrr. I'm AGAINST **ironing boards** too.

Common Pronunciations

Common **ON** reading: **HAN** (ハ ン)
Common **kun** reading: none

Less Common Pronunciations

Less common **ON** reading: **TAN** (タ ン);
HON (ホ ン)
Less common **kun** readings: **so** (そ)

COMMON WORDS AND COMPOUNDS		
反転	against + roll = *roll over; reverse*	**HAN·TEN** ハン・テン
反動	against + move = *reaction; recoil*	**HAN·DŌ** ハン・ドウ
反対	against + versus = *opposition; resistance*	**HAN·TAI** ハン・タイ

KANJI 288

 GOOD

BUILDING THIS KANJI
Jelly Bean ⟍ + Frog 艮 = 良

Meaning
Good.

Remembering this kanji
When the 'jelly bean' component looks like this, we'll think of it as balancing straight up and down.

"GOOD…GOOD…keep at it…"
It's a GOOD exercise getting a **jelly bean** to balance straight up and down on a **frog**. GOOD for developing patience, GOOD for steadying your movements, and GOOD for honing your vision. I'm not sure how GOOD it is for the **frog**, though.

Common Pronunciations
Common **ON** reading: **RYŌ** (リ ョ ウ)
Common **kun** reading: **yo** (よ)

Less Common Pronunciations
Less common **ON** reading: none
Less common **kun** readings: none

COMMON WORDS AND COMPOUNDS		
良い	good	**yo·i** よ・い
良心	good + heart = *conscience*	**RYŌ·SHIN** リ ョ ウ・シ ン
良好	good + like = *good; satisfactory*	**RYŌ·KO** リ ョ ウ・コ ウ

KANJI 289

 DISTRIBUTE

Meaning
Distribute.

BUILDING THIS KANJI
Whiskey Jug 酉 + Oneself (whip) 己 (214) = 配

Remembering this kanji

If you've ever seen a **whiskey jug** and taken a **whip** to it, the chances are you're a pretty serious teetotaler. Given that, it wouldn't be smart for you to get a job where you'd have to DISTRIBUTE whiskey jugs. No, you'd likely find it more rewarding to DISTRIBUTE advice to those sorry whiskey drinkers instead.

Common Pronunciations

Common **ON** reading: **HAI** (ハイ)
Common **kun** reading: **kuba** (く ば)

Less Common Pronunciations

Less common **ON** reading: none
Less common **kun** readings: none

COMMON WORDS AND COMPOUNDS		
配る	*distribute*	**kuba·ru** く ば·る
配水	distribute + water = *water supply*	**HAI·SUI** ハイ·スイ
心配	heart + distribute = *worry; anxiety*	**SHIN·PAI** シン·パイ

COMPONENT #290

SHERPA   呆

KANJI 290

遠   **FAR**

BUILDING THIS KANJI
Earth 土(87) + Sherpa 呆 + Seal 辶 = 遠

Meaning
Far.

Remembering this kanji

"I bring you this **earth** from FAR away," said the **sherpa**, placing his pile next to the **seal**'s flippers.
"How FAR is FAR, **sherpa**?" demanded the **seal**.
"From Nepal."

That *is* FAR, thought the **seal**, grinning. If this keeps up, I'll soon have all the earth I need.

Common Pronunciations

Common **ON** reading: **EN** (エン)
Common **kun** reading: **tō** (と お)

Less Common Pronunciations

Less common **ON** reading: **ON** (オン)
Less common **kun** readings: none

COMMON WORDS AND COMPOUNDS		
遠い	*far; distant*	**tō·i** と お·い
遠足	far + leg = *excursion*	**EN·SOKU** エン·ソク
永遠	eternal + far = *eternity*	**EI·EN** エイ·エン

KANJI 291

 FORGET

| ' | 一 | 亡 | 亡 | 忘 | 忘 | 忘 | | |

BUILDING THIS KANJI
Perish 亡(254) + Heart 心 (25) = 忘

Meaning
Forget.

Remembering this kanji
"What does it mean to **FORGET**?" she asked her disciple. "Does everything **perish** in the **heart**?"
"Oh, darn it," he said, "I should be able to get this one. I have a feeling you told me earlier, but I **FORGET**."

Common Pronunciations
Common **ON** reading: **BŌ** (ボウ)
Common **kun** reading: **wasu** (わす)

Less Common Pronunciations
Less common **ON** reading: none
Less common **kun** readings: none

COMMON WORDS AND COMPOUNDS		
忘れる	*forget*	**wasu**·reru わす·れる
忘れ物	forget + thing = *something left behind*	**wasu**·re mono わす·れ もの
忘年会	forget + year + meet = *year-end party*	BŌ·NEN·KAI ボウ·ネン·カイ

KANJI 292

 PERFECT

| ' | ﾉ | 宀 | 宀 | 宁 | 宁 | 完 | | |

BUILDING THIS KANJI
Pincers 宀 + Basis 元(53) = 完

Meaning
Perfect, complete.

Remembering this kanji
"Hey boss," he asked, "when it comes to **pincers**, what is the **basis** of a **PERFECT** set?"
The **pincer** maker smiled. "Son, some will tell you the **basis** is **PERFECT** welding, others that it is **PERFECT** riveting. But don't be fooled: the **basis** of **PERFECT pincers** has – and always will be – how well they pick stuff up."

Common Pronunciations
Common **ON** reading: **KAN** (カン)
Common **kun** reading: none

Less Common Pronunciations
Less common **ON** reading: none
Less common **kun** readings: none

COMMON WORDS AND COMPOUNDS		
完全	perfect + complete = *perfection; completeness*	**KAN**·ZEN カン·ゼン
完成	perfect + become = *completion; accomplishment*	**KAN**·SEI カン·セイ
完結	perfect + bind = *completion; conclusion*	**KAN**·KETSU カン·ケツ

且 BESIDES

Meaning
Besides, moreover.

Remembering this kanji
We will assign this character the unrelated meaning of a **filing cabinet**. Why, you ask? Well, like 又 ('Again', which we know from Entry 159 as our 'ironing board'), it's obscure and not very common on its own. BESIDES, it has to be learned given that it pops up as a component in other kanji. BESIDES that, it looks like a **filing cabinet**.

Common Pronunciations
Common **ON** reading: none
Common **kun** reading: **ka** (か)

Less Common Pronunciations
Less common **ON** reading: **SHO** (ショ)
Less common **kun** readings: none

COMMON WORDS AND COMPOUNDS		
且つ	*besides*	ka·tsu か・つ

COMPONENT #294

VETERAN YODELER 阝

Just as we met the 'good figure skater' and 'poor figure skater' earlier, we will now meet a pair of yodelers. This present fellow is clearly a veteran yodeler: the raised-leg form and chubby physique are classic, and he projects his voice beautifully into open air. It is this latter fact, actually, that distinguishes the veteran yodeler; he always appears on the right-hand side of a kanji so that nothing interferes with his sound.

KANJI 294

 都 METROPOLIS

BUILDING THIS KANJI
Individual 者(93) + Veteran Yodeler 阝 = 都

Meaning
Metropolis, large city.

Remembering this kanji
Look, an **individual** can only succeed in getting heard in this METROPOLIS if they're like a **veteran yodeler**. I mean, it's a great big METROPOLIS for goodness sakes, and only a **veteran yodeler** could get noticed in such a noisy environment.

Common Pronunciations

Common **ON** reading: **TO** (ト)
Common **kun** reading: **miyako** (み や こ)

Less Common Pronunciations

Less common **ON** reading: **TSU** (ツ)
Less common **kun** readings: none

You will only meet this **on-yomi** in two compounds, the first being 都合 (**TSU·GŌ** / ツ· ゴウ) 'circumstances, arrangements' composed of the kanji 'metropolis' and 'match', the second

都度 (**TSU·DO** / ツ·ド) 'each time, whenever' from the kanji 'metropolis' and 'degree'.

COMMON WORDS AND COMPOUNDS		
都	*metropolis; capital*	miyako み や こ
京都	capital + metropolis = *Kyoto*	KYŌ·TO キョウ·ト
首都	neck + metropolis = *capital city*	SHU·TO シュ·ト

COMPONENT #295

NOVICE YODELER 阝

What a sorry sight! As we can see by the horrible posture and skinny physique, this is obviously a novice yodeler. And as the next kanji makes clear, he needs to learn not to yodel into other objects; sadly, however, he always does so by only showing up on the left-hand side of any kanji in which he appears.

KANJI 295

 DESCEND

゛	⻏	阝	阝'	阝⁷	阝夂	阝夂	降
降							

BUILDING THIS KANJI
Novice Yodeler 阝 + Running Chicken 夂 + Whirling Dervish 牛 = 降

Meaning

Descend, fall, surrender. This is the character used when describing the 'falling' of rain or snow, etc.

Remembering this kanji

You can never tell what will happen when a plane DESCENDS. On my last flight, for instance, I was sitting between a terrible **novice yodeler** who started to yodel when a **running chicken** flapped by him, and a **whirling dervish** who began to whirl. The whole episode made me a little nervous… I dunno, maybe I'm just one of those guys who doesn't like to DESCEND.

Common Pronunciations

Common **ON** reading: **KŌ** (コウ)
Common **kun** reading: **fu** (ふ)

Less Common Pronunciations

Less common **ON** reading: none
Less common **kun** readings: **o** (お)

This reading forms an intransitive/transitive verb pair (降りる / 降ろす) that has the same pronunciation as one we met earlier with the kanji 下 (Entry 31): 下りる / 下ろす. The characters are sometimes used interchangeably, although you are more likely to see them written as 下りる and 下ろす.

COMMON WORDS AND COMPOUNDS

降る	fall (rain / snow)	**fu**·ru ふ·る
降下	descend + lower = descent; landing	**KŌ**·KA コウ·カ
降水	descend + water = precipitation	**KŌ**·SUI コウ·スイ

KANJI 296

婚 **MARRIAGE**

| く | ノ | 女 | 女ゝ | 女ヒ | 女匕 | 女氏 | 女氏 | 婚 |
| 婚 | 婚 | | | | | | | |

BUILDING THIS KANJI
Woman 女(16) + Surname 氏(234) + Sun 日
(6) = 婚

Meaning
Marriage.

Remembering this kanji
MARRIAGE, in a lot of cultures, means that a **woman** essentially tosses her **surname** into the **sun**. She assumes another **surname**, of course, but there is disagreement nowadays as to whether this requirement of MARRIAGE is out-of-date.

Common Pronunciations
Common **ON** reading: **KON** (コン)
Common **kun** reading: none

Create your **on-yomi** keyword and enter it in the table at the back of the book. After that, write your sentence to remember the **on-yomi** reading in the box below.

Less Common Pronunciations
Less common **ON** reading: none
Less common **kun** readings: none

COMMON WORDS AND COMPOUNDS

離婚	separate + marriage = divorce	**RI**·**KON** リ·コン
結婚	bind + marriage = marriage	**KEK**·**KON** ケッ·コン
婚期	marriage + period = marriageable age	**KON**·KI コン·キ

KANJI 297

祭 **FESTIVAL**

| ノ | ク | タ | タ | タフ | 祭 | 祭 | 祭 | 祭 |
| 祭 | 祭 | | | | | | | |

BUILDING THIS KANJI
Moon 月 (11) + **Again (ironing board)** 又 (159) + **Show** 示 (247) = 祭

Meaning
Festival. This kanji can also have some religious overtones in the senses of ritual and worship. Note that the first stroke of 'again' is clipped off in some fonts so that it does not pass through the second.

Remembering this kanji
"You here **moon** FESTIVAL? I **show** you. Nice price. No?...What?...**Ironing board** FESTIVAL? There is **ironing board** FESTIVAL? No, no, come back! I **show** you **ironing board** FESTIVAL! Then **moon** FESTIVAL."

Common Pronunciations
Common **ON** reading: **SAI** (サイ)
Common **kun** reading: **matsu** (まつ)

Less Common Pronunciations
Less common **ON** reading: none
Less common **kun** readings: none

COMMON WORDS AND COMPOUNDS		
祭り	*festival*	**matsu·ri** まつ・り
祭日	festival + sun (day) = *festival day*	**SAI·JITSU** サイ・ジツ
百年祭	hundred + year + festival = *centennial*	**HYAKU·NEN·SAI** ヒャク・ネン・サイ

KANJI 298

指 **FINGER**

| 一 | 十 | 才 | 扌 | 扛 | 指 | 指 | 指 | 指 |

BUILDING THIS KANJI
Finger 扌 + **Gist** 旨 (244) = 指

Meaning
Finger, along with the senses of indicating and pointing. Note that this kanji never appears as a component in other characters; any reference to "finger" in future stories, therefore, will always be to 扌.

Remembering this kanji
Look, it makes sense for the **finger** component to be in the kanji for FINGER. That's the **gist** of it, anyway.

Common Pronunciations
Common **ON** reading: **SHI** (シ)
Common **kun** reading: **yubi** (ゆび); **sa** (さ)

As the second example shows, **sa** can become voiced outside of the first position.

Less Common Pronunciations
Less common **ON** reading: none
Less common **kun** readings: none

COMMON WORDS AND COMPOUNDS		
指	*finger*	**yubi** ゆび
目指す	eye + finger = *aim at*	me za·su め ざ・す
指名	finger + name = *nomination; designation*	**SHI·MEI** シ・メイ

DENTIST LIGHT

Ensure that you note the difference between this component and 厶, the 'broken crutch', introduced prior to Entry 131.

KANJI 299

BEFOREHAND

BUILDING THIS KANJI
Dentist Light ⊽ + Harpoon 亅 = 予

Meaning
Beforehand, previously. As you may have guessed, it's unusual for a component to show up in different positions in the same kanji like this.

Remembering this kanji
I'd had a sense **BEFOREHAND** that it wasn't going to be routine, and started to worry the moment my orthodontist turned on the **dentist light**.

"Hmm," she said, holding the **harpoon** first evenly, then straight up and down. My assistant told me **BEFOREHAND** that you had a whale of a cavity, but I wasn't expecting this. You should have taken care of it **BEFOREHAND**."

Common Pronunciations
Common **ON** reading: **YO** (ヨ)
Common **kun** reading: none

Create your **on-yomi** keyword and enter it in the table at the back of the book. After that, write your sentence to remember the **on-yomi** reading in the box below.

Less Common Pronunciations
Less common **ON** reading: none
Less common **kun** readings: none

COMMON WORDS AND COMPOUNDS		
予言	beforehand + say = *prediction*	**YO·GEN** ヨ·ゲン
予定	beforehand + fixed = *prearrangement; plan*	**YO·TEI** ヨ·テイ
予期	beforehand + period = *anticipation; expectation*	**YO·KI** ヨ·キ

KANJI 300

 ACTIVE

`	丶	氵	氵	氵	汗	汗	活	活

BUILDING THIS KANJI
Splash 氵 + Tongue 舌(110) = 活

Meaning
Active, lively.

Remembering this kanji

"Look at that **tongue splash** around in the pool over there."

"Yeah, it does laps to keep **ACTIVE**."

Common Pronunciations

Common **ON** reading: **KATSU** (カ ツ)

Common **kun** reading: none

Create your **on-yomi** keyword and enter it in the table at the back of the book. After that, write your sentence to remember the **on-yomi** reading in the box below.

Less Common Pronunciations

Less common **ON** reading: none

Less common **kun** readings: none

COMMON WORDS AND COMPOUNDS		
生活	life + active = *life; livelihood*	**SEI·KATSU** セイ·カツ
活気	active + spirit = *liveliness; vigor*	**KAK·KI** カッ·キ
活動	active + move = *activity; action*	**KATSU·DŌ** カツ·ドゥ

KANJI 301

和 **HARMONY**

⟋	一	千	千	禾	禾	和	和

BUILDING THIS KANJI

Crops 禾 + Mouth (vampire) 口 (8) = 和

Meaning

Harmony, peace. This kanji is also used as an abbreviation for Japan in much the same way ' 日 ' is (the final compound offers an example of this usage).

Remembering this kanji

Crops have nothing to fear from **vampires**, since **vampires** have no interest in **crops**. Thus, there is **HARMONY** between them.

Common Pronunciations

Common **ON** reading: **WA** (ワ)

Common **kun** reading: none

Less Common Pronunciations

Less common **ON** reading: **O** (オ)

Less common **kun** readings: **yawa** (やわ);
nago (なご)

IRREGULAR READING		
大和	large + harmony = *ancient Japan*	**yamato** やまと
日和	sun + harmony = *fine weather*	hi·**yori** ひ·より

COMMON WORDS AND COMPOUNDS		
和	*harmony*	**WA** ワ
平和	flat + harmony = *peace*	**HEI·WA** ヘイ·ワ
和食	harmony (Japan) + eat = *Japanese food*	**WA·SHOKU** ワ·ショク

KANJI 302

 VIA

| ㇏ | ㇙ | ㇰ | 糸 | 糸 | 糸 | 紀 | 紹 | 経 |
| 経 | 経 | | | | | | | |

BUILDING THIS KANJI
Thread 糸 (196) + **Again (ironing board)** 又 (159) + **Earth** 土 (87) = 経

Meaning
Via, in the sense of things passing or elapsing. A secondary meaning related to Buddhist sutras makes use of the less common **on-yomi**.

Remembering this kanji
"I will help you find me in the labyrinth," she promised.
"But how?" he asked.
She turned to the **ironing board**. "**VIA** this."
"**VIA** the **ironing board**? I don't get it."
"No. **VIA** this **thread**. I'll let it trail behind me over the **earth** so that you can follow me."
"I'm not sure," he said. "Don't you feel it might be easier to find you VIA a trail of **ironing boards** instead?"

Common Pronunciations
Common **ON** reading: **KEI** (ケイ)
Common **kun** reading: **he** (ヘ)

Less Common Pronunciations
Less common **ON** reading: **KYŌ** (キョウ)
Less common **kun** readings: none

COMMON WORDS AND COMPOUNDS		
経る	*elapse; pass through*	**he**·ru ヘ・る
経由	via + cause = *via; by way of*	**KEI·YU** ケイ・ユ
経験	via + test = *experience*	**KEI·KEN** ケイ・ケン

COMPONENT #303

GUY WEARING A BARREL

KANJI 303

頭 HEAD

| 一 | 丆 | 丆 | 冖 | 冝 | 豆 | 豆 | 豆 | 豆' |
| 豇 | 頭 | 頭 | 頭 | 頭 | 頭 | 頭 | | |

BUILDING THIS KANJI
Bean 豆 (280) + **Guy Wearing a Barrel** 頁 = 頭

Meaning
Head.

Remembering this kanji
So I gave a **bean** to this **guy wearing** a **barrel**. "What's this for?" he asked. "For your HEAD," I answered. "Why should I put a **bean** on my HEAD?" he said. "Well," I replied, "you have to begin your wardrobe somewhere, don't you? Why not with a beanie for your HEAD?"

Common Pronunciations

Common **ON** reading: **TŌ** (トウ)
Common **kun** reading: **atama** (あたま)

Less Common Pronunciations

Less common **ON** reading: **ZU** (ズ); **TO** (ト)
Less common **kun** readings: **kashira** (かしら)

You are most likely to encounter the first of these **on-yomi** in only a pair of words: 頭上 (**ZU·JŌ** / ズ・ジョウ) "overhead" from the kanji "head" and "upper", and the final sample compound of Entry 461.

COMMON WORDS AND COMPOUNDS		
頭	*head*	atama あたま
先頭	precede + head = *at the lead; at the head*	SEN·TŌ セン・トウ
店頭	shop + head = *storefront; shopwindow*	TEN·TŌ テン・トウ

KANJI 304

魚 **FISH**

ノ	⺈	⼔	匄	甶	魚	魚	魚	魚
魚	魚							

BUILDING THIS KANJI
Little Red Riding Hood ⺈ + Rice Field 田
(73) + Gas Stove 灬 = 魚

Meaning
Fish.

Remembering this kanji

"What's **Little Red Riding Hood** doing in that **rice field**?" someone cried. "And there's smoke! Maybe she's the one!"

The mob rushed through the **rice field**, but slowed on catching sight of the **gas stove**. "It's not her, guys," someone said. "She's just grilling a **FISH**."

Common Pronunciations

Common **ON** reading: **GYO** (ギョ)
Common **kun** reading: **sakana** (さかな)

Create your **on-yomi** keyword and enter it in the table at the back of the book. Then, after creating your **kun-yomi** keyword, write your sentence to remember the **on-yomi** and **kun-yomi** readings in the box below.

Less Common Pronunciations

Less common **ON** reading: none
Less common **kun** readings: **uo** (うお)

COMMON WORDS AND COMPOUNDS		
魚	*fish*	sakana さかな
金魚	gold + fish = *goldfish*	KIN·GYO キン・ギョ
人魚	person + fish = *mermaid; merman*	NIN·GYO ニン・ギョ

KANJI 305

実 **ACTUAL**

`	｀	宀	宀	宑	宣	宣	実

BUILDING THIS KANJI

Pincers 宀 + Three (full hamburger) 三(5) + Person 人(2) = 実

Meaning

This kanji has to do with the actual nature or reality of things.

Remembering this kanji

So this **person** made an ACTUAL **full hamburger** that was bigger than he was! Unfortunately, he had to get lifted up by an ACTUAL set of **pincers** after he ate it. They had to be ACTUAL **pincers**, of course, because he was an ACTUAL **person**.

Common Pronunciations

Common **ON** reading: **JITSU** (ジツ)

Common **kun** reading: none

Less Common Pronunciations

Less common **ON** reading: none

Less common **kun** readings: **mi** (み);
mino (みの)

These two readings relate to a secondary meaning of this kanji that has to do with seeds, berries and nuts, etc.

COMMON WORDS AND COMPOUNDS		
事実	matter + actual = *fact*	**JI·JITSU** ジ・ジツ
実用	actual + utilize = *practical use; utility*	**JITSU·YŌ** ジツ・ヨウ
実行	actual + go = *put into practice; execute*	**JIK·KŌ** ジッ・コウ

CHAPTER 14 REVIEW EXERCISES

A. Please match the following kanji to their meanings.

1.	指	a.	Roof
2.	完	b.	Descend
3.	遠	c.	Perfect
4.	魚	d.	Marriage
5.	婚	e.	Finger
6.	経	f.	Arrow
7.	降	g.	Good
8.	屋	h.	Far
9.	良	i.	Via
10.	矢	j.	Fish

B. Please match the following meanings to their kanji, and these to their **on** or **kun-yomi**.

1.	Distribute	a. 配	1.	**wasu** (わす)
2.	Metropolis	b. 的	2.	**KATSU** (カツ)
3.	Harmony	c. 実	3.	**atama** (あたま)
4.	Actual	d. 反	4.	**WA** (ワ)
5.	Target	e. 活	5.	**kuba** (くば)
6.	Festival	f. 頭	6.	**JITSU** (ジツ)
7.	Active	g. 和	7.	**TO** (ト)
8.	Forget	h. 祭	8.	**HAN** (ハン)
9.	Against	i. 忘	9.	**TEKI** (テキ)
10.	Head	j. 都	10.	**matsu** (まつ)
	(**kun-yomi**)			

C. Please choose the best answer(s) to the following questions.

1. Which is the correct reading of 降る?
   a. **ka·ru** (か・る)
   b. **ku·ru** (く・る)
   c. **a·ru** (あ・る)
   d. **fu·ru** (ふ・る)

2. Which of the following readings apply to the kanji 遠?
   a. **kō** (こお)
   b. **KEN** (ケン)
   c. **EN** (エン)
   d. **IN** (イン)
   e. **tō** (とお)

3. Which of the following kanji has the most number of strokes?
   a. 祭　b. 配　c. 屋　d. 降　e. 界

4. I'm afraid of ___ , so please don't make me go to the public aquarium.
   a. 婚　b. 各　c. 界　d. 魚　e. 和

5. Which of the following readings apply to the kanji 形?
   a. **KA** (カ)　　　　b. **KI** (キ)
   c. **KEI** (ケイ)　　d. **kata** (かた)
   e. **katachi** (かたち)

D. Please match the following compounds to their meanings and pronunciations.

1. 世界　a. Nomination　1. **KIN·GYO** (キン・ギョ)
2. 予定　b. Kyoto　2. **RYŌ·SHIN** (リョウ・シン)
3. 金魚　c. Conscience　3. **KAK·KI** (カッ・キ)
4. 目的　d. Prearrangement　4. **KAN·ZEN** (カン・ゼン)
5. 指名　e. Liveliness / Vigor　5. **SE·KAI** (セ・カイ)
6. 京都　f. The world　6. **MOKU·TEKI** (モク・テキ)
7. 活気　g. Purpose / Aim　7. **KYŌ·TO** (キョウ・ト)
8. 完全　h. Divorce　8. **SHI·MEI** (シ・メイ)
9. 離婚　i. Perfection　9. **RI·KON** (リ・コン)
10. 良心　j. Goldfish　10. **YO·TEI** (ヨ・テイ)

E. Please read the passage below and answer the questions that follow.

"来月京都のお祭りへ行きますか。"
"はい。学校の遠足で。あなたも行きますか。"
"いいえ。ここで大事な用事があります。"

1. What is happening next month?
2. Where is it taking place?
3. Why is one of these people able to go?
4. Will both of these people be going?
5. What does one of these people have to take care of?

Kanji #306—330

KANJI 306

ACHIEVE

一	ナ	土	去	去	幸	幸	査	幸
達	達	達						

BUILDING THIS KANJI
Earth 土(87) + Sheep 羊(262) + Seal 辶 = 達

Meaning
Achieve, attain. When used as a suffix this kanji also serves to indicate the plural, although the second compound below can refer to only one person as well.

Remembering this kanji
So the extent of what you'd like to ACHIEVE is to put **earth** on a **sheep**? Big deal. Why not do something no one has ever ACHIEVED, and plop that **earth**-covered **sheep** on a **seal**! You do that and you'll have really ACHIEVED something, since you'd not only have to haul the **sheep** over a kelp-covered beach, but chase down the **seal** as well.

Common Pronunciations
Common **ON** reading: **TATSU** (タツ)
Common **kun** reading: **tachi** (たち)

The second example shows how the **kun-yomi** can become voiced; this reading never appears in first position.

Create your **on-yomi** keyword and enter it in the table at the back of the book. Then, after creating your **kun-yomi** keyword, write your sentence to remember the **on-yomi** and **kun-yomi** readings in the box below.

Less Common Pronunciations
Less common **ON** reading: none
Less common **kun** reading: none

COMMON WORDS AND COMPOUNDS		
上達	upper + achieve = *improvement; progress*	**JŌ·TATSU** ジョウ・タツ
友達	friend + achieve = *friend(s)*	tomo·**dachi** とも・だち
発達	discharge + achieve = *correspondence*	**HAT·TATSU** ハッ・タツ

KANJI 307

 CONTINUE

∠	∠	幺	糸	糸	糸	糸	糸	糸
続	続	続	続					

BUILDING THIS KANJI
Thread 糸(196) + Sell 売(92) = 続

Meaning
Continue.

Remembering this kanji
If it's **thread** you'd like to **sell**, you must understand this fact: you can only CONTINUE to **sell** it for as long as it CONTINUES to come off the spool.

Common Pronunciations
Common **ON** reading: **ZOKU**(ゾク)
Common **kun** reading: **tsuzu**(つづ)

Create your **on-yomi** keyword and enter it in the table at the back of the book. Then, after creating your **kun-yomi** keyword, write your sentence to remember the **on-yomi** and **kun-yomi** readings in the box below.

Less Common Pronunciations
Less common **ON** reading: none
Less common **kun** reading: none

COMMON WORDS AND COMPOUNDS		
続く (intr)	*continue*	**tsuzu**·ku つづ·く
続ける (tr)	*continue*	**tsuzu**·keru つづ·ける
手続き	hand + continue = *formalities; procedure*	te **tsuzu**·ki て つづ·き
接続	join + continue = *connection; joining*	SETSU·**ZOKU** セツ·ゾク

COMPONENT #308

PINBALL

KANJI 308

弱 **WEAK**

ㄱ	ㄱ	弓	弓	弓	弓	弓	弱	弱
弱								

BUILDING THIS KANJI
Bow 弓(143) + Pinball ⼁ + Bow 弓(143) + Pinball ⼁ = 弱

Meaning
Weak.

Remembering this kanji
Note that the story below emphasizes that there are two of each of these components.

Geez, I'm WEAK. I tried to do curls with a couple of **bows** but was too WEAK to lift them. So I went to my **pinball** machine to have some fun, but I couldn't even get the pair of flippers to budge. Yeah, I'm that WEAK.

Common Pronunciations
Common **ON** reading: **JAKU** (ジャク)
Common **kun** reading: **yowa** (よわ)

Create your **on-yomi** keyword and enter it in the table at the back of the book. Then, after creating your **kun-yomi** keyword, write your sentence to remember the **on-yomi** and **kun-yomi** readings in the box below.

Less Common Pronunciations
Less common **ON** reading: none
Less common **kun** reading: none

COMMON WORDS AND COMPOUNDS		
弱い	*weak*	**yowa**·i よわ·い
弱点	weak + point = *weak point;* *shortcoming*	**JAKU**·TEN ジャク・テン
弱肉強食	weak + meat + strong + eat = *survival* *of the fittest*	**JAKU**·NIKU·KYŌ· SHOKU ジャク・ニク・ キョウ・ショク

KANJI 309

短 **SHORT**

BUILDING THIS KANJI
Arrow 矢(285) + Bean 豆(280) = 短

Meaning
Short.

Remembering this kanji
In SHORT, a SHORT distance makes it easier to shoot an **arrow** into a **bean**.

Common Pronunciations
Common **ON** reading: **TAN** (タン)
Common **kun** reading: **mijika** (みじか)

Less Common Pronunciations
Less common **ON** reading: none
Less common **kun** reading: none

COMMON WORDS AND COMPOUNDS		
短い	*short*	**mijika**·i みじか·い
最短	most + short = *shortest*	**SAI**·**TAN** サイ・タン
短期	short + period = *short-term*	**TAN**·KI タン・キ

KANJI 310

辞 **RESIGN**

ノ	⼆	⼗	千	舌	舌	舌ˋ	舌ˊ	舌ˊ
舌ˊ	辞	辞	辞					

BUILDING THIS KANJI
Tongue 舌 (110) + Spicy 辛 (267) = 辞

Meaning
Resign, quit. A second meaning relates to phrases and words; this sense is reflected in the final two compounds.

Remembering this kanji
"You had to RESIGN?! What happened?"
"It was the curry I had for lunch. It made my **tongue** too **spicy** to be a judge in the pie-tasting competition; I had no choice but to RESIGN."

Common Pronunciations
Common **ON** reading: **JI** (ジ)
Common **kun** reading: **ya** (や)

Less Common Pronunciations
Less common **ON** reading: none
Less common **kun** reading: none

COMMON WORDS AND COMPOUND		
辞める	*resign; quit*	**ya**·meru や·める
辞書	resign (phrase) + write = *dictionary*	**JI**·SHO ジ·ショ
お世辞	society + resign (phrase) = *flattery; compliment*	o SE·**JI** お セ·ジ

COMPONENT #311

BUCKTEETH

KANJI 311

免 **EXEMPTION**

ノ	⼉	⼏	夕	刍	刍	免	免	

BUILDING THIS KANJI
Little Red Riding Hood ⼎ + Buckteeth ⼝ + Ballet 儿 = 免

Meaning
Exemption, permission.

Remembering this kanji
"But **Little Red Riding Hood** doesn't have **buckteeth**, so how can she be in our **buckteeth** ballet?"
"Because I gave her an EXEMPTION, all right?"
"How come? Without **buckteeth** she can't even…"
"Don't you realize we're doing "**Little Red Riding Hood**: The **Ballet**" this season? It makes sense to give her an EXEMPTION!"

Common Pronunciations
Common **ON** reading: **MEN** (メン)
Common **kun** reading: none

Create your **on-yomi** keyword and enter it in the table at the back of the book. After that, write

your sentence to remember the **on-yomi** reading in the box below.

Less common **ON** reading: none
Less common **kun** reading: **manuka** (まぬか)

COMMON WORDS AND COMPOUNDS		
免じる	*to exempt; dismiss*	**MEN**·jiru メン・じる

KANJI 312

 SONG

BUILDING THIS KANJI
Possible 可 (252) + Possible 可 (252) + **Lack** 欠 (246) = 歌

Meaning
Song, singing. In a few compounds this character can also mean poetry.

Remembering this kanji
"What's up with that SONG? It seems to **lack** something."
"Is it the **lack** of rhythm?"
"It's **possible**."
"How about the **lack** of melody or nice singing?"
"That's *doubly* **possible**."
"Hmm. Maybe it just **lacks** everything needed to be a decent SONG."

Common Pronunciations
Common **ON** reading: **KA** (カ)
Common **kun** reading: **uta** (う た)

The **on-yomi** is the more common reading.

Less Common Pronunciations
Less common **ON** reading: none
Less common **kun** reading: none

COMMON WORDS AND COMPOUNDS		
歌	*song; poem*	**uta** う た
歌手	song + hand = *singer*	**KA**·SHU カ・シュ
国歌	country + song = *national anthem*	KOK·**KA** コッ・カ

COMPONENT #313

OPERA SINGER

KANJI 313

 SEND

`	ˊ	⼆	⼆	⺰	关	`关	₃关	送

BUILDING THIS KANJI
Opera Singer 关 + Seal ⻌ = 送

Meaning
Send.

Remembering this kanji
"SEND it away!" said the **opera singer**. "I've told you countless times: I realize he's a fan, but I don't want that **seal** to SEND me buckets of bait."

Common Pronunciations
Common **ON** reading: **SŌ** (ソ ウ)
Common **kun** reading: **oku** (お く)

Although there are a few compound verbs (such as the second example below) making use of the **kun-yomi**, the **on-yomi** is the more common reading.

Less Common Pronunciations
Less common **ON** reading: none
Less common **kun** reading: none

COMMON WORDS AND COMPOUNDS		
送る	*to send*	**oku**·ru お く・る
見送る	see + send = *see (someone) off*	mi·**oku**·ru み お く・る
送別	send + different = *farewell; send off*	**SŌ**·BETSU ソ ウ・ベ ツ

KANJI 314

払 **PAY**

⼀	⼁	⼿	払	払		

BUILDING THIS KANJI
Finger ⺘ + Broken Crutch ム = 払

Meaning
Pay. A secondary meaning relates to the idea of 'driving / sweeping away' something.

Remembering this kanji
Recall from Entry 298 that the word 'finger' in this and all future stories indicates the component ⺘, <u>not</u> the kanji 指.

"You're gonna PAY for that!" he said, pointing (with his **finger**) at the **broken crutch**.
"I'm not going to PAY for anything," I shot back. "You asked me to break it!"

Common Pronunciations
Common **ON** reading: none
Common **kun** reading: **hara** (は ら)

This **kun-yomi** will often become voiced in second and third position when forming nouns, as in the final compound. It never becomes voiced, however, when forming verbs.

Less Common Pronunciations
Less common **ON** reading: **FUTSU** (フ ツ)
Less common **kun** reading: none

COMMON WORDS AND COMPOUNDS		
払う	*pay; sweep away*	**hara**·u は ら・う
先払い	precede + pay = *payment in advance*	saki·**bara**·i さ き ば ら・い

KANJI 315

夫 **HUSBAND**

BUILDING THIS KANJI
One (hamburger patty) 一(3) + Large (sumo wrestler) 大(17) = 夫

Meaning
Husband. This is a good time to ensure that you can clearly distinguish the following five kanji based on our sumo wrestler: 大 "large" from Entry 17, 天 "heaven" from Entry 123, 夫 "husband" from here, as well as the two that included a hammer component, 失 "lose" from Entry 142, and 矢 "arrow" from Entry 285.

Remembering this kanji
If you're looking for a HUSBAND, a quick way to get one is to offer a **hamburger patty** to a **sumo wrestler**. Do that and you'll have a HUSBAND right away.

Common Pronunciations
Common **ON** reading: **FU** (フ)
Common **kun** reading: **otto** (おっと)

Less Common Pronunciations
Less common **ON** reading: **FŪ** (フウ)
Less common **kun** reading: none

You are only likely to encounter this reading in the final compound of Entry 504, as well as in the word 工夫 (KU·FŪ / ク・フウ) 'device, invention', from the kanji for 'craft' and 'husband' ('工' being read here with its less common **on-yomi**).

COMMON WORDS AND COMPOUNDS		
夫	*husband*	**otto** おっと
夫人	husband + person = *wife; Mrs.*	**FU·JIN** フ・ジン

COMPONENT #316

FRISKING 亦

KANJI 316

変 **ALTER**

BUILDING THIS KANJI
Frisking 亦 + Running Chicken 夂 = 変

Meaning
Alter, change. In some compounds the idea of an accident or mishap is present.

Remembering this kanji
It's not easy **frisking** a **running chicken**, given how quickly they're able to ALTER their course. And even if you do find contraband on them, you'll need some skill to get a confession; they're famous for being able to ALTER their story on a moment's notice.

Common Pronunciations
Common **ON** reading: **HEN** (ヘ ン)
Common **kun** reading: **ka** (か)

HEN is the overwhelming choice in first position. The **kun-yomi** becomes voiced in second position according to the same rules we learned for 付 back in Entry 226.

Create your **on-yomi** keyword and enter it in the table at the back of the book. Then, after creating your **kun-yomi** keyword, write your sentence to remember the **on-yomi** and **kun-yomi** readings in the box below.

Less Common Pronunciations
Less common **ON** reading: none
Less common **kun** reading: none

COMMON WORDS AND COMPOUNDS		
変わる (intr)	*change; be different*	**ka**·waru か・わる
変える (tr)	*alter; change*	**ka**·eru か・える
変化	alter + change = *change; transformation*	**HEN·KA** ヘン・カ
大変	large + alter = *serious; very*	**TAI·HEN** タイ・ヘン

KANJI 317

EAT

BUILDING THIS KANJI
Umbrella 八 + Good 良 (288) = 食

Meaning
Eat.

Remembering this kanji
"Umbrella good!"
"Yeah, but don't EAT it."

Common Pronunciations
Common **ON** reading: **SHOKU** (ショク)
Common **kun** reading: **ta** (た)

Create your **on-yomi** keyword and enter it in the table at the back of the book. Then, after creating your **kun-yomi** keyword, write your sentence to remember the **on-yomi** and **kun-yomi** readings in the box below.

Less Common Pronunciations
Less common **ON** reading: **JIKI** (ジキ)
Less common **kun** reading: **ku** (く)

This **kun-yomi** is often found in words conveying a negative aspect of eating.

COMMON WORDS AND COMPOUNDS		
食べる	*eat*	**ta**·beru た・べる
食べ物	eat + thing = *food*	**ta**·be mono た・べ もの
定食	fixed + eat = *set meal*	**TEI·SHOKU** テイ・ショク

KANJI 318

動 MOVE

丿	一	亡	盲	盲	盲	重	重	重
動	動							

BUILDING THIS KANJI
Heavy 重 (249) + Strength 力 (63) = 動

Meaning
Move.

Remembering this kanji
Advice from a professional mover, on how to MOVE stuff:

"If it's **heavy**, you'll need **strength** to MOVE it."

Common Pronunciations
Common **ON** reading: **DŌ** (ド ウ)
Common **kun** reading: **ugo** (う ご)

Less Common Pronunciations
Less common **ON** reading: none
Less common **kun** reading: none

COMMON WORDS AND COMPOUNDS		
動く (intr)	*move*	**ugo·ku** う ご・く
動かす (tr)	*move*	**ugo·kasu** う ご・か す
動物	move + thing = *animal*	**DŌ·BUTSU** ド ウ・ブ ツ
自動	self + move = *automatic*	**JI·DŌ** ジ・ド ウ

KANJI 319

泉 SPRING(S)

丿	丶	宀	白	白	宁	身	泉	泉

BUILDING THIS KANJI
White 白 (7) + Water 水 (61) = 泉

Meaning
Spring(s) (as in a source of water).

Remembering this kanji
"Excuse me, how do I find the SPRINGS?"
"Well, can you spot that **white** froth on the **water** over there? Those are your SPRINGS."

Common Pronunciations
Common **ON** reading: **SEN** (セ ン)
Common **kun** reading: **izumi** (い ず み)

Less Common Pronunciations
Less common **ON** reading: none
Less common **kun** reading: none

COMMON WORDS AND COMPOUNDS		
泉	*spring(s)*	**izumi** い ず み
温泉	warm + springs = *hot spring; spa*	**ON·SEN** オ ン・セ ン

KANJI 320

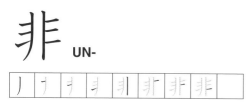

UN-

ノ	ｺ	ｮ	ｮ	刔	非	非	非

Meaning

This curious-looking character is another important negating prefix, much like '不' ('Not', from Entry 186). In this and future stories we will assign it the external meaning of "amoebas". Take care with the stroke order—though the first line of the 'merging' component is the initial stroke of this kanji, the second comes after the three amoebas on the left. Also keep in mind that the six amoebas are always written left to right.

Remembering this kanji

What could be more "UN-" than amoebas? They're UNcoordinated, and their blobby physique is UNattractive. They're also UNdisciplined; if told to **merge** in an orderly fashion (as these were), at least one will be UNcooperative and fail to do so. It's obvious from the illustration which one was UNwilling to listen in this case.

Common Pronunciations

Common **ON** reading: **HI** (ヒ)
Common **kun** reading: none

Less Common Pronunciations

Less common **ON** reading: none
Less common **kun** reading: none

COMMON WORDS AND COMPOUNDS		
非売品	un- + sell + goods = *"item not for sale"*	**HI·BAI·HIN** ヒ·バイ·ヒン
是非	approve + un- = *without fail; by any means*	**ZE·HI** ゼ·ヒ
非公式	un- + public + type = *unofficial; informal*	**HI·KŌ·SHIKI** ヒ·コウ·シキ

COMPONENT #321

SPILLING COFFEE

This is the second of our special family of five components (the first being 七). As you can see, it differs from 'ghost' by virtue of an additional stroke at the end. An important thing to keep in mind with this component (and the next two members of the family) is that if anything ever appears underneath the horizontal line (such as 工 in Entry 353), it is always written immediately after it, thus breaking the normal stroke order of the component.

KANJI 321

SUBSTITUTE

ノ	亻	亻	代	代			

BUILDING THIS KANJI
Giraffe 亻 + Spilling Coffee 弋 = 代

Meaning

Substitute. This interesting kanji also carries some important secondary meanings—it can indicate a 'fee' for some type of good or service (think of the fee as a 'substitute' for what is received), as well as convey the idea of 'generations' in compounds related to eras or reigns (as in the third example below).

Remembering this kanji

The **giraffe** slammed down her cup, **spilling coffee** on the counter. "You put a SUBSTITUTE in this coffee, didn't you?" she said. "I told you not to do that; you can't imagine what it's like having a SUBSTITUTE sweetener going down this throat of mine."

Common Pronunciations

Common **ON** reading: **DAI** (ダイ)
Common **kun** reading: **ka** (か)

Though sharing the same pronunciation, note the subtle difference in meaning between the intransitive/transitive verb pair shown here and the pair in Entry 316.

Less Common Pronunciations

Less common **ON** readings: **TAI** (タイ)
Less common **kun** reading: **yo** (よ)

COMMON WORDS AND COMPOUNDS		
代わる (intr)	take the place of	**ka·**waru か・わる
代える (tr)	substitute; exchange	**ka·**eru か・える
時代	time + substitute = era; age	**JI·DAI** ジ・ダイ
代表	substitute + express = representative	**DAI·**HYŌ ダイ・ヒョウ

KANJI 322

記 NOTE

`	一	二	言	言	言	言	言	記
記								

BUILDING THIS KANJI
Say 言 (80) + **Oneself (whip)** 己 (214) = 記

Meaning

Note, write down.

Remembering this kanji

"Hey, there's a NOTE on this **whip**."
"Really? What's it **say**?"
"It **says**: 'This is a **whip**'."
"Hmm. That's a very useful NOTE."

Common Pronunciations

Common **ON** reading: **KI** (キ)
Common **kun** reading: none

Less Common Pronunciations

Less common **ON** reading: none
Less common **kun** reading: **shiru** (しる)

COMMON WORDS AND COMPOUNDS		
記者	note + individual = (newspaper) reporter / writer	**KI·**SHA キ・シャ
日記	sun (day) + note = diary; journal	NIK·**KI** ニッ・キ
暗記	dark + note = memorization	AN·**KI** アン・キ

映 REFLECT

| 丨 | 冂 | 日 | 日 | 日¹ | 日⁷ | 日⁼ | 映 | 映 |

BUILDING THIS KANJI
Sun 日(6) + Center 央(140) = 映

Meaning
Reflect (an image, etc.), project.

Remembering this kanji
The **sun** is at the **center** of our orbit, so a lot of stuff will REFLECT it.

Common Pronunciations
Common **ON** reading: **EI** (エイ)
Common **kun** reading: **utsu** (うつ)

Less Common Pronunciations
Less common **ON** reading: none
Less common **kun** reading: **ha** (は)

COMMON WORDS AND COMPOUNDS		
映る (intr)	*reflect*	**utsu·ru** うつ·る
映す (tr)	*reflect (something)*	**utsu·su** うつ·す
映画	reflect + painting = *movie; film*	**EI·GA** エイ·ガ

MAGNET

Here we have another component with a 'broken' stroke order similar to that of the 'prison'. In this case, whatever is inside the magnet is always written following the first stroke. It is subsequently enclosed by the final one.

医 DOCTOR

| 一 | 丆 | 丆 | 三 | 医 | 矢 | 医 | | |

BUILDING THIS KANJI
Magnet 匚 + Arrow 矢(285) = 医

Meaning
Doctor, healing, cure.

Remembering this kanji
"I should be able to get that **arrow** out with this **magnet**," said the DOCTOR.
"Are you sure that's how it's supposed to be done?" I asked.
"Oh, I didn't realize you were a DOCTOR," he said.
"Sorry, DOCTOR," I replied.

Common Pronunciations
Common **ON** reading: **I** (イ)
Common **kun** reading: none

Less Common Pronunciations
Less common **ON** reading: none
Less common **kun** reading: none

COMMON WORDS AND COMPOUNDS		
医者	doctor + individual = *doctor; physician*	**I·SHA** イ·シャ
医学	doctor + study = *medical science*	**I·GAKU** イ·ガク
医院	doctor + institution = *doctor's office; clinic*	**I·IN** イ·イン

洋 **OCEAN**

BUILDING THIS KANJI
Splash 氵 + Sheep 羊(262) = 洋

Meaning
Ocean. This kanji is also used to denote things from the 'West' (as opposed to the Orient); the first compound provides an example of this usage.

Remembering this kanji
"Ah, the **splash** of **sheep** in the OCEAN," he sighed.
"Um…those **sheep** look like they're pretty desperate to get back to shore," she said. "Why are you tossing them into the OCEAN anyway?"

Common Pronunciations
Common **ON** reading: **YŌ** (ヨ ウ)
Common **kun** reading: none

Less Common Pronunciations
Less common **ON** reading: none
Less common **kun** reading: none

COMMON WORDS AND COMPOUNDS		
洋服	ocean (Western) + clothes = *(Western-type) clothes*	**YŌ**·FUKU ヨ ウ · フ ク
大西洋	large + west + ocean = *the Atlantic Ocean*	TAI·SEI·**YŌ** タ イ · セ イ · ヨ ウ
海洋学	sea + ocean + study = *oceanography*	KAI·**YŌ**·GAKU カ イ · ヨ ウ · ガ ク

1950'S ROCK STAR 夭

橋 **BRIDGE**

BUILDING THIS KANJI
Tree 木(13) + **1950's Rock Star** 夭 + **Mouth (vampire)** 口(8) + **Gorilla** 冂 + **Mouth (vampire)** 口(8) = 橋

Meaning
Bridge.

Remembering this kanji
Several aspects of BRIDGE are represented in this kanji. Most important is the **tree**, which has long given us wood for BRIDGES. The **1950's rock star** BRIDGES the gap nicely between big band jazz and psychedelic rock, and though we can't fathom what the misunderstanding might be between this **pair of vampires**, the kanji obviously has the **gorilla** acting as a BRIDGE here so that they can BRIDGE their differences.

Common Pronunciations

Common **ON** reading: **KYŌ** (キョウ)

Common **kun** reading: **hashi** (はし)

The **kun-yomi** can become voiced outside of first position (as in the final compound).

Less Common Pronunciations

Less common **ON** reading: none

Less common **kun** reading: none

COMMON WORDS AND COMPOUNDS		
橋	*bridge*	**hashi** はし
歩道橋	walk + road + bridge = *pedestrian bridge*	HO·DŌ·**KYŌ** ホ·ド ウ·キョウ
石橋	stone + bridge = *stone bridge*	ishi·**bashi** いし·ばし

KANJI 327

現 **PRESENT**

BUILDING THIS KANJI

King 王(23) + See 見(42) = 現

Meaning

Present (in terms of time). A related meaning has to do with the ideas of revealing and expressing things. The overall sense is one of things being present or brought into being.

Remembering this kanji

Even the greatest **king** can **see** only what the rest of us **see**: nothing but the PRESENT.

Common Pronunciations

Common **ON** reading: **GEN** (ゲン)

Common **kun** reading: **arawa** (あらわ)

The **kun-yomi** is the usual verb stem for the first and second examples below. A quirk with this kanji, however, is that you may occasionally see these verbs written as 現われる and 現わす. Think of these two verbs as things either presenting themselves (in the first instance) or being presented in some way.

Less Common Pronunciations

Less common **ON** reading: none

Less common **kun** reading: none

COMMON WORDS AND COMPOUNDS		
現れる (intr)	*appear; come out*	**arawa**·reru あらわ·れる
現す (tr)	*reveal*	**arawa**·su あらわ·す
現実	present + actual = *actuality; reality*	**GEN**·JITSU ゲン·ジツ

COMPONENT #328

HUCKLEBERRY FINN 也

KANJI 328

地 **GROUND**

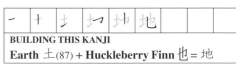

BUILDING THIS KANJI

Earth 土(87) + Huckleberry Finn 也 = 地

Meaning

Ground. Whereas 土 is primarily concerned with the idea of actual earth and soil, this kanji has more to do with the **surface** of things in the sense of 'land', 'district' and 'region', for example. This concept of a 'base' is even extended to include such things as the fabric or texture of objects like cloth, as well as the background of a person's character or voice.

Remembering this kanji

Tom Sawyer: "Golly! Why ya got **earth** on your pants, **Huckleberry Finn**?"
Huckleberry Finn: "Well, look at me in this kanji, Tom: I'm sittin' on the GROUND."

Common Pronunciations

Common ON reading: **CHI** (チ); JI (ジ)
Common **kun** reading: none

CHI is by far the more common of these readings, especially in second and third position, where **JI** appears in only a few compounds primarily related to cloth. In the first position the situation is a bit less precise, although even here **CHI** will be encountered more often. Note that the second compound uses the less common on-yomi of 土 (**TO** / ト); this is the only word in which the kanji has this reading. Recall from Entry 25 that 心 in the first example below has an irregular reading of **koko** / こ こ.

Create your **on-yomi** keyword for "チ" and enter it in the table at the back of the book. After that, write your sentence to remember the **on-yomi** readings in the box below.

Less Common Pronunciations

Less common **ON** reading: none
Less common **kun** reading: none

COMMON WORDS AND COMPOUNDS		
心地	heart + ground = *feeling*	koko·CHI こ こ·チ
土地	earth + ground = *land*	TO·CHI ト·チ
地所	ground + location = *piece of land*	**JI·SHO** ジ·シ ョ

KANJI 329

伝 TRANSMIT

BUILDING THIS KANJI
Giraffe イ + Spy 云 = 伝

Meaning

Transmit, communicate.

Remembering this kanji

"We were shocked," said the **giraffe**." He said he just wanted to graze with us."
"So none of you realized he was a **spy**?"
"Not until we caught him in the act; it seems the lions were having him TRANSMIT our whereabouts."

Common Pronunciations

Common ON reading: **DEN** (デン)
Common **kun** reading: **tsuta** (つた)

The kun-yomi can become voiced in second position according to the same rules for 付 (Entry 226).

Less Common Pronunciations
Less common **ON** reading: **TEN** (テ ン)
Less common **kun** reading: none

COMMON WORDS AND COMPOUNDS		
伝える	*transmit; convey*	**tsuta·eru** つた·える
伝来	transmit + come = *transmission; handing down*	**DEN·RAI** デン·ライ
伝記	transmit + note = *biography*	**DEN·KI** デン·キ

KANJI 330

BIND

'	幺	幺	糸	糸	糸	糸	紅	紅	結
結	結	結							

BUILDING THIS KANJI
Thread 糸 (196) + **Lucky** 吉 (269) = 結

Meaning
Bind, as well as the senses of 'tying up' such things as a contract or marriage, for example.

Remembering this kanji
"Yeah, I knocked him out with the spool and was able to **BIND** him with the **thread**."
"That was sure **lucky**. It sounds like you were in a real **BIND**."

Common Pronunciations
Common **ON** reading: **KETSU** (ケ ツ)
Common **kun** reading: **musu** (む す)

Less Common Pronunciations
Less common **ON** reading: none
Less common **kun** reading: **yu** (ゆ)

COMMON WORDS AND COMPOUNDS		
結ぶ	*bind; connect*	**musu·bu** むす·ぶ
結婚	bind + marriage = *marriage*	**KEK·KON** ケッ·コン
結合	bind + match = *union; combination*	**KETSU·GŌ** ケツ·ゴウ

CHAPTER 15 REVIEW EXERCISES

A. Please match the following kanji to their meanings.

1. 代   a. Substitute
2. 変   b. Ocean
3. 続   c. Send
4. 映   d. Reflect
5. 達   e. Springs
6. 夫   f. Continue
7. 送   g. Achieve
8. 洋   h. Alter
9. 伝   i. Husband
10. 泉   j. Transmit

B. Please match the following meanings to their kanji, and these to their **on-** or **kun-yomi**.

1. Song   a. 非   1. **I** (イ)
2. Present   b. 短   2. **HI** (ヒ)
3. Weak   c. 医   3. **ugo** (う ご)
4. Short   d. 歌   4. **GEN** (ゲ ン)
5. Doctor   e. 動   5. **uta** (う た)

6. Bridge   f. 弱   6. **hashi** (はし)
7. Move   g. 結   7. **mijika** (みじか)
8. Un-   h. 橋   8. **MEN** (メン)
9. Bind   i. 現   9. **musu** (むす)
10. Exemption   j. 免   10. **yowa** (よわ)

C. Please choose the best answer(s) to the following questions.

1. Which of the following readings apply to the kanji 地?
   a. **JI** (ジ)   b. **JO** (ジョ)
   c. **SHI** (シ)   d. **SHO** (ショ)
   e. **CHI** (チ)

2. She needed to relax, so went on a holiday to a hot ____ resort.
   a. 医   b. 夫   c. 泉   d. 記   e. 橋

3. Which is the correct reading of 食べる?
   a. **ka·beru** (か・べる)
   b. **sa·beru** (さ・べる)
   c. **shira·beru** (しら・べる)
   d. **ta·beru** (た・べる)

4. Which of the following kanji has the most number of strokes?
   a. 辞   b. 短   c. 続   d. 歌   e. 達

5. Which is the correct reading of 払う?
   a. **ka·u** (か・う)
   b. **hara·u** (はら・う)
   c. **uba·u** (うば・う)
   d. **kura·u** (くら・う)

D. Please match the following compounds to their meanings and pronunciations.

1. 日記   a. Set meal   1. **DŌ·BUTSU** (ドウ・ブツ)

2. 心地   b. Doctor   2. **TEI·SHOKU** (テイ・ショク)

3. 動物   c. Change   3. **I·SHA** (イ・シャ)

4. 時代   d. Diary / Journal   4. **EI·GA** (エイ・ガ)

5. 変化   e. Animal   5. **KEK·KON** (ケッ・コン)

6. 映画   f. Dictionary   6. **JI·DAI** (ジ・ダイ)

7. 辞書   g. Era / Age   7. **HEN·KA** (ヘン・カ)

8. 結婚   h. Feeling   8. **NIK·KI** (ニッ・キ)

9. 定食   i. Movie   9. **JI·SHO** (ジ・ショ)

10. 医者   j. Marriage   10. **koko·CHI** (ここ・チ)

E. Please read the passage below and answer the questions that follow.

　　先週末、私の小学校からの友達が
　　結婚しました。"
"だれですか。"
"本田さんです。"
"本田さんは新聞記者ですよね。"
"いいえ。医者です。"

1. What did Honda-san recently do?
2. When did this happen?
3. What is the relationship of the first person to Honda-san?
4. What did the second person believe Honda-san did for a living?
5. What is Honda-san's actual profession?

Kanji #331—360

KANJI 331

 TASTE

㇇	口	口	口一	口一	吁	味	味

BUILDING THIS KANJI
Mouth (vampire) 口(8) + Not yet 未(276) = 味

Meaning
Taste, flavor.

Remembering this kanji
"I only want a TASTE," murmured the **vampire**, drawing closer.
"**Not yet**!" she said.
"**Not yet**!?" he cried. "C'mon, there's hardly any cookie dough left!"
"Well, I'm sorry," she said, "but if I give you a TASTE, I'll have to let everyone have a TASTE."

Common Pronunciations
Common **ON** reading: **MI** (ミ)
Common **kun** reading: **aji** (あ じ)

Less Common Pronunciations
Less common **ON** reading: none
Less common **kun** reading: none

IRREGULAR READING		
美味しい	beautiful + taste = *delicious*	**oi**·shii おい・しい

COMMON WORDS AND COMPOUNDS		
味	*taste*	**aji** あじ
気味	spirit + taste = *feeling; sensation*	**KI·MI** キ・ミ
意味	mind + taste = *meaning; significance*	**I·MI** イ・ミ

KANJI 332

尺 **MEASUREMENT**

㇇	コ	尸	尺				

BUILDING THIS KANJI
Flag 尸 + Comet 一 = 尺

Meaning

Measurement. This kanji derives from an old Japanese unit of measurement equivalent to about 30.3 cm; it is of most use as a component in other characters.

Remembering this kanji

So you're going to put a **flag** on a **comet**, are you? Well, you better get some MEASUREMENTS. And not just a MEASUREMENT for the **flag**, because that's easy. No, you'll have to get out there and come up with a MEASUREMENT for the **comet**, too.

Create your **on-yomi** keyword and enter it in the table at the back of the book. After that, write your sentence to remember the **on-yomi** reading in the box below.

Less Common Pronunciations

Less common ON reading: none
Less common kun reading: none

COMMON WORDS AND COMPOUNDS		
尺八	measurement + eight = *shakuhachi flute*	**SHAKU·HACHI** シャク・ハチ
尺度	measurement + degree = *linear measure; scale*	**SHAKU·DO** シャク・ド

Common Pronunciations

Common ON reading: **SHAKU** (シャク)
Common kun reading: none

FLAT

BUILDING THIS KANJI

One (top of a bun) 一 (3) + **Rabbit** ゛ノ + **Ten** (scarecrow) 十 (28) = 平

Meaning

Flat, with extended meanings such as ordinary and peaceful.

Remembering this kanji

She laid the blanket out FLAT, and after flattening down the **top of the bun**, bit into her ham and cheese. The noise of crunching lettuce startled a nearby **rabbit** — it held its ears FLAT in surprise. Did she sense this? She looked up, but as always there was only the **scarecrow** watching her, tied FLAT to its boards.

Common Pronunciations

Common ON reading: **HEI** (ヘイ)
Common kun reading: **hira** (ひら)

HEI is the more common of these readings.

Create your **on-yomi** keyword and enter it in the table at the back of the book. Then, after creating your kun-yomi keyword, write your sentence to remember the **on-yomi** and **kun-yomi** readings in the box below.

COMMON WORDS AND COMPOUNDS		
平たい	*flat; level*	**hira**·tai ひら・たい
平和	flat + harmony = *peace*	**HEI**·WA ヘイ・ワ
太平洋	fat + flat + ocean = *the Pacific Ocean*	TAI·**HEI**·YŌ タイ・ヘイ・ヨウ

Less Common Pronunciations
Less common **ON** reading: **BYŌ** (ビョウ)
Less common **kun** reading: **tai** (たい)

COMPONENT #334

CLIFF DIVER

KANJI 334

度 **DEGREE**

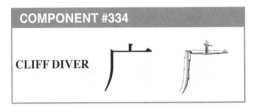

BUILDING THIS KANJI
Cliff Diver 广 + Straw 艹 + Again (ironing board) 又(159) = 度

Meaning
Degree, extent. As the second compound shows, this kanji can also mean 'times' in the sense of 'how many times'.

Remembering this kanji
"For me it's about the **DEGREE** of difficulty," said the **cliff diver**.
"For me it's the **DEGREE** of temperature," said the **ironing board**. "I can't have it too high."
The **straw** had been sitting quietly between them. "I just realized something," he said. "When I get put in a drink I'm always stuck at some angle between 0 and 90 **DEGREES**. No wonder I'm so bored."

Common Pronunciations
Common **ON** reading: **DO** (ド)
Common **kun** reading: **tabi** (たび)

Less Common Pronunciations
Less common **ON** reading: **TAKU** (タク);
TO (ト)
Less common **kun** reading: none

COMMON WORDS AND COMPOUNDS		
度々	degree + degree = *often; over and over*	**tabi**·**tabi** たび・たび
一度	one + degree (times) = *once; one time*	ICHI·**DO** イチ・ド
丁度	block + degree = *exactly*	CHŌ·**DO** チョウ・ド

KANJI 335

際 **EDGE**

| ⁷ | ³ | ₱ | ⁴ ₱ | ⁵ ₱ | ₱ | ₱ | ₱⁷ | 隊 |
| 陜 | 陛 | 際 | 際 | 際 | | | | |

BUILDING THIS KANJI
Novice Yodeler ß + Festival 祭 (297) = 際

Meaning
Edge, limit. A secondary meaning has to do with an 'occasion'.

Remembering this kanji
"Geez, honey, does it have to be another amateur yodeling **festival**? If I have to listen to any more **novice yodelers** it'll drive me over the EDGE."

Common Pronunciations
Common **ON** reading: **SAI** (サイ)
Common **kun** reading: **kiwa** (きわ)

The **kun-yomi** is always voiced outside of first position with the exception of '一際' (hito·**kiwa** / ひと・きわ), 'remarkably, conspicuously'; recall from Entry 224 that no kanji becomes voiced following 一 when it is read with its **kun-yomi** of **hito** (ひと).

Less Common Pronunciations
Less common **ON** reading: none
Less common **kun** reading: none

COMMON WORDS AND COMPOUNDS		
水際	water + edge = *water's edge; waterside*	mizu·**giwa** みず・ぎわ
国際	country + edge = *international*	**KOKU·SAI** コク・サイ
実際	actual + edge = *in practice; in actuality*	JIS·**SAI** ジッ・サイ

KANJI 336

貸 **LEND**

| ノ | イ | 亻 | 代 | 代 | 代 | 伫 | 停 | 貸 |
| 貸 | 貸 | 貸 | | | | | | |

BUILDING THIS KANJI
Substitute 代 (321) + Shellfish 貝 (21) = 貸

Meaning
Lend.

Remembering this kanji
"But there is no **substitute** for **shellfish**. Just LEND me yours."
"All right, then, I'll LEND them to you for tonight. But if you don't have them home at a decent hour I'll never LEND you anything else."

Common Pronunciations
Common **ON** reading: none
Common **kun** reading: **ka** (か)

As the last two examples show, this kanji can absorb its hiragana accompaniment when forming compounds. This reading is also frequently voiced when not in first position.

Less Common Pronunciations
Less common **ON** reading: **TAI** (タ イ)
Less common **kun** reading: none

COMMON WORDS AND COMPOUNDS		
貸す	*lend*	**ka·su** か・す
貸切	lend + cut = *reserved; chartered*	**kashi·**kiri か し・き り
貸主	lend + primary = *lender; landlord*	**kashi·**nushi か し・ぬ し

PAINT SPRAYER

This component is unusual in that it is often abbreviated when either handwritten or presented in a more calligraphic font, as in the next entry. In such instances it becomes the "dentist light" component we learned prior to Entry 299. It only appears, incidentally, in the following kanji, although this kanji finds its way into other characters as a component.

KANJI 337

 COMMAND

ノ	人	𠆢	今	令			

BUILDING THIS KANJI
Umbrella 𠆢 + One (hamburger patty) 一(3)
+ Paint Sprayer 丁 = 令

Meaning
Command, order. This kanji is also used as an honorific prefix in certain compounds. Note that the kanji appears in the next section (as background for the illustration) in its more formal rendering, and thus contains the hamburger patty and paint sprayer components listed above.

Remembering this kanji
Though his **umbrella** was shielding the **hamburger patty**, he flinched on hearing the COMMAND.

"I COMMAND you to put down your **umbrella** and step away from the **patty**," said the girl with the **paint sprayer**.

"But it's done nothing wrong!" he cried.

And yet...even he had suspected that this would happen, and as the **paint sprayer** hissed, he knew that somehow, in some way, the COMMAND had needed to be given.

Common Pronunciations
Common **ON** reading: **REI** (レ イ)
Common **kun** reading: none

Create your **on-yomi** keyword and enter it in the table at the back of the book. After that, write your sentence to remember the **on-yomi** reading in the box below.

Less Common Pronunciations

Less common **ON** reading: none

Less common **kun** reading: none

COMMON WORDS AND COMPOUNDS		
指令	finger + command = *order; directive*	SHI·**REI** シ・レイ
号令	title + command = *command; order*	GŌ·**REI** ゴウ・レイ

KANJI 338

野
FIELD

╮	⌐	⊢	⊟	甲	甲	里	里	野⁷	野
野	野								

BUILDING THIS KANJI

Hamlet 里 (180) + Beforehand 予 (299) = 野

Meaning

Field, the wild. Interestingly, this kanji is used to denote a political party in opposition.

Remembering this kanji

Everyone in the **hamlet** came out as I approached. "You'd do well to understand something **beforehand**," said the **hamlet** leader. "We care for our FIELDS here. We'll tend a FIELD, and if the FIELD sees fit it'll give us its bounty. So you'd better tell us **beforehand** if you don't get along with FIELDS."

Common Pronunciations

Common **ON** reading: **YA** (ヤ)

Common **kun** reading: **no** (の)

This is a tougher character than might be expected; both readings will be encountered frequently, although **YA** appears more often in the second position.

Less Common Pronunciations

Less common **ON** reading: none

Less common **kun** reading: none

COMMON WORDS AND COMPOUNDS		
野心	field + heart = *ambition*	**YA**·SHIN ヤ・シン
分野	part + field = *field (of study, etc.)*	BUN·**YA** ブン・ヤ
野原	field + original = *field(s)*	**no**·hara の・はら

KANJI 339

広
WIDE

﹅	￢	广	広	広			

BUILDING THIS KANJI

Cliff Diver 厂 + Broken Crutch ム = 広

Meaning

Wide, broad, spacious.

Remembering this kanji

The **cliff diver** peered down and saw a **broken crutch** strewn over a WIDE area. "How could anyone have believed they could do this on crutches?" he thought, spreading his arms WIDE before diving in a WIDE arc.

Common Pronunciations

Common **ON** reading: **KŌ** (コ ウ)
Common **kun** reading: **hiro** (ひ ろ)

Less Common Pronunciations

Less common **ON** reading: none
Less common **kun** reading: none

COMMON WORDS AND COMPOUNDS		
広い	wide; spacious	**hiro·i** ひろ·い
広島	wide + island = *Hiroshima*	**hiro·shima** ひろ·しま
広大	wide + large = *extensive; immense*	**KŌ·DAI** コウ·ダイ

KANJI 340

石   **STONE**

BUILDING THIS KANJI
One (top of a bun) 一(3) + Comet 丿 +
Mouth (vampire) 口(8) = 石

Meaning
Stone.

Remembering this kanji

If you leave it long enough, the **top of a bun** will eventually turn into a STONE. Like the STONE in a **comet**. Oh, or the STONE that a **vampire** would dislike (since he realizes like everyone else that there are certain things you can't get from a STONE).

Common Pronunciations

Common **ON** reading: **SEKI** (セ キ)
Common **kun** reading: **ishi** (い し)

Both readings are used frequently in compounds, although **SEKI** is more common outside of first position.

Less Common Pronunciations

Less common **ON** readings: **SHAKU** (シ ャ ク);
KOKU (コ ク)
Less common **kun** reading: none

COMMON WORDS AND COMPOUNDS		
石	stone	**ishi** いし
化石	change + stone = *fossil*	**KA·SEKI** カ·セキ
一石二鳥	one + stone + two + bird = *kill two birds with one stone*	**IS·SEKI·NI·CHŌ** イッ·セキ·ニ·チョウ

COMPONENT #341

GIRL WITH A HULA HOOP

KANJI 341

 CHINA

BUILDING THIS KANJI
Splash 氵 + Wreath 艹 + Girl With A Hula
Hoop 夫 = 漢

Meaning
China, the Han dynasty. The first compound
below may be familiar to you.

Remembering this kanji
"And this is us **splashing** in the Yangtze…"
"Where's that?"
"It's in CHINA. And here I am laying a **wreath**
at a monument to Confucius…"
"Where was he from?"
"From CHINA. And this **girl with a hula
hoop**…"
"Where…"
"It was in CHINA, OK! At a circus in CHINA!
The slides are all from CHINA!"

Common Pronunciations
Common **ON** reading: **KAN** (カン)
Common **kun** reading: none

Less Common Pronunciations
Less common **ON** reading: none
Less common **kun** reading: none

COMMON WORDS AND COMPOUNDS		
漢字	China + character = *kanji*	**KAN·JI** カン・ジ
漢方	China + direction = *Chinese medicine*	**KAN·PŌ** カン・ポウ

KANJI 342

 DIFFERENT

BUILDING THIS KANJI
Mouth (vampire) 口 (8) + Chair 力 + Chisel 刂
= 別

Meaning
Different, as well as the ideas of separation and
farewell.

Remembering this kanji
"You're DIFFERENT from my usual custom-
ers," she said as the **vampire** took a **chair** in her
salon. "I mean, I'm going to need a **chisel** to get
through that hair gel!"
"It's Transylvanian," said the **vampire**. "We
prefer a DIFFERENT brand there."

Common Pronunciations
Common **ON** reading: **BETSU** (ベツ)
Common **kun** reading: **waka** (わか)

Create your **on-yomi** keyword and enter it in the table at the back of the book. Then, after creating your **kun-yomi** keyword, write your sentence to remember the **on-yomi** and **kun-yomi** readings in the box below.

Less Common Pronunciations
Less common **ON** reading: none
Less common **kun** reading: **wa** (わ)

COMMON WORDS AND COMPOUNDS		
別れる	*part company; branch off*	**waka**·reru わか·れる
別々	different + different = *separate; individual*	**BETSU·BETSU** ベツ・ベツ
送別	send + different = *farewell; send-off*	**SŌ·BETSU** ソウ・ベツ

KANJI 343

GARDEN

BUILDING THIS KANJI
Prison □ + Earth 土(87) + Sherpa 朶 = 園

Meaning
Garden.

Remembering this kanji
"Geez, warden, that **sherpa** hasn't adjusted to our **prison** very well, has he? I mean, what's the deal with him hauling that **earth** everywhere?"
"He said he wants to create a GARDEN so that it'll remind him of the nature in Nepal."
"Isn't that a bit risky? I could be wrong, but something tells me the other cons won't be too thrilled to see their basketball court turned into a GARDEN."

Common Pronunciations
Common **ON** reading: **EN** (エン)
Common **kun** reading: none

Recall from Entry 318 that the first two characters of the final compound mean "animal" when taken together.

Less Common Pronunciations
Less common **ON** reading: none
Less common **kun** reading: **sono** (その)

COMMON WORDS AND COMPOUNDS		
公園	public + garden = *park*	**KŌ·EN** コウ・エン
学園	study + garden = *educational institute*	**GAKU·EN** ガク・エン
動物園	animal + garden = *zoo*	**DŌ·BUTSU·EN** ドウ・ブツ・エン

KANJI 344

皆   **ALL**

一	ヒ	ヒ	比	比	比	皆	皆	皆

BUILDING THIS KANJI
Compare 比(240) + White 白(7) = 皆

Meaning
All.

Remembering this kanji
"Listen up, ALL of you," she said. "I want you
ALL to **compare** this **white** stuff."
We stared at her in disbelief.
"That is ALL!" she yelled.

Common Pronunciations
Common **ON** reading: none
Common **kun** reading: **mina** (みな)

In spoken Japanese, this reading is often
pronounced **minna** (みんな) for emphasis.

Less Common Pronunciations
Less common **ON** reading: **KAI** (カイ)
Less common **kun** reading: none

COMMON WORDS AND COMPOUNDS		
皆	*all; everybody*	**mina** みな
皆様	all + manner = *"ladies and gentlemen"*	**mina**·sama みな・さま

COMPONENT #345

BILLIONAIRE   貝

Note the difference between this component
and 貝, our "frog" introduced prior to Entry 230.

KANJI 345

即   **IMMEDIATE**

⁊	⁊	∃	∃	艮	即	即

BUILDING THIS KANJI
Billionaire 貝 + Fern ⌐ = 即

Meaning
Immediate, at once.

Remembering this kanji
If a **billionaire** wants a **fern** it means he needs it
IMMEDIATELY, so take IMMEDIATE action
and get him one. And yes, even if it's for something weird it's still your IMMEDIATE concern.

Common Pronunciations
Common **ON** reading: **SOKU** (ソク)
Common **kun** reading: none

Less Common Pronunciations
Less common **ON** reading: none
Less common **kun** reading: none

COMMON WORDS AND COMPOUNDS		
即日	immediate + sun (day) = *on the same day*	**SOKU**·JITSU ソク・ジツ
即死	immediate + death = *instant death*	**SOKU**·SHI ソク・シ
即売	immediate + sell = *sale on the spot*	**SOKU**·BAI ソク・バイ

KANJI 346

店 **SHOP**

BUILDING THIS KANJI
Cliff Diver 广 + Occupy 占 (255) = 店

Meaning
Shop, store.

Remembering this kanji
"I don't get it. What made the **cliff diver occupy** that SHOP?"
"Hasn't anyone told you? That SHOP makes low-cost artificial **cliff divers**. His livelihood is at stake; he had no choice but to **occupy** it."

Common Pronunciations
Common **ON** reading: **TEN** (テ ン)
Common **kun** reading: **mise** (み せ)

The **on-yomi** is the more common reading.

Less Common Pronunciations
Less common **ON** reading: none
Less common **kun** reading: none

COMMON WORDS AND COMPOUNDS		
店	*shop; store*	mise み せ
開店	open + shop = *shop/store opening*	KAI·TEN カ イ · テ ン
書店	write + shop = *bookstore*	SHO·TEN シ ョ · テ ン

KANJI 347

院 **INSTITUTION**

BUILDING THIS KANJI
Novice Yodeler 阝 + Perfect 完 (292) = 院

Meaning
Institution, in the sense of public buildings such as a hospitals, or bodies such as legislatures.

Remembering this kanji
For a **novice yodeler** who wants to be **perfect**, there is only one INSTITUTION: the INSTITUTION for **Perfect** Yodeling. But what about a **novice yodeler** who doesn't want to be **perfect**? Well, someone like that belongs in an INSTITUTION.

Common Pronunciations
Common **ON** reading: **IN** (イ ン)
Common **kun** reading: none

Less Common Pronunciations
Less common **ON** reading: none
Less common **kun** reading: none

COMMON WORDS AND COMPOUNDS		
入院	enter + institution = *be admitted to hospital*	NYŪ·**IN** ニュウ・イン
学院	study + institution = *academy*	GAKU·**IN** ガク・イン
病院	illness + institution = *hospital*	BYŌ·**IN** ビョウ・イン

COMPONENT #348

SHARK ATTACK

KANJI 348

登 **CLIMB**

フ	ブ	ヺ	癶	癶	癶	癶	啓	啓
啓	啓	登						

BUILDING THIS KANJI
Shark Attack 癶 + Bean 豆 (280) = 登

Meaning
Climb. An important secondary meaning has to do with attendance (the first compound offers an example).

Remembering this kanji
I kept CLIMBING and CLIMBING, but this was no run-of-the-mill **shark attac**k.
"The **beans**, Jack," someone yelled at me from below, "maybe it just wants **beans**!"
   It didn't seem likely. I mean, if I was able to CLIMB up a beanstalk, it was only logical that a shark could attack me by CLIMBING one too.

Common Pronunciations
Common **ON** reading: **TŌ** (ト ウ)
Common **kun** reading: none

Less Common Pronunciations
Less common **ON** reading: **TO** (ト)
Less common **kun** reading: **nobo** (のぼ)

You are most likely to encounter the **on-yomi** in one word: 登山 (**TO**·ZAN / ト・ザン) "mountain climbing", with 山 being voiced. The **kun-yomi** for this kanji serves as an alternate form of 上る (**nobo**·ru / のぼ·る), which we met in Entry 30.

COMMON WORDS AND COMPOUNDS		
登校	climb (attend) + school = *attend school*	**TŌ**·KŌ トウ・コウ
登場	climb + place = *make an entrance;* *show up*	**TŌ**·JŌ トウ・ジョウ

KANJI 349

原 **ORIGINAL**

一	厂	厂	斤	戸	戸	盾	原	原
原								

BUILDING THIS KANJI
Cliff 厂 + White 白 (7) + Small 小 (20) = 原

Meaning
Original, in the sense of things in their original or primitive state. Many compounds with this character also convey the idea of a plain or field (the first two examples below, for instance). Think of this in connection to "original" as a place that is unspoiled or wilderness-like.

Remembering this kanji
"It seems that the ORIGINAL inhabitants of this **cliff** not only painted themselves **white**, but were very **small**," said the tour guide. "Can anyone tell me who they were?"

"The **Whites** and the **Smalls**?" someone asked with a smirk.

"Gee, that's ORIGINAL," she said.

Common Pronunciations
Common **ON** reading: **GEN** (ゲン)
Common **kun** reading: **hara** (はら)

Less Common Pronunciations
Less common **ON** reading: none
Less common **kun** reading: none

IRREGULAR READING		
川原	river + original = *dry riverbed*	kawa·**ra** かわ・ら

COMMON WORDS AND COMPOUNDS		
野原	field + original = *field(s)*	no·**hara** の・はら
高原	tall + original = *plateau; tableland*	**KŌ·GEN** コウ・ゲン
原子力	original + child + strength = *atomic energy; nuclear power*	**GEN·SHI·RYOKU** ゲン・シ・リョク

KANJI 350

晩 **LATE**

丨	冂	日	日	日'	日⁷	旷	昭	晩
晩	晩	晩						

BUILDING THIS KANJI
Sun 日 (6) + Exemption 免 (311) = 晩

Meaning
Late, evening. This kanji also imparts the idea of late in a number of more poetic words—the first two compounds below offer examples.

Remembering this kanji

"The orderly told me it's getting LATE," she said. "I should probably be on my way."

"No, you don't have to," he said. "It won't get LATE until I let it get LATE. If the **sun** doesn't ask me for an **exemption**, it can't set."

So this is it, she thought. This is what the LATE stages will be like.

Common Pronunciations

Common **ON** reading: **BAN** (バン)

Common **kun** reading: none

Less Common Pronunciations

Less common **ON** reading: none

Less common **kun** reading: none

COMMON WORDS AND COMPOUNDS		
晩秋	late + autumn = *late autumn*	**BAN·SHŪ** バン・シュウ
晩年	late + year = *one's later years*	**BAN·NEN** バン・ネン
今晩は	now + late = *"good evening"*	KON·**BAN**·wa コン・バン・は

KANJI 351

 ENTWINE

ノ	㇄	㇄	㇄	糸	糸	糸′	糸⁷	終
絡	絡	絡						

BUILDING THIS KANJI

Thread 糸(196) + Each 各(282) = 絡

Meaning

Entwine, become entangled.

Remembering this kanji

"We are as **thread**," he whispered, "in that **each** of our lives will ENTWINE with the other."

Common Pronunciations

Common **ON** reading: **RAKU** (ラク)

Common **kun** reading: **kara** (から)

Less Common Pronunciations

Less common **ON** reading: none

Less common **kun** reading: none

COMMON WORDS AND COMPOUNDS		
絡む	*entwine; become entangled*	**kara·mu** から・む
絡み付く	entwine + attach = *cling to; coil around*	**kara·mi tsu·ku** から・み つ・く
短絡	short + entwine = *short circuit*	TAN·**RAKU** タン・ラク

COMPONENT #352

SPRINTER

As we will meet a few other components that look similar to this one in the pages ahead, it would be a good idea to spend some time here in order to clearly see how each line contributes to the illustration. You may find it useful to compare this component to the lower half of 呆, the sherpa we learned prior to Entry 290. Keep in mind as well that the sprinter's arms and starting line are written as a single stroke.

KANJI 352

表 **EXPRESS**

BUILDING THIS KANJI
Candlestick Holder 圭 + Sprinter 仪 = 表

Meaning

To express, often one's feelings and beliefs, etc. This idea of bringing things into the open extends to this kanji's other primary meanings, namely surfaces and charts.

Remembering this kanji

The **candlestick holder** was awarded, and the **sprinter** made an attempt to EXPRESS his feelings. "I'd like to EXPRESS my thanks," he said, but I would rather EXPRESS my gratitude. With this **candlestick holder** I can sprint with candles. It's so…so…I'm sorry, it's more than I can EXPRESS."

Common Pronunciations

Common **ON** reading: **HYŌ** (ヒョウ)
Common **kun** reading: **omote** (おもて);
arawa (あらわ)

HYŌ is the more common of these readings. **arawa** forms the two verbs in the second and third examples below; you may recognize these as being pronounced identically to 現れる and 現す from Entry 327. Not surprisingly, the pair here can also be seen written at times as 表わ れる and 表わす. Though these characters are similar in some respects, this kanji is used more for the idea of "expressing" things such as feelings, thoughts and opinions.

Create your **on-yomi** keyword and enter it in the table at the back of the book. Then, after creating your **kun-yomi** keywords, write your sentence to remember the **on-yomi** and **kun-yomi** readings in the box below.

Less Common Pronunciations

Less common **ON** reading: none
Less common **kun** reading: none

COMMON WORDS AND COMPOUNDS		
表	surface; front	**omote** おもて
表れる (intr)	be expressed	**arawa**·reru あらわ·れる
表す (tr)	express; reveal	**arawa**·su あらわ·す
表現	express + present = expression	**HYŌ**·GEN ヒョウ·ゲン

KANJI 353

 TYPE

BUILDING THIS KANJI
Spilling Coffee 弋 + Craft 工(47) = 式

Meaning
The primary meaning is that of a type or style of something (as in the second compound). It is also very commonly used, however, in the sense of "ceremony" (as is evident in the final example). Take care with the stroke order of this kanji; recall what was written about the "spilling coffee" component when it was introduced prior to Entry 321.

Remembering this kanji
"Hey, watch it! What TYPE of an idiot are you?"
"The TYPE who **spills coffee** on others. That TYPE."
"Oh. Well then, you've really mastered your **craft**. Forgive me for being rude, you're obviously a decent TYPE."

Common Pronunciations
Common **ON** reading: **SHIKI** (シ キ)
Common **kun** reading: none

Create your **on-yomi** keyword and enter it in the table at the back of the book. After that, write your sentence to remember the **on-yomi** reading in the box below.

Less Common Pronunciations
Less common **ON** reading: none
Less common **kun** reading: none

COMMON WORDS AND COMPOUNDS		
形式	form + type = *form; formality*	KEI·**SHIKI** ケイ・シキ
自動式	self + move + type = *automatic*	JI·DŌ·**SHIKI** ジ・ドウ・シキ
成人式	become + person + type = *Coming of Age ceremony*	SEI·JIN·**SHIKI** セイ・ジン・シキ

KANJI 354

 PASSAGE

BUILDING THIS KANJI
Dentist Light ⌐ + Utilize 用(270) + Seal ⻌ = 通

Meaning
The general concept is of passing through and along. This is a very versatile kanji that can mean a variety of things, from "street" (it often appears on road signs), to the ideas of thoroughly getting to know a subject or having things go according to plan.

Remembering this kanji

On hearing that the **dentist light** could finally be **utilized**, she forced her way through the PASSAGE. Moments later she identified the SEAL'S problem: a blocked PASSAGE!

Common Pronunciations

Common **ON** reading: **TSŪ** (ツウ)
Common **kun** reading: **tō** (と お)

In the first position, **TSŪ** is by far the more common reading. Both occur frequently in the second position, and the **kun-yomi** is often voiced (although it never becomes so when forming verbs).

Create your **on-yomi** keyword and enter it in the table at the back of the book. Then, after creating

your **kun-yomi** keyword, write your sentence to remember the **on-yomi** and **kun-yomi** readings in the box below.

Less Common Pronunciations

Less common **ON** reading: **TSU** (ツ)
Less common **kun** reading: **kayo** (か よ)

COMMON WORDS AND COMPOUNDS		
通る (intr)	*go along; pass by*	**tō·**ru と お·る
通す (tr)	*pierce; let through*	**tō·**su と お·す
大通り	large + passage = *a main street*	**ō dō·**ri おお どお·り
交通	mix + passage = *traffic;* *communication*	**KŌ·TSŪ** コウ·ツウ

KOI STREAMERS

KANJI 355

昨 **PAST**

丨	冂	日	日	日ʹ	日�	昨	昨	昨

BUILDING THIS KANJI
Sun 日 (6) + Koi Streamers 乍 = 昨

Meaning

Past.

Remembering this kanji

"The **sun** was dazzling that day…**koi streamers** twirled in the sky…"
"Yes," she said, "but the PAST is the PAST."

Common Pronunciations

Common **ON** reading: **SAKU** (サ ク)
Common **kun** reading: none

Create your **on-yomi** keyword and enter it in the table at the back of the book. After that, write your sentence to remember the **on-yomi** reading in the box below.

Less Common Pronunciations

Less common **ON** reading: none
Less common **kun** reading: none

IRREGULAR READING		
昨日	past + sun (day) = *yesterday*	**kinō** きのう

COMMON WORDS AND COMPOUNDS		
昨年	past + year = *last year*	**SAKU·NEN** サク・ネン
昨夜	past + night = *last night*	**SAKU·YA** サク・ヤ
昨今	past + now = *recently;* *nowadays*	**SAK·KON** サッ・コン

This compound can also be read using the characters' normal on-yomi (**SAKU·JITSU** / サク・ジツ), giving the word a more formal tone.

KANJI 356

BUNDLE

BUILDING THIS KANJI
Tree 木 (13) + Mouth (vampire) 口 (8) = 束

Meaning
Bundle, bunch. Note that the writing order of this kanji does not follow the components as listed above, with "mouth" written after the initial horizontal stroke. It is similar in this respect to the character for "east" (東) from Entry 76.

Remembering this kanji
Crouched behind the **tree**, the **vampire** was a **BUNDLE** of nerves. "They're getting closer," he thought. "I'd better get rid of this **BUNDLE**."

Common Pronunciations
Common **ON** reading: **SOKU** (ソク)
Common **kun** reading: **taba** (たば)

Less Common Pronunciations
Less common **ON** reading: none
Less common **kun** reading: **tsuka** (つか)

COMMON WORDS AND COMPOUNDS		
束	*bundle; bunch*	**taba** たば
花束	flower + bunch = *bouquet*	**hana·taba** はな・たば
結束	bind + bunch = *union;* *combination*	**KES·SOKU** ケッ・ソク

KANJI 357

SPECIAL

BUILDING THIS KANJI
Cow 牛 (100) + Temple 寺 (104) = 特

Meaning
Special.

Remembering this kanji
"There was a **cow** in that **temple** the other day. I didn't realize they were so **SPECIAL** here."
"They are. But speaking of **cows**, the deli downtown has a great **SPECIAL** on sirloin today."

Common Pronunciations
Common **ON** reading: **TOKU** (トク)
Common **kun** reading: none

Create your **on-yomi** keyword and enter it in the table at the back of the book. After that, write

your sentence to remember the **on-yomi** reading in the box below.

Less Common Pronunciations

Less common **ON** reading: none
Less common **kun** reading: none

COMMON WORDS AND COMPOUNDS		
特別	special + different = *special; extraordinary*	**TOKU·BETSU** ト ク・ベ ツ
特売	special + sell = *bargain; special buy*	**TOKU·BAI** ト ク・バ イ
特急	special + hasten = *special express (train)*	**TOKU·KYŪ** ト ッ・キ ュ ウ

KANJI 358

 TRUE

一	十	广	宀	古	吉	百	直	真
真								

BUILDING THIS KANJI
Ten (scarecrow) 十(28) + Tool 具(177) = 真

Meaning

True, genuine. This interesting kanji often intensifies the quality of the character that follows it—the irregular readings and first compound below offer examples of this. As this kanji is very similar to some others we will learn, make sure you clearly see that it breaks apart into "ten (scarecrow)" and "tool".

Remembering this kanji

"You are a **scarecrow**?"
"TRUE."
"Then giving you this **TOOL** would be kind of pointless, wouldn't it?"
"That is also TRUE."

It was looking like he would have to fix the barn on his own; that which he had feared more than anything else was coming TRUE.

Common Pronunciations

Common **ON** reading: **SHIN** (シ ン)
Common **kun** reading: **ma** (ま)

Less Common Pronunciations

Less common **ON** reading: none
Less common **kun** reading: none

IRREGULAR READINGS		
真赤	true + red = *deep red*	**mak·ka** ま っ・か
真青	true + blue = *deep blue; horribly pale*	**mas·sao** ま っ・さ お

These are the only two words in which the readings of the kanji that follow 真 change in such a radical way. More common examples include 真白 (**mas**·shiro / ま っ・し ろ) "snow white" and 真暗 (**mak**·kura / ま っ・く ら) "pitch dark". You may also see these compounds written as 真っ赤, 真っ青, and 真っ白, etc. Keep an eye out as well for a few words such as 真中 (**man**·naka / ま ん・な か) "right in the middle", which is also sometimes written as 真ん中.

COMMON WORDS AND COMPOUNDS		
真新しい	true + new = *brand-new*	**ma** atara·shii ま あたら・しい
真実	true + actual = *truth; reality*	**SHIN·JITSU** シ ン・ジ ツ

COMPONENT #359

COMPONENT #359

CRANE

KANJI 359

局 **OFFICE**

| ┐ | ⁻ | 尸 | 弓 | 局 | 局 | 局 | | |

BUILDING THIS KANJI
Flag 尸 + Crane ⊐ + Mouth (vampire) 口 (8)
= 局

Meaning

Office, bureau. In a few words this kanji can also mean the "situation", or state of something (the first compound is an example).

Remembering this kanji

"The **flag** is torn," said the foreman. "We gotta replace it."
"Can I get up there with the **crane**, boss?" asked the **vampire**.
"Why do that? Just head through their OFFICE."
The **vampire** took off his hard hat. "Really," he said. "Imagine me strolling by those power suits, cubicles and computers. I'd look ridiculous in an OFFICE."

Common Pronunciations

Common **ON** reading: **KYOKU** (キョク)
Common **kun** reading: none

Recall from Entry 122 that the first two kanji of the second compound mean "water supply system" when taken together

Create your **on-yomi** keyword and enter it in the table at the back of the book. After that, write your sentence to remember the **on-yomi** reading in the box below.

Less Common Pronunciations

Less common **ON** reading: none
Less common **kun** reading: none

COMMON WORDS AND COMPOUNDS		
結局	bind + office (situation) = *after all; in the long run*	KEK·**KYOKU** ケッ・キョク
水道局	water supply system + office = *water bureau*	SUI·DŌ·**KYOKU** スイ・ドウ・キョク
薬局	medicine + office = *pharmacy*	YAK·**KYOKU** ヤッ・キョク

KANJI 360

集 **GATHER**

| ′ | ′ | ′ | ′ | 亻 | 什 | 件 | 隹 | 隹 |
| 隹 | 集 | 集 | | | | | | |

BUILDING THIS KANJI
Squirrels 隹 + Tree 土 (13) = 集

Meaning

Gather, assemble.

Less Common Pronunciations

Less common **ON** reading: none

Less common **kun** reading: tsudo (つど)

Remembering this kanji

"**Squirrels** sure like to GATHER in that **tree**, don't they?"

"Yeah, they GATHER nuts and then GATHER afterward to chat about how much they GATH-ERED."

COMMON WORDS AND COMPOUNDS		
集まる (intr)	gather; come together	**atsu**·maru あつ・まる
集める (tr)	gather; collect	**atsu**·meru あつ・める
集中	gather + middle = concentration	**SHŪ·CHŪ** シュウ・チュウ

Common Pronunciations

Common **ON** reading: **SHŪ** (シュウ)

Common **kun** reading: **atsu** (あつ)

CHAPTER 16 REVIEW EXERCISES

A. Please match the following kanji to their meanings.

1. 通
2. 集
3. 晩
4. 野
5. 石
6. 園
7. 別
8. 真
9. 院
10. 広

a. Field
b. Late
c. Passage
d. True
e. Garden
f. Wide
g. Stone
h. Different
i. Gather
j. Institution

B. Please match the following meanings to their kanji, and these to their **on-** or **kun-yomi**.

1. Special
2. Taste
3. Flat
4. Office
5. Original
6. Shop
7. Edge
8. All
9. Past
10. Lend

a. 昨
b. 局
c. 特
d. 店
e. 味
f. 貸
g. 際
h. 原
i. 平
j. 皆

1. **GEN** (ゲン)
2. **KYOKU** (キョク)
3. **mise** (みせ)
4. **ka** (か)
5. **TOKU** (トク)
6. **mina** (みな)
7. **hira** (ひら)
8. **SAI** (サイ)
9. **SAKU** (サク)
10. **aji** (あじ)

C. Please choose the best answer(s) to the following questions.

1. Which of the following kanji has the most number of strokes?
a. 表   b. 皆   c. 野   d. 通   e. 真

2. Which of the following readings apply to the kanji 表?
a. **arawa** (あらわ)
b. **kara** (から)
c. **SHI** (シ)
d. **JO** (ジョ)
e. **omote** (おもて)

3. I will not rest until I ___ Mr. Everest!
a. 味   b. 貸   c. 集   d. 登   e. 絡

4. Which is the correct reading of 通る?
a. **no·ru** (の・る)
b. **tō·ru** (とお・る)
c. **kō·ru** (こお・る)
d. **so·ru** (そ・る)

5. Which is the correct reading of 広い?
  a. **hira·i** (ひ ら·い)
  b. **hara·i** (は ら·い)
  c. **hiro·i** (ひ ろ·い)
  d. **kuro·i** (く ろ·い)

D. Please match the following compounds to their meanings and pronunciations.

1. 国際   a. Special   1. **KAN·JI** (カ ン·ジ)

2. 動物園   b. Automatic   2. **I·MI** (イ·ミ)

3. 特別   c. Fossil   3. **SOKU·SHI** (ソ ク·シ)

4. 丁度   d. Instant death   4. **DŌ· BUTSU·EN** (ド ウ· ブ ツ· エ ン)

5. 意味   e. Zoo   5. **KOKU·SAI** (コ ク· サ イ)

6. 漢字   f. Meaning   6. **TOKU· BETSU** (ト ク· ベ ツ)

7. 自動式   g. Exactly   7. **KA·SEKI** (カ·セ キ)

8. 指令   h. Order / Directive   8. **SHI·REI** (シ·レ イ)

9. 即死   i. Kanji   9. **CHŌ·DO** (チ ョ ウ· ド)

10. 化石   j. International   10. **JI·DŌ· SHIKI** (ジ·ド ウ· シ キ)

E. Please read the passage below and answer the questions that follow.

先月私は夫と広島へ行きました。
県立動物園へ行って付近の山をハ
イキングしました。とても楽しか
ったです。来年は北海道へ行く予
定です。

1. Where did she go last month?
2. With whom did she go?
3. Where did they visit in the city?
4. What did they do outside the city?
5. Where do they plan to go next year?

CUMULATIVE REVIEW EXERCISES FOR
CHAPTERS 1 - 16

A. Please match the following kanji to their meanings.

1. 若   a. Clothes

2. 界   b. Bundle

3. 可   c. World

4. 服   d. Beforehand

5. 束   e. Filial piety

6. 且   f. Appearance

7. 孝   g. Besides

8. 仕   h. Serve

9. 予   i. Young

10. 采   j. Possible

B. Which kanji does not belong in the group?

1. a.野   b.泉   c.忘   d.石   e.洋

2. a.楽   b.羊   c.牛   d.魚   e.馬

3. a.進   b.動   c.走   d.登   e.県

4. a.姉   b.夫   c.兄   d.医   e.母

5. a.亡   b.死   c.和   d.泣   e.弔

6. a.洋   b.歌   c.海   d.魚   e.泉

7. a.暗   b.低   c.短   d.若   e.番

8. a.弱   b.吉   c.良   d.美   e.完

9. a.指   b.酒   c.足   d.頭   e.耳

10. a.現   b.予   c.昨   d.晩   e.信

C. Identify the kanji n each group having the most number of strokes.

1. a.兄   b.反   c.予   d.手   e.尺

2. a.各   b.州   c.旨   d.令   e.医

3. a.県   b.店   c.配   d.即   e.茶

4. a.姉   b.屋   c.実   d.良   e.画

5. a.楽   b.際   c.遠   d.漢   e.続

6. a.事   b.形   c.式   d.送   e.定

7. a.己   b.亡   c.代   d.文   e.戸

8. a.理   b.神   c.紙   d.降   e.記

9. a.用   b.両   c.払   d.民   e.未

10. a.銀   b.遊   c.園   d.質   e.橋

D. Please list the following kanji in the order indicated (alphabetical).

1. Arrow / End / Husband / Not yet / Spicy
   a.辛   b.夫   c.矢   d.未   e.末

2. Against / Door / Measurement / Office / Roof
   a.反   b.尺   c.戸   d.局   e.屋

3. Lend / People / Substitute / Surname / Type
   a.民   b.式   c.貸   d.氏   e.代

4. Cause / Declare / God / Painting / Utilize
   a.神   b.申   c.画   d.用   e.由

5. Bind / Continue / Entwine / Picture / Via
   a.続   b.結   c.絵   d.経   e.絡

6. Active / Cry / Ocean / Saké / Wash
   a.洋   b.洗   c.酒   d.活   e.泣

7. Direction / Flat / Literature / Perish / Proper
    a. 方   b. 文   c. 正   d. 平   e. 亡

8. Achieve / Advance / Passage / Play / Send
    a. 進   b. 遊   c. 送   d. 通   e. 達

9. Besides / Prefecture / Quality / True / Wear
    a. 着   b. 且   c. 質   d. 真   e. 県

10. Against / Original / Shop / Stone / Wide
    a. 反   b. 広   c. 店   d. 原   e. 石

E. Please choose the best answer to the following
    questions.

1. There's nothing nicer than an afternoon
    cup of ____.
    a. 洋   b. 魚   c. 茶   d. 民   e. 羊

2. Don't you dare wag your ____ at me!
    a. 神   b. 質   c. 都   d. 野   e. 指

3. Have you ever tasted a more delicious
    Japanese ____ than this one?
    a. 園   b. 橋   c. 矢   d. 束   e. 酒

4. Congratulations on your recent ____!
    a. 県   b. 婚   c. 軍   d. 味   e. 食

5. My boss wants to speak with me about
    an important ____.
    a. 洗   b. 非   c. 重   d. 事   e. 至

F. Please choose the best answer to the following
    questions.

1. Which is the correct reading of 比べる?
    a. shira·beru (しら・べる)
    b. ara·beru (あら・べる)
    c. fu·beru (ふ・べる)
    d. kura·beru (くら・べる)

2. Which is the correct reading of 楽しい?
    a. tano·shii (たの・しい)
    b. taka·shii (たか・しい)
    c. tada·shii (ただ・しい)
    d. tama·shii (たま・しい)

3. Which is the correct reading of 付ける?
    a. a·keru (あ・ける)
    b. u·keru (う・ける)
    c. tsu·keru (つ・ける)
    d. ma·keru (ま・ける)

4. Which is the correct reading of 辞める?
    a. de·meru (で・める)
    b. shi·meru (し・める)
    c. ka·meru (か・める)
    d. ya·meru (や・める)

5. Which is the correct reading of 占う?
    a. makana·u (まかな・う)
    b. urana·u (うらな・う)
    c. fuka·u (ふか・う)
    d. tama·u (たま・う)

G. Please choose the best answer to the following
    questions.

1. Which is the correct reading of 登山?
    a. KO·ZAN (コ・ザン)
    b. O·ZAN (オ・ザン)
    c. TO·ZAN (ト・ザン)
    d. DO·SAN (ド・サン)

2. Which is the correct reading of 頭上?
    a. MU·JŌ (ム・ジョウ)
    b. ZU·JŌ (ズ・ジョウ)
    c. SU·JŌ (ス・ジョウ)
    d. KU·JŌ (ク・ジョウ)

3. Which is the correct reading of 茶道?
    a. KA·DŌ (カ・ドウ)
    b. TA·DŌ (タ・ドウ)
    c. HA·DŌ (ハ・ドウ)
    d. SA·DŌ (サ・ドウ)

4. Which is the correct reading of 大和?
    a. amato (あまと)
    b. sabaku (さばく)
    c. yamato (やまと)
    d. sabato (さばと)

5. Which is the correct reading of 文字?
   a. **MO·JI** (モ·ジ)
   b. **FU·JI** (フ·ジ)
   c. **HI·JI** (ヒ·ジ)
   d. **U·JI** (ウ·ジ)

6. Which is the correct reading of 人形?
   a. **hito·GYŌ** (ひと·ギョウ)
   b. **NIN·GYŌ** (ニン·ギョウ)
   c. **NIN·JI** (ニン·ジ)
   d. **NIN·JA** (ニン·ジャ)

7. Which is the correct reading of 気付く?
   a. **KI fu·ku** (キ ふ·く)
   b. **KI zu·ku** (キ づ·く)
   c. **KI chi·ku** (キ ち·く)
   d. **KI ma·ku** (キ ま·く)

8. Which is the correct reading of 美味しい?
   a. **oi·shii** (おい·しい)
   b. **ko·shii** (こ·しい)
   c. **i·shii** (い·しい)
   d. **uru·shii** (うる·しい)

9. Which is the correct reading of 川原?
   a. **kawa·na** (かわ·な)
   b. **kawa·ba** (かわ·ば)
   c. **kawa·sa** (かわ·さ)
   d. **kawa·ra** (かわ·ら)

10. Which is the correct reading of 世間?
    a. **SO·KEN** (ソ·ケン)
    b. **SA·KEN** (サ·ケン)
    c. **SE·KEN** (セ·ケン)
    d. **SE·KAN** (セ·カン)

H. Please match the following compounds to their meanings and pronunciations.

1. 酒屋   a. District /   1. **RAKU·EN**
              Region   (ラク·エン)

2. 活動   b. Definite /   2. **hana·taba**
              Concrete   (はな·たば)

3. 楽園   c. Excursion /   3. **HO·DŌ·KYŌ**
              Day trip   (ホ·ドウ·キョウ)

4. 具体的 d. Form /   4. **KEI·SHIKI**
              Formality   (ケイ·シキ)

5. 送別   e. Liquor   5. **HYAKU·NEN·SAI**
              store   (ヒャク·ネン·サイ)

6. 花束   f. Bouquet   6. **saka·ya**
                                  (さか·や)

7. 地方   g. Activity   7. **TAI·SEI·YŌ**
                                  (タイ·セイ·ヨウ)

8. 百年歳 h. Atlantic   8. **GAKU·IN**
              Ocean   (ガク·イン)

9. 学院   i. Pacific   9. **KATSU· DŌ**
              Ocean   (カツ·ドウ)

10. 大西洋 j. Worry /   10. **SHIN·PAI**
              Anxiety   (シン·パイ)

11. 太平洋 k. Farewell /   11. **EN·SOKU**
              Send-off   (エン·ソク)

12. 遠足   l. Pedestrian   12. **CHI·HŌ**
              bridge   (チ·ホウ)

13. 歩道橋 m.Academy   13. **SŌ·BETSU**
                                  (ソウ·ベツ)

14. 心配   n. Paradise   14. **TAI·HEI·YŌ**
                                  (タイ·ヘイ·ヨウ)

15. 形式   o. Centennial   15. **GU·TAI·TEKI**
                                  (グ·タイ·テキ)

CHAPTER SEVENTEEN

Kanji #361—385

KANJI 361

HARD

BUILDING THIS KANJI
Prison 囗 + Old 古(58) = 固

Meaning
Hard, solid.

Remembering this kanji
"You don't wanna be in **prison** when you're **old** like me," he said. "The walls are HARD, the cells are HARD, the cots are HARD, even the grub is HARD. I dunno…I'd just like to figure out what it is about being here that makes my attitude so HARD."

Common Pronunciations
Common **ON** reading: **KO** (コ)
Common **kun** reading: **kata** (か た)

Less Common Pronunciations
Less common **ON** reading: none
Less common **kun** reading: none

COMMON WORDS AND COMPOUNDS		
固い	*hard; solid*	**kata·i** か た·い
固体	hard + body = *a solid*	**KO·TAI** コ·タイ
固定	hard + fixed = *fixed; settled*	**KO·TEI** コ·テイ

KANJI 362

COOL

BUILDING THIS KANJI
Ice Hockey 冫 + Command 令(337) = 冷

Meaning
Cool, cold. The sense here is of objects that are cool or cold to the touch (the idea of cold weather, however, is generally conveyed by the kanji in Entry 446). Remember that the 'paint sprayer' component in the character for command will often change to マ (the 'dentist light') when handwritten or in a more calligraphic-style font.

Remembering this kanji

You're in an **ice hockey** game, and have to take **command**. It's COOL in the arena; you'll need to be even COOLER than that.

Common Pronunciations

Common **ON** reading: **REI** (レイ)
Common **kun** reading: **tsume** (つめ)

Less Common Pronunciations

Less common **ON** reading: none
Less common **kun** reading: **hi** (ひ); **sa** (さ)

COMMON WORDS AND COMPOUNDS		
冷たい	*cool*	**tsume**·tai つめ・たい
冷気	cool + spirit = *chill; cold weather*	**REI·KI** レイ・キ
寒冷	cold + cool = *cold; chilly*	KAN·**REI** カン・レイ

COMPONENT #363

CHIMNEY　　土

KANJI 363

昔　LONG AGO

一	十	卅	土	甘	节	昔	昔

BUILDING THIS KANJI
Chimney 土 + Sun 日 (6) = 昔

Meaning
Long ago, old times.

Remembering this kanji

"LONG AGO," he said, "when Santa used to go down the **chimney** on the **sun**…"

"What are you talking about?" the girl interrupted. "There could never have been a **chimney** on the **sun**. It's a superheated ball of gas."

"Jeez, I guess you really did give up on fairy tales LONG AGO."

Common Pronunciations

Common **ON** reading: none
Common **kun** reading: **mukashi** (むかし)

Less Common Pronunciations

Less common **ON** reading: **SEKI** (セキ);
SHAKU (シャク)
Less common **kun** reading: none

COMMON WORDS AND COMPOUNDS		
昔	*long ago*	**mukashi** むかし
昔話	long ago + speak = *old story; folklore*	**mukashi**·banashi むかし・ばなし

KANJI 364

究 **INQUIRY**

`	'	宀	宀	宀	究	究		

BUILDING THIS KANJI
Weightlifter 宀 + Nine 九 (39) = 究

Meaning

Inquiry, often with the sense of this being done thoroughly or extensively.

Remembering this kanji

Even if a **weightlifter** can raise **99.99%** of the weight given him, he will still have failed in his task. If he wants to succeed, he must make INQUIRY upon INQUIRY into how he can lift up the rest.

Common Pronunciations

Common **ON** reading: **KYŪ** (キュウ)
Common **kun** reading: **kiwa** (きわ)

Less Common Pronunciations

Less common **ON** reading: none
Less common **kun** reading: none

COMMON WORDS AND COMPOUNDS		
究める	*investigate thoroughly; master*	kiwa·meru きわ·める
研究	polish + inquiry = *research*	KEN·KYŪ ケン·キュウ

KANJI 365

薬 **MEDICINE**

一	丷	丗	丗	艻	苩	苩	苩	莆
苩	蓲	薴	薴	蕐	薬	薬		

BUILDING THIS KANJI
Wreath ⺾ + Music 楽 (216) = 薬

Meaning

Medicine. In a few compounds this kanji can mean 'chemical'.

Remembering this kanji

If you realize that someone's laying a **wreath** over you, and that the **music** playing is Chopin's funeral march…chances are you didn't get the right MEDICINE.

Common Pronunciations

Common **ON** reading: **YAKU** (ヤク)
Common **kun** reading: **kusuri** (くすり)

The **kun-yomi** is always voiced outside of first position, as in the second compound below.

Create your **on-yomi** keyword and enter it in the table at the back of the book. After that, write your sentence to remember the **on-yomi** and **kun-yomi** readings in the box below.

Less Common Pronunciations
Less common **ON** reading: none
Less common **kun** reading: none

COMMON WORDS AND COMPOUNDS		
薬	medicine	**kusuri** くすり
目薬	eye + medicine = eye drops	me·**gusuri** め・ぐすり
薬局	medicine + office = pharmacy	**YAK·KYOKU** ヤッ・キョク

 LINE

BUILDING THIS KANJI
Thread 糸(196) + Springs 泉(319) = 線

Meaning
Line.

Remembering this kanji
"I really dislike being in LINE to get tickets like this," said the **thread**.
"I don't understand why," said the **springs**. "You *are* a LINE."
"Very funny, but I wouldn't be joking about LINES if I were you; look at the wet LINE you're leaving on the carpet here."

Common Pronunciations
Common **ON** reading: **SEN**(セン)
Common **kun** reading: none

Less Common Pronunciations
Less common **ON** reading: none
Less common **kun** reading: none

COMMON WORDS AND COMPOUNDS		
本線	main + line = main railway line	**HON·SEN** ホン・セン
前線	before + line = front line; (weather) front	**ZEN·SEN** ゼン・セン
配線	distribute + line = wiring	**HAI·SEN** ハイ・セン

COMPONENT #367

VASE

Ensure that you can see how this component differs from 立, the kanji for 'stand' in Entry 112.

KANJI 367

 FACE

`	一	亠	ソ	立	产	产	彦	彦
彦	彦	顔	顔	顔	顔	顔	顔	顔

BUILDING THIS KANJI

Vase ☆ + Cliff 厂 + Scratches 彡 +
Guy Wearing a Barrel 頁 = 顔

Meaning
Face.

Remembering this kanji
So there's this **vase** on the top of a **cliff**, and a
guy wearing a barrel wants to get it. But as he
scratches his way up the FACE of the **cliff** he
gets a lot of **scratches** of his own. Especially
on his FACE. Fortunately for him, the **vase** has
FACE cream in it.

Common Pronunciations
Common **ON** reading: **GAN** (ガン)
Common **kun** reading: **kao** (かお)

The **kun-yomi** is almost always voiced when not
in first position, as in the third compound.

Less Common Pronunciations
Less common **ON** reading: none
Less common **kun** reading: none

COMMON WORDS AND COMPOUNDS		
顔	*face*	kao かお
洗顔	wash + face = *washing one's face*	SEN·GAN セン·ガン
横顔	sideways + face = *profile*	yoko·gao よこ·がお

KANJI 368

族   TRIBE

`	一	ゟ	方	方'	扩	扩	抗	族
族	族							

BUILDING THIS KANJI

Direction 方 (223) + Hammer ⼢ + Arrow 矢
(285) = 族

Meaning
Tribe, family.

Remembering this kanji
In one **direction** was a TRIBE of fierce carpen-
ters, **hammers** at the ready. In another **direction**, a more traditional TRIBE with **arrows**.
Hammers or **arrows**... We weren't afraid
of either, I thought, until I looked back and
wondered where the rest of my TRIBE had gone.

Common Pronunciations
Common **ON** reading: **ZOKU** (ゾク)
Common **kun** reading: none

Less Common Pronunciations
Less common **ON** reading: none
Less common **kun** reading: none

COMMON WORDS AND COMPOUNDS		
家族	house + tribe = *family*	KA·ZOKU カ·ゾク
民族	people + tribe = *race; a people*	MIN·ZOKU ミン·ゾク
水族館	water + tribe + manor = *(public) aquarium*	SUI·ZOKU·KAN スイ·ゾク·カン

COMPONENT #369

CHEERLEADERS

In comparison to our short and squat 'running chicken' component, the 'cheerleaders' presented here are taller and thinner. It's important to remember that this component is written with *four* strokes, not three, and that the feet of the top cheerleader will always poke out a bit on the side.

Remembering this kanji

Since they're usually so popular and able to get what they want, **cheerleaders** often have little **filial piety**…

"We have to TEACH her!"
"Oh, let them TEACH her in the classroom."
"Honey, how could they TEACH anyone not to toss their pom-poms into the gravy on our dinner table?"

KANJI 369

教 **TEACH**

| 一 | 十 | 土 | ﾉ | 耂 | 考 | 孝 | 孝 | 孝 |
| 教 | 教 | | | | | | | |

BUILDING THIS KANJI
Filial piety 孝(273) + Cheerleaders 攵 = 教

Meaning
Teach. A religious element can be present in this kanji, as shown in the second compound below.

Common Pronunciations
Common **ON** reading: **KYŌ** (キョウ)
Common **kun** reading: **oshi** (おし)

Less Common Pronunciations
Less common **ON** reading: none
Less common **kun** reading: **oso** (おそ)

COMMON WORDS AND COMPOUNDS		
教える	*teach*	**oshi·eru** おし・える
教会	teach + meet = *church*	**KYŌ·KAI** キョウ・カイ
教科書	teach + course + write = *textbook; school book*	**KYŌ·KA·SHO** キョウ・カ・ショ

KANJI 370

丙 **THIRD**

| 一 | 一 | 冂 | 内 | 丙 | | | | |

BUILDING THIS KANJI
One (top of a bun) 一 (3) + Inside 内 (34) = 丙

Meaning
You will rarely meet this kanji on its own; its value for us is as a component in other more common characters. It is, however, found in documents of a more official nature, where it is used to indicate the third item or clause in a list.

Remembering this kanji

Sure, you can look at the **top of a bun** and get a sense of its width and height. It is only by being **inside** it, however, that you can appreciate its THIRD dimension.

Common Pronunciations
Common **ON** reading: **HEI** (ヘイ)
Common **kun** reading: none

Less Common Pronunciations
Less common **ON** readings: none
Less common **kun** reading: none

COMMON WORDS AND COMPOUNDS		
丙	*third (in a series)*	**HEI** ヘイ

KANJI 371

 LODGING

'	'	宀	宀	宀	宀	宀	宀	宿
宿	宿							

BUILDING THIS KANJI
Pincers 宀 + Giraffe 亻 + Hundred 百 (51)
= 宿

Meaning
Lodging, from inns to hotels.

Remembering this kanji
Even with **pincers** able to deposit them onto the balconies of their suites, it's still hopeless: **giraffes** are a **hundred** percent likely to be uncomfortable with their LODGING.

Common Pronunciations
Common **ON** reading: **SHUKU** (シュク)
Common **kun** reading: **yado** (やど)

Create your **on-yomi** keyword and enter it in the table at the back of the book. Then, after creating your kun-yomi keyword, write your sentence to remember the **on-yomi** and **kun-yomi** readings in the box below.

Less Common Pronunciations
Less common **ON** reading: none
Less common **kun** reading: none

COMMON WORDS AND COMPOUNDS		
宿	*lodging; inn*	**yado** やど
下宿	lower + lodging = *lodgings; boarding house*	**GE·SHUKU** ゲ・シュク
宿題	lodging + topic = *homework*	**SHUKU·DAI** シュク・ダイ

KANJI 372

 TRY

`	一	ニ	三	言	言	言	言
訂	言	試	試				

BUILDING THIS KANJI
Say 言 (80) + Type 式 (353) = 試

Meaning
Try.

Remembering this kanji
"You **say** you're the **type** who will TRY anything. Would you care to TRY this?"
"Uh…I would TRY it, but…"
"But what? If you **say** you're that **type**…"
"OK, OK, I'll TRY it."

Common Pronunciations
Common **ON** reading: **SHI** (シ)
Common **kun** reading: **kokoro** (こころ);
tame (ため)

The two **kun-yomi** are verb stems for the first and second examples below. Though they both mean to 'try', 試す (**tame**·su / ため·す) has the added implication of testing something so as to ascertain its value or validity. Note the mix of **on** and **kun-yomi** in the third compound.

Less Common Pronunciations
Less common **ON** reading: none
Less common **kun** reading: none

COMMON WORDS AND COMPOUNDS		
試みる	*try*	**kokoro**·miru こころ・みる
試す	*try; test*	**tame**·su ため・す
試合	try + match = *game; match*	**SHI**·ai シ・あい

PIRANHA

KANJI 373

ANEW

一	厂	冂	百	更	更	更		

BUILDING THIS KANJI
One (top of a bun) 一(3) + Sun 日(6) +
Piranha 乂 = 更

Meaning
This kanji conveys a sense of doing things anew, be it through revision, reform or renewal, amongst others. A secondary meaning (expressed with the less common **kun-yomi**) has to do with staying up late or the day growing late.

Remembering this kanji
The **tops of buns** baked ANEW when the **sun** rises, feeding those as hungry as **piranhas**. And so the day begins ANEW…

Common Pronunciations
Common **ON** reading: KŌ (コウ)
Common **kun** reading: sara (さら)

Less Common Pronunciations
Less common **ON** reading: none
Less common **kun** reading: **fu** (ふ)

COMMON WORDS AND COMPOUNDS		
更に	*anew; furthermore*	**sara**·ni さら・に
更生	anew + life = *rebirth; revival*	**KŌ**·SEI コウ・セイ
変更	alter + anew = *alteration; change*	HEN·**KŌ** ヘン・コウ

KANJI 374

SYSTEM

一	幺	幺	系	系	系	系		

BUILDING THIS KANJI
Comet 一 + Thread 糸(196) = 系

Meaning
System. As you can see from the final compounds below, this kanji also appears in words related to lineage and genealogy.

Remembering this kanji
I asked a **comet** if it was tough to **thread** its way through the space debris of a planetary SYSTEM like ours. "Of course it is," he said, "but what can you do? You can't fight the SYSTEM."

Common Pronunciations

Common **ON** reading: **KEI** (ケイ)
Common **kun** reading: none

Less Common Pronunciations

Less common **ON** reading: none
Less common **kun** reading: none

COMMON WORDS AND COMPOUNDS		
体系	body + system = *system*	**TAI·KEI** タイ・ケイ
系図	system + diagram = *family tree; genealogy*	**KEI·ZU** ケイ・ズ
日系	sun (Japan) + system = *of Japanese descent*	**NIK·KEI** ニッ・ケイ

KANJI 375

去　**DEPART**

BUILDING THIS KANJI
Earth 土(87) + Broken Crutch ム = 去

Meaning

Depart, leave.

Remembering this kanji

Covered in **earth**, the **broken crutch** looked up. "You must DEPART from me," it said. "I'm broken and can no longer do anything for you." It was a wrenching moment, but she realized the **broken crutch** was right. Placing the last of the **earth** over it, she turned to DEPART.

Common Pronunciations

Common **ON** reading: **KYO** (キョ)
Common **kun** reading: **sa** (さ)

Create your **on-yomi** keyword and enter it in the table at the back of the book. Then, after creating your **kun-yomi** keyword, write your sentence to remember the **on-yomi** and **kun-yomi** readings in the box below.

Less Common Pronunciations

Less common **ON** reading: **KO** (コ)
Less common **kun** reading: none

COMMON WORDS AND COMPOUNDS		
去る	*depart; leave*	**sa·ru** さ・る
去年	depart + year = *last year*	**KYO·NEN** キョ・ネン
飛び去る	fly + depart = *fly away*	**to·bi sa·ru** と・び さ・る

COMPONENT #376

BALLROOM DANCERS

Ensure that you can quickly spot the difference between this component and 开, the "picnic table" introduced prior to Entry 106.

KANJI 376

鼻　**NOSE**

BUILDING THIS KANJI
Self 自 (33) + Rice Field 田 (73) + Ballroom Dancers 廾 = 鼻

Meaning

Nose.

Remembering this kanji

"Wow, that guy has a pretty inflated sense of **self**, doesn't he? Look at his NOSE sticking up!"
"No, you're mistaken. He wants to figure out which **rice field** over there got a fresh load of manure; that's why his NOSE is up like that."
"Oh. Well, he still looks like a snooty **ballroom dancer** with his NOSE in the air."

Common Pronunciations

Common **ON** reading: none
Common **kun** reading: **hana** (は な)

Less Common Pronunciations

Less common **ON** reading: **BI** (ビ)
Less common **kun** reading: none

COMMON WORDS AND COMPOUNDS		
鼻	*nose*	**hana** は な
鼻歌	nose + song = *humming*	**hana·uta** は な・う た
鼻水	nose + water = *runny nose*	**hana·mizu** は な・み ず

KANJI 377

亜 ASIA

Meaning

This kanji can stand for Asia in the same way that 日 does for Japan and 中 does for China. In a few other compounds it can act like the English prefix 'sub-'. It's an uncommon character, however, and will prove more useful as a component.

Remembering this kanji

What does an overhead view of a train track have to do with ASIA? Well, the Trans-Siberian is mostly in ASIA isn't it? And Japan, also in ASIA, is famous for the bullet train.

Common Pronunciations

Common **ON** reading: **A** (ア)
Common **kun** reading: none

After creating your **on-yomi** keyword and entering it in the table at the back of the book, write your sentence to remember the **on-yomi** reading in the box below.

Less Common Pronunciations

Less common **ON** reading: none
Less common **kun** reading: none

COMMON WORDS AND COMPOUNDS		
東亜	east + Asia = *East Asia*	**TŌ·A** ト ウ・ア

KANJI 378

接 JOIN

BUILDING THIS KANJI
Finger 扌 + Stand 立(112) + Woman 女(16)
= 接

Meaning
Join, contact.

Remembering this kanji
"Let us **JOIN fingers** and **stand** up for our rights as one **woman**!" they cried. "**JOIN** us! **JOIN** us!"

Common Pronunciations
Common **ON** reading: **SETSU** (セツ)
Common **kun** reading: none

Less Common Pronunciations
Less common **ON** reading: none
Less common **kun** reading: none

	COMMON WORDS AND COMPOUNDS	
接続	join + continue = *joining; connection*	SETSU·ZOKU セツ·ゾク
接着	join + wear = *adhesion*	SET·CHAKU セッ·チャク
面接	mask + join = *interview*	MEN·SETSU メン·セツ

TELEVISION 兌 兌

KANJI 379

 OPINION

Remembering this kanji
They asked me to **say** something on **television**. So I did. Yeah, that's right, I gave them just what they wanted: my **OPINION**.

BUILDING THIS KANJI
Say 言 (80) + Television 兌 = 説

Meaning
Opinion, theory.

Common Pronunciations
Common **ON** reading: **SETSU** (セツ)
Common **kun** reading: none

Less Common Pronunciations
Less common **ON** reading: **ZEI** (ゼイ)
Less common **kun** reading: **to** (と)

	COMMON WORDS AND COMPOUNDS	
説明	opinion + bright = *explanation*	SETSU·MEI セツ·メイ
伝説	transmit + opinion = *legend*	DEN·SETSU デン·セツ
小説	small + opinion = *a novel*	SHŌ·SETSU ショウ·セツ

KANJI 380

 MAKE

BUILDING THIS KANJI
Giraffe 亻 + Koi Streamers 乍 = 作

Meaning
Make. A secondary meaning relates to crops and harvesting.

Remembering this kanji

Giraffes are clueless when it comes to **koi streamers**, so don't ask any of them to MAKE one. They can't MAKE the cloth, they can't MAKE the design…they can't even MAKE the wire frame! About the only thing they can MAKE is a giant mess with those clumsy hooves of theirs.

Common Pronunciations

Common **ON** reading: **SAKU** (サ ク); **SA** (サ)
Common **kun** reading: **tsuku** (つ く)

SAKU is by far the more commonly used of these readings. The **kun-yomi** is usually voiced outside of first position.

Create your **on-yomi** keyword for **SA** (サ) and enter it in the table at the back of the book. Then, after creating your **kun-yomi** keyword, write your sentence to remember the **on-yomi** and **kun-yomi** readings in the box below.

Less Common Pronunciations

Less common **ON** reading: none
Less common **kun** reading: none

COMMON WORDS AND COMPOUNDS		
作る	*make*	**tsuku·ru** つく·る
作者	make + individual = *author; writer*	**SAKU·SHA** サク·シャ
動作	move + make = *action; movement*	**DŌ·SA** ド ウ·サ

節 JOINT

ノ	┝	⺮	⺮	⺮	⺮	⺮	⺮	⺮
⺮	⺮	節	節					

BUILDING THIS KANJI
Machine Guns ⺮ + Immediate 即 (345) = 節

Meaning

This interesting character refers to a joint or a section of something. It is used in a variety of words, and can refer to everything from a 'joint' between seasons (the second common word provides an example), a knot in wood, or a melody in music, for instance. It can also convey a sense of moderation or economizing; think of this in terms of a narrowing joint that squeezes off the use of something such as a flow of money.

Remembering this kanji

The **machine guns** went off, and my reaction was **immediate**: they're aiming for my JOINT!

Common Pronunciations

Common **ON** reading: **SETSU** (セ ツ)
Common **kun** reading: **fushi** (ふ し)

Less Common Pronunciations

Less common **ON** reading: **SECHI** (セ チ)
Less common **kun** reading: none

COMMON WORDS AND COMPOUNDS		
節	*joint; melody; knot*	**fushi** ふし
節分	joint + part = *last day of winter*	**SETSU·BUN** セ ツ·ブ ン
調節	tone + joint = *adjustment; regulaton*	**CHŌ·SETSU** チ ョ ウ·セ ツ

KANJI 382

則 RULE

1	冂	冃	月	目	貝	貝	則	則

BUILDING THIS KANJI
Shellfish 貝 (21) + Chisel 刂 = 則

Meaning
Rule, in the sense of a law or regulation.

Remembering this kanji
Be careful! There's a very important RULE to remember when prying apart **shellfish** with a **chisel**. Unfortunately, though, I have a RULE not to tell that RULE to anyone.

Common Pronunciations
Common **ON** reading: **SOKU** (ソ ク)
Common **kun** reading: none

Less Common Pronunciations
Less common **ON** reading: none
Less common **kun** reading: none

COMMON WORDS AND COMPOUNDS		
定則	fixed + rule = *established rule*	TEI·SOKU テイ・ソク
原則	original + rule = *principle; general rule*	GEN·SOKU ゲン・ソク
法則	law + rule = *rule; law*	HŌ·SOKU ホウ・ソク

COMPONENT #383

ELBOW

KANJI 383

今 NOW

ノ	人	今	今				

BUILDING THIS KANJI
Umbrella 人 + One (hamburger patty) 一 (3) + Elbow コ = 今

Meaning
Now.

Remembering this kanji
Even though I was hidden by the **umbrella**, I grew nervous when the **hamburger patty** was placed on my **elbow**. "Get it off me," I was soon pleading, "NOW!" They remained calm, however, and only smiled. "NOW, NOW," one of them said, "don't be like that."

Common Pronunciations
Common **ON** reading: **KON** (コン)
Common **kun** reading: **ima** (いま)

Less Common Pronunciations
Less common **ON** reading: **KIN** (キン)
Less common **kun** reading: none

IRREGULAR READING		
今日	now + sun (day) = *today*	kyō きょう
今朝	now + morning = *this morning*	kesa けさ
今年	now + year = *this year*	ko·toshi こ・とし

We met the first two of these compounds in Entries 6 and 85, as the readings of both kanji were irregular. The third we encounter here, as **toshi** is the normal **kun-yomi** for 年. Also note how the addition of the **hiragana** は in the second example below (which creates the most famous of all Japanese greetings) can change the readings of both kanji from the first example above.

COMMON WORDS AND COMPOUNDS		
今	*now*	**ima** いま
今日は	now + sun (day) = *Good morning / afternoon; Hello!*	**KON·NICHI-wa** コン・ニチ・は
今週	now + week = *this week*	**KON·SHŪ** コン・シュ ウ

KANJI 384

永 **ETERNAL**

`	丿	刁	永	永			

BUILDING THIS KANJI
Jelly Bean ヽ + Water 水(61) = 永

Meaning

Eternal, forever. Much as we did for 未 and 末 (Entries 276 and 277), we will learn this and the next entry as a pair in order to solidify the differences between these easily confused kanji. Refer back to the kanji for "water" (Entry 61) in order to see how the "harpoon" component of that character has become transformed in this one.

Remembering this kanji

How long do you suppose it would take for a **jelly bean** dropping onto the kanji for "**water**" to turn its harpoon into a crane? It's tough to imagine, isn't it? Obviously we're dealing with something ETERNAL here.

Common Pronunciations

Common **ON** reading: **EI** (エ イ)
Common **kun** reading: **naga** (な が)

Less Common Pronunciations

Less common **ON** reading: none
Less common **kun** reading: none

COMMON WORDS AND COMPOUNDS		
永い	*long (in terms of time)*	**naga·i** な が·い
永遠	eternal + far = *eternity*	**EI·EN** エ イ·エ ン

KANJI 385

氷 **ICE**

丿	丶	刁	氷	氷			

BUILDING THIS KANJI
Water 水(61) + Jelly Bean ヽ = 氷

Meaning

Ice. As you can see, this kanji is very similar visually to 永. The only other thing to keep in mind here is that the stroke order of the 'water' component is broken—the jelly bean is written immediately after the initial harpoon stroke.

Remembering this kanji
…stuck on the **water**…hungry…shivering…

"I'm going to get that **jelly bean** floating over there," he told her in a daze.

She barely kept him from jumping out of their dinghy into the frigid **water**. "That's not a **jelly bean**," she said desperately. "It's not. It's ICE. Nothing but ICE."

Common Pronunciations
Common **ON** reading: **HYŌ** (ヒョウ)
Common **kun** reading: **kōri** (こおり)

Less Common Pronunciations
Less common **ON** reading: none
Less common **kun** reading: none

COMMON WORDS AND COMPOUNDS		
氷	*ice*	kōri こおり
氷山	ice + mountain = *iceberg*	HYŌ·ZAN ヒョウ·ザン
氷結	ice + bind = *freeze over*	HYŌ·KETSU ヒョウ·ケツ

CHAPTER 17 REVIEW EXERCISES

A. Please match the following kanji to their meanings.

1.	薬	a.	Nose
2.	氷	b.	Medicine
3.	永	c.	Long ago
4.	教	d.	Hard
5.	系	e.	Try
6.	昔	f.	Eternal
7.	接	g.	Teach
8.	固	h.	Ice
9.	試	i.	Join
10.	鼻	j.	System

B. Please match the following meanings to their kanji, and these to their **on-** or **kun-yomi**.

1.	Face	a. 亜	1.	**REI** (レイ)
2.	Asia	b. 今	2.	**SEN** (セン)
3.	Now	c. 去	3.	**yado** (やど)
4.	Line	d. 顔	4.	**ZOKU** (ゾク)
5.	Cool	e. 線	5.	**sa** (さ)
6.	Opinion	f. 説	6.	**SETSU** (セツ)
7.	Depart	g. 族	7.	**fushi** (ふし)
8.	Lodging	h. 節	8.	**A** (ア)
9.	Joint	i. 宿	9.	**ima** (いま)
	(**kun-yomi**)			
10.	Tribe	j. 冷	10.	**kao** (かお)

C. Please choose the best answer(s) to the following questions.

1. Which of the following readings apply to the kanji 作?
   a. **tsu** (つ)
   b. **SEI** (セイ)
   c. **SA** (サ)
   d. **tsuku** (つく)
   e. **SAKU** (サク)

2. Which is the correct reading of 固い?
   a. **ama·i** (あま·い)
   b. **kata·i** (かた·い)
   c. **kita·i** (きた·い)
   d. **kota·i** (こた·い)

3. Which of the following kanji has the most number of strokes?
   a. 接   b. 族   c. 試   d. 宿   e. 教

4. You're darn right it hurt. I got hit smack on the _____ .
   a. 氷   b. 鼻   c. 薬   d. 丙   e. 則

5. Which is the correct reading of 冷たい?
   a. **mika·tai** (みか・たい)
   b. **kami·tai** (かみ・たい)
   c. **tsume·tai** (つめ・たい)
   d. **hari·tai** (はり・たい)

D. Please match the following compounds to their meanings and pronunciations.

1. 民族　a. Adhesion　1. **MIN·ZOKU** (ミン・ゾク)

2. 今週　b. This week　2. **TEI·SOKU** (テイ・ソク)

3. 試合　c. Game / Match　3. **KŌ·SEI** (コウ・セイ)

4. 接着　d. Established rule　4. **SHI·ai** (シ・あい)

5. 薬局　e. Humming　5. **SET·CHAKU** (セッ・チャク)

6. 昔話　f. Old story / Folklore　6. **hana·uta** (はな・うた)

7. 永遠　g. Race / A people　7. **EI·EN** (エイ・エン)

8. 鼻歌　h. Rebirth / Revival　8. **YAK·KYOKU** (ヤッ・キョク)

9. 更生　i. Pharmacy　9. **KON·SHŪ** (コン・シュウ)

10. 定則　j. Eternity　10. **mukashi· banashi** (むかし・ばなし)

E. Please read the passage below and answer the questions that follow.

今日は冷たい雨が降った。私の小さい家の上に黒い鳥が集まった。晩秋だ。今年も一人です。

1. What happened today?
2. What time of year is it?
3. Do I have a spacious house?
4. What has happened above my house?
5. Am I surrounded by friends this year?

Kanji #386—410

KANJI 386

 LAW

`丶 氵 汁 汁 汁 注 法 法`

BUILDING THIS KANJI
Splash 氵 + Depart 去(375) = 法

Meaning
Law, method. A religious meaning (particularly Buddhist) is also conveyed in some specialized compounds that include this kanji.

Remembering this kanji
"I can't believe you'd just **splash** someone like that and **depart**!" he exclaimed. "Don't you realize you broke the **LAW**!?"

Common Pronunciations
Common **ON** reading: **HŌ** (ホ ウ)
Common **kun** reading: none

Less Common Pronunciations
Less common **ON** reading: **HA-** (ハ ッ);
HO- (ホ ッ)
Less common **kun** reading: none

As we saw in the less common **on-yomi** for 合 back in Entry 250 [**GA-** (ガ ッ) and **KA-** (カ ッ)], these two readings always "double up" with the **on-yomi** of the kanji that follow. The compounds in which they appear are obscure.

	COMMON WORDS AND COMPOUNDS	
方法	direction + law = *method; way*	HO·**HŌ** ホ ウ·ホ ウ
文法	literature + law = *grammar*	BUN·**PŌ** ブ ン·ポ ウ
立法	stand + law = *legislation; law making*	RIP·**PŌ** リ ッ·ポ ウ

COMPONENT #387

DRAGON

`一 十 土 圹 圻 坍 坍 坍 埕`
`場 場 場`

BUILDING THIS KANJI
Earth 土(87) + Sun 日(6) + Dragon 㿟 = 場

Meaning
A place.

KANJI 387

 PLACE

Remembering this kanji

I grabbed a handful of crumbly **earth** and squinted up at the **sun** as the **dragon** landed nearby. "What is this terrible PLACE?" I asked. "How can you not recognize it?" she said. "It's the PLACE you have always wished to be."

Common Pronunciations

Common **ON** reading: **JŌ** (ジ ョ ウ)
Common **kun** reading: **ba** (ば)

As both readings are used extensively, compounds containing this kanji need to be learned on a word by word basis. You may find it useful to employ the same strategy that was suggested for the **on-yomi** of 所 back in Entry 242. Note the mix of **on-** and **kun-yomi** in the second example below, a very common word.

Less Common Pronunciations

Less common **ON** reading: none
Less common **kun** reading: none

COMMON WORDS AND COMPOUNDS		
工場	craft + place = *factory; plant*	**KŌ·JŌ** コウ・ジョウ
場所	place + location = *place; location*	**ba·SHO** ば・ショ
場合	place + match = *circumstances; situation*	**ba·ai** ば・あい

科 **COURSE**

BUILDING THIS KANJI
Crops 禾 + Dipper 斗 (278) = 科

Meaning

Course (of study), as well as other ideas largely related to scholarly matters. This character is used to denote the departments and faculties of educational institutions, for example.

Remembering this kanji

"You obviously care a lot about **crops**, so take a farming COURSE."
"Yeah, but what about this **dipper** I've got?"
"Well, look at this COURSE: 'Crop harvesting with a **dipper**'."
"Hey, that does seem like an interesting COURSE!"

Common Pronunciations

Common **ON** reading: **KA** (カ)
Common **kun** reading: none

Less Common Pronunciations

Less common **ON** reading: none
Less common **kun** reading: none

COMMON WORDS AND COMPOUNDS		
科学	course + study = *science*	**KA·GAKU** カ・ガク
科目	course + eye = *academic subject; course*	**KA·MOKU** カ・モク
教科書	teach + course + write = *textbook*	**KYŌ·KA·SHO** キョウ・カ・ショ

KANJI 389

 YOUNGER BROTHER

BUILDING THIS KANJI
Rabbit ` ´ + Mourn 弔 (228) + Comet 一
= 弟

Meaning
Younger brother. This kanji can also refer to the disciples or pupils of an accomplished master. Ensure that you can easily see the difference between this character and 第 ("No.", from Entry 243).

Remembering this kanji
So my YOUNGER BROTHER had this pet **rabbit** that ended up dying on him, and geez did he ever **mourn**. So we got him a **comet** to cheer him up, but he just kept on **mourning** for that silly **rabbit**. I mean, the **comet** took him to other planets and he still wasn't happy! I'm starting to wonder if my YOUNGER BROTHER'S a bit spoiled.

Common Pronunciations
Common **ON** reading: none
Common **kun** reading: **otōto** (おとうと)

Less Common Pronunciations
Less common **ON** reading: **TEI** (テイ);
DAI (ダイ); **DE** (デ)
Less common **kun** reading: none

Interestingly, the last two **on-yomi** appear in only one word each, although the words themselves are commonly used. The first is 兄弟 (KYŌ·DAI / キョウ·ダイ) 'brothers (as well as sisters)' from the kanji 'elder brother' and 'younger brother'. This is the only compound, incidentally, in which 兄 is read with it's less common **on-yomi** of KYŌ. The only word in which 弟 is read with DE is 弟子 (**DE**·SHI / デ·シ) 'disciple; pupil', from the kanji 'younger brother' and 'child'.

COMMON WORDS AND COMPOUNDS		
弟	= younger brother	**otōto** おとうと

COMPONENT #390

LONG-TAILED BUTTERFLY

KANJI 390

 MANNER

BUILDING THIS KANJI
Tree 木 (13) + Rabbit ` ´ + Three (full hamburger) 三 (5) + Long-tailed Butterfly 氺
= 様

Meaning
Manner, way. When following a family name, this kanji acts as a very polite form of 'Mr.', 'Mrs.', or 'Miss'.

Remembering this kanji
Beside a **tree**—growing in a gnarled **MANNER**—is a **rabbit** sitting over a **full hamburger**. Yet it is interested only in the lettuce, and chews this in a halting **MANNER**. Until, that is, it is startled by the tail of a **long-tailed butterfly's** fluttery **MANNER**…

Common Pronunciations

Common **ON** reading: **YŌ** (ヨ ウ)
Common **kun** reading: **sama** (さ ま)

The **kun-yomi** is the reading used to convey the polite form of 'Mr.', 'Mrs.' or 'Miss' mentioned above: 山本様 (yama·moto·**sama** / や ま·も と·さ ま), 'Mr. / Mrs. / Miss Yamamoto', for example.

Less Common Pronunciations

Less common **ON** readings: none
Less common **kun** reading: none

	COMMON WORDS AND COMPOUNDS		
皆様	all + manner = *Ladies and Gentlemen!*; *all (of you)*	mina·**sama** みな·さ ま
神様	God + manner = *God; god*	kami·**sama** か み·さ ま
様式	manner + type = *mode; form*	**YŌ**·SHIKI ヨ ウ·シ キ

KANJI 391

虫 **INSECT**

丶	一	口	中	虫	虫			

Meaning

Insect. No story required. Take note that the long vertical line is not combined into a single stroke with the horizontal line at the bottom when writing this kanji; there are thus six strokes to the character here, not five.

Common Pronunciations

Common **ON** reading: **CHŪ** (チ ュ ウ)
Common **kun** reading: **mushi** (む し)

The **kun-yomi** is the more common reading.

Less Common Pronunciations

Less common **ON** reading: none
Less common **kun** reading: none

	COMMON WORDS AND COMPOUNDS	
虫	*insect; bug*	**mushi** む し
泣き虫	cry + insect = *crybaby*	na·ki **mushi** な·き む し
成虫	become + insect = *adult insect*	SEI·**CHŪ** セ イ·チ ュ ウ

KANJI 392

駅 **STATION**

l	厂	Ｆ	Ｆ	馬	馬	馬	馬	馬
馬	馬	馬	駅	駅				

BUILDING THIS KANJI
Horse 馬(144) + Measurement 尺(332) = 駅

Meaning

Train station.

Remembering this kanji

"Forelock…mane… Ma'am, will you please keep your **horse** still so that I can take the **measurements**?"

"Look, I don't even understand what the heck you're doing!"

"Hey, you're the one who pulled into a **horse measurement STATION**."

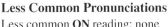

Common Pronunciations
Common **ON** reading: **EKI** (エキ)
Common **kun** reading: none

Note the mix of **on** and **kun-yom**i in the second example.

Create your **on-yomi** keyword and enter it in the table at the back of the book. After that, write your sentence to remember the **on-yom**i reading in the box below.

Less Common Pronunciations
Less common **ON** reading: none
Less common **kun** reading: none

COMMON WORDS AND COMPOUNDS		
駅	*train station*	**EKI** エキ
駅前	station + before = *in front of the station*	**EKI**·mae エキ・まえ
駅伝	station + transmit = *long-distance relay race*	**EKI**·DEN エキ・デン

DIAMOND RING 冋

商 COMMERCE

'	一	亠	产	产	冋	产	商	商
商	商							

BUILDING THIS KANJI
Diamond Ring 冋 + Ballet 儿 + Mouth
(vampire) 口 (8) = 商

Meaning
Commerce, trade.

Remembering this kanji
Dracula flashed a **diamond ring**, and the **ballet dancer** came closer. "It goes with your tutu," said the **vampire**, "and it's yours for this cheap introductory price."
"Oh," she replied, "I didn't realize you were so into COMMERCE."
"You'd be surprised," he said. "What with rent and the cost of coffins, I'd be crazy not to be doing at least some COMMERCE."

Common Pronunciations
Common **ON** reading: **SHŌ** (ショウ)
Common **kun** reading: none

Less Common Pronunciations
Less common **ON** reading: none
Less common **kun** reading: akina (あきな)

COMMON WORDS AND COMPOUNDS		
商人	commerce + person = *merchant; dealer*	**SHŌ**·NIN ショウ・ニン
商売	commerce + sell = *commerce; trade*	**SHŌ**·BAI ショウ・バイ
商店	commerce + shop = *shop; store*	**SHŌ**·TEN ショウ・テン

KANJI 394

 BAD

| 一 | 厂 | 戸 | 戸 | 甲 | 甲 | 亜 | 亜 | 悪 |
| 悪 | 悪 | | | | | | | |

BUILDING THIS KANJI
Asia 亜(377) + Heart 心(25) = 悪

Meaning
Bad, wrong, inferior...this kanji is bad news all around.

Remembering this kanji
Imagine the entire continent of **Asia** weighing down on your **heart**. That would be pretty BAD.

Common Pronunciations
Common **ON** reading: **AKU** (アク)
Common **kun** reading: **waru** (わる)

Create your **on-yomi** keyword and enter it in the table at the back of the book. Then, after creating your **kun-yomi** keyword, write your sentence to remember the **on-yomi** and **kun-yomi** readings in the box below.

Less Common Pronunciations
Less common **ON** reading: **O** (オ)
Less common **kun** reading: none

COMMON WORDS AND COMPOUNDS		
悪い	bad	**waru**·i わる·い
最悪	most + bad = *worst*	**SAI**·**AKU** サイ·アク
悪意	bad + mind = *evil intention*	**AKU**·I アク·イ

KANJI 395

 KNOW

| ノ | ト | 匕 | 仁 | 矢 | 矢 | 知 | 知 |

BUILDING THIS KANJI
Arrow 矢(285) + Mouth (vampire) 口(8) = 知

Meaning
Know, information.

Remembering this kanji
Oh yeah? Well, I'll bet you didn't KNOW that an **arrow** is useless on a **vampire**, did you? Oh, you *did* KNOW. Hmm, I wonder why I didn't KNOW that...

Common Pronunciations
Common **ON** reading: **CHI** (チ)
Common **kun** reading: **shi** (し)

Less Common Pronunciations
Less common **ON** reading: none
Less common **kun** reading: none

COMMON WORDS AND COMPOUNDS		
知る	*know*	**shi**·ru し·る
知らせ	*notice; information*	**shi**·rase し·らせ
知人	know + person = *acquaintance*	**CHI**·JIN チ·ジン

KANJI 396

借 **BORROW**

ノ	亻	亠	什	仕	什	借	借	借
借								

BUILDING THIS KANJI
Giraffe 亻 + Long Ago 昔 (363) = 借

Meaning
Borrow.

Remembering this kanji
"That **giraffe** really bugs me."
"Why's that?"
"Oh, it's something that happened **long ago**."
"Allow me to guess: you let it **BORROW** some of your stuff and you didn't get it back."
"Yeah, that's right! Did it **BORROW** something from you as well?"
"My tennis racket. I learned **long ago** that a **giraffe** will **BORROW** anything."

Common Pronunciations
Common **ON** reading: **SHAKU** (シャク)
Common **kun** reading: **ka** (か)

As you can see by the second example, this is another of those kanji whose verb form can incorporate its **hiragana** ending when forming nouns.

Less Common Pronunciations
Less common **ON** reading: none
Less common **kun** reading: none

COMMON WORDS AND COMPOUNDS		
借りる	*borrow*	**ka·riru** か・りる
借手	borrow + hand = *borrower*	**kari·te** かり・て
借金	borrow + gold (money) = *loan; a debt*	**SHAK·KIN** シャッ・キン

COMPONENT #397

PERISCOPE

KANJI 397

決 **DECIDE**

`	丶	氵	汀	江	汁	決		

BUILDING THIS KANJI
Splash 氵 + Periscope ユ + Person 人 (2) = 決

Meaning
Decide.

Remembering this kanji

I looked up when hit by the **splash** and found myself right in front of a **periscope**. A **person** appeared moments later. "Are you crazy?!" he yelled. "What the heck made you DECIDE to snorkel through a naval base?"

Common Pronunciations

Common **ON** reading: **KETSU** (ケ ツ)
Common **kun** reading: **ki** (き)

Less Common Pronunciations

Less common **ON** reading: none
Less common **kun** reading: none

COMMON WORDS AND COMPOUNDS		
決まる (intr)	*to be decided / settled*	**ki**·maru き・まる
決める (tr)	*to decide / settle*	**ki**·meru き・める
決心	decide + heart = *determination; resolution*	**KES**·**SHIN** ケッ・シン

KANJI 398

区 **PARTITION**

BUILDING THIS KANJI
Magnet 匚 + Banana Peels メ = 区

Meaning

Partition, division. This character is used to indicate zones or areas. You will often see this kanji in mailing addresses, as it's used to denote a ward or district of a city; the final compound below, a famous area of Tokyo, offers an example.

Remembering this kanji

A **magnet** would only be OK as a PARTITION, as anything not magnetic could get through it. **Banana peels** would do a better job, as they're slippery and would discourage crossings. So why, then, doesn't someone invent a **magnet** made of **banana peels**? I mean, that would obviously be the best PARTITION ever, wouldn't it?

Common Pronunciations

Common **ON** reading: **KU** (ク)
Common **kun** reading: none

Less Common Pronunciations

Less common **ON** reading: none
Less common **kun** reading: none

COMMON WORDS AND COMPOUNDS		
区分	partition + part = *partition; division*	**KU**·**BUN** ク・ブン
区別	partition + different = *distinction; difference*	**KU**·**BETSU** ク・ベツ
新宿区	new + lodging + partition = *Shinjuku ward (in Tokyo)*	**SHIN**·**JUKU**·**KU** シン・ジュク・ク

KANJI 399

発 DISCHARGE

BUILDING THIS KANJI
Shark Attack 𛰝 + Picnic Table 开 = 発

Meaning
Discharge, break out.

Remembering this kanji
It's necessary here to DISCHARGE an unusual fact: this is the only time the '**picnic table**' component will appear with both its legs broken (although this entire character does figure as part of another more complex kanji). That it should look like this is hardly surprising, as there's an enormous DISCHARGE of energy whenever a **shark attack** occurs on a **picnic table**.

Common Pronunciations
Common **ON** reading: **HATSU** (ハツ)
Common **kun** reading: none

Create your **on-yomi** keyword and enter it in the table at the back of the book. After that, write your sentence to remember the **on-yomi** reading in the box below.

Less Common Pronunciations
Less common **ON** reading: **HOTSU** (ホツ)
Less common **kun** reading: none

COMMON WORDS AND COMPOUNDS		
発音	discharge + sound = *pronunciation*	**HATSU·ON** ハツ·オン
出発	exit + discharge = *departure*	**SHUP·PATSU** シュッ·パツ
新発売	new + discharge + sell = *"Now on Sale"*	**SHIN·HATSU·BAI** シン·ハツ·バイ

COMPONENT #400

KILLER BEE   戈

The addition of another stroke gives us the third member of our special component family, following 七 'ghost', and 弋 'spilling coffee'. Remember that anything appearing underneath the horizontal line (the next entry provides an example), is always written immediately after it, interrupting the stroke order of this component.

KANJI 400

幺幺 HOW MANY

BUILDING THIS KANJI
Frustration 幺 + Frustration 幺 + Killer Bee 戈 + Person 人(2) = 幾

Meaning
How many, how much. Another meaning is conveyed when this character precedes a 'number' kanji (as in the final example); in these cases the character means 'some' or 'several'. Take care with the stroke order of this kanji, remembering that 'person' is written immediately after the horizontal line of the killer bee component. And don't forget that bee!

Remembering this kanji

Oh, **frustration** upon **frustration**. That's right, *double* **frustration**! HOW MANY instances must there be of a **killer bee** scaring a **person**? I ask you: HOW MANY must flee from HOW MANY **killer bees**?

Common Pronunciations

Common **ON** reading: none
Common **kun** reading: **iku** (い く)

Less Common Pronunciations

Less common **ON** reading: **KI** (キ)
Less common **kun** reading: none

You are only likely to meet this reading in one compound: 幾何学 (**KI·KA·GAKU** / キ・カ・ガク) 'geometry', from the kanji 'how many', 'what', and 'study'.

COMMON WORDS AND COMPOUNDS		
幾つ	*how many; how much*	**iku·tsu** い く・つ
幾ら	*how much*	**iku·ra** い く・ら
幾百	how many + hundred = *some / several hundreds*	**iku·HYAKU** い く・ヒャク

室 **ROOM**

BUILDING THIS KANJI
Pincers 宀 + Reach 至 (239) = 室

Meaning

Room, chamber. As they're visually similar, make sure not to confuse this character with 屋, the kanji for 'roof' we learned back in Entry 281.

Remembering this kanji

"What are you doing in this ROOM?"
"Don't you remember? This was the only ROOM the **pincers** couldn't **reach** me."
"Oh, so this is the ROOM!"
"Yes. I'm only alive today because I was able to **reach** this ROOM."

Common Pronunciations

Common **ON** reading: **SHITSU** (シツ)
Common **kun** reading: none

Less Common Pronunciations

Less common **ON** reading: none
Less common **kun** reading: **muro** (むろ)

COMMON WORDS AND COMPOUNDS		
室内	room + inside = *indoor(s)*	**SHITSU·NAI** シツ・ナイ
室外	room + outside = *outdoor(s)*	**SHITSU·GAI** シツ・ガイ
温室	warm + room = *hothouse; greenhouse*	**ON·SHITSU** オン・シツ

KANJI 402

 FALL

一	⺡	⺿	⺿	⺿	艻	艿	茨	茨
茨	落	落						

BUILDING THIS KANJI

Wreath ⺿ + Splash ⺡ + Each 各 (282) = 落

Meaning
Fall, fail.

Remembering this kanji
"How could you not have realized that the **wreath** needed care? Did I not tell you to **splash** it **each** day, **each** of you, so that the petals and leaves would not FALL off? But you didn't, and so they did FALL… Oh, the lot of you should FALL to your knees!"

Common Pronunciations
Common **ON** reading: **RAKU** (ラ ク)
Common **kun** reading: **o** (お)

The verbs in the first and second examples below can sometimes absorb their **hiragana** endings when forming words with other kanji.

Less Common Pronunciations
Less common **ON** reading: none
Less common **kun** reading: none

COMMON WORDS AND COMPOUNDS		
落ちる (intr)	*to fall*	o·chiru お・ち る
落とす (tr)	*to let fall / drop*	o·tosu お・と す
急落	hasten + fall = *sudden drop/decline*	KYŪ·**RAKU** キュ ウ・ラ ク

KANJI 403

 FAST

一	⼀	⼁	三	申	束	束	束	涑
速								

BUILDING THIS KANJI

Bundle 束 (356) + Seal ⻌ = 速

Meaning
Fast, in terms of speed and movement. Recall that 早 ("early", Entry 29) is more concerned with the idea of "fast" in terms of time.

Remembering this kanji
"Look kid, if you're gonna **bundle** up a **seal** at this rodeo, you'd better be FAST. 'Cause believe you me, when they get those flippers flappin', they're FAST."

Common Pronunciations
Common **ON** reading: **SOKU** (ソ ク)
Common **kun** reading: **haya** (は や)

Less Common Pronunciations
Less common **ON** reading: none
Less common **kun** reading: **sumi** (す み)

COMMON WORDS AND COMPOUNDS		
速い	*fast*	**haya**·i は や・い
高速	tall + fast = *high-speed*	**KŌ·SOKU** コ ウ・ソ ク
速度	fast + degree = *speed*	**SOKU·DO** ソ ク・ド

COMPONENT #404

SHOPPING CART

KANJI 404

色 COLOR

BUILDING THIS KANJI
Little Red Riding Hood 勹 + Shopping Cart
巴 = 色

Meaning
Color. Interestingly, this kanji also conveys a decidedly erotic meaning to many compounds in which it appears (as it does in the second example below).

Remembering this kanji
"Hello, I'm **Little Red Riding Hood**, and I've got a **shopping cart**! Isn't it a nice COLOR?"
"First of all, miss, **Little Red Riding Hood** would have a basket, not a **shopping cart**. But even if she had one it wouldn't be purple; didn't anyone tell you she's only into one COLOR?"

Common Pronunciations
Common **ON** reading: **SHOKU** (ショク)
Common **kun** reading: **iro** (いろ)

Both these readings are used frequently in compounds, although **iro** is more common in the first position and **SHOKU** more common in the second and third.

Less Common Pronunciations
Less common **ON** reading: **SHIKI** (シキ)
Less common **kun** reading: none

COMMON WORDS AND COMPOUNDS		
色	color	**iro** いろ
色目	color + eye = *amorous glance*	**iro·me** いろ・め
原色	original + color = *primary color*	**GEN·SHOKU** ゲン・ショク

KANJI 405

始 START

BUILDING THIS KANJI
Woman 女 (16) + Platform 台 (264) = 始

Meaning
Start.

Remembering this kanji
"Look, there's a **woman** on the **platform**."
"That means they're ready to START."
"Why's that?"
"Because it's the starter's **platform**. In a moment she'll call out 'START your engines'."

Common Pronunciations

Common **ON** reading: **SHI** (シ)
Common **kun** reading: **haji** (はじ)

Less Common Pronunciations

Less common **ON** reading: none
Less common **kun** reading: none

COMMON WORDS AND COMPOUNDS		
始まる (intr)	to start	**haji**·maru はじ·まる
始める (tr)	to start (something)	**haji**·meru はじ·める
原始	original + start = primitive	GEN·**SHI** ゲン·シ

是 APPROVE

丿	冂	日	日	日	旦	早	문	是	是

BUILDING THIS KANJI
Sun 日 (6) + Surfer 疋 = 是

Meaning

Approve, to be right.

Remembering this kanji

The **sun** looked down on a **surfer**. "I APPROVE of how you're surfing," it said.
"Well yeah," said the **surfer**. "I APPROVE of your approval."

Common Pronunciations

Common **ON** reading: **ZE** (ゼ)
Common **kun** reading: none

Create your **on-yomi** keyword and enter it in the table at the back of the book. After that, write your sentence to remember the **on-yomi** reading in the box below.

Less Common Pronunciations

Less common **ON** reading: none
Less common **kun** reading: none

COMMON WORDS AND COMPOUNDS		
是非	approve + un- = by any means; without fail	**ZE**·HI ゼ·ヒ

直 STRAIGHT

一	十	十	古	市	直	直	直

BUILDING THIS KANJI
Ten (scarecrow) 十 (28) + Eye (cyclops) 目 (15) + Forklift ∟ = 直

Meaning

Straight, direct, at once. By extension comes the idea of things being correct or corrected (best illustrated by the intransitive/transitive verb pair below). An important aspect of these two verbs can be seen when they attach to the end of other kanji as a suffix (as in the third example). In such cases, this character gives the compound a sense of 'redoing' whatever the first kanji represents. Ensure that you can clearly see the difference between this kanji and 真 ('true', from Entry 358).

Remembering this kanji

If there's a **scarecrow** on top of a **Cyclops**, the only way you can lift them with a **forklift** is if they pose as STRAIGHT as the **forklift**. The **Cyclops** in this illustration is obviously keeping as STRAIGHT as he can, and the **scarecrow** is balancing with his arms out STRAIGHT.

Common Pronunciations

Common **ON** reading: **CHOKU** (チ ョ ク)
Common **kun** reading: **nao** (な お)

Create your **on-yomi** keyword and enter it in the table at the back of the book. Then, after creating your **kun-yomi** keyword, write your sentence to remember the **on-yomi** and **kun-yomi** readings in the box below.

Less Common Pronunciations

Less common **ON** reading: **JIKI** (ジ キ)
Less common **kun** reading: **tada** (た だ)

You will encounter the **kun-yomi** in only one word: 直ちに (**tada**·chi ni / た だ・ち に) 'immediately, at once'.

COMMON WORDS AND COMPOUNDS		
直る (intr)	to be corrected / repaired	**nao·ru** な お・る
直す (tr)	to correct / repair / fix	**nao·su** な お・す
書き 直す	write + straight = rewrite; write again	ka·ki **nao·su** か・き な お・す
直線	straight + line = straight line	**CHOKU·SEN** チ ョ ク・セ ン

COMPONENT #408

LEMMINGS

Lemmings jumping off a cliff. This component usually appears in characters whose meaning has some connection to illness or disease.

KANJI 408

病 **ILLNESS**

BUILDING THIS KANJI
Lemmings 疒 + **Third** 丙 (370) = 病

Meaning

Illness, disease.

Remembering this kanji

If you couldn't tell from the couple of **lemmings** in the illustration who have already gone over, it should be obvious looking at the **third** who's about to: these are creatures with an ILLNESS.

Common Pronunciations

Common **ON** reading: **BYŌ** (ビ ョ ウ)
Common **kun** reading: none

Note that the final compound below uses the less common **on-yomi** for 持.

Less Common Pronunciations
Less common **ON** reading: **HEI** (ヘイ)
Less common **kun** reading: **ya** (や);
yamai (やまい)

COMMON WORDS AND COMPOUNDS		
病気	illness + spirit = *illness*	**BYŌ·KI** ビョウ·キ
病院	illness + institution = *hospital*	**BYŌ·IN** ビョウ·イン
持病	hold + illness = *chronic disease*	**JI·BYŌ** ジ·ビョウ

KANJI 409

共 **TOGETHER**

BUILDING THIS KANJI
Chimney 土 + Eight (volcano) 八(19) = 共

Meaning
Together.

Remembering this kanji
Have you ever noticed that **chimneys** and **volcanoes** are linked TOGETHER? Well they are, because a volcano is simply a **chimney** for a planet. So it's only right that they should be thought of TOGETHER.

Common Pronunciations
Common **ON** reading: **KYŌ** (キョウ)
Common **kun** reading: **tomo** (とも)

Less Common Pronunciations
Less common **ON** reading: none
Less common **kun** reading: none

COMMON WORDS AND COMPOUNDS		
共	*together*	**tomo** とも
共同	together + same = *cooperation; collaboration*	**KYŌ·DŌ** キョウ·ドウ
共和国	together + harmony + country = *republic*	**KYŌ·WA·KOKU** キョウ·ワ·コク

KANJI 410

願 **DESIRE**

BUILDING THIS KANJI
Original 原(349) + Guy Wearing a Barrel 頁
= 願

Meaning

Desire, petition. This character carries a polite tone of entreaty.

Common Pronunciations

Common **ON** reading: **GAN** (ガン)
Common **kun** reading: **nega** (ねが)

Less Common Pronunciations

Less common **ON** reading: none
Less common **kun** reading: none

Remembering this kanji

"We've been told that you're the **original guy wearing a barrel**. We DESIRE to ask you something."

"Oh really? Well, *my* DESIRE is to put on something other than a ridiculous looking barrel; this outfit could only appeal to someone with a DESIRE to get slivers."

COMMON WORDS AND COMPOUNDS		
願う	*desire; request politely*	**nega**·u ねが・う
お願い します	*please*	o **nega**·i shimasu お ねが・い します
願書	*desire + write = written application / request*	**GAN**·SHO ガン・ショ

CHAPTER 18 REVIEW EXERCISES

A. Please match the following kanji to their meanings.

1. 落	a. Straight
2. 病	b. Desire
3. 虫	c. Law
4. 科	d. Know
5. 法	e. Fall
6. 知	f. Illness
7. 発	g. Decide
8. 直	h. Course
9. 願	i. Discharge
10. 決	j. Insect

B. Please match the following meanings to their kanji, and these to their **on-** or **kun-yomi**.

1. Place	a. 弟	1. **iku** (い く)
2. Partition	b. 速	2. **haya** (は や)
3. Station	c. 場	3. **SHITSU** (シ ツ)
4. Younger brother	d. 共	4. **EKI** (エ キ)
5. Fast	e. 幾	5. **KU** (ク)

6. How many	f. 様	6. **KYŌ** (キョウ)
7. Manner	g. 駅	7. **haji** (は じ)
8. Start	h. 始	8. **YŌ** (ヨウ)
9. Room	i. 室	9. **otōto** (おとうと)
10. Together	j. 区	10. **ba** (ば)

C. Please choose the best answer(s) to the following questions.

1. If you don't hurry up and get to the _____ , you'll miss your train.
   a. 虫   b. 願   c. 駅   d. 病   e. 科

2. Which is the correct reading of 落ちる?
   a. **a·chiru** (あ・ちる)
   b. **i·chiru** (い・ちる)
   c. **o·chiru** (お・ちる)
   d. **u·chiru** (う・ちる)

3. Which of the following kanji has the most number of strokes?
   a. 是   b. 病   c. 直   d. 弟   e. 発

4. Which of the following readings apply to the kanji 色?
   a. **iro** (い ろ)
   b. **SHŌ** (ショウ)
   c. **kuro** (く ろ)
   d. **SHOKU** (ショク)
   e. **SAKU** (サク)

5. Which is the correct reading of 借りる?
   a. **mina·riru** (みな·りる)
   b. **ko·riru** (こ·りる)
   c. **ake·riru** (あけ·りる)
   d. **ka·riru** (か·りる)

D. Please match the following compounds to their meanings and pronunciations.

1. 最悪　　a. Speed / Velocity　　1. **HATSU·ON** (ハツ·オン)
2. 商店　　b. Straight line　　2. **BYŌ·KI** (ビョウ·キ)
3. 場所　　c. Pronunciation　　3. **SHŌ·TEN** (ショウ·テン)
4. 発音　　d. Indoor(s)　　4. **CHOKU·SEN** (チョク·セン)
5. 是非　　e. Shop / Store　　5. **SHITSU·NAI** (シツ·ナイ)

6. 直線　　f. By any means　　6. **KA·GAKU** (カ·ガク)
7. 科学　　g. Illness　　7. **SOKU·DO** (ソク·ド)
8. 病気　　h. Worst　　8. **SAI·AKU** (サイ·アク)
9. 速度　　i. Place / Location　　9. **ZE·HI** (ゼ·ヒ)
10. 室内　　j. Science　　10. **ba·SHO** (ば·ショ)

E. Please read the passage below and answer the questions that follow.

テレビを買いに新宿駅前の店へ行きました。。。

“すみません、新発売のテレビは幾らですか”
“二十五万円です”

その夜、私は弟に借金をお願いしました。

1. What do I want to buy?
2. Where did I go to find it?
3. About which specific one did I ask?
4. How much was it?
5. What did I do that evening?

Kanji #411—440

KANJI 411

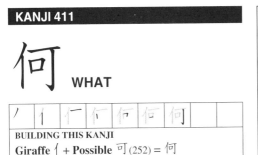

何 **WHAT**

| ノ | イ | 仁 | 仁 | 何 | 何 | 何 | | |

BUILDING THIS KANJI
Giraffe 亻 + Possible 可 (252) = 何

Meaning

What, although the sense of 'how many' can also be expressed in certain compounds (such as the first example of Entry 488). This is obviously a common word that appears often in the stories of this book. Unless accompanied by a string of exclamation and question marks (as shown below), however, the word "what" in future stories will have no connection to this kanji. There is, incidentally, only one character in the 2,136 general-use list that uses this kanji as a component—you will meet it in Entry 466. Take care with the stroke order of the right-hand side here.

Remembering this kanji

"If you can convince the **giraffe** to do it" he whispered, "it's **possible**."
"WHAT!!!???"

Common Pronunciations

Common **ON** reading: none
Common **kun** reading: **nan** (なん); **nani** (なに)

nan is the more common of these readings.

Less Common Pronunciations

Less common **ON** reading: **KA** (カ)
Less common **kun** reading: none

This reading is found in only one compound, which we met back in Entry 400: 幾何学 (**KI·KA·GAKU** / キ・カ・ガク) 'geometry', from the kanji 'how many', 'what', and 'study'.

COMMON WORDS AND COMPOUNDS		
何	*what; What!*	**nani** なに
何時	what + time = *What time?*	**nan·JI** なん・ジ

KANJI 412

 POLISH

BUILDING THIS KANJI
Stone 石 (340) + Picnic Table 开 = 研

Meaning
To polish.

Remembering this kanji
"Look what you did to that **picnic table**! Why did you have to POLISH your **stone** on it?"
"Hey, I didn't care about POLISHING the **stone**. I wanted to POLISH the **picnic table**."

Common Pronunciations
Common **ON** reading: **KEN** (ケン)
Common **kun** reading: none

Less Common Pronunciations
Less common **ON** reading: none
Less common **kun** reading: **to** (と)

	COMMON WORDS AND COMPOUNDS	
研究	polish + inquiry = *research*	**KEN·KYŪ** ケン・キュウ
研究所	research + location = *laboratory; research institute*	**KEN·KYŪ·JO** ケン・キュウ・ジョ

COMPONENT #413

ACTOR

Like any good actor, this component is all about sentiment; it usually shows up in kanji having to do with feelings and emotions.

KANJI 413

 BUSY

BUILDING THIS KANJI
Actor 忄 + Perish 亡 (254) = 忙

Meaning
Busy.

Remembering this kanji
"You landed another role? Wow, you sure are BUSY."
"An **actor** must always be BUSY. Those who aren't BUSY, **perish**."

Common Pronunciations
Common **ON** reading: **BŌ** (ボウ)
Common **kun** reading: **isoga** (いそが)

Less Common Pronunciations
Less common **ON** reading: none
Less common **kun** reading: none

	COMMON WORDS AND COMPOUNDS	
忙しい	*busy*	isoga·shii いそが・しい
多忙	many + busy = *busy; work pressure*	**TA·BŌ** タ・ボウ

KANJI 414

 SLOW

⁀	⁼	厂	尸	尸	戸	屵	屵	犀
犀	遅	遅						

BUILDING THIS KANJI

Flag 尸 + Sheep 羊 (262) + Seal ⻌ = 遅

Common Pronunciations

Common **ON** reading: none
Common **kun** reading: **oku** (お く); **oso** (お そ)

Less Common Pronunciations

Less common **ON** reading: **CHI** (チ)
Less common **kun** reading: none

COMMON WORDS AND COMPOUNDS		
遅い	slow; delayed	**oso·i** おそ·い
遅れる	be late / delayed	**oku·reru** おく·れる

Meaning

Slow, and the ideas of being late or delayed.

Remembering this kanji

Ah, it seemed to be SLOW everywhere that day…the **flag** shifted SLOWLY in the air, **sheep** grazed SLOWLY in the pastures, and a **seal** lolled SLOWLY on the tide.

KANJI 415

 FEE

`	⁞	⁼	十	半	米	米	米	料
料								

BUILDING THIS KANJI

Rice 米 (32) + Dipper 斗 (278) = 料

Meaning

Fee, charge. Another meaning relates to 'materials' (the second compound of Entry 440 provides an example). Ensure that you can clearly distinguish this kanji from 科 ('course', Entry 388).

Remembering this kanji

"The **rice** is piled over there with a **dipper** on top. Grab as much as you need."
"Is there a FEE?"
"There's a FEE for the **rice**, but no FEE for getting it with the **dipper**."

Common Pronunciations
Common **ON** reading: **RYŌ** (リ ョ ウ)
Common **kun** reading: none

Less Common Pronunciations
Less common **ON** reading: none
Less common **kun** reading: none

COMMON WORDS AND COMPOUNDS		
料金	fee + gold (money) = *fee; charge*	**RYŌ·KIN** リョウ・キン
料理	fee + reason = *cooking; food*	**RYŌ·RI** リョウ・リ
入場料	enter + place + fee = *admission fee*	NYŪ·JŌ·RYŌ ニュウ・ジョウ・リョウ

COMPONENT #416

QUICKSAND

KANJI 416

業 **BUSINESS**

ﾉ	ﾉ	ﾘﾉ	ﾘﾉ	一	业	业	业	业
业	丵	芉	業					

BUILDING THIS KANJI
Quicksand 业 + **Sheep** 羊 (262) + **Umbrella**
入 = 業

Meaning
Business, industry.

Remembering this kanji
"Look at that **quicksand**, Rocco. You'd never guess we tossed that **sheep** in there."
"Well, BUSINESS is BUSINESS, ain't it Vinnie?"
"Yeah. He shoulda known better than to butt into our **umbrella** BUSINESS."

Common Pronunciations
Common **ON** reading: **GYŌ** (ギ ョ ウ)
Common **kun** reading: none

Create your **on-yomi** keyword and enter it in the table at the back of the book. After that, write your sentence to remember the **on-yomi** reading in the box below.

Less Common Pronunciations
Less common **ON** reading: **GŌ** (ゴ ウ)
Less common **kun** reading: **waza** (わ ざ)

COMMON WORDS AND COMPOUNDS		
工業	craft + business = *industry*	**KŌ·GYŌ** コウ・ギョウ
事業	matter + business = *undertakings; tasks*	**JI·GYŌ** ジ・ギョウ
商業	commerce + business = *commerce; business*	**SHŌ·GYŌ** ショウ・ギョウ

KANJI 417

泳 SWIM

丶 丶 氵 汀 汀 泳 泳 泳

BUILDING THIS KANJI
Splash 氵 + Eternal 永 (384) = 泳

Meaning
Swim.

Remembering this kanji
"When you SWIM," she said, "SWIM efficiently by keeping your **splashes** down."
"But what if I'm on an **eternal** SWIM, coach?" someone asked.
"Well, in that case, **splash** away," she answered, "since you'll probably do it out of sheer boredom if you're on an **eternal** SWIM."

Common Pronunciations
Common **ON** reading: **EI** (エイ)
Common **kun** reading: **oyo** (およ)

Less Common Pronunciations
Less common **ON** reading: none
Less common **kun** reading: none

COMMON WORDS AND COMPOUNDS		
泳ぐ	*swim*	**oyo**·gu および·ぐ
平泳ぎ	flat + swim = *breaststroke*	hira **oyo**·gi ひら およ·ぎ
水泳	water + swim = *swimming*	**SUI·EI** スイ·エイ

KANJI 418

係 CONNECTION

ノ イ 亻 仵 侁 係 係 係 係

BUILDING THIS KANJI
Giraffe 亻 + System 系 (374) = 係

Meaning
Connection, often with the sense of being concerned with or involved in something. When used on its own or as a suffix, however, this kanji usually indicates a person working at a certain type of job—ticket collectors, tellers, receptionists and sales clerks are a few examples of compounds making use of this character.

Remembering this kanji
"You should ask that **giraffe** over there. He understands the **system** better than I do."
"Really?"
"Yeah. You gotta have CONNECTIONS here. You need a bit of extra food? He has a CONNECTION to the zookeeper. You want your pen hosed down? He has a CONNECTION to the cleaning guy. Believe me, a **giraffe** like you will find this **system** tough without CONNECTIONS."

Common Pronunciations
Common **ON** reading: **KEI** (ケイ)
Common **kun** reading: **kakari** (かかり)

kakari is the reading used as a suffix to denote the types of jobs mentioned above. It is always voiced when in this final position (as in the second example below).

Less Common Pronunciations
Less common **ON** reading: none
Less common **kun** reading: none

COMMON WORDS AND COMPOUNDS		
係	*clerk*	**kakari** かかり
受付係	receive + attach + connection = *receptionist;* *information clerk*	uke·tsuke·**gakari** うけ・つけ・ がかり
関係	checkpoint + connection = *connection;* *relationship*	**KAN·KEI** カン・ケイ

COMPONENT #419

良

GLUTTON

Something tells me that cupcake won't be there for long. Fittingly, the glutton usually appears in kanji related to food and drink; he invariably tries to hide his shameful behavior under an umbrella, as in the next entry. Make sure to note the difference between this component and 且, the 'billionaire' that was introduced prior to Entry 345.

KANJI 419

飲 **DRINK**

ノ	ハ	ケ	今	今	合	食	食	食
飲	飲	飲						

BUILDING THIS KANJI
Umbrella へ + Glutton 良 + Lack 欠 (246) = 飲

Meaning
Drink.

Remembering this kanji
Bring an **umbrella** if you'll be close to a **glutton** with a DRINK. If you don't, his **lack** of manners will result in a lot of that DRINK ending up on you.

Common Pronunciations
Common **ON** reading: **IN** (イ ン)
Common **kun** reading: **no** (の)

Less Common Pronunciations
Less common **ON** reading: none
Less common **kun** reading: none

COMMON WORDS AND COMPOUNDS		
飲む	*drink*	**no**·mu の・む
飲み物	drink + thing = *a drink*	**no**·mi mono の・み もの
飲食	drink + eat = *drinking and eating;* *food and drink*	**IN**·SHOKU イン・ショク

KANJI 420

黄 **YELLOW**

一	十	卄	艹	苫	芢	莳	苗	苗
黄	黄							

BUILDING THIS KANJI
Chimney 土 + Cause 由 (236) + Eight
(volcano) (19) = 黄

Meaning
Yellow.

Remembering this kanji
"I can't understand why my **chimney's** turning
YELLOW."
"Maybe sulphur's the **cause**."
"How so?"
"Well, it's YELLOW isn't it? Plus, I saw some
on a **volcano** once, and soon after that I came
down with YELLOW fever."

Common Pronunciations
Common **ON** reading: **Ō** (オ ウ); **KŌ** (コ ウ)
Common **kun** reading: **ki** (き)

This is an odd character when it comes to pronunciations, as it has three common readings despite
there being very few compounds containing the
kanji. In addition, several of these compounds
can be read with either of the **on-yom**i; in such
cases, though, one of them will invariably be the
more widely used.

Less Common Pronunciations
Less common **ON** reading: none
Less common **kun** reading: **ko** (こ)

You will only encounter this reading as an alternate
to the second compound below: 黄金 (**ko·gane**
/ こ·がね) 'gold' or 'money'. Nevertheless, it
is far more common for 黄金色 (**ko·gane·iro** /
こ·がね·いろ) 'gold color', to be read with the
kun-yomi of these kanji.

COMMON WORDS AND COMPOUNDS		
黄色	yellow	**ki**·iro き·いろ
黄金	yellow + gold = *gold; money*	**Ō**·GON オウ·ゴン
黄海	yellow + sea = *the Yellow Sea*	**KŌ**·KAI コウ·カイ

KANJI 421

答 **ANSWER**

ノ	𠂉	ﾉ	ﾉﾉ	ﾉﾟ	ﾉﾉ	ﾉﾟ	欠	答
答	答	答						

BUILDING THIS KANJI
Machine Guns ⺮ + Match 合 (250) = 答

Meaning
Answer.

Remembering this kanji
They fired their **machine gun**s and we were
forced to **match** them in ANSWER. "No!" a
peacenik cried, jumping between us. "This is
not the ANSWER!"

Common Pronunciations
Common **ON** reading: **TŌ** (ト ウ)
Common **kun** reading: **kota** (こ た)

The final compound below is the only instance in which the **on-yomi** becomes voiced.

Less Common Pronunciations
Less common **ON** reading: none
Less common **kun** reading: none

COMMON WORDS AND COMPOUNDS		
答え	*answer; response*	**kota·e** こた・え
答える	*to answer; respond*	**kota·eru** こた・える
問答	question + answer = *questions and answers*	MON·DŌ モン・ドウ

CROSSING GATE

Take some time to review 呆, our 'sherpa' component that preceded Entry 290, and 仏, the 'sprinter' we met prior to Entry 352 in order to solidify the differences between these three components.

KANJI 422

 TRAVEL

'	二	方	方	扩	扩	扩	旅
旅							

BUILDING THIS KANJI
Direction 方 (223) + **Hammer** 丆 + **Crossing Gate** 仏 = 旅

Meaning
Travel, journey.

Remembering this kanji
So you want to TRAVEL? Great, but you'd better pick a **direction**, because you obviously can't TRAVEL without one. Oh, and you also have to make sure that someone hasn't taken a **hammer** and put up a **crossing gate** somewhere in that **direction**, as that means you probably can't TRAVEL there.

Common Pronunciations
Common **ON** reading: **RYO** (リョ)
Common **kun** reading: **tabi** (たび)

Create your **on-yomi** keyword and enter it in the table at the back of the book. Then, after creating your **kun-yomi** keyword, write your sentence to remember the **on-yomi** and **kun-yomi** readings in the box below.

Less Common Pronunciations
Less common **ON** reading: none
Less common **kun** reading: none

COMMON WORDS AND COMPOUNDS		
旅	*travel; trip*	**tabi** たび
旅人	travel + person = *traveler*	**tabi·**bito たび・びと
旅行	travel + go = *travel; trip*	**RYO·KŌ** リョ・コウ

KANJI 423

皿 **DISH**

| 丨 | 冂 | 冂 | 皿 | 皿 | | | |

Meaning
Dish, plate. No story required.

Common Pronunciations
Common **ON** reading: none
Common **kun** reading: **sara** (さ ら)

Less Common Pronunciations
Less common **ON** reading: none
Less common **kun** reading: none

COMMON WORDS AND COMPOUNDS		
皿	*dish*	**sara** さ ら
皿洗い	dish + wash = *dishwashing*	**sara** ara·i さ ら あ ら・い

KANJI 424

治 **GOVERN**

| ` | ⺀ | ⺀ | 氵 | 氵 | 汾 | 治 | 治 | 治 |

BUILDING THIS KANJI
Splash 氵 + Platform 台 (264) = 治

Meaning
This interesting kanji conveys a sense of governing or having things under control. It's a meaning that can extend to the idea of managing one's health or having an illness cured. Make sure to clearly distinguish this character from 法 ("law", Entry 386), as the two are visually similar.

Remembering this kanji
The president struggled to GOVERN her emotions. "If you feel you must **splash** me whenever I address you from this **platform**," she said, "how can you expect me to GOVERN?"

Common Pronunciations
Common **ON** reading: CHI (チ); JI (ジ)
Common **kun** reading: **osa** (お さ); **nao** (な お)

Though we're dealing with four common readings here, things are much simpler than they appear at first glance. The **kun-yomi** are only found in the two intransitive/transitive verb pairs below, and **CHI** is the more common of the **on-yomi**.

Less Common Pronunciations
Less common **ON** reading: none
Less common **kun** reading: none

COMMON WORDS AND COMPOUNDS		
治まる (intr)	*to be tranquil; calm down*	**osa**·maru お さ・ま る
治める (tr)	*to govern / administer*	**osa**·meru お さ・め る
治る (intr)	*to get well / recover*	**nao**·ru な お・る
治す (tr)	*to heal*	**nao**·su な お・す
自治	self + govern = *self-government;* *autonomy*	**JI·CHI** ジ・チ
明治	bright + govern = *Meiji (period / emperor)*	**MEI·JI** メ イ・ジ

COMPONENT #425

RATTLESNAKE

KANJI 425

与 **CONFER**

BUILDING THIS KANJI
Rattlesnake 与 + One (hamburger patty) 一
(3) = 与

Meaning
Confer, give.

Remembering this kanji
"I CONFER on you, **rattlesnake**, the prize for best rattling noise. I was going to CONFER it on you, **hamburger patty**, but then I realized you were sizzling instead."

Common Pronunciations
Common **ON** reading: **YO** (ヨ)
Common **kun** reading: **ata** (あ た)

Less Common Pronunciations
Less common **ON** reading: none
Less common **kun** reading: none

COMMON WORDS AND COMPOUNDS		
与える	*confer; give*	**ata**·eru あた・える
授与	grant + confer = *conferment; awarding*	**JU·YO** ジュ・ヨ

KANJI 426

昼 **DAYTIME**

BUILDING THIS KANJI
Measurement 尺(332) + Dawn 旦(183) = 昼

Meaning
Daytime, midday.

Remembering this kanji
It's pointless to make a **measurement** of **dawn**, because really, when does it begin and end? No, a more useful **measurement** would be to calculate the hours of DAYTIME instead.

Common Pronunciations

Common **ON** reading: **CHŪ** (チュウ)
Common **kun** reading: **hiru** (ひる)

Less Common Pronunciations

Less common **ON** reading: none
Less common **kun** reading: none

COMMON WORDS AND COMPOUNDS		
昼	*daytime; midday*	**hiru** ひる
昼間	daytime + interval = *daytime; during the day*	**hiru·ma** ひる・ま
昼食	daytime + eat = *lunch*	**CHŪ·SHOKU** チュウ・ショク

KANJI 427

 PRODUCE

'	一	十	宀	立	产	产	产	産
産	産							

BUILDING THIS KANJI
Vase ⌎ + Cliff 厂 + Life 生 (99) = 産

Meaning
Produce, give birth to.

Remembering this kanji
A **vase** teeters on a **cliff**, its **life** in the balance…
What kind of feeling does this **PRODUCE** in
you?

Common Pronunciations

Common **ON** reading: **SAN** (サン)
Common **kun** reading: **u** (う)

The **kun-yomi** forms the intransitive/transitive
verb pair 産まれる / 産む (**u**·mareru / **u**·mu)
'to be born / to give birth to'; these verbs have
the same meaning as the identically pronounced
生まれる/ 生む , which we learned back in
Entry 99. The **on-yomi** can become voiced in the
second position, but only in a few compounds
related to childbirth.

Less Common Pronunciations

Less common **ON** reading: none
Less common **kun** reading: **ubu** (うぶ)

IRREGULAR READING		
土産	earth + produce = *souvenir*	**miyage** みやげ

The honorary prefix 'o-' is often attached to this
word: お土産 .

COMMON WORDS AND COMPOUNDS		
産院	produce + institution = *maternity hospital*	**SAN·IN** サン・イン
生産	life + produce = *production*	**SEI·SAN** セイ・サン
水産	water + produce = *marine products*	**SUI·SAN** スイ・サン

COMPONENT #428

RAT

This component is written with three strokes, not two.

KANJI 428

  CONSTRUCT

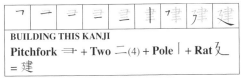

BUILDING THIS KANJI
Pitchfork ⱻ + Two 二(4) + Pole ｜ + Rat 爻
= 建

Meaning

Construct, build. You may notice that the 'pole' component in this character extends all the way through the kanji for 'two', whereas it stops short in 書 ('write', from Entry 136). The reason for this is simple: the sun burnt off the bottom of the pole in 書.

Remembering this kanji

"So you were able to **CONSTRUCT** a barn, but you've already got **rats**, huh?"

"Yeah, should I **CONSTRUCT** a **rat** hotel for them somewhere else so that they'll leave?"

"Well, if you do you'll need **two** objects to get rid of them: a **pitchfork** to scare them out of their hiding spots, and a **pole** to herd them off. It might be cheaper to just **CONSTRUCT** some **rat** traps for them instead."

Common Pronunciations

Common **ON** reading: **KEN** (ケン)
Common **kun** reading: **ta** (た)

As the second example shows, this is another kanji whose verb form can incorporate its **hiragana** ending in certain compounds.

Less Common Pronunciations

Less common **ON** reading: **KON** (コン)
Less common **kun** reading: none

COMMON WORDS AND COMPOUNDS		
建てる	*construct; build*	**ta·**teru た・てる
建物	construct + thing = *building*	**tate·**mono たて・もの
建国	construct + country = *founding of a country*	**KEN·KOKU** ケン・コク

KANJI 429

  YOUNGER SISTER

BUILDING THIS KANJI
Woman 女(16) + Not Yet 未(276) = 妹

Meaning

Younger sister.

Remembering this kanji

"What's up with that **woman** over there?"

"They keep telling her it's **not yet** her turn, so she's upset."

"Doesn't she realize what's going to happen?"

"She's been pretty sheltered, so probably not; that's Marie Antoinette's **YOUNGER SISTER**."

Common Pronunciations
Common **ON** reading: **MAI** (マイ)
Common **kun** reading: **imōto** (いもうと)

Less Common Pronunciations
Less common **ON** reading: none
Less common **kun** reading: none

COMMON WORDS AND COMPOUNDS		
妹	*younger sister*	**imōto** いもうと
姉妹	elder sister + younger sister = *sisters*	**SHI·MAI** シ・マイ

KANJI 430

 POND

`	`	シ	⺍	汁	池			

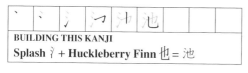

BUILDING THIS KANJI
Splash シ + Huckleberry Finn 也 = 池

Common Pronunciations
Common **ON** reading: **CHI** (チ)
Common **kun** reading: **ike** (いけ)

Less Common Pronunciations
Less common **ON** reading: none
Less common **kun** reading: none

COMMON WORDS AND COMPOUNDS		
池	*pond*	**ike** いけ
電池	electric + pond = *battery*	**DEN·CHI** デン・チ

Meaning
Pond, reservoir.

Remembering this kanji
"What was that **splash**, **Huckleberry Finn**?" asked Tom Sawyer. "Did you toss something into the POND?"
"Uh…yeah, that was it."

COMPONENT #431

CLOWN   巿   巿

KANJI 431

 REGULATION

ノ	⺊	乞	乍	匂	岜	制	制

BUILDING THIS KANJI
Jelly Bean ヽ + Clown 巿 + Chisel リ = 制

Meaning
Regulation, control.

Remembering this kanji

"Look, a REGULATION is a REGULATION — you have to get rid of the big **jelly bean**."

"But why?" asked the **clown**. "Mr. **Jelly Bean** has always been the highlight of my act."

"And that's the issue. You've had it so long it's covered in mold; you're going to need a **chisel** to get it off your hat."

"Geez, who would have thought I was breaking a health REGULATION?"

Common Pronunciations
Common **ON** reading: **SEI** (セイ)
Common **kun** reading: none

Less Common Pronunciations
Less common **ON** reading: none
Less common **kun** reading: none

COMMON WORDS AND COMPOUNDS		
自制	self + regulation = *self-control*	JI·SEI ジ·セイ
制服	regulation + clothes = *uniform*	SEI·FUKU セイ·フク
制度	regulation + degree = *system*	SEI·DO セイ·ド

KANJI 432

 TRANSPORT

'	一	一	冖	冖	宀	宣	宣	軍
軍	運	運						

BUILDING THIS KANJI
Army 軍(260) + Seal 辶 = 運

Meaning
Transport. A second important meaning (as can be seen in the final example below) relates to luck.

Remembering this kanji
"The **army** is furious with you. Didn't you get the navy **seals** to TRANSPORT the weapons?"

"Oops, I thought you wanted me to get real **seals** to TRANSPORT them."

Common Pronunciations
Common **ON** reading: **UN** (ウン)
Common **kun** reading: **hako** (はこ)

Create your **on-yomi** keyword and enter it in the table at the back of the book. Then, after creating your **kun-yomi** keyword, write your sentence to remember the **on-yomi** and **kun-yomi** readings in the box below.

Less Common Pronunciations
Less common **ON** reading: none
Less common **kun** reading: none

COMMON WORDS AND COMPOUNDS		
運ぶ	*transport; carry*	hako·bu はこ·ぶ
運送	transport + send = *transportation; shipping*	UN·SŌ ウン·ソウ
不運	not + transport (luck) = *bad luck; misfortune*	FU·UN フ·ウン

KANJI 433

 MECHANISM

BUILDING THIS KANJI
Tree 木 (13) + **How Many** 幾 (400) = 機

Meaning

The general sense is of mechanisms and things employing some type of mechanistic action (the final compound below provides an interesting example). This kanji also conveys the idea of 'opportunity' or 'chance' in some of the compounds in which it appears (as in the first compound). This is, incidentally, the only time in the general-use kanji that the character for 'how many' figures as a component in another character.

Remembering this kanji

Whenever DaVinci looked at a **tree** he imagined **how many** MECHANISMS it could yield; a clock MECHANISM, a loom MECHANISM, and a gear MECHANISM, for example.

Common Pronunciations

Common **ON** reading: **KI** (キ)
Common **kun** reading: none

Less Common Pronunciations

Less common **ON** reading: none
Less common **kun** reading: **hata** (は た)

COMMON WORDS AND COMPOUNDS		
機会	mechanism + meet = *chance; opportunity*	**KI**·KAI キ·カイ
電動機	electric + move + mechanism = *electric motor*	DEN·DŌ·**KI** デン·ドウ·キ
有機体	have + mechanism + body = *organism*	YŪ·**KI**·TAI ユウ·キ·タイ

KANJI 434

 STRONG

ㄱ	ㄴ	弓	弓'	弘	弘	弘	弘	強
強	強							

BUILDING THIS KANJI
Bow 弓 (143) + **Broken Crutch** ム + **Insect** 虫
(391) = 強

Meaning
Strong.

Remembering this kanji

I took out my **bow** but couldn't scare it. I whacked it with my crutch, but this only left me with a **broken crutch**. I had only one thought as the **insect** came closer: "Wow, this insect is STRONG."

Common Pronunciations

Common **ON** reading: **KYŌ** (キョウ)
Common **kun** reading: **tsuyo** (つよ)

The **kun-yomi** is usually voiced when in second position.

Less Common Pronunciations
Less common **ON** reading: **GŌ** (ゴ ウ)
Less common **kun** reading: **shi** (し)

This **on-yomi** usually appears in words that carry a violent or negative connotation.

COMMON WORDS AND COMPOUNDS		
強い	*strong*	**tsuyo·i** つよ·い
強化	strong + change = *strengthening;* *intensification*	**KYŌ·KA** キョウ·カ
強制	strong + regulation = *compulsion; coercion*	**KYŌ·SEI** キョウ·セイ

COMPONENT #435

ROCKET LAUNCH

KANJI 435

光 **SHINE**

丨	丶	丷	半	半	光		

BUILDING THIS KANJI
Rocket Launch + One (hamburger patty)
一(3) + Ballet 儿 = 光

Meaning
Shine, light.

Remembering this kanji
"What a **rocket launch**," she said. "Look at the SHINE coming off the rocket!"
"It's even making the grease on my **hamburger patty** SHINE," he said.
"You're right. It's shining just like the sequins on my **ballet** outfit."

Common Pronunciations
Common **ON** reading: **KŌ** (コ ウ)
Common **kun** reading: **hika** (ひ か);
hikari (ひ か り)

Less Common Pronunciations
Less common **ON** reading: none
Less common **kun** reading: none

COMMON WORDS AND COMPOUNDS		
光る	*shine*	**hika·ru** ひか·る
光	*light; ray*	**hikari** ひかり
日光	sun + shine = *sunshine; sunlight*	**NIK·KŌ** ニッ·コウ

KANJI 436

 DIFFICULT

BUILDING THIS KANJI
Wreath ⁺⁺ + Girl with a Hula Hoop 夨 +
Squirrels 隹 = 難

Meaning
Difficult.

Remembering this kanji
"Is it DIFFICULT to put a **wreath** on a girl **with a hula hoop**?"
"It's a bit DIFFICULT, because you have to watch for the hula hoop spinning about. But at least it's easier than doing it to those **squirrels** on that brick wall over there; they're so DIFFICULT they won't even let the **wreath** appear above them in this kanji."

Common Pronunciations
Common **ON** reading: **NAN** (ナン)
Common **kun** reading: **muzuka** (むずか);
kata (かた)

It's only fitting that this kanji is a bit difficult. **NAN**, however, is by far the most common reading, and the two **kun-yomi** form adjectives. When in the second position, **kata** becomes voiced and makes an adjective of the type shown in the second example below.

IRREGULAR READING		
有 り 難 う	have + difficult = *Thank you; Thanks*	a·ri **gatō** あ·り がと·う

Less Common Pronunciations
Less common **ON** reading: none
Less common **kun** reading: none

COMMON WORDS AND COMPOUNDS		
難 しい	*difficult*	**muzuka**·shii むずか·しい
言い難い	say + difficult = *difficult to say*	i·i **gata**·i い·い がた·い
難民	difficult + people = *refugees*	**NAN·MIN** ナン·ミン

KANJI 437

 COMPANY

BUILDING THIS KANJI
Whittling 衤 + Earth 土(87) = 社

Meaning
Company. This kanji also refers to Shinto shrines; note how the second compound below can encompass both meanings.

Remembering this kanji
"My COMPANY? Oh, it's involved in **whittling earth**."
"So you've got a landscaping COMPANY then?"
"There's no need to be rude. We prefer to call it a **whittling earth** COMPANY."

Common Pronunciations
Common **ON** reading: **SHA** (シャ)
Common **kun** reading: none

The final compound below is the only instance in which the **on-yomi** becomes voiced.

Less Common Pronunciations
Less common **ON** reading: none
Less common **kun** reading: **yashiro** (やしろ)

COMMON WORDS AND COMPOUNDS		
会社	meet + company = *company; corporation*	KAI·SHA カイ・シャ
本社	main + company = *head office; main temple*	HON·SHA ホン・シャ
神社	god + company = *Shinto shrine*	JIN·JA ジン・ジャ

笑 LAUGH

ノ	ー	⺮	⺮	⺮⼁	⺮⼁	⺉	𥝱	笑
笑								

BUILDING THIS KANJI
Machine Guns ⺮ + 1950's Rock Star 天 = 笑

Meaning
Laugh.

Remembering this kanji
"So that's when he started performing with **machine guns**?"

"Yeah, I suppose he was desperate. Nobody wanted to listen to a **1950's rock star** any more."

"How did he react when the crowd began to LAUGH?"

"Well, it was a little dicey for a while—I mean, he did have **machine guns**—but fortunately he ended up as a comedian. It turns out he enjoyed making others LAUGH."

Common Pronunciations
Common **ON** reading: **SHŌ** (ショウ)
Common **kun** reading: **wara** (わら)

Less Common Pronunciations
Less common **ON** reading: none
Less common **kun** reading: **e** (え)

COMMON WORDS AND COMPOUNDS		
笑う	*laugh; smile*	**wara**·u わら・う
高笑い	tall + laugh = *loud laughter*	taka **wara**·i たか わら・い
失笑	lose + laugh = *burst out laughing*	SHIS·**SHŌ** シッ・ショウ

COMPONENT #439

ECCENTRIC PROFESSOR

As befits an eccentric, this fellow will have an umbrella no matter what the weather.

KANJI 439

 TEST

BUILDING THIS KANJI
Horse 馬(144) + Eccentric Professor 僉 = 験

Meaning
Test, examine.

Remembering this kanji
Bolting into the classroom on a **horse**, the **eccentric professor** threw out the TEST. "This is an important TEST," he said. "It will TEST if you can pass a TEST in the presence of a **horse**."

Common Pronunciations
Common **ON** reading: **KEN** (ケン)
Common **kun** reading: none

Less Common Pronunciations
Less common **ON** reading: **GEN** (ゲン)
Less common **kun** reading: none

COMMON WORDS AND COMPOUNDS		
試験	try + test = *test; examination*	SHI·KEN シ・ケン
受験	receive + test = *take an examination*	JU·KEN ジュ・ケン
実験	actual + test = *experiment*	JIK·KEN ジッ・ケン

KANJI 440

史 **HISTORY**

BUILDING THIS KANJI
Mouth (vampire) 口(8) + Piranha 乂 = 史

Meaning
History. It's worth taking a moment to see clearly that this kanji does <u>not</u> function as a component in 更 ('anew', from Entry 373).

Remembering this kanji
"Excuse me, I'm looking for a book about **vampires** and **piranhas**."
"What's it called?"
"'Scary Stuff That Bites: A HISTORY'."

Common Pronunciations

Common **ON** reading: **SHI** (シ)

Common **kun** reading: none

Note that the first two kanji in the final compound mean 'literature' when taken together.

Less Common Pronunciations

Less common **ON** reading: none

Less common **kun** reading: none

	COMMON WORDS AND COMPOUNDS	
史学	history + study = *history; historical studies*	**SHI·GAKU** シ・ガク
史料	history + fee (materials) = *historical materials/records*	**SHI·RYŌ** シ・リョウ
文学史	literature + history = *literary history*	**BUN·GAKU·SHI** ブン・ガク・シ

CHAPTER 19 REVIEW EXERCISES

A. Please match the following kanji to their meanings.

1.	泳	a.	Travel
2.	験	b.	What
3.	妹	c.	Test
4.	何	d.	Busy
5.	料	e.	Mechanism
6.	旅	f.	Produce
7.	機	g.	Younger sister
8.	難	h.	Fee
9.	忙	i.	Difficult
10.	産	j.	Swim

B. Please match the following meanings to their kanji, and these to their **on-** or **kun-yomi**.

1.	Dish	a.	昼	1.	**GYŌ**(ギョウ)
2.	Regulation	b.	遅	2.	**UN**(ウン)
3.	Pond	c.	飲	3.	**IN**(イン)
4.	Shine	d.	制	4.	**ike**(いけ)
5.	Slow	e.	皿	5.	**hikari**(ひかり)
6.	Drink	f.	運	6.	**SHI**(シ)
7.	Daytime	g.	光	7.	**oso**(おそ)
8.	History	h.	業	8.	**sara**(さら)
9.	Business	i.	史	9.	**SEI**(セイ)
10.	Transport	j.	池	10.	**hiru**(ひる)

C. Please choose the best answer(s) to the following questions.

1. Which of the following kanji has the most number of strokes?
   a. 強 b. 旅 c. 答 d. 料 e. 産

2. Which of the following readings apply to the kanji 治?
   a. **CHI**(チ)   b. **osa**(おさ)   c. **JI**(ジ)
   d. **SHI**(シ)   e. **nao**(なお)

3. He fell in the pond, and she couldn't help but _____ .
   a. 光 b. 旅 c. 研 d. 笑 e. 与

4. Which of the following readings apply to the kanji 黄?
   a. **KŌ**(コウ)   b. **SHŌ**(ショウ)
   c. **ku**(く)   d. **Ō**(オウ)
   e. **ki**(き)

5. Which is the correct reading of 遅れる?
   a. **aka·reru**(あか·れる)
   b. **chika·reru**(ちか·れる)
   c. **oku·reru**(おく·れる)
   d. **hama·reru**(はま·れる)

D. Please match the following compounds to their meanings and pronunciations.

1. 神社   a. Sunshine

2. 強化   b. Travel

3. 料理   c. Shinto shrine

4. 難民   d. Refugees

5. 建物   e. Cooking / Food

6. 日光   f. Yellow

7. 電池   g. Battery

8. 研究   h. Research

9. 黄色   i. Strengthening

10. 旅行   j. Building

1. **NAN·MIN**
（ナン・ミン）

2. **RYŌ·RI**
（リョウ・リ）

3. **ki·iro**
（き・いろ）

4. **RYŌ·KŌ**
（リョ・コウ）

5. **NIK·KŌ**
（ニッ・コウ）

6. **DEN·CHI**
（デン・チ）

7. **tate·mono**
（たて・もの）

8. **JIN·JA**
（ジン・ジャ）

9. **KEN·KYŪ**
（ケン・キュウ）

10. **KYŌ·KA**
（キョウ・カ）

E. Please read the passage below and answer the questions that follow.

"今何時ですか。"

"二時半です。バスが遅れていますね。"

"そうですね。先週から大通りで工事をしています。"

"ああ～忘れていました。いつまでですか。"

"年末まで続きます"

1. What did the first person initially want to know?
2. For what form of transportation are these two people waiting?
3. Why is it running late?
4. When had this work begun?
5. For how long will it continue?

Kanji #441—465

階 **FLOOR**

⁷	³	�ß	ß⁻	ß⌐	ßᵘ	ßᵘᵗ	ßᵗᵗ	ßᵗᵗᵢ
階	階	階						

BUILDING THIS KANJI
Novice Yodeler ß + All 皆 (344) = 階

Meaning
Floor, story (of a building). Related to this idea of layers, 階 can also refer to the rank or social stratum to which a person or group of people belong.

Remembering this kanji
The **novice yodeler yodeled**, and was so terrible that **all** of them dropped to the FLOOR. And not just those on the FLOOR he was on, I'm talking everyone on **all** the FLOORS in the building.

Common Pronunciations
Common **ON** reading: **KAI** (カイ)
Common **kun** reading: none

Less Common Pronunciations
Less common **ON** reading: none
Less common **kun** reading: none

COMMON WORDS AND COMPOUNDS		
一階	one + floor = *first floor; ground floor*	IK·KAI イッ·カイ
階上	floor + upper = *upstairs*	**KAI**·JŌ カイ·ジョウ
階下	floor + lower = *downstairs*	**KAI**·KA カイ·カ

点 **POINT**

1	⊦	⼁⼂	⼇	占	占	点	点	点

BUILDING THIS KANJI
Occupy 占 (255) + Gas Stove 灬 = 点

Meaning
Point, mark.

Remembering this kanji
"Organization is everything," our chef told us before the exam, "so have your frying pan nicely **occupy** the top of the **gas stove**. You will get maximum POINTS for doing this, and may even earn a bonus POINT."

Common Pronunciations
Common **ON** reading: **TEN** (テ ン)
Common **kun** reading: none

Less Common Pronunciations
Less common **ON** reading: none
Less common **kun** reading: none

COMMON WORDS AND COMPOUNDS		
点火	point + fire = *ignition*	**TEN·KA** テン·カ
重点	heavy + point = *important point; emphasis*	**JŪ·TEN** ジュウ·テン
氷点	ice + point = *freezing point*	**HYŌ·TEN** ヒョウ·テン

COMPONENT #443

BUNK BEDS 目

KANJI 443

官 **OFFICIAL**

'	'	宀	宁	宁	宁	官	官

BUILDING THIS KANJI
Pincers 宀 + Bunk Beds 目 = 官

Meaning
Official, government. This kanji is often used as a suffix to indicate an official with some sort of governmental or bureaucratic authority.

Remembering this kanji
The refugees looked on as an OFFICIAL watched a set of **pincers** offload **bunk beds**. "I've heard he's the OFFICIAL in charge of **pincers**," one of them said.
"Really? Why isn't the **bunk bed** OFFICIAL here then?" asked another.
"Oh, she's over there, talking with the mattress OFFICIAL and the bed frame OFFICIAL," replied the first.

Common Pronunciations
Common **ON** reading: **KAN** (カ ン)
Common **kun** reading: none

Recall that the first two kanji of the second compound mean 'test' or 'examination' (from Entry 439), and that the first two kanji of the final compound mean 'foreign policy' (from Entry 185) when taken together.

Less Common Pronunciations
Less common **ON** reading: none
Less common **kun** reading: none

COMMON WORDS AND COMPOUNDS		
教官	teach + official = *instructor*	**KYŌ·KAN** キョウ·カン
試験官	examination + official = *examiner*	**SHI·KEN·KAN** シ·ケン·カン
外交官	foreign policy + official = *diplomat*	**GAI·KŌ·KAN** ガイ·コウ·カン

KANJI 444

羽 **FEATHER**

﹁	﹁	刁	刁	羽	羽			

BUILDING THIS KANJI

Crane ﹁ + Pinball ⸍ + Crane ﹁ + Pinball ⸍ = 羽

Meaning

Feather. This kanji can also refer to the wings of birds, insects and airplanes, etc.

Remembering this kanji

"Look what I found, grandpa!"

"That's a **FEATHER**, sweetheart."

"Really? What can you do with it?"

"Well, you can have a **FEATHER** pillow and a **FEATHER** duvet, for instance. You wouldn't want a **FEATHER** crane, though, as even a couple of those would be pretty useless. Oh, and I wouldn't want a pair of **FEATHER** **pinball** flippers either, as that would really ruin the game."

Common Pronunciations

Common **ON** reading: none

Common **kun** reading: **ha** (は); **hane** (は ね)

hane tends to be the reading used when the kanji appears on its own, while **ha** is the more common in compounds. Note that the odd word in the final example below uses one of the less common **on-yomi** of 合 (**KA-** / カ ッ); this is the only time 合 is read with this pronunciation.

Less Common Pronunciations

Less common **ON** reading: **U** (ウ)

Less common **kun** reading: none

COMMON WORDS AND COMPOUNDS		
羽	*feather; wing*	**hane** は ね
合羽	match + feather = *raincoat*	KAP·pa カ ッ ·ぱ

KANJI 445

温 **WARM**

`	⸍	⸍	氵	汩	汩	汩	泗	泗

温	温	温						

BUILDING THIS KANJI

Splash 氵 + Sun 日 (6) + Dish 皿 (423) = 温

Meaning

Warm.

Remembering this kanji

"Whew! It's really **WARM** isn't it?"

"It sure is. Let me **splash** this on you."

"OK...oh yuck, what did you just **splash** me with?"

"Relax, it's only butter; the **sun** melted it in the **dish**. Do you feel how **WARM** it is?"

Common Pronunciations
Common **ON** reading: **ON** (オン)
Common **kun** reading: **atata** (あたた)

Less Common Pronunciations
Less common **ON** reading: none
Less common **kun** reading: none

COMMON WORDS AND COMPOUNDS		
温かい	*warm*	**atata**·kai あたた·かい
気温	spirit + warm = *(air) temperature*	**KI·ON** キ·オン
温泉	warm + springs = *hot spring; spa*	**ON·SEN** オン·セン

COMPONENT #446

TIC TAC TOE

KANJI 446

寒 **COLD**

BUILDING THIS KANJI

Pincers 宀 + Tic Tac Toe ## + Seesaw 六 +
Jelly Bean ヽ + Jelly Bean ヽ = 寒

Meaning
Cold.

Remembering this kanji
"Aren't you COLD out here?"
"Sure I'm COLD, but what of it? I couldn't pick up a date in that club if I had **pincers**."
"What about that girl you had a game of **tic tac toe** with? She seemed nice."
"She was until I won. Then she turned COLD."
"Well you can't just sit here on this **seesaw**, staring at a couple of discarded **jelly beans** no one will ever care for. I mean, that even makes me feel COLD."

Common Pronunciations
Common **ON** reading: **KAN** (カン)
Common **kun** reading: **samu** (さむ)

Note that the second compound below can also be read as (**samu**·KE / さむ·ケ); meaning 'chill (from a sickness, etc)', it uses the less common **on-yomi** of 気.

Less Common Pronunciations
Less common **ON** reading: none
Less common **kun** reading: none

COMMON WORDS AND COMPOUNDS		
寒い	*cold*	**samu**·i さむ·い
寒気	cold + spirit = *coldness; the cold*	**KAN·KI** カン·キ
寒冷 前線	cold + cool + before + line = *cold front*	**KAN·REI·ZEN·SEN** カン·レイ· ゼン·セン

DILIGENCE

| ノ | ﾉ | ㇏ | ㇒ | 免 | 免 | 免 | 免 | 勉 |
| 勉 | | | | | | | | |

BUILDING THIS KANJI
Exemption 免(311) + Strength 力(63) = 勉

Meaning
Diligence. This is the only one of the general-use kanji in which the character for exemption is stretched out in such a way; the story and illustration takes this into account.

Remembering this kanji
He got an **exemption** because of his **strength**, but stressed that it was also due to his DILI-GENCE. "**Strength** alone," he said, "could not have done this. It took forever, and I could not have stretched out the kanji for '**exemption**' the way I have without a lot of DILIGENCE."

Common Pronunciations
Common **ON** reading: **BEN** (ベン)
Common **kun** reading: none

Create your **on-yomi** keyword and enter it in the table at the back of the book. After that, write your sentence to remember the **on-yomi** reading in the box below.

Less Common Pronunciations
Less common **ON** reading: none
Less common **kun** reading: none

COMMON WORDS AND COMPOUNDS		
勉学	diligence + study = *diligent study*	**BEN·GAKU** ベン・ガク
勉強	diligence + strong = *studying*	**BEN·KYŌ** ベン・キョウ

 TECHNIQUE

| ノ | ノ | 彳 | 彳 | 彳 | 彳 | 術 | 術 | 術 |
| 術 | 術 | | | | | | | |

BUILDING THIS KANJI
Go 行(173) + Zombie 朮 + Jelly Bean ヽ = 術

Meaning
Technique, skill. The most striking thing about this kanji is that the character for 'go' is split in half. 行 is, in fact, unusual in this respect, for with the exception of its appearance in one obscure kanji [桁* (keta·けた) "beam; girder"] it is the only character in the general-use list that <u>always</u> does this when functioning as a component in other kanji. As a result, it will be the only one that retains its original meaning despite breaking apart in this way.

Remembering this kanji

"Go!" she said to the **zombie**, but of course it wouldn't leave.

"TECHNIQUE…" it said, "…practice…"

"Oh, all right," she sighed. "I'll toss the **jelly bean**, you catch it. I still don't understand why you want to master this silly TECHNIQUE, though."

Common Pronunciations

Common **ON** reading: **JUTSU** (ジュツ)

Common **kun** reading: none

Create your **on-yomi** keyword and enter it in the table at the back of the book. After that, write your sentence to remember the **on-yomi** reading in the box below.

[blank box]

Less Common Pronunciations

Less common **ON** reading: none

Less common **kun** reading: none

COMMON WORDS AND COMPOUNDS		
美術	beautiful + technique = *art; the fine arts*	BI·**JUTSU** ビ・ジュツ
手術	hand + technique = *surgical operation*	SHU·**JUTSU** シュ・ジュツ
話術	speak + technique = *storytelling*	WA·**JUTSU** ワ・ジュツ

KANJI 449

身 **PERSONAL**

BUILDING THIS KANJI

Self 自 (33) + Comet 一 = 身

Meaning

This odd-looking kanji has to do with things 'personal', in the sense of someone's own body (as in the first compound) or a specific thing's characteristics (as in the third). Take care with the stroke order here; though deformed by the comet, the kanji is written in the order of the components as listed.

Remembering this kanji

"No, it's not your PERSONAL affair, **comet**! Your behavior is affecting other kanji in a very PERSONAL way. I mean, look what you've done to 'self' here by blazing across it like this: you've made the Cyclops drop his club!"

"Hey, the jelly bean's still there."

"So what? I'm telling you, the other kanji are talking, and it's going to get PERSONAL."

Common Pronunciations

Common **ON** reading: **SHIN** (シン)

Common **kun** reading: **mi** (み)

You will encounter both readings frequently, although **mi** predominates in the first position and **SHIN** in the second.

Less Common Pronunciations
Less common **ON** reading: none
Less common **kun** reading: none

COMMON WORDS AND COMPOUNDS		
身体	personal + body *= the body; physical*	**SHIN**·TAI シン・タイ
出身	exit + body *= one's hometown*	SHUS·**SHIN** シュッ・シン
中身	middle + body *= contents*	naka·**mi** なか・み

MATADOR

Ensure that you can see the difference between this component and 扌, our component for 'whittling' introduced prior to Entry 253.

KANJI 450

 BEGINNING

BUILDING THIS KANJI
Matador 衤 + Sword 刀 (117) = 初

Meaning
Beginning.

Remembering this kanji
We watched as the **matador** drew his **sword**. "It's BEGINNING!" she yelled to me over the roar of the crowd. "It's finally BEGINNING!"

Common Pronunciations
Common **ON** reading: SHO (ショ)
Common **kun** reading: **haji** (はじ); **hatsu** (はつ)

SHO is the most common of these three readings. **haji** appears only in the initial word below and one other: 初めて (**haji**·mete / はじ・めて) 'for the first time'. **hatsu** tends to have a more poetic shade of meaning and appears with only a few compounds in the first position.

Less Common Pronunciations
Less common **ON** reading: none
Less common **kun** reading: **so** (そ)

COMMON WORDS AND COMPOUNDS		
初め	*beginning; outset*	**haji**·me はじ・め
初雪	beginning + snow *= first snowfall of the year*	**hatsu**·yuki はつ・ゆき
初日	beginning + sun (day) *= first day; opening day*	**SHO**·NICHI ショ・ニチ

KANJI 451

 DISTRESS

| 丨 | 冂 | 冃 | 困 | 困 | 困 | 困 | |

BUILDING THIS KANJI
Prison 囗 + Tree 木(13) = 困

Meaning
Distress.

Remembering this kanji
I'm never in more DISTRESS than when I catch sight of a **tree** in **prison**. I mean, the thought of it being rooted to one spot while the other cons stroll about the yard chatting…I can't imagine the DISTRESS it must feel.

Common Pronunciations
Common **ON** reading: **KON** (コン)
Common **kun** reading: **koma** (こま)

Less Common Pronunciations
Less common **ON** reading: none
Less common **kun** reading: none

COMMON WORDS AND COMPOUNDS		
困る	*be distressed; suffer*	**koma·ru** こま・る
困難	distress + difficult = *distress; difficulty*	**KON·NAN** コン・ナン

KANJI 452

 PUT

| 丶 | 一 | 一 | 一 | 一 | 一 | 平 | 平 | 罘 |
| 罘 | 置 | 置 | 置 | | | | | |

BUILDING THIS KANJI
Bandage ⊞ + Straight 直(407) = 置

Meaning
Put, place, leave behind. It's worth spending a moment to ensure that you can clearly see the differences between this kanji and two others learned earlier: 直 ('straight', Entry 407) and 真 ('true', Entry 358).

Remembering this kanji
"PUT it on! PUT it on!"
"Calm down. I want the **bandage** to be nice and **straight**."
"Who cares? PUT it on before I lose consciousness!"

Common Pronunciations
Common **ON** reading: **CHI** (チ)
Common **kun** reading: **o** (お)

The **kun-yomi** is invariably the reading in the first position, with the **on-yom**i more common in the second. As you can see from the middle compound below, this is another kanji that can absorb its accompanying **hiragana**.

Less Common Pronunciations
Less common **ON** reading: none
Less common **kun** reading: none

COMMON WORDS AND COMPOUNDS		
置く	*put; place; leave*	**o·ku** お・く
置場	put + place = *place (for something)*	**oki·ba** おき・ば
配置	distribute + put = *arrangement; layout*	**HAI·CHI** ハイ・チ

KANJI 453

個 **SOLO**

ノ	イ	イ	們	们	們	個	個	個
個								

BUILDING THIS KANJI
Giraffe イ + Hard 固(361) = 個

Meaning

This kanji emphasizes the separateness of individual objects (including people). It is, in fact, used as a general counter for 'pieces' — the final compound shows this aspect of its meaning.

Remembering this kanji

"What with predators about," he said, " a **giraffe** had better be **hard** if he's gonna graze SOLO."

Common Pronunciations

Common **ON** reading: **KO** (コ)
Common **kun** reading: none

Less Common Pronunciations

Less common **ON** reading: none
Less common **kun** reading: none

COMMON WORDS AND COMPOUNDS		
個人	solo + person = *an individual*	**KO·JIN** コ・ジン
個別	solo + different = *individually;* *one by one*	**KO·BETSU** コ・ベツ
三個	three + solo = *three (pieces)*	SAN·**KO** サン・コ

COMPONENT #454

PIRATE 戊 戊

Here we have the fourth member of our special family of components. As with 弋 'spilling coffee' and 戈 'killer bee', the stroke order is broken here by anything that appears underneath the horizontal line (the following kanji provides an example). And finally, don't ever forget to include the doubloon with this component — the pirate is known to become very angry if someone takes away his money.

KANJI 454

成 **BECOME**

ノ	厂	万	成	成	成			

BUILDING THIS KANJI
Pirate 戊 + Crane フ = 成

Meaning

Become. Pay close attention to the stroke order of this kanji, as the sword of the pirate is always written <u>before</u> the horizontal line (thus making these initial strokes the opposite of 厂, the "cliff" learned prior to Entry 287. Remember also that the crane breaks the stroke order of the pirate by following immediately after the horizontal line.

Remembering this kanji

"If you want to BECOME a **pirate** these days," Blackbeard told me, "you'll need to have a **crane**."
"Why's that?" I asked.
"Well, have you seen the size of those supertankers? You even attempt to scale one of those with ropes and you'll BECOME a laughingstock."

Common Pronunciations

Common **ON** reading: **SEI** (セイ)
Common **kun** reading: **na** (な)

The **kun-yomi** can incorporate its **hiragana** ending in certain compounds.

Less Common Pronunciations

Less common **ON** reading: **JŌ** (ジョ ウ)
Less common **kun** reading: none

COMMON WORDS AND COMPOUNDS		
成る	become	**na·ru** な・る
成年	become + year = *adult; age of majority*	**SEI**·NEN セイ・ネン
成立	become + stand = *formation*	**SEI**·RITSU セイ・リツ

 WORK

BUILDING THIS KANJI
Giraffe イ + **Move** 動(318) = 働

Meaning
Work.

Remembering this kanji
"Do you ever notice that **giraffes** always seem to be on the **move**?"
"That's because a lot of them are unemployed. They're looking for **WORK**."

Common Pronunciations

Common **ON** reading: none
Common **kun** reading: **hatara** (はたら)

Less Common Pronunciations

Less common **ON** reading: **DŌ** (ド ウ)
Less common **kun** reading: none

COMMON WORDS AND COMPOUNDS		
働く	*work*	**hatara·ku** はたら・く
働き口	work + mouth = *job; position*	**hatara·ki** guchi はたら・き ぐち

COMPONENT #456

CRAB WITH A MOHAWK

This is a good place to review a number of similar-looking components. In addition to the present one, ensure that you are able to easily identify ⼧ 'pincers', ⼀ 'UFO', ⼋ "claw", ⼍ 'weightlifter', ⼎ 'stroller', ⼀ 'quicksand', and ⼋ 'rocket launch'.

KANJI 456

堂 **HALL**

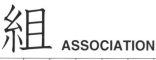

BUILDING THIS KANJI
Crab With a Mohawk ⼧ + Mouth (vampire)
口 (8) + Earth 土 (87) = 堂

Meaning
This kanji refers to a larger-sized hall, usually in a public building.

Remembering this kanji
The HALL was in a bloodthirsty uproar, as the **crab with a mohawk** had unexpectedly pinned the **vampire**. Moments later, however, the HALL fell silent, and we watched as the **crab** helped the **vampire** to his feet and brushed the **earth** from his cape. I was not alone in feeling ashamed, for no one in that HALL had ever witnessed such sportsmanship.

Common Pronunciations
Common ON reading: DŌ (ド ウ)
Common kun reading: none

Less Common Pronunciations
Less common ON reading: none
Less common kun reading: none

COMMON WORDS AND COMPOUNDS		
食堂	eat + hall = *dining hall; cafeteria*	SHOKU·DŌ ショク・ドウ
本堂	main + hall = *main hall; main temple*	HON·DŌ ホン・ドウ

KANJI 457

組 **ASSOCIATION**

BUILDING THIS KANJI
Thread 糸 (196) + Besides (filing cabinet) 且 (293) = 組

Association, set. This kanji has to do with things coming together or being put together in groups.

Remembering this kanji
"**Thread**?" she said. "Yes, of course we do. I'll get you some from the **filing cabinet** over there."

And so, she thought, it goes on…will I ever get free from the clutches of the Quilter's ASSOCIATION?

Common Pronunciations
Common ON reading: none
Common kun reading: **ku** (く); **kumi** (く み)

These readings become voiced in the second position according to the rules we learned for 付 in Entry 226. Note the mix of **on-** and **kun-yomi** in the final compound.

Less Common Pronunciations
Less common **ON** reading: **SO** (ソ)
Less common **kun** reading: none

COMMON WORDS AND COMPOUNDS		
組む	*put together; form*	**ku**·mu く・む
組合	association + match = *association; (labor) union*	**kumi**·ai く み・あい
番組	order + association = *a program*	BAN·**gumi** バン・ぐみ

KANJI 458

起 ARISE

一	十	土	尹	走	走	走	起	起
起								

BUILDING THIS KANJI
Run 走(212) + Oneself (whip) 己(214) = 起

Meaning
Arise, get up, happen. The kanji for 'run' always stretches out like this when appearing on the left of another character as a component.

Remembering this kanji
If you **run** with a **whip** and yell 'ARISE!', it's pretty likely that something or someone will in fact ARISE.

Common Pronunciations
Common **ON** reading: **KI** (キ)
Common **kun** reading: **o** (お)

The first two examples below function as a normal intransitive/transitive verb pair.

Less Common Pronunciations
Less common **ON** reading: none
Less common **kun** reading: none

COMMON WORDS AND COMPOUNDS		
起こる (intr)	*to happen; come to pass*	**o**·koru お・こる
起こす (tr)	*to bring about; raise up*	**o**·kosu お・こす
起きる (intr)	*to get up / rise*	**o**·kiru お・きる
起点	arise + point = *starting point*	**KI·TEN** キ・テン

KANJI 459

争 DISPUTE

ノ	⼕	⼚	刍	刍	争		

BUILDING THIS KANJI
Little Red Riding Hood ⼚ + Pitchfork ⼹ + Harpoon 亅 = 争

Meaning
Dispute, argue.

Remembering this kanji
Little Red Riding Hood is a country girl, so it was natural that she'd grab a **pitchfork**. What was odd, though, was how she managed to get a **harpoon**...had she really gone down to the docks? Anyway, what was beyond DISPUTE was that she was finally ready for any DISPUTE.

Common Pronunciations

Common **ON** reading: **SŌ** (ソウ)
Common **kun** reading: **araso** (あらそ)

Less Common Pronunciations

Less common **ON** reading: none
Less common **kun** reading: none

COMMON WORDS AND COMPOUNDS		
争う	*dispute; contend*	araso·u あらそ・う
争点	dispute + point = *point of dispute*	SŌ·TEN ソウ・テン
内争	inside + dispute = *internal dispute*	NAI·SŌ ナイ・ソウ

COMPONENT #460

NUCLEAR REACTOR

There's no need to be concerned about what's leaking out of the right-hand side of the reactor here; this is only an illustration.

KANJI 460

風 WIND

BUILDING THIS KANJI
Nuclear Reactor 几 + Comet 一 + Insect 虫 (391) = 風

Meaning

Wind (as in breeze). An important secondary meaning relates to the ideas of style and appearance; the final compound provides an example.

Remembering this kanji

"You expect me to believe that the **nuclear reactor** was struck by a **comet**?" I asked.
"Look, pal," said the giant mutating **insect**, "I'm only suggesting you might want to stay ahead of the WIND."

Common Pronunciations

Common **ON** reading: **FŪ** (フウ)
Common **kun** reading: **kaza** (かざ); **kaze** (かぜ)

FŪ is the more common of the three readings, while **kaza** appears only in the first position. **kaze** is the reading used when the kanji stands on its own; it rarely occurs in the first position but is as common as **FŪ** when this character is the last in a compound. **FŪ** is the reading used in those compounds relating to style and appearance.

Create your **on-yomi** keyword and write it in the table at the back of the book. Then, after creating your **kun-yomi** keywords, write your sentence to remember the on-yomi and kun-yomi readings in the box below.

Less Common Pronunciations

Less common **ON** reading: **FU** (フ)
Less common **kun** reading: none

This reading is primarily useful for its appearance in the well-known Japanese word for 'bath': 風呂* (**FU·RO** / フ・ロ), from the kanji 'wind' and 'spine'. The latter character, incidentally, is not presented in this book, but can be easily remembered as a straight pictogram of a spine, or as a pair of *katakana* **RO** (ロ) strung together.

COMMON WORDS AND COMPOUNDS		
風	*wind*	kaze かぜ
風車	wind + car = *windmill*	kaza·guruma かざ・ぐるま
台風	platform + wind = *typhoon*	TAI·FŪ タイ・フウ
日本風	Japan + wind (style) = *Japanese style*	NI·HON·FŪ ニ・ホン・フウ

KANJI 461

 PAIN

BUILDING THIS KANJI
Lemmings 疒 + Dentist Light マ + Utilize 用
(270) = 痛

Meaning
Pain.

Remembering this kanji
I watched as the **lemmings** carefully positioned the **dentist light** above me. At least they're able to **utilize** that, I thought. Nevertheless, I couldn't shake the feeling that my root canal was about to leave me in a lot of **PAIN**.

Common Pronunciations
Common **ON** reading: **TSŪ** (ツ ウ)
Common **kun** reading: **ita** (い た)

Recall from Entry 303 that the final compound below uses a less common **on-yomi** for 頭.

Less Common Pronunciations
Less common **ON** reading: none
Less common **kun** reading: none

COMMON WORDS AND COMPOUNDS		
痛い	*painful*	**ita**·i いた·い
痛み止め	pain + stop = *painkiller*	**ita**·mi do·me いた·み ど·め
頭痛	head + pain = *headache*	**ZU**·**TSŪ** ズ·ツ ウ

KANJI 462

 OFFICER

BUILDING THIS KANJI
One (hamburger patty) 一(3) + History 史
(440) = 吏

Meaning
An officer or official, typically one of lower standing. We will find more use for this kanji as a component than as a character on its own.

Remembering this kanji
"What is it I do? I'm a **hamburger patty history OFFICER**."
"Is that so?"
"Yes, well the **hamburger patty** has an interesting **history**. I mean, anything that's gone from a slab of gristle-clogged beef to the status of culinary icon needs someone to tell its story. Who else is more qualified than a **hamburger patty history OFFICER**?"

Common Pronunciations
Common **ON** reading: **RI** (リ)
Common **kun** reading: none

Less Common Pronunciations
Less common **ON** reading: none
Less common **kun** reading: none

COMPONENT #463

JUGGLER

KANJI 463

寝 SLEEP

'	｀	´´	宀	宀	宀	宀	宀	宀
宀	宀	寝	寝					

BUILDING THIS KANJI
Pincers 宀 + Juggler ⺆ + Comb ⼹ + UFO
⼍ + Again (ironing board) 又(159) = 寝

Meaning
Sleep.

Remembering this kanji
The stress of a modern lifestyle, it seemed, was starting to be too much.
"SLEEP...SLEEP..." he said softly.
"But I can't SLEEP!" she exclaimed. "I've got so much to do, I feel like there's a huge set of **pincers** hovering over me. I mean, I'm like a **juggler**! I always have to keep up my appearance with this **comb**..."
"Just SLEEP..."
"But how can I? Since the aliens in the **UFO** gave me the **ironing board** and told me to take better care of the family..."
"Sssshhh...you just need to SLEEP..."

Common Pronunciations
Common **ON** reading: SHIN (シ ン)
Common **kun** reading: ne (ね)

The **kun-yomi** is the more common reading here.

Less Common Pronunciations
Less common **ON** reading: none
Less common **kun** reading: none

COMMON WORDS AND COMPOUNDS		
寝る	*sleep*	ne·ru ね・る
昼寝	daytime + sleep = *afternoon nap*	hiru·ne ひる・ね
寝室	sleep + room = *bedroom*	SHIN·SHITSU シン・シツ

KANJI 464

関 CHECKPOINT

| 丨 | 冂 | 冂 | 戶 | 戶 | 門 | 門 | 門 | 門 |
| 門 | 閂 | 関 | 関 | 関 | | | | |

BUILDING THIS KANJI
Gate 門(96) + Opera Singer 关 = 関

Meaning
Checkpoint, barrier.

Remembering this kanji
We approached the **gate** but found our way blocked by an **opera singer**. "This is a CHECK-POINT," she said.
I was frightened, but you were not. "I'm not sure I understand," you replied. "Is the **gate** the CHECKPOINT, or are you the CHECK-POINT?"

Common Pronunciations
Common **ON** reading: **KAN** (カン)
Common **kun** reading: **seki** (せき)

Less Common Pronunciations
Less common **ON** reading: none
Less common **kun** reading: none

COMMON WORDS AND COMPOUNDS		
関	*checkpoint; barrier*	**seki** せき
機関	mechanism + checkpoint = *engine; organization*	KI·KAN キ・カン
関係	checkpoint + connection = *relationship; connection*	KAN·KEI カン・ケイ

KANJI 465

側 SIDE

| ノ | 亻 | 亻 | 佀 | 俏 | 但 | 俱 | 俱 | 俱 |
| 俱 | 側 | | | | | | | |

BUILDING THIS KANJI
Giraffe 亻 + Rule 則(382) = 側

Meaning
Side.

Remembering this kanji
"**Giraffes** have a **rule**," he said. "When they graze, everyone else has to step to the SIDE. It's always been like that here on the savanna."
"Well, you might be happy to watch from the SIDE," she said, "but I'm not. Those arrogant **giraffes** and their **rules** won't force me to the SIDE forever."

Common Pronunciations
Common **ON** reading: **SOKU** (ソク)
Common **kun** reading: **gawa** (がわ)

Less Common Pronunciations

Less common **ON** reading: none

Less common **kun** reading: none

COMMON WORDS AND COMPOUNDS		
側	*side*	**gawa** がわ
左側	left + side = *left side*	hidari·**gawa** ひだり・がわ
側近	side + near = *close associate*	**SOK·KIN** ソッ・キン

CHAPTER 20 REVIEW EXERCISES

A. Please match the following kanji to their meanings.

1.	困	a.	Cold
2.	寒	b.	Point
3.	点	c.	Personal
4.	働	d.	Dispute
5.	争	e.	Pain
6.	痛	f.	Warm
7.	組	g.	Feather
8.	身	h.	Distress
9.	羽	i.	Work
10.	温	j.	Association

B. Please match the following meanings to their kanji, and these to their on- or kun-yomi.

1.	Checkpoint	a. 置	1.	**KAI** (カイ)	
2.	Become	b. 堂	2.	**kaze** (かぜ)	
3.	Arise	c. 術	3.	**DŌ** (ドウ)	
	(on-yomi)				
4.	Side	d. 関	4.	**JUTSU** (ジュツ)	
5.	Sleep	e. 起	5.	**KI** (キ)	
6.	Put	f. 成	6.	**seki** (せき)	
	(kun-yomi)				
7.	Wind	g. 風	7.	**gawa** (がわ)	
8.	Technique	h. 階	8.	**o** (お)	
9.	Floor	i. 側	9.	**ne** (ね)	
10.	Hall	j. 寝	10.	**na** (な)	

C. Please choose the best answer(s) to the following questions.

1. Which is the correct reading of 働く?
   a. **hara·ku** (はら・く)
   b. **hatara·ku** (はたら・く)
   c. **kotara·ku** (こたら・く)
   d. **hikera·ku** (ひけら・く)

2. Which of the following readings apply to the kanji 初?
   a. **haji** (はじ)　　b. **SHO** (ショ)
   c. **SHŌ** (ショウ)　　d. **ha** (は)
   e. **hatsu** (はつ)

3. Rembrandt's _____ is known for its subtlety.
   a. 側　b. 風　c. 官　d. 術　e. 羽

4. Which is the correct reading of 寒い?
   a. **ubu·i** (うぶ・い)
   b. **kamu·i** (かむ・い)
   c. **samu·i** (さむ・い)
   d. **kayu·i** (かゆ・い)

5. Which of the following kanji has the most number of strokes?
   a. 風　b. 身　c. 官　d. 困　e. 初

D. Please match the following compounds to their meanings and pronunciations.

1. 台風	a. Headache	1. **ZU·TSŪ** (ズ・ツウ)	
2. 勉強	b. An individual	2. **BAN·gumi** (バン・ぐみ)	
3. 個人	c. Afternoon nap	3. **KO·JIN** (コ・ジン)	
4. 温泉	d. Point of dispute	4. **SŌ·TEN** (ソウ・テン)	
5. 頭痛	e. Typhoon	5. **TAI·FŪ** (タイ・フウ)	
6. 関係	f. Connection	6. **SHUS·SHIN** (シュッ・ シン)	
7. 番組	g. Hot spring / Spa	7. **ON·SEN** (オン・セン)	
8. 出身	h. A program	8. **BEN·KYŌ** (ベン・ キョウ)	
9. 争点	i. Studying	9. **KAN·KEI** (カン・ケイ)	
10. 昼寝	j. One's hometown	10. **hiru·ne** (ひる・ね)	

E. Please read the passage below and answer the questions that follow.

科学の勉強をしている時に気温が下がって初雪が降りました。寒いのでクラスの後、温泉に行く事に決めました。二人の友達と行って楽しかったです。

1. What was this person studying?
2. What happened during this time?
3. What did this person decide to do after class?
4. With whom did this person go?
5. What made them decide to do this?

Kanji #466—490

KANJI 466

 CARGO

一	十	卄	ナ	汁	芢	芢	荷	芢
荷								

BUILDING THIS KANJI
Wreath 艹 + What 何(411) = 荷

Meaning
Cargo, burden. As mentioned in Entry 411, this is the only general-use kanji in which the character for 'what' appears as a component. As there, it will be highlighted in the story below by a string of exclamation and question marks.

Remembering this kanji
"A **wreath**," she said quietly.
"**What**!!!???"
"I couldn't believe it either. We looked everywhere, but that was the only CARGO."

Common Pronunciations
Common **ON** reading: **KA** (カ)
Common **kun** reading: **ni** (に)

The **kun-yomi** is by far the more common reading. Note that the second compound (a combination of **on-** and **kun-yomi**) uses the less common **on-yomi** of 物 ("thing", from Entry 125).

Less Common Pronunciations
Less common **ON** reading: none
Less common **kun** reading: none

COMMON WORDS AND COMPOUNDS		
重荷	heavy + cargo = *heavy burden / load*	omo·**ni** おも・に
荷物	cargo + thing = *luggage; baggage*	**ni**·MOTSU に・モツ
出荷	exit + cargo = *shipment; shipping*	SHUK·**KA** シュッ・カ

KANJI 467

 PORT

`	`	⺡	⺡	汁	汁	洪	洪	洪
港	港	港						

BUILDING THIS KANJI
Splash ⺡ + Together 共(409) + Oneself (whip)
己(214) = 港

Meaning
Port, harbor.

Remembering this kanji
I was woken by a **splash** and looked up; we were
still **together** on the raft, but the elements were
lashing us like a **whip**. The PORT, I thought,
would we ever make it to the PORT?

Common Pronunciations
Common **ON** reading: **KŌ** (コウ)
Common **kun** reading: **minato** (みなと)

Less Common Pronunciations
Less common **ON** reading: none
Less common **kun** reading: none

COMMON WORDS AND COMPOUNDS		
港	port; harbor	**minato** みなと
入港	enter + port = *entering port; arrival*	NYŪ·KŌ ニュウ・コウ
空港	empty (sky) + port = *airport*	KŪ·KŌ クウ・コウ

KANJI 468

 HIT

一	丁	扌	扌	打			

BUILDING THIS KANJI
Finger 扌 + Block 丁 (165) = 打

Meaning
Hit, strike.

Remembering this kanji
"It's rough here, so for goodness sakes don't
wag your **finger** at anyone in this **block**. You'll
get HIT."

Common Pronunciations
Common **ON** reading: **DA** (ダ)
Common **kun** reading: **u** (う)

u is the more common reading. This is another
kanji that will often incorporate its accompanying
hiragana when forming nouns.

Create your **on-yomi** keyword and enter it in the
table at the back of the book. Then, after creating
your **kun-yomi** keyword, write your sentence to
remember the **on-yomi** and **kun-yomi** readings in
the box below.

Less Common Pronunciations

Less common **ON** reading: none
Less common **kun** reading: none

COMMON WORDS AND COMPOUNDS		
打つ	*hit; strike*	**u**·tsu う・つ
打ち切る	hit + cut = *stop doing something; break off*	**u**·chi ki·ru う・ち き・る
打者	hit + individual = *batter; hitter (in baseball)*	**DA**·SHA ダ・シャ

JUNGLEMAN

KANJI 469

列 **ROW**

一	ﾉ	ﾗ	歹	列	列		

BUILDING THIS KANJI
Jungleman 歹 + Chisel 刂 = 列

Meaning

Row (as in a row of objects).

Remembering this kanji

"It really bugs me that it's so messy here in
the jungle," said the **jungleman**, "and since it
can be easy to misplace stuff because of that,
it's important that I keep everything tidy and
ID my possessions with this **chisel**. Here, for
instance, are my spears: you'll notice they're
nicely arranged in a ROW. Over there are my
animal skulls—also in a ROW—and of course
my leopard-skin shorts. And yes, those are in a
ROW, too."

Common Pronunciations

Common **ON** reading: **RETSU** (レ ツ)
Common **kun** reading: none

Create your **on-yomi** keyword and enter it in the
table at the back of the book. After that, write
your sentence to remember the **on-yomi** reading
in the box below.

Less Common Pronunciations

Less common **ON** reading: none
Less common **kun** reading: none

COMMON WORDS AND COMPOUNDS		
列島	row + island = *island chain; archipelago*	**RET**·TŌ レッ・トウ
列車	row + car = *train*	**RES**·SHA レッ・シャ
系列	system + row = *series; corporate group*	**KEI**·**RETSU** ケイ・レツ

KANJI 470

丸 **ROUND**

ノ	九	丸						

BUILDING THIS KANJI
Nine 九 (39) + Jelly Bean ヽ = 丸

Meaning
Round. By extension are the ideas of completion and wholeness, etc.

Remembering this kanji
"Yes, I realize you're dressed to the **nines** and look great. But if you keep eating one **jelly bean** after another like this...I'm telling you, you're going to get ROUND."

Common Pronunciations
Common **ON** reading: none
Common **kun** reading: **maru** (ま る)

Less Common Pronunciations
Less common **ON** reading: **GAN** (ガ ン)
Less common **kun** reading: none

COMMON WORDS AND COMPOUNDS		
丸い	*round*	**maru**·i ま る·い
丸める	*to make round*	**maru**·meru ま る·め る
日の丸	sun + round = *the Japanese (rising sun) flag*	hi no **maru** ひ の ま る

KANJI 471

館 **MANOR**

ノ	ハ	ベ	今	今	今	食	食	食'
食'	飠	館	飣	館	館	館		

BUILDING THIS KANJI
Umbrella 𠆢 + Glutton 𩙿 + Official 官 (443)
= 館

Meaning
Manor, although this kanji can appear in compounds referring to anything from stately embassies to simple country inns.

Remembering this kanji
Though an **umbrella** was covering the **glutton**, the **official** at the MANOR was not fooled. "I'm not letting you in," she said. "This wine and cheese is only for **officials** who have been invited to the MANOR."

Common Pronunciations
Common **ON** reading: **KAN** (カ ン)
Common **kun** reading: none

Recall from Entry 448 that the first two kanji of the final compound mean 'art' when taken together.

Less Common Pronunciations
Less common **ON** reading: none
Less common **kun** reading: none

旅館	travel + manor = *Japanese-style inn*	RYO·KAN リョ・カン
図書館	diagram + write + manor = *library*	TO·SHO·KAN ト・ショ・カン
美術館	art + manor = *art museum*	BI·JUTSU·KAN ビ・ジュツ・カン

COMPONENT #472

HUMMINGBIRD   飞

KANJI 472

飛 FLY

⺇	⺄	飞	⻏	飞	飛	飛	飛	飛

BUILDING THIS KANJI
Hummingbird 飞 + Pole | + Giraffe 亻 +
Hummingbird 飞 = 飛

Meaning
Fly. You will need to take care with the stroke order of this very unusual-looking character; it may help when writing it to think of your pen moving in the odd pattern of left to right, back to left, and once again to right.

Remembering this kanji
A couple of **hummingbirds** can obviously FLY, but what about a **pole**? Well, it can FLY through the air if you toss it, right? And don't even bring up the **giraffe**; anyone who looks at its shape in this kanji can tell that it's FLYING.

Common Pronunciations
Common **ON** reading: **HI** (ヒ)
Common **kun** reading: **to** (と)

The **kun-yomi** can absorb its accompanying **hiragana** when forming nouns. When taken together, the first two kanji in the final compound mean 'flight' or 'flying'.

Less Common Pronunciations
Less common **ON** reading: none
Less common **kun** reading: none

飛ぶ	*fly*	**to**·bu と・ぶ
飛び出す	fly + exit = *fly out; jump out*	**to**·bi da·su と・び だ・す
飛行機	flight + mechanism = *airplane*	**HI·KŌ·KI** ヒ・コウ・キ

NUMBER

ヽ	゛	一	十	米	米	米	娄
娄	娄	数	数				

BUILDING THIS KANJI
Rice 米 (32) + Woman 女 (16) + Cheerleaders
夂 = 数

Meaning
Number. When in the first position, this kanji will sometimes carry the meaning of 'several' of whatever is indicated by the character following (years, persons, days, etc.).

Remembering this kanji
"The NUMBER of **rice** grains that you can stack on this **woman** is very important," she said. "It will determine which of you **cheerleaders** pass the tryout."

"Uh, excuse me?" said the **woman**. "What kind of ridiculous job is this? I'm supposed to just sit here and get covered with **rice**? No wonder a NUMBER of **women** told me not to apply."

Common Pronunciations
Common **ON** reading: **SŪ** (スウ)
Common **kun** reading: **kazu** (かず); **kazo** (かぞ)

SŪ is the most common reading, and the one used to express the idea of 'several' mentioned above. **kazu** is the general word for 'number' and forms only a few compounds, while **kazo** is a verb stem (for the verb in the second example below). On rare occasions the **on-yomi** can become voiced; the final compound is an example.

Create your **on-yomi** keyword and write it in the table at the back of the book. Then, after creating your **kun-yomi** keywords, write your sentence to remember the **on-yomi** and **kun-yomi** readings in the box below.

Less Common Pronunciations
Less common **ON** reading: **SU** (ス)
Less common **kun** reading: none

COMMON WORDS AND COMPOUNDS		
数	*number*	**kazu** かず
数える	*count*	**kazo·eru** かぞ·える
数学	number + study = *mathematics*	**SŪ·GAKU** スウ·ガク
人数	person + number = *number of persons*	**NIN·ZŪ** ニン·ズウ

習 LEARN

フ	�ヲ	ヨ	羽	羽	羽	羽	羽	習
習	習							

BUILDING THIS KANJI
Feather 羽 (444) + White 白 (7) = 習

Meaning
Learn. Take care not to confuse this kanji with 皆 ('all', from Entry 344).

Remembering this kanji

"If you drop a **feather** on something **white**," said the guru. "What will you LEARN? Assuming the **feather** is **white**, of course."

"I couldn't care less," he said.

"Oh. Well you obviously have much to LEARN."

Common Pronunciations

Common **ON** reading: **SHŪ** (シュウ)
Common **kun** reading: **nara** (なら)

Less Common Pronunciations

Less common **ON** reading: none
Less common **kun** reading: none

COMMON WORDS AND COMPOUNDS		
習う	learn; take lessons	**nara·u** なら・う
自習	self + learn = learning by oneself	**JI·SHŪ** ジ・シュウ
習字	learn + character = penmanship	**SHŪ·JI** シュウ・ジ

COMPONENT #475

PLAYGROUND   衣   衣

As this is the last of several similar-looking components, it's now a good idea for us to compare it to the others: 呆 'sherpa', 衣 'sprinter', 仐 'crossing gate'.

KANJI 475

展   **DISPLAY**

BUILDING THIS KANJI
Flag 尸 + Wreath 艹 + Playground 衣 = 展

Meaning
Display, spread.

Remembering this kanji

"DISPLAY the **flag**! She's here!"

And we did so without complaint, for this was our champion, her victory **wreath** on full DISPLAY. Even those in the **playground**, it must be said, were unable to swing or slide, being awestruck by the entire DISPLAY.

Common Pronunciations

Common **ON** reading: **TEN** (テン)
Common **kun** reading: none

Less Common Pronunciations

Less common **ON** reading: none
Less common **kun** reading: none

COMMON WORDS AND COMPOUNDS		
展開	display + open = unfolding; development	**TEN·KAI** テン・カイ
展示	display + show = display; exhibition	**TEN·JI** テン・ジ
発展	discharge + display = development; expansion	**HAT·TEN** ハッ・テン

KANJI 476

MASK

Meaning
Mask, aspect, face. Underlying the meaning of this character is a sense of the surface appearance of things. You've no doubt seen enough kanji by now to realize what a unique-looking character we're dealing with here; you'll need to take your time with the stroke order, as it's unlike any other kanji you'll meet.

Common Pronunciations
Common **ON** reading: **MEN** (メ ン)
Common **kun** reading: **omote** (お も て);
omo (お も)

MEN is the far more common reading.

Less Common Pronunciations
Less common **ON** reading: none
Less common **kun** reading: **tsura** (つ ら)

IRREGULAR READING		
真面目	true + mask + eye = *honest; earnest*	ma·ji·me ま·じ·め

COMMON WORDS AND COMPOUNDS		
面	*surface; face*	omote おもて
面白い	mask + white = *interesting*	omo shiro·i おも しろ·い
面接	mask + join = *interview*	MEN·SETSU メ ン·セ ツ

KANJI 477

SELECT

BUILDING THIS KANJI
Oneself (whip) 已(214) + Oneself (whip) 已 (214) + **Together** 共(409) + **Seal** 辶 = 選

Meaning
Select, choose.

Remembering this kanji
It was my turn to SELECT, but just like the other rookies I could only do it with a couple of **whips**. The herd, of course, attempted to stick **together** at first, but I was eventually able to force a **seal** to stray from the rest. Quite honestly, though, I should have been able to SELECT a better one.

Common Pronunciations
Common **ON** reading: **SEN** (セン)
Common **kun** reading: **era** (えら)

Less Common Pronunciations
Less common **ON** reading: none
Less common **kun** reading: none

COMMON WORDS AND COMPOUNDS		
選ぶ	*select; choose*	**era·bu** えら·ぶ
選手	select + hand = *athlete*	**SEN·SHU** セン·シュ
特選	special + select = *special selection*	TOKU·**SEN** トク·セン

COMPONENT #478

CHILI PEPPER

KANJI 478

帰
HOMEWARD

BUILDING THIS KANJI
Chili Pepper ⺈ + Comb ⦀ + UFO ⌒ + Cloth 巾 (162) = 帰

Meaning
Homeward, in the sense of going back or returning.

Remembering this kanji
A glance HOMEWARD…

I am a **chili pepper** in a foreign land, and they are looking for those like me with a fine-toothed **comb**. They call me an alien, and I feel, sometimes, as if I *had* dropped here from a **UFO**. And yet I am needed here, to draw a **cloth** across my sweating brow doing jobs that others feel are beneath them. It is unbearable, and yet for the sake of my loved ones, I cannot turn HOMEWARD…

Common Pronunciations
Common **ON** reading: **KI** (キ)
Common **kun** reading: **kae** (かえ)

The **kun-yomi** becomes voiced (as in the second compound) according to the same rules as those for 付 (Entry 226).

Less Common Pronunciations
Less common **ON** reading: none
Less common **kun** reading: none

COMMON WORDS AND COMPOUNDS		
帰る	*go back*	**kae·ru** かえ·る
日帰り	sun (day) + homeward = *day trip*	hi **gae·ri** ひ がえ·り
帰国	homeward + country = *go back to one's country*	**KI**·KOKU キ·コク

KANJI 479

部 SECTION

'	二	宀	立	立	立	音	音	音
部	部							

BUILDING THIS KANJI
Stand 立(112) + Mouth (vampire) 口(8) +
Veteran Yodeler 阝= 部

Meaning
Section, department, category.

Remembering this kanji
"Why can't I **stand** in this SECTION?" asked
the **vampire**. "I'd prefer to be…"
He was interrupted by a yodel. A magnificent,
soaring, yodel.
"I'm so sorry," he said. "I didn't realize this was
the **veteran yodeler** SECTION."

Common Pronunciations
Common **ON** reading: **BU** (ブ)
Common **kun** reading: none

Create your **on-yomi** keyword and enter it in the
table at the back of the book. After that, write
your sentence to remember the **on-yomi** reading
in the box below.

Less Common Pronunciations
Less common **ON** reading: none
Less common **kun** reading: none

IRREGULAR READING		
部屋	section + roof = *room (of a house, etc.)*	he·ya へ・や

COMMON WORDS AND COMPOUNDS		
全部	complete + section = *all; the whole*	ZEN·BU ゼン・ブ
上部	upper + section = *upper section / part*	JŌ·BU ジョウ・ブ
部分	section + part = *part; portion*	BU·BUN ブ・ブン

KANJI 480

題 TOPIC

'	乛	甲	日	旦	早	早	是	是
是	是'	趸	題	題	題	題	題	題

BUILDING THIS KANJI
Approve 是(406) + Guy Wearing a Barrel 頁
= 題

Meaning
Topic, theme. This is the only instance in the
general-use kanji in which the character for
'approve' is stretched out; the story takes this
into account.

Remembering this kanji
"What's the TOPIC?"

"It's 'Do you **approve** of a **guy wearing a barrel** being a component in kanji?'"

"Hmmm. That's a troubling TOPIC, given the way he's so rudely distorting the **approve** component in TOPIC."

Common Pronunciations
Common **ON** reading: **DAI** (ダイ)
Common **kun** reading: none

Less Common Pronunciations
Less common **ON** reading: none
Less common **kun** reading: none

COMMON WORDS AND COMPOUNDS		
問題	question + topic = *problem; issue*	MON·DAI モン・ダイ
宿題	lodging + topic = *homework*	SHUKU·DAI シュク・ダイ
主題	primary + topic = *theme; subject*	SHU·DAI シュ・ダイ

COMPONENT #481

PARFAIT

Like any good parfait, there are three layers of ice cream here: chocolate, strawberry and vanilla (or whichever others you may prefer).

KANJI 481

期 **PERIOD**

BUILDING THIS KANJI
Parfait 其 + Moon 月 (11) = 期

Meaning
Period (of time).

Remembering this kanji
"**Parfaits**?" said the **moon**. "Yes, there's a PERIOD in a month when I binge on them until I'm full. But after that it seems I can't bear to look at them, and for an equal PERIOD I just waste away."

Common Pronunciations
Common **ON** reading: **KI** (キ)
Common **kun** reading: none

Less Common Pronunciations
Less common **ON** reading: **GO** (ゴ)
Less common **kun** reading: none

COMMON WORDS AND COMPOUNDS		
期間	period + interval = *period of time*	KI·KAN キ・カン
期待	period + wait = *expectation*	KI·TAI キ・タイ
定期	fixed + period = *fixed period*	TEI·KI テイ・キ

KANJI 482

 GRANT

BUILDING THIS KANJI
Finger 扌 + Receive 受(191) = 授

Meaning
To grant, impart.

Remembering this kanji
She watched nervously as one **finger** after another was scrutinized; would she finally **receive** the manicure? At last the famous beautician looked up. "Yes," she said, "I will GRANT it."

Common Pronunciations
Common **ON** reading: **JU** (ジュ)
Common **kun** reading: none

Less Common Pronunciations
Less common **ON** reading: none
Less common **kun** reading: **sazu** (さず)

COMMON WORDS AND COMPOUNDS		
授業	grant + business = *lesson; instruction*	**JU·GYŌ** ジュ・ギョウ
授与	grant + confer = *awarding; conferring*	**JU·YO** ジュ・ヨ
教授	teach + grant = *teaching; a professor*	KYŌ·JU キョウ・ジュ

KANJI 483

便 **DELIVERY**

BUILDING THIS KANJI
Giraffe 亻 + Anew 更(373) = 便

Meaning
This character has an array of meanings, from postal services, convenience and opportunity to—believe it or not—bodily functions such as defecation and urination. Underlying everything, when you think about it though, is a sense of (ahem) 'delivering' things or of things being delivered in some way.

Remembering this kanji
The **giraffe** was suffering **anew**. "Has the DELIVERY truck been here yet?" she asked the clerk hoarsely. "I'm really hoping you get that DELIVERY of throat lozenges today."

Common Pronunciations
Common **ON** reading: **BEN** (シン);
BIN (ビン)
Common **kun** reading: none

BEN is the reading used in compounds related to both convenience and bodily functions (as in the first two examples below), while **BIN** appears in compounds having to do with mail (such as in the final example) and opportunity. Recall from Entry

239 that the first two kanji in the final compound mean 'urgent' when taken together.

Create your **on-yomi** keyword for **BIN** (ビン) and enter it in the table at the back of the book. After that, write your sentence to remember the **on-yomi** readings in the box below.

Less Common Pronunciations
Less common **ON** reading: none
Less common **kun** reading: **tayo** (たよ)

	COMMON WORDS AND COMPOUNDS	
便利	delivery + profit = *convenient; handy*	**BEN·RI** ベン·リ
便所	delivery + location = *toilet; lavatory*	**BEN·JO** ベン·ジョ
至急便	urgent + delivery = *express (mail)*	**SHI·KYŪ·BIN** シ·キュウ·ビン

KANJI 484

歳 **ANNUAL**

BUILDING THIS KANJI
Stop 止 (43) + Pirate 戊 + One (hamburger patty) 一 (3) + Small 小 (20) = 歳

Meaning

Annual, year, age. When used as a suffix (as in the final example below), this kanji translates as '…years old'. Pay close attention to the intricate stroke order of this character, keeping in mind that anything underneath the horizontal line of the pirate component is always written immediately after it.

Remembering this kanji

"If we intend to **stop** this **pirate**," he said, "we should offer him a **hamburger patty**."

"But he won't care about that," she said. "It's way too **small**."

"Hmmm. You're right. I'm sure he has a lot of ANNUAL expenses, but his ANNUAL income is still probably more than my ANNUAL salary."

Common Pronunciations
Common **ON** reading: **SAI** (サイ)
Common **kun** reading: none

The famous word in the second example is the only time this reading becomes voiced; recall from Entry 89 that 万 is read with its less common **on-yomi** here. Recall as well from Entry 411 that 何 (in the first compound) can express the idea of 'how many' in addition to 'what'.

Less Common Pronunciations
Less common **ON** reading: **SEI** (セイ)
Less common **kun** reading: none

	IRREGULAR READING	
二十歳	twenty + annual = *twenty years old*	**hatachi** はたち

	COMMON WORDS AND COMPOUNDS	
何歳	what + annual = *how many years old*	nan·**SAI** なん·サイ
万歳	ten thousand + annual = *Hurrah!*	**BAN·ZAI** バン·ザイ
五歳	five + annual = *five years old*	**GO·SAI** ゴ·サイ

COMPONENT #485

CHURCH

KANJI 485

専 **EXCLUSIVE**

BUILDING THIS KANJI
Church 甫 + Tiny (soccer player) 寸 (103) =
専

Meaning
Exclusive.

Remembering this kanji
"I'd ask you into our **church**," said the **tiny soccer player**, "but unfortunately it's EXCLUSIVE."

"Oh, I'm sorry. I didn't realize there was a **church** for **tiny soccer players**."

"Yes, but don't worry. There's an EXCLUSIVE **church** for medium-sized soccer players down the street."

Common Pronunciations
Common **ON** reading: **SEN** (セン)
Common **kun** reading: none

Less Common Pronunciations
Less common **ON** reading: none
Less common **kun** reading: **moppa** (もっぱ)

COMMON WORDS AND COMPOUNDS		
専門	exclusive + gate = *specialty*	**SEN·MON** セン·モン
専用	exclusive + utilize = *exclusive use; private use*	**SEN·YŌ** セン·ヨウ
専有	exclusive + have = *exclusive possession*	**SEN·YŪ** セン·ユウ

KANJI 486

向 **ORIENT**

BUILDING THIS KANJI
Jelly Bean 丶 + Gorilla 冂 + Mouth (vampire)
口 (8) = 向

Meaning
To orient, to look on. The overall sense is of things either orienting themselves or being oriented in a literal or figurative direction. When used as a suffix as in the second compound below, the meaning becomes 'intended for' or 'suited to'. Take care not to confuse this kanji with 同 'same' from Entry 197.

Remembering this kanji

Since **jelly beans** are a **gorilla's** favorite party food, you can always ORIENT one toward the snack table by placing some there. Attempting to ORIENT a **vampire**, however, will be a lot more tricky and dangerous, but then, I keep telling you that you shouldn't even invite one.

Common Pronunciations

Common **ON** reading: **KŌ** (コ ウ)
Common **kun** reading: **mu** (む)

Although the **kun-yomi** usually acts as a verb stem (as in the first example below), it's worth being aware that the word 向こう (**mu·kō** / む·こう) is actually a noun meaning 'the other side/party' or 'beyond'.

Less Common Pronunciations

Less common **ON** reading: none
Less common **kun** reading: none

COMMON WORDS AND COMPOUNDS		
向かう	*face on; be opposite*	**mu**·kau む·かう
夏向き	summer + orient = *for summer*	natsu **mu**·ki なつ む·き
向学心	orient + study + heart = *love of learning*	**KŌ**·GAKU·SHIN コ ウ·ガ ク·シ ン

 TRAIN

BUILDING THIS KANJI
Thread 糸(196) + **East** 東(76) = 練

Meaning
To train, knead.

Remembering this kanji

So I grabbed my **thread** and headed off to the **East**. If I wanted to be a kimono maker, I thought, where better to TRAIN?

Common Pronunciations

Common **ON** reading: **REN** (レ ン)
Common **kun** reading: **ne** (ね)

Create your **on-yomi** keyword and enter it in the table at the back of the book. Then, after creating your kun-yomi keyword, write your sentence to remember the **on-yomi** and **kun-yomi** readings in the box below.

Less Common Pronunciations

Less common **ON** reading: none
Less common **kun** reading: none

COMMON WORDS AND COMPOUNDS		
練る	*to train; knead*	**ne**·ru ね·る
練習	train + learn = *practice; exercise*	**REN**·SHŪ レ ン·シ ュ ウ
訓練	instruction + train = *training; discipline*	KUN·**REN** ク ン·レ ン

COMPONENT #488

MERMAID

KANJI 488

育 **RAISE**

BUILDING THIS KANJI
Mermaid 云 + Moon 月 (21) = 育

Meaning
To raise, bring up (as in children).

Remembering this kanji
I was unsure if I could RAISE a family, so I thought I'd practice first with a **mermaid**. Unfortunately, it didn't turn out well, as she'd flip her tail and disappear whenever I approached. So I attempted to RAISE the **moon** instead, but this was even worse; it would never stay home, and paid no attention to me at all. Darn it. I'm obviously not fit to RAISE anything.

Common Pronunciations
Common **ON** reading: **IKU** (イ ク)
Common **kun** reading: **soda** (そ だ)

Create your **on-yomi** keyword and enter it in the table at the back of the book. Then, after creating your **kun-yomi** keyword, write your sentence to remember the **on-yomi** and **kun-yomi** readings in the box below.

Less Common Pronunciations
Less common **ON** reading: none
Less common **kun** reading: none

COMMON WORDS AND COMPOUNDS		
育てる	*raise; bring up*	**soda**·teru そだ·てる
教育	teach + raise = *education*	**KYŌ·IKU** キョウ·イク
体育	body + raise = *physical education*	**TAI·IKU** タイ·イク

KANJI 489

考 **CONSIDER**

BUILDING THIS KANJI
Earth 土 (87) + Comet 一 + Rattlesnake 与
= 考

Meaning
Consider, think about.

Remembering this kanji

CONSIDER this: there was nothing else to do but pile **earth** on top of the **rattlesnake** after the **comet** crashed through this kanji. Should you be shocked? Hardly, when you CONSIDER that the **rattlesnake** was so horribly squashed that its head needs to be written from right to left here. What to do with this troublesome **comet**? Fine it? Scold it? It appears we'll have to CONSIDER everything.

Common Pronunciations

Common **ON** reading: **KŌ** (コ ウ)
Common **kun** reading: **kanga** (か ん が)

Less Common Pronunciations

Less common **ON** reading: none
Less common **kun** reading: none

COMMON WORDS AND COMPOUNDS		
考える	consider; think about	kanga·eru かんが·える
思考	think + consider = *thinking; consideration*	SHI·KŌ シ·コウ
考古学	consider + old + study = *archaeology*	KŌ·KO·GAKU コウ·コ·ガク

KANJI 490

員 MEMBER

ヽ	⁻	冖	冖	月	月	冃	冒	員
員								

BUILDING THIS KANJI
Mouth (vampire) 口 (8) + Shellfish 貝 (21) = 員

Meaning
Member.

Remembering this kanji

"I wish to be a MEMBER," said the **vampire**. "Um…this is the **Shellfish** Club," she said, "and I can't imagine you have anything in common with **shellfish**."
"Well, I shut myself up in my coffin like a **shellfish**."
"Oh, you're right. In that case, fine. We'd be happy to have you as a MEMBER."

Common Pronunciations

Common **ON** reading: **IN** (イ ン)
Common **kun** reading: none

Less Common Pronunciations

Less common **ON** reading: none
Less common **kun** reading: none

COMMON WORDS AND COMPOUNDS		
全員	complete + member = *all members; the whole staff*	ZEN·IN ゼン·イン
店員	shop + member = *clerk; store assistant*	TEN·IN テン·イン
社員	company + member = *employee; member*	SHA·IN シャ·イン

CHAPTER 21 REVIEW EXERCISES

A. Please match the following kanji to their meanings.

1.	飛	a.	Consider
2.	歳	b.	Manor
3.	考	c.	To train
4.	港	d.	Period
5.	帰	e.	Fly
6.	展	f.	Homeward
7.	期	g.	Port
8.	練	h.	Row
9.	館	i.	Display
10.	列	j.	Annual

B. Please match the following meanings to their kanji, and these to their **on-** or **kun-yomi**.

1.	Number	a. 授	1.	**BU** (ブ)	
2.	Topic	b. 育	2.	**SHŪ** (シュウ)	
3.	Grant	c. 部	3.	**u** (う)	
4.	Member	d. 向	4.	**JU** (ジュ)	
5.	Orient	e. 打	5.	**IN** (イン)	
6.	Learn	f. 丸	6.	**soda** (そだ)	
7.	Hit	g. 数	7.	**maru** (まる)	
8.	Round	h. 員	8.	**mu** (む)	
9.	Section	i. 題	9.	**DAI** (ダイ)	
10.	Raise	j. 習	10.	**kazu** (かず)	

C. Please choose the best answer(s) to the following questions.

1. Which of the following readings apply to the kanji 面?
   a. **omo** (おも)
   b. **MEN** (メン)
   c. **omote** (おもて)
   d. **MON** (モン)
   e. **omono** (おもの)

2. Which is the correct reading of 数える?
   a. **kama·eru** (かま·える)
   b. **kita·eru** (きた·える)
   c. **kazo·eru** (かぞ·える)
   d. **kota·eru** (こた·える)

3. Which of the following kanji has the most number of strokes?
   a. 港 b. 授 c. 飛 d. 歳 e. 期

4. Grandma went down to the dockyard, as it seemed her ＿＿＿ had just come in.
   a. 館 b. 打 c. 題 d. 育 e. 荷

5. Which of the following readings apply to the kanji 便?
   a. **BON** (ボン)
   b. **BIN** (ビン)
   c. **KAN** (カン)
   d. **BEN** (ベン)
   e. **HIN** (ヒン)

D. Please match the following compounds to their meanings and pronunciations.

1.	数学	a. Specialty	1.	**TEN·JI** (テン·ジ)	
2.	専門	b. Expectation	2.	**KŪ·KŌ** (クウ·コウ)	
3.	荷物	c. Airport	3.	**ni·MOTSU** (に·モツ)	
4.	展示	d. Display / Exhibition	4.	**SEN·SHU** (セン·シュ)	
5.	選手	e. Mathematics	5.	**SŪ·GAKU** (スウ·ガク)	
6.	空港	f. Inn / Hotel	6.	**RYO·KAN** (リョ·カン)	
7.	練習	g. Practice / Exercise	7.	**KYŌ·IKU** (キョウ· イク)	
8.	期待	h. Education	8.	**REN·SHŪ** (レン· シュウ)	
9.	教育	i. Luggage / Baggage	9.	**SEN·MON** (セン·モン)	
10.	旅館	j. Athlete	10.	**KI·TAI** (キ·タイ)	

E. Please read the passage below and answer the questions that follow.

図書館で美術の本を読むのが大好きです。一番好きなのは、古い日本画です。色が美しいし、形と顔がとても面白いと思います。

1. What does this person really like to do?
2. Where do they go to do this?
3. Which type of art do they like most?
4. What do they find beautiful about it?
5. How do they feel about the forms and faces?

Kanji #491—520

KANJI 491

写 **COPY**

BUILDING THIS KANJI
UFO ⌒ + Confer 与(425) = 写

Meaning
Copy, photograph.

Remembering this kanji
The **UFO** hovered overhead as the alien stepped forward to **confer** the award. "With this **COPY**," it began, "we would…"
"Hang on a sec," she interrupted. "This is a **COPY**? Where's the real one?"

Common Pronunciations
Common **ON** reading: **SHA** (シ ャ)
Common **kun** reading: **utsu** (う つ)

Less Common Pronunciations
Less common **ON** reading: none
Less common **kun** reading: none

COMMON WORDS AND COMPOUNDS		
写す	*copy; take a photograph*	**utsu**·su う つ・す
写真	copy + true = *photograph*	**SHA**·**SHIN** シ ャ・シ ン
写生	copy + life = *sketch; sketching*	**SHA**·SEI シ ャ・セ イ

COMPONENT #492

JACK IN THE BOX   壬   壬

Compare the jack in the box to 关, the 'opera singer' preceding Entry 313, and 禾, the '1950's rock star' preceding Entry 326 so as to solidify the differences between these similar-looking components.

KANJI 492

廷   COURT

| ´ | ´¯ | 千 | 壬 | 7壬 | 7廷 | 廷 | |

BUILDING THIS KANJI
Jack in the Box 壬 + Rat 乂 = 廷

Meaning
Court. This kanji can refer to courts of law (as in the initial two compounds below) and imperial courts (as in the last).

Remembering this kanji
Suddenly, the **jack in the box** popped up and pointed right at the **rat**.
"How dare you **rat** me out!" the **rat** squealed. There was chaos in the COURT.

Common Pronunciations
Common **ON** reading: **TEI** (シ ン)
Common **kun** reading: none

Less Common Pronunciations
Less common **ON** reading: none
Less common **kun** reading: none

COMMON WORDS AND COMPOUNDS		
法廷	law + court = *law court*	HŌ·TEI ホウ・テイ
出廷	exit + court = *appear in court*	SHUT·TEI シュッ・テイ
朝廷	morning (dynasty) + court = *the imperial court*	CHŌ·TEI チョウ・テイ

KANJI 493

横   SIDEWAYS

| ― | 十 | 才 | 木 | 木¯ | 朾 | 朾 | 桙 | 桙 |
| 桙 | 桙 | 横 | 横 | 横 | 横 | | | |

BUILDING THIS KANJI
Tree 木 (13) + Yellow 黄 (420) = 横

Meaning
Sideways, horizontal.

Remembering this kanji
I had given it only a SIDEWAYS glance, but realized in an instant that something in the **tree** was **yellow**. A lemon, perhaps? I carefully turned SIDEWAYS to make sure…

Common Pronunciations
Common **ON** reading: **Ō** (オ ウ)
Common **kun** reading: **yoko** (よ こ)

The **kun-yomi** is the more common reading.

Less Common Pronunciations

Less common **ON** reading: none
Less common **kun** reading: none

COMMON WORDS AND COMPOUNDS		
横	*sideways; horizontal*	**yoko** よこ
横切る	sideways + cut = *go across; traverse*	**yoko** gi·ru よこ ぎ·る
横転	sideways + roll = *turn sideways; barrel roll*	**Ō·TEN** オウ·テン

KANJI 494

 CERTAIN

BUILDING THIS KANJI
Heart 心(25) + Comet ⼀ = 必

Meaning

Certain, sure. Despite its simplicity, writing this kanji is difficult due to 'heart' being written in an entirely different stroke order.

Remembering this kanji

This much is CERTAIN: when a **comet** goes through a **heart** there will be a major disruption. In the case of the kanji for 'heart', this means that its stroke order gets totally scrambled. Given how our **comet** has been behaving, it was pretty much CERTAIN that this would happen.

Common Pronunciations

Common **ON** reading: **HITSU** (ヒ ツ)
Common **kun** reading: **kanara** (か な ら)

Create your **on-yomi** keyword and enter it in the table at the back of the book. Then, after creating your **kun-yomi** keyword, write your sentence to remember the **on-yomi** and **kun-yomi** readings in the box below.

Less Common Pronunciations

Less common **ON** reading: none
Less common **kun** reading: none

COMMON WORDS AND COMPOUNDS		
必ず	*certain; for sure*	**kanara**·zu か な ら·ず
必要	certain + essential = *essential; necessary*	**HITSU·YŌ** ヒ ツ·ヨ ウ
必死	certain + death = *certain death; desperate*	**HIS·SHI** ヒ ッ·シ

COMPONENT #495

POLO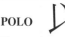

Ensure that you can see the difference between this component and 冫 (the 'ice hockey' component that was introduced prior to Entry 271), and 丶, the 'pinball' component that first appeared before Entry 308.

KANJI 495

 WITH

BUILDING THIS KANJI
Polo 以 + Person 人(2) = 以

Meaning

This odd-looking but useful character works together with the kanji that follows it, and with its companion sets some type of condition on the kanji preceding them (you can see how it functions in the compounds below). As with the kanji for 'what' (Entry 411) we will distinguish this character from all other occurrences of the word 'with' by a string of exclamation or question marks.

Common Pronunciations

Common **ON** reading: **I** (イ)
Common **kun** reading: none

Less Common Pronunciations

Less common **ON** reading: none
Less common **kun** reading: none

COMMON WORDS AND COMPOUNDS		
六十 以上	sixty + with + upper = *more than sixty*	ROKU·JU·I·JŌ ロク・ジュウ・ イ・ジョウ
十度 以内	ten + degree + with + inside = *within ten degrees*	JŪ·DO·I·NAI ジュウ・ド・ イ・ナイ
私以外	private (I) + with + outside = *except for me*	watashi·I·GAI わたし・イ・ガイ

Remembering this kanji

"You mean…you want a game of **polo**…but it has to be *with* a **person**?"
"That's right."
"WITH!!!???"
"Yes, for goodness sakes, WITH!!!"

KANJI 496

単 **SINGLE**

BUILDING THIS KANJI
Claw ⅞ + Sun 日 (6) + Ten (scarecrow) 十 (28) = 単

Meaning

Single, simple. Take care when writing this character to have the scarecrow be in <u>front</u> of the sun (not under it as in 早 , 'early' from Entry 29). The story below emphasizes this point.

Remembering this kanji

"Did you realize," said the **scarecrow**, "that it's a SINGLE **claw** that brings up the **sun**?"
"There isn't a SINGLE bit of truth in that," she said. "And anyway, how could you tell? Everything happens behind you."

There was just no impressing her, the **scarecrow** thought. She wasn't believing a SINGLE statement he made.

Common Pronunciations
Common **ON** reading: **TAN** (タ ン)
Common **kun** reading: none

Less Common Pronunciations
Less common **ON** reading: none
Less common **kun** reading: none

COMMON WORDS AND COMPOUNDS		
単語	single + words = *word*	**TAN·GO** タ ン · ゴ
単数	single + number = *singular* *(opposite of plural)*	**TAN·SŪ** タ ン · ス ウ
単刀 直入	single + sword + straight + enter = *straight to the point; frank*	**TAN·TŌ·CHOKU· NYŪ** タ ン · ト ウ · チ ョ ク · ニ ュ ウ

KANJI 497

 VERSUS

'	一	㇆	文	文	対	対		

BUILDING THIS KANJI
Police 一 + Banana Peels メ + Tiny (soccer
player) 寸(103) = 対

Meaning
Versus. The general sense is of things opposing
each other in a confrontational way, or simply
facing each other in a more neutral manner.

Common Pronunciations
Common **ON** reading: **TAI** (タ イ)
Common **kun** reading: none

Less Common Pronunciations
Less common **ON** reading: **TSUI** (ツ イ)
Less common **kun** reading: none

COMMON WORDS AND COMPOUNDS		
対立	versus + stand = *opposition; confrontation*	**TAI·RITSU** タ イ · リ ツ
対比	versus + compare = *comparison; contrast*	**TAI·HI** タ イ · ヒ
反対	against + versus = *opposite; contrary*	**HAN·TAI** ハ ン · タ イ

Remembering this kanji
Then one of the **police** threw down a **banana
peel**, but the **tiny soccer player's** cleats prevented
him from skidding. The game was getting nasty,
as it always did when it was **police VERSUS tiny
soccer players**.

KANJI 498

 MEAL

ノ	人	㇟	今	合	今	貪	食	食一
飣	飯	飯						

BUILDING THIS KANJI
Umbrella 𠆢 + Glutton 良 + Against 反(287)
= 飯

Meaning
Meal, (cooked) rice.

Remembering this kanji

Unable to sneak in under his **umbrella**, the **glutton** lowered it and spoke. "Why are you always **against** me?" he asked.

"Look," we said. "This is a buffet, and we have to make sure that everyone gets a MEAL."

Common Pronunciations

Common **ON** reading: **HAN** (ハン)
Common **kun** reading: **meshi** (めし)

Note that ' ご ' in the second example below can also be written with the honorific prefix 御* (not included in this book).

Less Common Pronunciations

Less common **ON** reading: none
Less common **kun** reading: none

COMMON WORDS AND COMPOUNDS		
飯	*meal; (cooked) rice*	meshi めし
ご飯	*meal; (cooked) rice*	go·**HAN** ご・ハン

LIGHTNING

号 **TITLE**

ヽ	冖	口	口	号			

BUILDING THIS KANJI
Mouth (vampire) 口 (8) + Lightning 丂 = 号

Meaning

Title, sign. This is a versatile kanji that can refer to everything from traffic signals to newspaper editions. The idea of a title or sign, however, is usually present in some way.

Remembering this kanji

The **vampire** swooped down like **lightning**. "I am Count Dracula," he said. "What is *your* TITLE?"

"Uh...I'm a librarian."

"Wonderful. Tell me, then, do you have this TITLE?"

Common Pronunciations

Common **ON** reading: **GŌ** (ゴウ)
Common **kun** reading: none

Less Common Pronunciations

Less common **ON** reading: none
Less common **kun** reading: none

COMMON WORDS AND COMPOUNDS		
信号	trust + title = *signal*	SHIN·**GŌ** シン・ゴウ
番号	order + title = *number*	BAN·**GŌ** バン・ゴウ
年号	year + title = *name of an era*	NEN·**GŌ** ネン・ゴウ

KANJI 500

卒 **GRADUATE**

BUILDING THIS KANJI
Police 宀 + Person 人(2) + Person 人(2) +
Ten (scarecrow) 十(28) = 卒

Meaning
Graduate, come to an end. A secondary meaning
relates to soldiers.

Remembering this kanji
"You have earned the right," said the **police**
chief, "to GRADUATE from the academy."
First one **person** then another **person** marched
by, but when the **scarecrow** attempted to do so he
was held back by being tied to his boards. "I'm
sorry," he was told, "but unless you can get up
here, you can't GRADUATE."

Common Pronunciations
Common **ON** reading: **SOTSU** (シ ン)
Common **kun** reading: none

Note that the second compound below is a short-
ening of 大学卒業者 (DAI·GAKU·**SOTSU**·
GYŌ·SHA / ダ イ · ガ ク · ソ ツ · ギ ョ ウ · シ ャ),
from 'university, 'graduation', and 'individual'.
This type of word creation is a common feature
of Japanese.

Create your **on-yomi** keyword and enter it in the
table at the back of the book. After that, write
your sentence to remember the **on-yomi** reading
in the box below.

Less Common Pronunciations
Less common **ON** reading: none
Less common **kun** reading: none

COMMON WORDS AND COMPOUNDS		
卒業	graduate + business = *graduation*	SOTSU·GYŌ ソ ツ · ギ ョ ウ
大卒	large + graduate = *university graduate*	DAI·SOTSU ダ イ · ソ ツ

KANJI 501

枚 **SHEET**

BUILDING THIS KANJI
Tree 木(13) + Cheerleaders 攵 = 枚

Meaning
Sheet. This is the counting word that Japanese
uses for flat, thin objects.

Remembering this kanji
"Yay, **tree**!" cheered the **cheerleaders**, holding
up a SHEET.

That seems really weird, she thought, watching
the scene nervously from a distance. Maybe I'll
be able to figure out what they're up to if I can
make out what's on that SHEET...

Common Pronunciations

Common **ON** reading: **MAI** (マ イ)
Common **kun** reading: none

Less Common Pronunciations

Less common **ON** reading: none
Less common **kun** reading: none

COMMON WORDS AND COMPOUNDS		
百枚	hundred + sheet = *one hundred sheets*	HYAKU·MAI ヒャク・マイ
枚数	sheet + number = *number of sheets*	MAI·SŪ マイ・スウ

KANJI 502

HOT

BUILDING THIS KANJI
Sun 日 (6) + **Individual** 者 (93) = 暑

Common Pronunciations

Common **ON** reading: **SHO** (シ ョ)
Common **kun** reading: **atsu** (あ つ)

Less Common Pronunciations

Less common **ON** reading: none
Less common **kun** reading: none

COMMON WORDS AND COMPOUNDS		
暑い	*hot (weather)*	atsu·i あつ・い
暑がる	*suffer from the heat*	atsu·garu あつ・がる
暑中	hot + middle = *height of summer; hot season*	SHO·CHŪ ショ・チュウ

Meaning

Hot. This kanji relates solely to air temperature and weather; it's opposite is thus 寒 , 'cold' (Entry 446).

Remembering this kanji

If the **sun** is hovering this closely over an **individual**, the conditions for them are probably pretty HOT. 'Cause the **sun**, from what I've been told, is always HOT.

COMPONENT #503

TORII

This component represents the famous gateway to a Shinto shrine. Note that its two straight legs distinguish it from 开 , our 'picnic table'.

KANJI 503

RIDE

BUILDING THIS KANJI
Comet ⼃ + **Torii** ⼲ + **Tree** 木 (13) = 乗

Meaning

Ride. A secondary meaning relates to deceiving someone or being deceived oneself (think of 'being taken for a ride'). Take care to write this character in the order of the components as listed above.

Remembering this kanji

She could hardly believe it, but there it was as the legend had foretold: a **comet** was passing over the **torii**! Scrambling down from the **tree**, she was rushing off on her bicycle moments later. "RIDE," was her only thought. "RIDE!"

Common Pronunciations

Common **ON** reading: **JŌ** (ジョウ)
Common **kun** reading: **no** (の)

The **kun-yomi** can incorporate its hiragana ending in certain compounds.

Less Common Pronunciations

Less common **ON** reading: none
Less common **kun** reading: none

COMMON WORDS AND COMPOUNDS		
乗る	ride; get onto	**no**·ru の·る
乗り場	ride + place = *(bus) stop; place to get on*	**no**·ri ba の·り ば
同乗	same + ride = *ride together; share a ride*	DŌ·**JŌ** ドウ·ジョウ

 LADY

く	㇅	女	女ㄱ	女コ	妲	妋	婦
婦	婦						

BUILDING THIS KANJI
Woman 女(16) + Comb ⺕ + UFO ⼍ + Cloth 巾(162) = 婦

Meaning

Lady, woman. It's worthwhile to see how this kanji differs visually from 寝 'sleep' (Entry 463), and 帰 'homeward' (Entry 478).

Remembering this kanji

"Hey, **woman**!"

She was so stunned that she turned with the **comb** still in her hair. "Who do you think you are?" she said. "That's no way to get my attention!"

"Forgive me," said the alien, fidgeting with a **cloth**. "I just came down from that **UFO** up there, and thought it was the custom on your planet to pick up a **woman's cloth** when she dropped it."

"Well, I don't care what you thought," she said. "I'm a LADY, understand? And you don't talk like that to a LADY."

Common Pronunciations

Common **ON** reading: **FU** (フ)
Common **kun** reading: none

Recall from Entry 315 that the final example below is one of the only instances where 夫 is read with its less common **on-yomi** of FŪ.

Less Common Pronunciations
Less common **ON** reading: none
Less common **kun** reading: none

COMMON WORDS AND COMPOUNDS		
婦人	lady + person = *lady; woman*	FU·JIN フ・ジン
婦人用	lady + person + utilize = *for ladies; women's*	FU·JIN·YŌ フ・ジン・ヨウ
夫婦	husband + lady = *husband and wife*	FŪ·FU フウ・フ

KANJI 505

 NATURE

ノ	ク	タ	タ	夕	夕	然	然	然
然	然	然						

BUILDING THIS KANJI
Moon 月 (11) + Dog 犬 (171) + Gas Stove ⺣
= 然

Meaning
Nature. This kanji emphasizes the nature or personality of the character preceding it.

Remembering this kanji
"Isn't NATURE intricate?"
"What do you mean?"
"Well, when the **moon** is out like this your **dog** howls. It's in his NATURE. And then, it's the NATURE of that **gas stove** there to have cooked your hot **dog**."
"Uh…is it in your NATURE to be this weird?"

Common Pronunciations
Common **ON** reading: ZEN (ゼン)
Common **kun** reading: none

Note that the second compound features the only instance of 自 being read with its less common **on-yomi** of SHI.

Less Common Pronunciations
Less common **ON** reading: NEN (ネン)
Less common **kun** reading: none

You are only likely to meet this reading in one compound (it's commonly used, however): 天然 (TEN·NEN / テン・ネン) 'natural', from the kanji 'heaven' and 'nature'.

COMMON WORDS AND COMPOUNDS		
全然	complete + nature = *entirely; (not) at all*	ZEN·ZEN ゼン・ゼン
自然	self + nature = *nature*	SHI·ZEN シ・ゼン

KANJI 506

 TONE

ヽ	一	三	言	言	言	言	言	訂
訂	調	調	調	調	調			

BUILDING THIS KANJI
Say 言 (80) + Around 周 (120) = 調

Meaning
Tone, tune. As an extension to toning and tuning comes the ideas of investigation, checking and preparation of things.

Remembering this kanji
"Just **say** it. There's nobody **around** but us."
"OK then, I will. He has no TONE, so tell him to TONE it down."

Common Pronunciations
Common **ON** reading: **CHŌ** (チ ョ ウ)
Common **kun** reading: **shira** (し ら)

Less Common Pronunciations
Less common **ON** reading: none
Less common **kun** reading: **totono** (と と の)

COMMON WORDS AND COMPOUNDS		
調べる	*investigate; inspect*	**shira·beru** し ら・べ る
強調	strong + tone = *emphasis; stress*	**KYŌ·CHŌ** キ ョ ウ・チ ョ ウ
単調	single + tone = *monotonous; dull*	**TAN·CHŌ** タ ン・チ ョ ウ

YOGA

Take a moment to compare this component with
匚 , our 'coat rack' introduced prior to Entry
234.

KANJI 507

KEEP

´	┗	䒑	㓁	㓁	㓁	留	留	留
留								

BUILDING THIS KANJI
Yoga 厶 + **Sword** 刀 (117) + **Rice Field** 田 (73)
= 留

Meaning
Keep, detain.

Remembering this kanji
He did **yoga** to KEEP in top shape, but would
also KEEP a **sword** at the ready. Because after
what almost happened in the **rice field**…well,
he realized he had to KEEP his wits about him.

Common Pronunciations
Common **ON** reading: **RYŪ** (リ ュ ウ)
Common **kun** reading: **to** (と)

The two verbs listed below have some overlap
with an identically pronounced pair we learned
back in Entry 43 (止 ま る / 止 め る). The two
here, however, have more of a sense of keeping
in place or being kept in place.

Create your **on-yomi** keyword and enter it in the
table at the back of the book. Then, after creating
your kun-yomi keyword, write your sentence to
remember the **on-yomi** and **kun-yomi** readings
in the box below.

Less Common Pronunciations
Less common **ON** reading: **RU** (ル)
Less common **kun** reading: none

COMMON WORDS AND COMPOUNDS		
留まる (intr)	*to be kept in place*	**to·maru** と・ま る
留める (tr)	*keep in place; detain*	**to·meru** と・め る
留置	keep + put = *detention; custody*	**RYŪ·CHI** リ ュ ウ・チ

KANJI 508

熱 **HEAT**

一	十	土	产	尤	查	幸	坴	孰
丸	熱	熱	熱	熱	熱			

BUILDING THIS KANJI
Earth 土(87) + Ballet 儿 + Earth 土(87) +
Round 丸(470) + Gas Stove 灬 = 熱

Meaning
Heat, hot (in aspects other than weather), and the
ideas of enthusiasm and passion. The opposite
to this kanji is 冷, 'cool' (Entry 362). Note
that the kanji for earth appears above and below
the ballet component (the story takes this into
account) and that certain fonts will 'round off'
the right-hand end of the kanji for 'round'.

Remembering this kanji
In the HEAT of their anger, the audience threw
earth at the **ballet dancer** from above and below
the stage. Once they had covered him with a
round pile, they began to HEAT it with a **gas
stove**. "Maybe this will generate a bit of HEAT
in his performance," someone muttered.

Common Pronunciations
Common **ON** reading: **NETSU** (ネ ツ)
Common **kun** reading: **atsu** (あ つ)

Create your **on-yomi** keyword and enter it in the
table at the back of the book. Then, after creating
your **kun-yomi** keyword, write your sentence to
remember the **on-yomi** and **kun-yomi** readings in
the box below.

Less Common Pronunciations
Less common **ON** reading: none
Less common **kun** reading: none

COMMON WORDS AND COMPOUNDS		
熱	*heat; a fever*	**NETSU** ネツ
熱い	*hot (to the touch); heated*	**atsu·i** あつ・い
熱愛	heat + love = *passionate love; devotion*	**NETSU·AI** ネツ・アイ

KANJI 509

使 **USE**

ノ	亻	亻	仨	俥	一	一	剕	使

BUILDING THIS KANJI
Giraffe 亻 + Officer 吏(462) = 使

Meaning
Use. This is the last of a group of five kanji
that we can now review as a whole. The building pattern for the present character has been as
follows: 史 'history' (Entry 440), to 吏 'officer'
(Entry 462), to 使. A pair of similar-looking but
unrelated kanji were constructed in this way: 更
'anew' (Entry 373), to 便 'delivery' (Entry 483).

Remembering this kanji

The **giraffe** sauntered up to the **officer**. "I wish to USE you," it said.

"For what?"

"Isn't it obvious? Something for which it's best to USE an **officer**."

Less Common Pronunciations

Less common **ON** reading: none

Less common **kun** reading: none

COMMON WORDS AND COMPOUNDS		
使う	*use*	**tsuka·u** つか·う
使用	use + utilize = *use; utilize*	**SHI·YŌ** シ・ヨウ
天使	heaven + use = *angel*	**TEN·SHI** テン・シ

Common Pronunciations

Common **ON** reading: **SHI** (シ)

Common **kun** reading: **tsuka** (つ か)

The **kun-yomi** can become voiced in second position, although never when forming verbs.

COMPONENT #510

DANCING SKELETON

Here at last we have the final member of our special component family, who would be well advised, incidentally, to dance with a little less energy given that his left forearm is flying off. Reviewing from the first, we have: 宀 'ghost' (preceding Entry 220), 弋 'spilling coffee' (preceding Entry 321), 戈 'killer bee' (preceding Entry 400), 戊 'pirate' (preceding Entry 454), and the present addition. Remember that the stroke order of the middle three is broken by anything appearing underneath their respective horizontal lines.

KANJI 510

 REMAIN

一	ア	歹	歹	歹	歹	歹	残	残
残								

BUILDING THIS KANJI

Jungleman 歹 + Dancing Skeleton 戋 = 残

Meaning

Remain. In an interesting connection, a secondary meaning relates to cruelty.

Remembering this kanji

The **jungleman** adjusts his leopard-skin shorts and exchanges an awkward glance with the **dancing skeleton**. The ball is over, and yet they REMAIN…

Common Pronunciations

Common **ON** reading: **ZAN** (ザ ン)

Common **kun** reading: **noko** (の こ)

Note the mix of on and **kun-yomi** in the final compound (and the voicing of 高).

Create your **on-yomi** keyword and enter it in the table at the back of the book. Then, after creating your **kun-yomi** keyword, write your sentence to remember the **on-yomi** and **kun-yomi** readings in the box below.

Less Common Pronunciations
Less common **ON** reading: none
Less common **kun** reading: none

COMMON WORDS AND COMPOUNDS		
残る	remain; be left	noko·ru のこ・る
残業	remain + business = overtime work	ZAN·GYŌ ザン・ギョウ
残高	remain + tall = (account) balance	ZAN·daka ザン・だか

KANJI 511

 QUIET

Common Pronunciations
Common **ON** reading: **SEI** (セイ)
Common **kun** reading: **shizu** (しず)

Less Common Pronunciations
Less common **ON** reading: **JŌ** (ジョウ)
Less common **kun** reading: none

BUILDING THIS KANJI
Blue 青 (86) + Dispute 争 (459) = 静

Meaning
Quiet.

COMMON WORDS AND COMPOUNDS		
静か	quiet; peaceful	shizu·ka しず・か
安静	ease + quiet = rest; repose	AN·SEI アン・セイ
静物画	quiet + thing + painting = still life	SEI·BUTSU·GA セイ・ブツ・ガ

Remembering this kanji
"They're feeling **blue**," she said, "so any **dispute** they have will be fairly **QUIET**."

KANJI 512

 GIFT

BUILDING THIS KANJI
Shellfish 貝 (21) + Rabbit `´ + Rice Field 田 (73) + Sun 日 (6) = 贈

Meaning
Gift, present.

Remembering this kanji

"I gave a GIFT of **shellfish**,
to a **rabbit** in a **rice field**,
that sparkled in the **sun**."

"Well, that's my poem so far. Do you like it?"
"It's OK, I guess. But what's with the **shellfish**
for a **rabbit**? I mean, that's just a totally useless
GIFT."

Common Pronunciations

Common **ON** reading: none
Common **kun** reading: **oku** (おく)

Less Common Pronunciations

Less common **ON** reading: **ZŌ** (ゾウ);
SŌ (ソウ)
Less common **kun** reading: none

COMMON WORDS AND COMPOUNDS		
贈る	*present (a gift)*	**oku·**ru おく・る
贈り物	gift + thing = *gift; present*	**oku·**ri mono おく・り もの

 VEGETABLE

一 艹 艹 艹 艹 艹 艹 艹 茟
茟 菜

BUILDING THIS KANJI
Wreath 艹 + Appearance 采 (259) = 菜

Common Pronunciations

Common **ON** reading: **SAI** (サイ)
Common **kun** reading: none

Less Common Pronunciations

Less common **ON** reading: none
Less common **kun** reading: **na** (な)

COMMON WORDS AND COMPOUNDS		
野菜	field + vegetable = *vegetables*	**YA·SAI** ヤ・サイ
菜食	vegetable + eat = *vegetarian diet*	**SAI·SHOKU** サイ・ショク
菜園	vegetable + garden = *vegetable garden*	**SAI·EN** サイ・エン

Meaning
Vegetable.

Remembering this kanji

"In order to get the champion's **wreath** at a
county fair, any VEGETABLE realizes that its
appearance must be flawless. A carrot must be
a sturdy and orange VEGETABLE, and a beet
must be a plump and purple VEGETABLE, for
example."

ノ 九 九 九 九 杂 杂 剎 剎
剎 剎 剎 雑 雑

BUILDING THIS KANJI
Nine 九 (39) + Tree 木 (13) + Squirrels 隹 = 雑

 MISCELLANEOUS

Meaning
Miscellaneous.

Remembering this kanji

"Did you realize that **99%** of **trees** have **squirrels** in them? And not only that, there are MISCEL-LANEOUS **trees** and MISCELLANEOUS **squirrels**!"

"Geez, I'm getting tired of you and your MISCELLANEOUS facts."

Common Pronunciations

Common **ON** reading: **ZATSU** (ザ ツ)
Common **kun** reading: none

Create your **on-yomi** keyword and enter it in the table at the back of the book. After that, write your sentence to remember the **on-yomi** reading in the box below.

Less Common Pronunciations

Less common **ON** reading: **ZŌ** (ゾ ウ)
Less common **kun** reading: none

COMMON WORDS AND COMPOUNDS		
雑音	miscellaneous + sound = *noise; interference*	**ZATSU·ON** ザ ツ・オ ン
雑事	miscellaneous + matter = *miscellaneous affairs*	**ZATSU·JI** ザ ツ・ジ
雑用	miscellaneous + utilize = *miscellaneous things to do*	**ZATSU·YŌ** ザ ツ・ヨ ウ

COMPONENT #515

SPIDER

KANJI 515

無 WITHOUT

/	一	二	仁	午	缶	無	無	無
無	無	無						

BUILDING THIS KANJI
Spider 無 + Gas Stove 灬 = 無

Meaning

Without. This is another important negating kanji, along with 不 'not' (Entry 186) and 非 'un-' (Entry 320). It imparts a sense of '-less' or '-free' in many of the compounds in which it appears.

Remembering this kanji

"I was tired of always dining of raw food," said the **spider**, "and so I got myself a **gas stove**. I mean, I can get by WITHOUT furniture or WITHOUT air con…but WITHOUT a **gas stove**? No, I can't imagine being WITHOUT one."

Common Pronunciations

Common **ON** reading: **MU** (ム); **BU** (ブ)
Common **kun** reading: **na** (な)

MU is by far the more common of these readings, although **BU** figures in a few important compounds as well. Except when it appears on its own (as in the first example below), **na** will be found only in the second or third position.

Create your **on-yomi** keyword for **MU** (ム) and enter it in the table at the back of the book. Then, after creating your **kun-yomi** keyword, write your sentence to remember the **on-yomi** and **kun-yomi** readings in the box below.

Less Common Pronunciations
Less common **ON** reading: none
Less common **kun** reading: none

COMMON WORDS AND COMPOUNDS		
無い	*there is no…*	na·i な·い
無料	without + fee = *free of charge*	MU·RYŌ ム·リョウ
無事	without + matter = *without incident; safe and sound*	BU·JI ブ·ジ

KANJI 516

YARD

'	一	广	广	庐	庐	庄	庭	庭
庭								

BUILDING THIS KANJI
Cliff Diver 广 + Court 廷(492) = 庭

Meaning
Yard, garden.

Remembering this kanji
"I swear I never meant to dive into that YARD," the **cliff diver** told the **court**. "I simply misjudged where I would land. Believe me, it's not very fun to miss the pool and crash into a YARD full of rose bushes when you're in a bathing suit."

Common Pronunciations
Common **ON** reading: **TEI** (テイ)
Common **kun** reading: **niwa** (にわ)

Less Common Pronunciations
Less common **ON** reading: none
Less common **kun** reading: none

COMMON WORDS AND COMPOUNDS		
庭	*yard; garden*	niwa にわ
庭園	yard + garden = *garden*	TEI·EN テイ·エン
家庭	house + yard = *home; household*	KA·TEI カ·テイ

KANJI 517

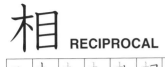

RECIPROCAL

一 十 扌 木 朾 机 机 相 相

BUILDING THIS KANJI
Tree 木(13) + Eye (Cyclops) 目(15) = 相

Meaning

Reciprocal, each other. An important secondary meaning is present when this kanji appears as the final character in certain compounds; in such instances it can indicate a government minister (as in the final example below).

Remembering this kanji

"Isn't it interesting what goes on between a **tree** and a **Cyclops**? Until the **tree** gives up its wood for the **Cyclops**' club, he keeps an **eye** on it."
"You're right. Their relationship is wonderfully RECIPROCAL."

Common Pronunciations

Common **ON** reading: **SŌ** (ソウ); **SHŌ** (ショウ)
Common **kun** reading: **ai** (あい)

SŌ is the most common reading here, with **SHŌ** only used outside of first position to indicate government ministers.

Less Common Pronunciations

Less common **ON** reading: none
Less common **kun** reading: none

COMMON WORDS AND COMPOUNDS		
相手	reciprocal + hand = *the other party; opponent*	**ai**·te あい・て
相続	reciprocal + continue = *inheritance; succession*	**SŌ**·ZOKU ソウ・ゾク
首相	neck (leader) + reciprocal (minister) = *prime minister*	SHU·**SHŌ** シュ・ショウ

COMPONENT #518

TOOTHBRUSH

You may wish to compare the final component of this book to 彐, our 'comb' from Entry 95.

KANJI 518

LONG

丨 厂 F E 三 長 長 長

BUILDING THIS KANJI
Toothbrush 髟 + Playground 衣 = 長

Meaning

Long. This kanji can also refer to the 'chief' or 'head' of entities such as cities and companies (the final compound provides an example).

Remembering this kanji

"Tough day?"
"Yeah. Boss gave me a **toothbrush** and told me to clean the **playground**."
"Yikes!"
"No kidding. The swings were easy enough, but some of those slides are really LONG."

Common Pronunciations

Common **ON** reading: **CHŌ** (チョウ)
Common **kun** reading: **naga** (なが)

Recall from Entry 384 that the identically pronounced 永い (naga·i / な が·い) refers to 'long' in terms of time.

Less Common Pronunciations
Less common **ON** reading: none
Less common **kun** reading: none

COMMON WORDS AND COMPOUNDS		
長い	*long*	**naga·i** な が·い
長期	long + period = *long-term*	**CHŌ·KI** チ ョ ウ·キ
社長	company + long (chief) = *company president*	**SHA·CHŌ** シ ャ·チ ョ ウ

KANJI 519

 COURTESY

`	フ	ネ	ネ	礼			

BUILDING THIS KANJI
Whittling ネ + Hook ㇄ = 礼

Common Pronunciations
Common **ON** reading: **REI** (レ イ)
Common **kun** reading: none

Less Common Pronunciations
Less common **ON** reading: **RAI** (ラ イ)
Less common **kun** reading: none

COMMON WORDS AND COMPOUNDS		
失礼	lose + courtesy = *discourtesy; rudeness*	**SHITSU·REI** シ ツ·レ イ
無礼	without + courtesy = *impoliteness; rudeness*	**BU·REI** ブ·レ イ
礼服	courtesy + clothes = *formal dress*	**REI·FUKU** レ イ·フ ク

Meaning
Courtesy, politeness.

Remembering this kanji
"You're really terrible at **whittling**. I'm surprised it would **hook** you like this."
"You're not much for **COURTESY**, are you?"

KANJI 520

 FINISH

く	幺	幺	糸	糸	糸	糸	終
終	終						

BUILDING THIS KANJI
Thread 糸 (196) + Winter 冬 (60) = 終

Meaning
Finish.

Remembering this kanji
They had followed the **thread** through the seasons, but when it ran out in **winter** they wondered: is it here that we must FINISH?

Common Pronunciations
Common **ON** reading: **SHŪ** (シュウ)
Common **kun** reading: **o** (お)

Less Common Pronunciations
Less common **ON** reading: none
Less common **kun** reading: none

COMMON WORDS AND COMPOUNDS		
終わる	*finish; come to an end*	o·waru お・わる
終結	finish + bind = *conclusion; end*	**SHŪ·KETSU** シュウ・ケツ
終点	finish + point = *last stop; end of the line*	**SHŪ·TEN** シュウ・テン

CHAPTER 22 REVIEW EXERCISES

A. Please match the following kanji to their meanings.

1.	長	a.	Ride
2.	熱	b.	Heat
3.	卒	c.	Court
4.	乗	d.	Vegetable
5.	静	e.	Nature
6.	必	f.	Quiet
7.	対	g.	Versus
8.	菜	h.	Certain
9.	廷	i.	Long
10.	然	j.	Graduate

B. Please match the following meanings to their kanji, and these to their on- or kun-yomi.

1.	Meal	a.	横	1.	**yoko** (よこ)
2.	Hot	b.	暑	2.	**I** (イ)
3.	With	c.	以	3.	**RYŪ** (リュウ)
4.	Sideways	d.	庭	4.	**GŌ** (ゴウ)
5.	Remain	e.	枚	5.	**ZAN** (ザン)
6.	Title	f.	残	6.	**tsuka** (つか)
7.	Sheet	g.	使	7.	**MAI** (マイ)
8.	Keep	h.	留	8.	**TEI** (テイ)
9.	Yard	i.	号	9.	**HAN** (ハン)
10.	Use	j.	飯	10.	**atsu** (あつ)

C. Please choose the best answer(s) to the following questions.

1. Which of the following readings apply to the kanji 無?
a. **BU** (ブ)   b. **GU** (グ)
c. **MU** (ム)   d. **CHŪ** (チュウ)
e. **SU** (ス)

2. Which is the correct reading of 静か?
a. **sazo·ka** (さぞ・か)
b. **shizu·ka** (しず・か)
c. **kazo·ka** (かぞ・か)
d. **tazo·ka** (たぞ・か)

3. Which of the following kanji has the most number of strokes?
a. 残   b. 然   c. 菜   d. 婦   e. 終

4. We have to be very ____ or we'll wake up that werewolf.
a. 菜   b. 贈   c. 長   d. 横   e. 静

5. Which is the correct reading of 必ず?
a. **tomura·zu** (とむら・ず)
b. **manaka·zu** (まなか・ず)
c. **chikara·zu** (ちから・ず)
d. **kanara·zu** (かなら・ず)

D. Please match the following compounds to their meanings and pronunciations.

1.	雑音	a. Nature	1.	**FU·JIN** (フ・ジン)
2.	無礼	b. Opposite	2.	**SHA·SHIN** (シャ・シン)
3.	写真	c. Conclusion	3.	**SOTSU·GYŌ** (ソツ・ギョウ)
4.	婦人	d. Photograph	4.	**SHŪ·KETSU** (シュウ・ケツ)
5.	相手	e. Lady / Woman	5.	**TAN·CHŌ** (タン・チョウ)

6. 反対　　f. Graduation

7. 終結　　g. Noise /
　　　　　　　Interference

8. 自然　　h. The other
　　　　　　　party

9. 単調　　i. Monotonous

10. 卒業　　j. Impoliteness

6. **HAN·TAI**
　（ハン・タイ）

7. **SHI·ZEN**
　（シ・ゼン）

8. **ZATSU·ON**
　（ザツ・オン）

9. **ai·te**
　（あい・て）

10. **BU·REI**
　（ブ・レイ）

"家庭菜園の野菜は美味しいで
すね。"

"はい、そうですね。でも一番
良いのは無料な事です。"

社長夫人はお金が大好きな人だ。

1. With whom did this person speak?
2. When did they speak with her?
3. What do they think is delicious?
4. What does the company president's wife like most about them?
5. What kind of person is the company president's wife?

E. Please read the passage below and answer the questions that follow.

今朝、社長夫人と話しました。。。

CUMULATIVE REVIEW EXERCISES FOR

CHAPTERS 1 - 22

A. Please match the following kanji to their meanings.

1. 辞　　　　　　a. Back

2. 笑　　　　　　b. Possible

3. 背　　　　　　c. Resign

4. 初　　　　　　d. Forget

5. 忘　　　　　　e. Degree

6. 可　　　　　　f. Exclusive

7. 選　　　　　　g. Laugh

8. 比　　　　　　h. Compare

9. 専　　　　　　i. Beginning

10. 度　　　　　　j. Select

B. Which kanji does not belong in the group?

1. a. 鼻　　b. 指　　c. 顔　　d. 頭　　e. 民

2. a. 妹　　b. 夫　　c. 兄　　d. 姉　　e. 弟

3. a. 橋　　b. 屋　　c. 戸　　d. 風　　e. 皿

4. a. 菜　　b. 酒　　c. 石　　d. 茶　　e. 豆

5. a. 熱　　b. 温　　c. 暑　　d. 氷　　e. 日

6. a. 笑　　b. 困　　c. 病　　d. 悪　　e. 痛

7. a. 虫　　b. 婦　　c. 魚　　d. 医　　e. 地

8. a. 利　　b. 社　　c. 商　　d. 業　　e. 食

9. a. 池　　b. 堂　　c. 氷　　d. 泉　　e. 洋

10. a. 則　　b. 法　　c. 晴　　d. 制　　e. 治

C. Identify the kanji in each group having the most number of strokes.

1. a. 定　　b. 育　　c. 始　　d. 是　　e. 身

2. a. 館　　b. 雑　　c. 静　　d. 熱　　e. 線

3. a. 重　　b. 建　　c. 幾　　d. 婚　　e. 勉

4. a. 永 b. 虫 c. 氷 d. 払 e. 令

5. a. 氏 b. 弔 c. 比 d. 区 e. 民

6. a. 薬 b. 顔 c. 機 d. 頭 e. 横

7. a. 無 b. 漢 c. 様 d. 園 e. 節

8. a. 色 b. 向 c. 両 d. 廷 e. 成

9. a. 働 b. 続 c. 痛 d. 歳 e. 銀

10. a. 都 b. 通 c. 弱 d. 乗 e. 特

D. Please list the following kanji in the order indicated (alphabetical).

1. Court / Original / Shop / Wide / Yard
   a. 原 b. 店 c. 廷 d. 庭 e. 広

2. Anew / Delivery / History / Officer / Use
   a. 史 b. 更 c. 吏 d. 便 e. 使

3. Business / Heavy / Move / Ride / Work
   a. 業 b. 働 c. 乗 d. 動 e. 重

4. Lend / People / Substitute / Surname / Type
   a. 民 b. 式 c. 代 d. 氏 e. 貸

5. All / Compare / Feather / Floor / Learn
   a. 羽 b. 階 c. 皆 d. 比 e. 習

6. Annual / Become / How many / Mechanism / Remain
   a. 残 b. 幾 c. 機 d. 歳 e. 成

7. Command / Match / Now / Orient / Same
   a. 向 b. 同 c. 今 d. 合 e. 令

8. Each / Lucky / Occupy / Platform / Stone
   a. 石 b. 台 c. 吉 d. 各 e. 占

9. Prefecture / Put / Straight / Tool / True
   a. 置 b. 真 c. 県 d. 具 e. 直

10. Display / Far / Garden / Long / Travel
    a. 旅 b. 展 c. 園 d. 遠 e. 長

E. Please choose the best answer to the following questions.

1. I really love the ____ of your eyes.
   a. 黄 b. 病 c. 束 d. 動 e. 色

2. The head chef served her creation in a beautiful ____ .
   a. 亜 b. 両 c. 皿 d. 申 e. 由

3. What will it take for people to live together in ____ ?
   a. 魚 b. 氷 c. 和 d. 菜 e. 画

4. The tiny country didn't have a chance against the ____ of its larger neighbor.
   a. 池 b. 紙 c. 酒 d. 味 e. 軍

5. You've really planted some fantastic flowers in your ____.
   a. 顔 b. 矢 c. 婚 d. 園 e. 争

F. Please choose the best answer to the following questions.

1. As 軽 is to 重 , 速 is to ____.
   a. 起 b. 遠 c. 遅 d. 達 e. 送

2. As 冷 is to 温 , 寒 is to ____.
   a. 場 b. 鼻 c. 旨 d. 暑 e. 単

3. As 兄 is to 弟 , 姉 is to ____.
   a. 婦 b. 婚 c. 数 d. 始 e. 妹

4. As 食 is to 飲 , 貸 is to ____.
   a. 昔 b. 是 c. 借 d. 共 e. 黄

5. As 強 is to 弱 , 長 is to ____.
   a. 豆 b. 頭 c. 矢 d. 短 e. 医

G. Please choose the best answer to the following questions.

1. Which is the correct reading of 土産?
   a. **karage** (からげ) b. **samage** (さまげ)
   c. **miyage** (みやげ) d. **takagi** (たかぎ)

2. Which is the correct reading of 今朝?
   a. **kyō** (きょう) b. **kesa** (けさ)
   c. **sage** (さげ) d. **kosu** (こす)

3. Which is the correct reading of 風呂?
   a. **KA·RO** (カ·ロ)   b. **MA·RO** (マ·ロ)
   c. **TA·RO** (タ·ロ)   d. **FU·RO** (フ·ロ)

4. Which is the correct reading of 天然?
   a. **TEN·KEN** (テン·ケン)
   b. **TEN·NEN** (テン·ネン)
   c. **SE·KEN** (セ·ケン)
   d. **SEN·NEN** (セン·ネン)

5. Which is the correct reading of 今年?
   a. **ko·toshi** (こ·とし)
   b. **ki·toshi** (き·とし)
   c. **ma·NEN** (ま·ネン)
   d. **ke·NEN** (け·ネン)

6. Which is the correct reading of 兄弟?
   a. **SAI·DAI** (サイ·ダイ)
   b. **NEN·DAI** (ネン·ダイ)
   c. **SHŌ·TAI** (ショウ·タイ)
   d. **KYŌ·DAI** (キョウ·ダイ)

7. Which is the correct reading of 合羽?
   a. **KI·ha** (キ·は)
   b. **KOP·pa** (コッ·ぱ)
   c. **mop·pa** (もっ·ぱ)
   d. **KAP·pa** (カッ·ぱ)

8. Which is the correct reading of 弟子?
   a. **DE·SHI** (デ·シ)   b. **KO·SHI** (コ·シ)
   c. **ta·ko** (た·こ)   d. **TAI·ko** (タイ·こ)

9. Which is the correct reading of 今日?
   a. **shō** (しょう)   b. **mō** (もう)
   c. **kyō** (きょう)   d. **kyū** (きゅう)

10. Which is the correct reading of 頭痛?
    a. **TO·TSŪ** (ト·ツウ)
    b. **ZU·TSŪ** (ズ·ツウ)
    c. **KA·TSŪ** (カ·ツウ)
    d. **SHI·TSŪ** (シ·ツウ)

H. Please match the following compounds to their meanings and pronunciations.

1. 暗示   a. Drinking   1. **BEN·RI**
               alcohol   (ベン·リ)

2. 去年   b. Peace   2. **HITSU·YŌ**
                               (ヒツ·ヨウ)

3. 昼食   c. Last year   3. **KAI·SHA**
                               (カイ·シャ)

4. 住民   d. Convenient   4. **IN·SHU**
                               (イン·シュ)

5. 便利   e. Festival   5. **KEK·**
               day   **KYOKU**
                               (ケッ·
                               キョク)

6. 自己   f. After all   6. **AN·JI**
                               (アン·ジ)

7. 祭日   g. Essential   7. **CHŪ·**
                               SHOKU
                               (チュウ·
                               ショク)

8. 必要   h. Hint   8. **JIS·SAI**
                               (ジッ·サイ)

9. 遊泳   i. Company /   9. **JI·KO**
               Corporation   (ジ·コ)

10. 平和   j. Oneself   10. **YŪ·EI**
                               (ユウ·エイ)

11. 実際   k. Lunch   11. **KYO·NEN**
                               (キョ·ネン)

12. 無料   l. Residents   12. **MU·RYŌ**
                               (ム·リョウ)

13. 飲酒   m. In actuality   13. **SAI·JITSU**
                               (サイ·ジツ)

14. 会社   n. Swimming   14. **JŪ·MIN**
                               (ジュウ·
                               ミン)

15. 結局   o. Free of   15. **HEI·WA**
               charge   (ヘイ·ワ)

ANSWER KEY FOR EXERCISES

CHAPTER 1

Section A
1. e	2. c	3. g	4. i	5. b
6. f	7. a	8. j	9. h	10. d

Section B
1. g – 8	2. j – 5	3. a – 10	4. i – 7
5. b – 3	6. h – 9	7. c – 1	8. f – 2
9. d – 6	10. e – 4		

Section C
1. b/c/d	2. c	3. d/e	4. a/d	5. a/d/e

Section D
1. d	2. e	3. b	4. d	5. b

Section E
1. f – 4	2. j – 9	3. a – 6	4. e – 5
5. b – 10	6. i – 2	7. h – 1	8. d – 7
9. c – 3	10. g - 8		

CHAPTER 2

Section A
1. c	2. j	3. f	4. h	5. e
6. a	7. i	8. g	9. d	10. b

Section B
1. d – 10	2. f – 4	3. a – 2	4. j – 9	5. h – 1
6. b – 3	7. g – 8	8. e – 7	9. c – 6	10. i – 5

Section C
1. a/b/d	2. a/b/d/e	3. b/d	4. d	5. a/b/c/d/e

Section D
1. b	2. c	3. a	4. d	5. c

Section E
1. g – 1	2. j – 6	3. a – 10	4. f – 3
5. i – 7	6. c – 2	7. h – 9	8. d – 5
9. b – 8	10. e - 4		

CHAPTER 3

Section A
1. d	2. h	3. j	4. b	5. i
6. g	7. c	8. f	9. a	10. e

Section B
1. i – 10	2. f – 2	3. d – 3	4. c – 7
5. a – 1	6. g – 8	7. b – 9	8. j – 4
9. h – 5	10. e – 6		

Section C
1. a/d	2. e	3. c/d	4. a/b/d	5. b/c/d

Section D
1. b	2. b	3. a	4. c	5. d

Section E
1. d – 6	2. b – 4	3. h – 2	4. j – 7
5. c – 9	6. f – 1	7. i – 5	8. g – 10
9. e – 3	10. a – 8		

CHAPTER 4

Section A
1. c	2. j	3. f	4. h	5. b
6. g	7. d	8. i	9. a	10. e

Section B
1. f – 4	2. c – 9	3. i – 2	4. g – 8
5. a – 6	6. j – 3	7. e – 7	8. d – 1
9. h – 5	10. b – 10		

Section C
1. a/b	2. b/c	3. a/d/e	4. d	5. b/e

Section D
1. d	2. b	3. c	4. d	5. a

Section E
1. c – 9	2. h – 6	3. f – 8	4. a – 3
5. j – 1	6. e – 10	7. i – 4	8. d – 7
9. g – 2	10. b – 5		

CHAPTER 5

Section A
1. h	2. b	3. e	4. g	5. c
6. j	7. f	8. i	9. d	10. a

Section B
1. d – 10	2. e – 5	3. a – 1	4. j – 3	5. g – 8
6. i – 6	7. b – 4	8. f – 9	9. h – 2	10. c – 7

Section C
1. c/e	2. a/b/d	3. e	4. d	5. b/d/e

Section D
1. b	2. c	3. d	4. b	5. d

Section E
1. f – 4	2. d – 7	3. h – 3	4. a – 9	5. c – 6
6. j – 8	7. e – 10	8. g – 1	9. b – 5	10. i – 2

CUMULATIVE REVIEW FOR CHAPTERS 1 - 5

Section A
1. f	2. d	3. i	4. a	5. h
6. c	7. j	8. e	9. g	10. b

Section B

1. c (not a body part)
2. a (not a person)
3. b (not something found in nature)
4. e (not a plant or animal)
5. a (not a direction)
6. d (not a number)
7. b (not a number)
8. c (not of water)
9. a (not a verb of motion)
10. h (not one of the kanji for days of the week)

Section C

1. b	2. d	3. a	4. d	5. e
6. c	7. a	8. b	9. e	10. c

Section D

1. d/c/a/e/b	2. b/d/a/e/c
3. c/e/d/a/b	4. c/b/e/a/d
5. a/e/d/c/b	6. b/c/d/e/a
7. e/c/a/d/b	8. a/d/b/e/c
9. c/b/d/a/e	10. b/a/d/e/c

Section E

1. e	2. b	3. d	4. d	5. c

Section F

1. a/b/e	2. a/b/d/e/f/g	3. a/b/c
4. a/b/c/d/e/g	5. a/b/c/e	

Section G

1. b	2. a	3. d	4. d	5. b
6. c	7. a	8. c	9. b	10. d

Section H

1. k – 3	2. e – 10	3. h – 14	4. m – 6
5. b – 12	6. f – 4	7. c – 9	8. n – 15
9. l – 7	10. g – 13	11. i – 2	12. o – 8
13. a – 5	14. j – 11	15. d – 1	

CHAPTER 6

Section A

1. f	2. c	3. g	4. a	5. b
6. e	7. i	8. j	9. d	10. h

Section B

1. i – 7	2. f – 2	3. h – 6	4. c – 10
5. a – 5	6. j – 3	7. d – 8	8. e – 9
9. g – 4	10. b – 1		

Section C

1. b/e	2. a/d	3. c	4. d/e	5. a/c

Section D

1. d	2. c	3. a	4. a	5. b/d

Section E

1. g – 3	2. d – 10	3. h – 1	4. j – 7
5. i – 5	6. b – 6	7. a – 4	8. e – 8
9. f – 2	10. c – 9		

CHAPTER 7

Section A

1. a	2. f	3. j	4. c	5. h
6. e	7. d	8. i	9. b	10. g

Section B

1. c – 5	2. h – 4	3. f – 1	4. i – 10
5. a – 7	6. j – 3	7. b – 9	8. d – 2
9. g – 8	10. e – 6		

Section C

1. b/c	2. a/e	3. c/d	4. d	5. a/e

Section D

1. b	2. d	3. c	4. a	5. a

Section E

1. i – 4	2. g – 9	3. e – 1	4. a – 7
5. c – 5	6. b – 8	7. f – 3	8. d – 10
9. j – 2	10. h – 6		

CHAPTER 8

Section A

1. b	2. d	3. a	4. i	5. g
6. j	7. f	8. c	9. e	10. h

Section B

1. j – 10	2. b – 1	3. f – 9	4. h – 4
5. c – 8	6. e – 7	7. a – 5	8. i – 3
9. d – 6	10. g – 2		

Section C

1. b/e	2. d	3. a/c	4. d/e	5. a/c/d

Section D

1. d	2. b	3. a	4. a	5. c

Section E

1. b – 5	2. h – 3	3. a – 9	4. f – 1
5. j – 6	6. d – 10	7. g – 8	8. i – 2
9. c – 4	10. e – 7		

CHAPTER 9

Section A

1. g	2. b	3. f	4. j	5. h
6. c	7. i	8. d	9. e	10. a

Section B

1. a – 8	2. b – 2	3. i – 9	4. g – 4
5. c – 1	6. h – 10	7. f – 6	8. e – 5
9. j – 3	10. d – 7		

Section C

1. a/c	2. b/e	3. b/d	4. c	5. a/b/c

Section D

1. d	2. a	3. b	4. c	5. d

Section E

1. j – 8	2. d – 3	3. g – 2	4. c – 10
5. a – 5	6. i – 9	7. h – 4	8. e – 6
9. f – 1	10. b – 7		

CHAPTER 10

Section A

1. h	2. i	3. e	4. b	5. c
6. j	7. a	8. g	9. f	10. d

Section B

1. d – 9	2. j – 3	3. a – 6	4. g – 10
5. h – 5	6. c – 2	7. i – 4	8. e – 7
9. b – 1	10. f – 8		

Section C

1. d/e	2. a/d	3. e	4. b/c	5. a/b/d/e

Section D

1. c	2. a	3. d	4. b	5. d

Section E

1. i – 7	2. h – 10	3. e – 1	4. g – 3
5. b – 8	6. a – 6	7. j – 2	8. d – 9
9. c – 4	10. f – 5		

CUMULATIVE REVIEW FOR CHAPTERS 1 - 10

Section A

1. f	2. e	3. g	4. c	5. i
6. b	7. h	8. j	9. a	10. d

Section B

1. d (not a time measurement)
2. b (not a color)
3. c (not a season)
4. c (not a population center)
5. a (not an animal)
6. e (not a direction)
7. b (not a body part)
8. a (not a time of the day)
9. d (not a man-made object)
10. e (not a positive thing)

Section C

1. e	2. c	3. a	4. d	5. c
6. d	7. b	8. d	9. e	10. b

Section D

1. b/c/d/a/e	2. a/d/e/b/c
3. c/b/a/d/e	4. c/a/b/d/e
5. e/c/d/b/a	6. e/d/c/b/a
7. c/d/a/e/b	8. d/b/a/c/e
9. b/e/c/d/a	10. d/c/b/e/a

Section E

1. e	2. c	3. e	4. d	5. a

Section F

1. a	2. d	3. b	4. e	5. b

Section G

1. b	2. d	3. a	4. a	5. c
6. d	7. a	8. c	9. b	10. d

Section H

1. c – 8	2. h – 1	3. a – 11	4. f – 14
5. o – 5	6. k – 7	7. m – 4	8. d – 12
9. i – 3	10. e – 15	11. n – 6	12. g – 13
13. b – 9	14. l – 2	15. j – 10	

CHAPTER 11

Section A

1. e	2. a	3. j	4. i	5. b
6. d	7. h	8. c	9. g	10. f

Section B

1. c – 2	2. f – 9	3. h – 1	4. g – 4
5. j – 6	6. a – 10	7. e – 3	8. b – 8
9. d – 7	10. i – 5		

Section C

1. b	2. b/c/d	3. d	4. c	5. a

Section D

1. a – 8	2. e – 5	3. g – 10	4. j – 2
5. c – 3	6. f – 1	7. b – 6	8. h – 9
9. d – 4	10. i – 7		

Section E

1. At 9AM.
2. To the university.
3. Their parents.
4. At the gate in front of the university.
5. By bicycle.

CHAPTER 12

Section A

1. f	2. j	3. g	4. e	5. c
6. b	7. i	8. d	9. a	10. h

Section B

1. f – 7	2. b – 9	3. a – 3	4. h – 1
5. e – 8	6. i – 2	7. g – 4	8. c – 6
9. j – 10	10. d – 5		

Section C

1. a/b/e	2. d	3. b	4. a	5. a

Section D

1. e – 7	2. f – 9	3. j – 6	4. c – 5
5. h – 1	6. b – 3	7. g – 2	8. a – 8
9. i – 10	10. d – 4		

Section E

1. At a bank.
2. Reception work.
3. Ten minutes.
4. An important interview.
5. At noon.

CHAPTER 13

Section A

1. e	2. j	3. c	4. g	5. d
6. h	7. f	8. i	9. b	10. a

Section B

1. d – 4	2. a – 9	3. i – 5	4. e – 7
5. g – 1	6. c – 8	7. b – 3	8. j – 2
9. h – 10	10. f – 6		

Section C

1. b	2. d	3. a/d/e	4. c	5. b/d

Section D

1. h – 5	2. j – 9	3. a – 7	4. b – 3
5. f – 1	6. i – 6	7. d – 4	8. e – 10
9. g – 8	10. c – 2		

Section E

1. Tea ceremony.
2. On the weekend.
3. On Kyushu.
4. Saturday.
5. By train.

CHAPTER 14

Section A

1. e	2. c	3. h	4. j	5. d
6. i	7. b	8. a	9. g	10. f

Section B

1. a – 5	2. j – 7	3. g – 4	4. c – 6
5. b – 9	6. h – 10	7. e – 2	8. i – 1
9. d – 8	10. f – 3		

Section C

1. d	2. c/e	3. a	4. d	5. c/d/e

Section D

1. f – 5	2. d – 10	3. j – 1	4. g – 6
5. a – 8	6. b – 7	7. e – 3	8. i – 4
9. h – 9	10. c – 2		

Section E

1. A festival.
2. In Kyoto.
3. There's a school trip.
4. No.
5. Some important business.

CHAPTER 15

Section A

1. a	2. h	3. f	4. d	5. g
6. i	7. c	8. b	9. j	10. e

Section B

1. d – 5	2. i – 4	3. f – 10	4. b – 7
5. c – 1	6. h – 6	7. e – 3	8. a – 2
9. g – 9	10. j – 8		

Section C

1. a/e	2. c	3. d	4. d	5. b

Section D

1. d – 8	2. h – 10	3. e – 1	4. g – 6
5. c – 7	6. i – 4	7. f – 9	8. j – 5
9. a – 2	10. b – 3		

Section E

1. He got married.
2. Last weekend.
3. They've been friends since elementary school.
4. That he worked as a newspaper reporter.
5. He's a doctor.

CHAPTER 16

Section A

1. c	2. i	3. b	4. a	5. g
6. e	7. h	8. d	9. j	10. f

Section B

1. c – 5	2. e – 10	3. i – 7	4. b – 2
5. h – 1	6. d – 3	7. g – 8	8. j – 6
9. a – 9	10. f – 4		

Section C

1. c	2. a/e	3. d	4. b	5. c

Section D

1. j – 5	2. e – 4	3. a – 6	4. g – 9
5. f – 2	6. i – 1	7. b – 10	8. h – 8
9. d – 3	10. c – 7		

Section E

1. To Hiroshima.
2. Her husband.
3. The prefectural zoo.
4. Hiked in the nearby mountains.
5. To Hokkaido.

CUMULATIVE REVIEW FOR CHAPTERS 1 - 16

Section A

1. i	2. c	3. j	4. a	5. b
6. g	7. e	8. h	9. d	10. f

Section B

1. c (not something found in nature)
2. a (not an animal)
3. e (not a verb of motion)
4. d (not a family member)
5. c (not something sad)
6. b (not something with a connection to water)
7. e (not an adjective)
8. a (not something positive)
9. b (not a body part)
10. e (not something to do with time)

Section C

1. a	2. e	3. c	4. b	5. b
6. d	7. c	8. a	9. b	10. e

Section D

1. c/e/b/d/a	2. a/c/b/d/e	3. c/a/e/d/b
4. e/b/a/c/d	5. b/a/e/c/d	6. d/e/a/c/b
7. a/d/b/e/c	8. e/a/d/b/c	
9. b/e/c/d/a	10. a/d/c/e/b	

Section E

1. c	2. e	3. e	4. b	5. d

Section F

1. d	2. a	3. c	4. d	5. b

Section G

1. c	2. b	3. d	4. c	5. a
6. b	7. b	8. a	9. d	10. c

Section H

1. e – 6	2. g – 9	3. n – 1	4. b – 15
5. k – 13	6. f – 2	7. a – 12	8. o – 5
9. m – 8	10. h – 7	11. i – 14	12. c – 11
13. l – 3	14. j – 10	15. d – 4	

CHAPTER 17

Section A

1. b	2. h	3. f	4. g	5. j
6. c	7. i	8. d	9. e	10. a

Section B

1. d – 10	2. a – 8	3. b – 9	4. e – 2
5. j – 1	6. f – 6	7. c – 5	8. i – 3
9. h – 7	10. g – 4		

Section C

1. c/d/e	2. b	3. c	4. b	5. c

Section D

1. g – 1	2. b – 9	3. c – 4	4. a – 5
5. i – 8	6. f – 10	7. j – 7	8. e – 6
9. h – 3	10. d – 2		

Section E

1. A cold rain fell.
2. Late autumn.
3. No, it's small.
4. Black birds have gathered.
5. No, I'm once again alone.

CHAPTER 18

Section A

1. e	2. f	3. j	4. h	5. c
6. d	7. i	8. a	9. b	10. g

Section B

1. c – 10	2. j – 5	3. g – 4	4. a – 9
5. b – 2	6. e – 1	7. f – 8	8. h – 7
9. i – 3	10. d – 6		

Section C

1. c	2. c	3. b	4. a/d	5. d

Section D

1. h – 8	2. e – 3	3. i – 10	4. c – 1
5. f – 9	6. b – 4	7. j – 6	8. g – 2
9. a – 7	10. d – 5		

Section E

1. A television.
2. A shop in front of Shinjuku statiion.
3. The new television that has just come on sale.
4. 250,000 yen.
5. I asked my younger brother for a loan.

CHAPTER 19

Section A

1. j	2. c	3. g	4. b	5. h 6. a
7. e	8. i	9. d	10. f	

Section B

1. e – 8	2. d – 9	3. j – 4	4. g – 5
5. b – 7	6. c – 3	7. a – 10	8. i – 6
9. h – 1	10. f – 2		

Section C

1. c	2. a/b/c/e	3. d	4. a/d/e	5. c

Section D

1. c – 8	2. i – 10	3. e – 2	4. d – 1
5. j – 7	6. a – 5	7. g – 6	8. h – 9
9. f – 3	10. b – 4		

Section E

1. What time it was.
2. A bus.
3. Because of construction on the main road.
4. The week before.
5. Until the end of the year.

CHAPTER 20

Section A

1. h	2. a	3. b	4. i	5. d
6. e	7. j	8. c	9. g	10. f

Section B

1. d – 6	2. f – 10	3. e – 5	4. i – 7
5. j – 9	6. a – 8	7. g – 2	8. c – 4
9. h – 1	10. b – 3		

Section C

1. b	2. a/b/e	3. d	4. c	5. a

Section D

1. e – 5	2. i – 8	3. b – 3	4. g – 7
5. a – 1	6. f – 9	7. h – 2	8. j – 6
9. d – 4	10. c – 10		

Section E

1. Science.
2. The temperature dropped, and the first snow of the year fell.
3. To go to a hot spring resort.
4. Two friends.
5. Because it was cold.

CHAPTER 21

Section A

1. e	2. j	3. a	4. g
5. f	6. i	7. d	8. c
9. b	10. h		

Section B

1. g – 10	2. i – 9	3. a – 4	4. h – 5
5. d – 8	6. j – 2	7. e – 3	8. f – 7
9. c – 1	10. b – 6		

Section C

1. a/b/c	2. c	3. d	4. e	5. b/d

Section D

1. e – 5	2. a – 9	3. i – 3	4. d – 1
5. j – 4	6. c – 2	7. g – 8	8. b – 10
9. h – 7	10. f – 6		

Section E

1. Read art books.
2. The library.
3. Old Japanese paintings.
4. The colors.
5. That they're very interesting.

CHAPTER 22

Section A

1. i	2. b	3. j	4. a	5. f
6. h	7. g	8. d	9. c	10. e

Section B

1. j – 9	2. b – 10	3. c – 2	4. a – 1
5. f – 5	6. i – 4	7. e – 7	8. h – 3
9. d – 8	10. g – 6		

Section C

1. a/c	2. b	3. b	4. e	5. d

Section D

1. g – 8	2. j – 10	3. d – 2	4. e – 1
5. h – 9	6. b – 6	7. c – 4	8. a – 7
9. i – 5	10. f – 3		

Section E

1. The company president's wife.
2. This morning.
3. Vegetables from the household vegetable garden.
4. That they're free.
5. Someone who really likes money.

CUMULATIVE REVIEW FOR CHAPTERS 1 - 22

Section A

1. c	2. g	3. a	4. i	5. d
6. b	7. j	8. h	9. f	10. e

Section B

1.   e (not a body part)
2.   b (not a brother or sister)
3.   d (not a man-made object)
4.   c (not a food or drink)
5.   d (not something hot or warm)
6.   a (not something negative)
7.   e (not something that lives)
8.   e (not something related to business)
9.   b (not something related to water)
10. c (not something related to governance)

Section C

1. d	2. a	3. c	4. b	5. e
6. b	7. c	8. d	9. e	10. a

Section D

1. c/a/b/e/d	2. b/d/a/c/e	3. a/e/d/c/b
4. e/a/c/d/b	5. c/d/a/b/e	6. d/e/b/c/a
7. e/d/c/a/b	8. d/c/e/b/a	9. c/a/e/d/b
10. b/d/c/e/a		

Section E

1. e	2. c	3. c	4. e	5. d

Section F

1. c	2. d	3. e	4. c	5. d

Section G

1. c	2. b	3. d	4. b	5. a
6. d	7. d	8. a	9. c	10. b

Section H

1. h – 6	2. c – 11	3. k – 7	4. l – 14
5. d – 1	6. j – 9	7. e – 13	8. g – 2
9. n – 10	10. b – 15	11. m – 8	12. o – 12
13. a – 4	14. i – 3	15. f – 5	

INDEX 1: STROKE COUNT

INDEX 2: KANJI NAMES

INDEX 3: ROMAJI